Lives of the Saints

Lives of the Saints

DAILY READINGS

by

Augustine Kalberer, O.S.B.

FRANCISCAN HERALD PRESS

1434 WEST 51st STREET • CHICAGO, 60609

Lives of the Saints: Daily Readings, by Augustine Kalberer O.S.B. Copyright ©1983 by Franciscan Herald Press, 1434 West 51st Street, Chicago, Illinois 60609. Made in the United States of America.

Library of Congress Cataloging in Publication Data
Kalberer, Augustine
  Lives of the saints.

  1. Christian saints. 2. Devotional calendars—
Catholic Church. I. Title.
BX4655.2K34   282'.092'2 (B)   74-10761
ISBN 0-8199-0539-9

Imprimi potest:
  +Eugene Medved, O.S.B.
  Abbot
  Westminster Abbey
Nihil Obstat:
  Mark Hegener O.F.M.
  Censor
Imprimatur:
  Msgr. Richard A. Rosemeyer, J.C.D.
  Vicar General, Archdiocese of Chicago

May, 1983

iv

The contents of this book are lives of the Saints and Blesseds of the Roman Catholic Church in harmony with the Calendar recently revised and in universal use. These "lives" will be short and succint summaries of the basic facts known about the saint or blessed and equivalent of what used to be called a "martyrology" which was read in connection with the canonical hour (one of the "hours" of the Divine Office) of Prime in the days before the entire liturgy was revised. This is the first attempt, as far as we know, to restore a daily reading of the lives of the saints for those who wish to make use of it.

—The Publishers.

"Be imitators of me as I am of Christ." — 1 **Cor.** 11:1.

"As we consider the lives of those who have faithfully followed Christ we are given fresh stimulus to seek the kingdom that is to come and at the same time we learn in a manner suited to each one's proper state and condition how to pass most securely through the changing things of this world so as to arrive at that perfect union with Christ which is holiness."
— II Vatican Council, **Church,** 50.

"Longum iter est per praecepta, breve et efficax per exempla — Example is the short and effective way, precept the long." — Seneca.

Preface to the First Edition

This book is the result of a work begun fifteen years ago to fill the need of a Benedictine community when the office of Prime was discontinued and the daily Roman Martyrology list of saints no longer read. The principal saints—the word is used in a broad sense to include both saints and blesseds—whose memory has been fostered in the Western Church will be found in this collection. The readings on each day's entries are short—preferably about three minutes—for easy insertion into an individual's or a community's daily schedule.

The characteristic of saints is their love of God. This quality is so attractive that their lives have special significance in terms of idealism and **inspiration**. But many of them were also outstanding teachers and prime witnesses to the Church's living **theology**. Then, too, their lives are an integral part of **history**. This book strives for a harmonious blend of the three elements of inspiration, theology and history.

In hagiography it is difficult to avoid the fanciful and legendary. One needs to be cautious without becoming hypercritical. A saint's own writings, if any remain, are the safest and best source material. "What I want to trace and study," John Henry Newman wrote in his Introductory to St. John Crysostom (**Historical Sketches,** Vol. 2), "is the real, hidden but human, life, or the **interior,** as it is called, of such glorious creations of God; and this I gain with difficulty from mere biographies. These biographies are most valuable both as being true and as being edifying; they are true to the letter, as far as they record facts and acts; I know it: but actions are not enough for sanctity; we must have saintly motives; and as to these motives, the actions themselves seldom carry the motives along with them. In consequence they are often supplied simply by the biographer out of his own head . . . On the other hand, when a saint is himself the speaker, he interprets his own action . . . I want to hear a saint converse; I am not content to look at him as a statue; his words are the index of his hidden life, as far as that life can be known to man . . . (pp. 219-220) A saint's writings are to me his real 'Life' (p. 227) . . . With a view to learning real devotion to him, I prefer, speaking for myself, to have any one action or event of his life drawn out minutely, with his own comments upon it, than a score of virtues, or of acts of one virtue, strung together in as many sentences . . ." (p. 229)

As saints have both their strength and their weaknesses it would be unreal if their **Lives** did not show something of both. Often, in fact, one finds special encouragement and support precisely in a saint's "ordinariness" or even in a saint's faults. Here too should be voiced Newman's complaint over "the perennial fidget which possess us about giving scandal. Facts are omitted in great histories, or glosses are put upon memorable acts, because they are thought not edifying, whereas of all scandals such omissions, such glosses, are the greatest." (p. 231)

In chronicling nearly a thousand holy men and women — usually two or three for each day — it was necessary to omit not only some shortcomings but also many virtues and memorable deeds. The major task throughout this book was that of selecting. I was ever occupied with the thought, "How significant is this piece of information? How interesting will it be if it is read again, year after year?"

On the theological level I have followed the faith of the Catholic Church as a guide in the choice of significant material. The reader will notice, for example, the importance given to historical documentation on the Eucharist and the Papacy.

The saints have generally been assigned to the day on which they died or the day on which their feast is celebrated. Saints with a place in the Universal Roman Calendar are put in capitals, like ST. BASIL and ST. GREGORY NAZIANZEN on January 2. In this way it is obvious at a glance which saints the Church honors at Mass on the respective days.

Religious orders and particular regions have their own calendar of feasts. Italics and footnotes are used to indicate saints who would thus be honored in particular churches on the respective days. Thus on January 4 the italics notations *United States*, *S.C.*, and *C.M.* above St. Elizabeth Bayley Seton indicate that, even though her name is not in capitals, her anniversary is celebrated on January 4 in the churches of the United States as well as among the Sisters of Charity (*S.C.*) and the Vincentians (*C.M.*).

It was not possible to consult the calendars of all the orders nor did it seem desirable in a general selection of saints to list all the "intra-mural" feasts of the various religious communities. There is also the further consideration that calendar information easily becomes incorrect or incomplete as changes are made and new saints are added.

I have not given a complete list of saints. The **Roman Sanctoral** (Roman Martyrology)—which is currently under revision— has several times as many. Interest, significance and space controlled my selection. The first day of the year will serve to illustrate both the wide range of choices and the method I followed.

A revised **Roman Sanctoral** list which the Congregation of Divine Worship circulated for study purposes in 1971 had the following as definite entries for January 1: THE SOLEMNITY OF MARY MOTHER OF GOD, St. Almachius (about 400 A.D.), St. Eugendus (about 510), St. Fulgentius (533), St. Agrippinus (about 580), St. Peter (837), St. Odilo (1049), St. Zdislava Berka (1252), Bl. Hugolinus (1260), Bl. Andrew of Segni (1302), Bl. Joseph Tommasi (1713), and St. Vincent Strambi (1824).

Of this group, the Augustinians celebrate St. Fulgentius on January 3; the Benedictines, St. Odilo on May 11; and the Passionists, St. Vincent Strambi on September 29. In order to make this book as serviceable as possible I have tried to put the saints on the dates where those most interested in them would like to find them. Thus St. Fulgentius is given on January 3, St. Odilo on May 11, and St. Vincent Strambi on September 25.

January 1 was thus left with THE SOLEMNITY OF MARY MOTHER OF GOD and eight other entries, most of them quite obscure. Mary's Solemnity and other aspects of New Year's Day required most of the available space and so there was room for only one or two of those who died on January 1. The saintly scholar Bl. Joseph Tommasi was selected because his life offered some quite distinctive material, such as his scrupulosity as a young priest and his liturgical research. The other seven saints and blesseds I omitted entirely.

It also happened that on certain days many "interesting" saints died while on other days few or none at all. And so in order to make the readings more even in length from day to day I moved some saints from the "crowded" to the "slack" days. Thus February 16 was quite empty and so St. Gilbert of Sempringham was brought in from February 4 and Bl. Francis de Laval was brought in from May 6.

The index of names at the back of the book will show, by means of dates in parenthesis, the saints I have moved from the position they will have—according to the day of death—in the **Roman Sanctoral.**

Butler's **Lives of the Saints** as revised by H. Thurston, S.J., and Donald Attwater (New York, 1956) deserves special mention as a work which has been consulted throughout, a work whose accuracy and balance one soon learns to appreciate.

I am grateful to my abbot and community for making available the opportunity to work on the lives of the saints, and I owe a large fraternal debt to the ongoing reaction and editorial assistance of the monks of this monastery where, in various revisions, this book has for so long been in daily use. Appreciative mention must also be made of the local Poor Clares who typed the manuscript and reacted to these lives as read in their convent during the past several years.

I am also grateful to Rt. Rev. Bonaventure Zerr, O.S.B., of Mt. Angel Abbey in Oregon and Rev. Richard Mugford, formerly of Anglican Theological College, Vancouver, British Columbia, for corrections and helpful suggestions on the manuscript, and to Rev. James Gandrau when he was editor of the **Catholic Northwest Progress**, Seattle, Washington, for initially suggesting that these daily readings might be serialized in a diocesan paper.

I am likewise indebted to the many religious who supplied information about the saints and the particular calendars of their orders, and I will welcome any further information that will make this work more reliable and useful.

Augustine Kalberer, O.S.B.
Westminster Abbey
Mission, B.C., Canada
March 21, 1975

Preface to the Second Edition

The principal reason for a new edition of the **Lives of the Saints** is the need to include those who have been beatified in the last few years. In the book thirty-eight additions have been made. Happily, names familiar in North America, and particularly Canada, are now in the list, such as Catherine Tekakwitha, Brother André founder of St. Joseph's Oratory in Montreal, Mother Marie Rose Durocher foundress of the Holy Names Sisters, Bishop Francis de Laval to whose Diocese of Quebec most of the United States and Canada once belonged, and Mother Marie of the Incarnation who was not only the superior of the first Ursuline convent and school in Quebec but a mystic of first rank.

Latin America is also represented with Pedro de San José Betancour of Guatemala City, Brother Michael Francis Febres Cordero of Ecuador, Bishop Ezechiel Moreno Díaz of Pasto in Colombia, and Father Joseph Anchieta, the great Jesuit missionary in Brazil.

Europe, of course, still dominates the new list with many attractive and significant entries such as Bl. Maria Teresa Ledóchowska who did so much for the African missions, Bl. Arnold Janssen who founded the Society of the Divine Word, Bl. Luigi Longo who as a layman established the Sanctuary of Pompei and did so much to promote the

Rosary, the diminutive Bl. Marie Rivier who founded the Presentation Sisters in the aftermath of the Reign of Terror to instruct girls, and Bl. Luigi Orione whose Little Work of Divine Providence gave the Church five new religious orders. There is also the gentle Croatian Capuchin, Leopoldo Mandić, who spent his last thirty-eight years hearing confessions in Padua, and the Good Shepherd nun, Bl. Mary Droeste zu Vischering, whose revelations prompted Pope Leo XIII to consecrate the human race to the Sacred Heart. Included also are two Italian doctors, Bl. Joseph Moscatti and Brother Richard Erminio Pampuri, as well as a French doctor who entered the priesthood and then became a missionary in Mauritius where he was one of the first members of Father Libermann's Society of the Immaculate Heart, Bl. Jacques Desire Laval. He is the first Holy Spirit Father to be raised to the Altar.

The most noticeable change in this edition is the use of photographs in place of sketches. The increasing number of nineteenth and twentieth century saints and **beati** makes this possible. A good picture of a saint carries a message deeper than words.

Those who use the **Lives of the Saints** for daily martyrology reading will notice that a few more saints have been shifted to days other than their own. This was done to lighten certain days and give more substance to calendar dates that previously were weak, particularly from February to April. This edition also profits from the corrections and suggestions sent in by kind readers and I wish to thank them most sincerely.

Augustine Kalberer, O.S.B.
Westminster Abbey
Mission, B.C. V2V 4J2
June 29, 1982

Abbreviations

The abbreviations used to indicate the particular calendars of various religious orders.

C.S.Sp.	Holy Spirit Fathers (Spiritans)
C.J.M.	Congregation of Jesus and Mary - Eudists
C.M.	Congregation of the Mission - Vincentians
C.N.D.	Sisters of the Congregation of Notre Dame
C.M.F.	Claretians
C.O.	Oratorians
C.P.	Passionists
C.PP.S.	Society of the Precious Blood
C.R.M.	Clerks Regular Minor
C.R.S.P.	Clerks Regular of St. Paul - Barnabites
C.S.C.	Congregation of the Holy Cross
C.SS.R.	Redemptorists
C.S.S.	Stigmatine Fathers and Brothers
D.C.	Daughters of the Cross
D.C.S.V.P.	Daughters of Charity of St. Vincent de Paul
F.D.P.	Sons of Divine Providence

F.M.A.	Daughters of Mary Help of Christians
F.M.S.	Marist Brothers
F.S.C.	Brothers of the Christian Schools
M.E.P.	Paris Foreign Mission Society
M.P.F.	Religious Teachers Filippini
O.A.R.	Augustinian Recollects
O. Carm.	Carmelites
O. Cart.	Carthusians
O.C.D.	Discalced Carmelites
O. Cist.	Cistercians
O.C.S.O.	Cistercians of the Strict Observance - Trappists
O.D.N.	Company of Mary
O.H.	Hospitaller Order of St. John of God
O.M.I.	Oblates of Mary Immaculate
O.P.	Dominicans
O. Praem.	Praemonstratensians - Norbertines
O.S.A.	Augustinians
O.S.B.	Benedictines
O.S.M.	Servites
O.SS.T.	Trinitarians
O.S.U.	Ursulines
P.M.	Sisters of the Presentation of Mary
P.M.C.	Little Missionary Sisters of Charity
R.C.	Congregation of Our Lady of the Retreat in the Cenacle
R.G.S.	Sisters of Our Lady of Charity of the Good Shepherd
R.S.C.J.	Society of the Sacred Heart
S.A.C.	Society of the Catholic Apostolate - Pallottine Fathers
S.C.	Sisters of Charity
Sch. P.	Piarist Fathers
S.C. J.	Congregation of the Priests of the Sacred Heart
S.D.B.	Salesians
S.J.	Jesuits
S.J.C.	Sisters of St. Joseph of Cluny
S.M.	Marist Fathers

S.M.M.	Montfort Missionaries
S.N.D.	Sisters of Notre Dame
S.N.J.M.	Sisters of the Holy Names of Jesus and Mary
S.S.D.	Sisters of St. Dorothy
S.S.S.	Congregation of the Blessed Sacrament
S.T.J.	Teresian Sisters
S.V.D.	Society of the Divine Word
II O.	Second Order
III O.	Third Order

Illustrations

The page numbers given here indicate the page after which the unnumbered illustrations are to be found.

JANUARY 1

THE SOLEMNITY OF MARY MOTHER OF GOD,New Year's Day, the Octave of Christmas, and World Day of Peace. Of the many themes associated with this day of celebration and good resolutions the Church gives first place to the Blessed Virgin under the title of Mother of God.

When fifth century Nestorians began to preach that Mary was the Mother of Christ but not the Mother of God, there was a strong reaction among lay people as well as theologians—similar —to what might be expected today if a new version of the **Hail Mary** read "Holy Mary, Mother of **Christ. . .**"

The Council of Ephesus in 431 vindicated the traditional title **Theotokos** (Mother of God), since it brings out so well Mary's unique dignity and expresses in a realistic way the true faith in the mystery of Christ: one Divine Person who is both true God and true man.

Today's feast also recalls the Circumcision eight days after the birth of Christ, when he received the name **Jesus** (the Lord saves).

In 1967 Pope Paul VI designated New Year's as the annual

World Day of Peace and invited all men of good will to join in prayer for peace.

1713

Bl. Joseph Tommasi, cardinal and scholar. Among the Theatines—whom he joined at fifteen—his aptitude for prayer and study found full scope, particularly as interior trials made him so scrupulous during his early years of priesthood that he was not allowed to preach or hear confessions. He is particularly remembered for his editions of unpublished sacramentaries and missals and his critical study of the Latin translations of the psalter. He served as consultor to many Roman congregations. As confessor to Cardinal Albani he imposed on him the obligation of accepting the papacy; but in his turn the new pope, Clement XI, ordered his confessor to accept the cardinalate.

JANUARY 2

379 and 389

ST. BASIL THE GREAT, principal organizer of monastic life in the Eastern Church, and **ST. GREGORY NAZIANZEN.** These two Cappadocian bishops and doctors belong to the group of oriental theologians to whom, under God, the Church owes right belief in the Trinity and Incarnation. Though they had already met in their home province of Cappadocia, it was only while studying rhetoric in Athens—along with the future emperor Julian the Apostate—that they became close friends. During their period as monks in Pontus they collaborated to produce St. Basil's two famous codes of the ascetic life, **The Longer** and **Shorter Rules.**

Basil, one of ten children in what is probably the church's most remarkable family of saints, became archbishop of his native Caesarea—now Kayseri in central Turkey—and the chief mainstay of orthodoxy after the death of St. Athanasius. Of his letters, 366 have survived. He commanded such prestige that Valens, the Arian emperor, was afraid in his case to carry out the policy of deposing non-Arian bishops. Gregory Nazianzen has preserved Basil's answer to the Prefect Modestus: "Confiscation means nothing to a man who has nothing, unless you covet these poor rags and a few books. . . . As for exile. . .I shall feel at home in any place to which I am sent. Or rather, I regard the whole earth as belonging to God, and I consider myself a stranger wherever I am. . . . As for death, this will be a benefit to me; for it will take me the sooner to God for whom I live. . . ." When the prefect remarked that no one had ever spoken to him like this before, Basil answered, "Perhaps that is because you have never had to deal with a bishop." He died worn out at forty-nine, just when the Catholic emperor, Theodosius the Great, was coming to power.

St. Gregory Nazianzen was of a contemplative and studious disposition, with none of Basil's talent for administration. He was ordained a priest against his will by his own father, St. Gregory Nazianzen the Elder, and ten years later reluctantly allowed Basil to ordain him bishop of Sasima, an outpost in Arian territory. After both ordinations he escaped into seclusion. Under the Theodosian restoration the Catholic party in Constantinople succeeded in transferring him to the imperial city, where Arians had dominated for over thirty years. He opened a small chapel in the house of a friend, consoling himself with the reflection that if the Arians were the stronger party his was the better cause; though they had the churches and the people, God and the angels were with him. In that small chapel he preached the famous **orations** on the Trinity that won him the title of "theologian" which he shares with St. John the Apostle. He presided for a time over the First Council of Constantinople in 381; but when the legitimacy of his transfer to Constantinople was contested by the Patriarch of Alexandria, he resigned in the cause of peace. He died on January 25 in 389 or 390.

JANUARY 3

Ca. 500

St. Genevieve, patroness of Paris. While historians question the reliability of the famous **Life of St. Genevieve,** she has proven herself a special protectress of Paris with miracles that made her tomb and church renowned throughout France. In times of calamity her reliquary would be carried in procession. In this way the fever of 1129 was stopped—an event still commemorated in Paris on November 26.

During the French Revolution her church was made the Pantheon and her body was burned. The remains of her relics were later re-enshrined in the church of St. Etienne du Mont where they continue to attract pilgrims.

The traditional story of her life shows Genevieve consecrating her virginity to God at fifteen. A few years later at a time of imminent danger of invasion she urged the people not to leave Paris but to do penance and trust in God while she and her devoted companions spent whole days in prayer until, at the last moment, Attila and his horde changed their course and by-passed Paris. And while the Franks—with whom she eventually got on very well—were besieging the city she managed to break through the blockade with several boatloads of grain for the starving population. Throughout the history of France she has been a symbol of Christian womanhood and of the fruitfulness of consecrated virginity.

553   [*O.S.A., O.A.R.*]

St. Fulgentius, abbot, bishop of Ruspe—now Kudiat Rosfa in Tunisia—author of some treatises against the Arian heresy and principal spokesman for the sixty African bishops banished to Sardinia by the Arian Vandals. He was attracted to the ascetic ideal by reading a sermon of St. Augustine on the brevity of human life.

JANUARY 4

1925

St. Raphaela Porras, foundress in Madrid of the Handmaids of the Sacred Heart, an institute devoted to education and retreats. At their beginning, before any of the sisters had vows, the small community fled from Cordova by night because the bishop there wanted to give them an entirely new rule. Bl. Raphaela spent the last thirty-two years at domestic work in the congregation's Roman house. Her own sister, who held views opposed to hers, had become superior general. "I will see the hand of God," she wrote, "in all that happens to me, attributing nothing to individuals—who are but instruments used by Him in the work of my sanctification." "My way," she would say, "is not to say many prayers, but to pray much."

1821   *[United States, S.C., C.M.]*

St. Elizabeth Ann Bayley Seton, foundress in 1809 at Emmitsburg, Maryland, of the first congregation of religious women in the United States, the Sisters of Charity, with a rule adapted from the Daughters of Charity of St. Vincent de Paul. She was a widow of thirty when her faith in the Eucharist led her along with her five children into the Catholic Church.

Works of mercy had always been a part of her life, and soon she opened a school in Baltimore. Others joined her. The religious ceremony of 1813 in which Mother Seton and seventeen companions pronounced their vows may be seen as the beginning of the immense parochial school system in the United States. Of the thousands who followed Mother Seton into religious life her own daughter Ann has a special place as the first one who took vows—a deathbed profession at the age of sixteen.

JANUARY 5

1066

St. Edward the Confessor, king of England from 1042 to 1066. His mother was from Normandy; and he was sent there for safety at the age of ten, returning to England only when called to the throne at the age of forty. His reign was peaceful and just; but his extensive Norman connections, sympathies, and even commitments led to the Norman Conquest upon his death. He made a vow to visit St. Peter's tomb; but because it would have been unwise for him to leave a realm plagued with problems of royal succession, Pope St. Leo IX commuted the vow requiring instead that the king give to the poor the sum he would have spent on the journey and that he repair or build and then endow a monastery in honor of St. Peter. Edward rebuilt and handsomely endowed the abbey of St. Peter on the isle of Thorney, called Westminster to distinguish it from the church of St. Paul in east London. According to William of Malmesbury, Edward was "so gentle that he would not say a word of reproach to the meanest person."

1860   [*United States, C.SS.R.*]

St. John Nepomucene Neumann, Redemptorist, beatified in 1963, the first United States bishop raised to the altar. He immigrated at twenty-five, penniless but with his theological studies completed and with a speaking knowledge of six—and later of twelve—languages. The archbishop of New York accepted him at once. In a matter of weeks he was ordained and sent as pastor of a territory in northern New York more extensive than the whole of his native Bohemia. Niagra Falls he referred to as "his baptismal font." Four years later he became a Redemptorist, the first to make profession in America. In twelve years he was superior of the entire mission band, a position which allowed him to keep the hardest work for himself, use a closet under the stairs as his room, and follow his own inclinations as to poverty of dress.

He put the Redemptorist order in the forefront of the parochial school movement, and as bishop achieved a nearly twenty-
fold increase of Catholic school attendance in the Philadelphia
diocese. He wrote two German catechisms and a Bible history
for school use. Children, sisters—he even founded a congregation of his own—and the poor were his fondest concern. He
had vowed not to waste a moment of time, and no one heard
more confessions.

At forty-nine he dropped dead on a Philadelphia street. A
poor man wearing one of the bishop's own shirts ran for a
priest. Under his patched suit was found a belt of sharply
pointed wires and in his coat pocket a rosary along with pieces
of candy he always carried for the children.

JANUARY 6

1611 [*O.SS.T.*]

St. John of Ribera, archbishop and viceroy of Valencia, whose
personal sanctity did not exempt him from the limited notions
of religious and political freedom then prevalent, or keep him
from taking a leading part in the expulsion of the Moriscos in
1609.

1937 [*Canada, C.S.C.*]

Bl. André Bessette, the "Frère André" whose name became a household word throughout French Canada, a Holy Cross brother credited
with thousands of cures—435 were recorded in 1916 alone—and
founder of Saint Joseph's Oratory in Montreal, today the world's principal shrine honoring St. Joseph. He died at 91, keeping to the end the
characteristic, teasing smile. Stricken with dizziness at the third
Christmas Mass twelve days before, he had to be helped to his room.
Prior to the burial an estimated million people came to the Oratory in
mid-winter to pay their last respects.

In 1910, when Brother André was 65, the Archbishop of Montreal
authorized an investigation of brother's ways, acceding to the com-

plaints of some doctors and churchmen that brother was a charlatan and an ignoramus. "I am ignorant," he admitted; "if there were anyone more ignorant the good God would choose him in my place." Of his cures he said, "I do what I feel I must." "It is St. Joseph that cures. I am nothing but his little dog."

The eighth child in a family of twelve at Saint-Gregoire d'Iberville, near Montreal and named Alfred at baptism, Brother André lost his carpenter father at 9 and his mother at 12. He remembered her as always smiling. "She kissed me more than was my turn," he said, explaining that he was always sickly and frail. His stomach would be a serious bother all his life. He grew to be hardly more than five feet tall and was unable to keep the various jobs he tried in his teens: shoemaking, baking, blacksmithing and farm work. Without schooling, he could hardly read or write. From the age of 20 for about three years he worked in textile factories in the United States.

At 15, on the advice of his closest priest friend, he applied to the Congregation of the Holy Cross, where he found natural expression for his special devotion to Our Lord's Passion and to St. Joseph, whose medal was part of a Holy Cross brother's habit. At the end of his novitiate he was rejected because of poor health and unsuitability for the Order; but the objections were eventually set aside by a good word from Bishop Bourget of Montreal and the reflection that the pious brother could at least pray.

He was soon assigned as porter at the College of Notre Dame, a job at which he would spend forty years until he was needed full-time at his shrine of St. Joseph on the slope of Mount Royal across the road from the college.

His St. Joseph cures began during his early years as porter. In time the crowds became too much for the college and visitors would gather at the trolley station across the road. Brother was 59 in 1904 when his first St. Joseph shrine was dedicated, a 15 by 18 ft chapel built by Brother Abundius with lumber purchased out of the $200 Br. André raised through 5¢ haircuts he gave the students and alms collected in the bowl he kept in front of the statue of St. Joseph.

In his later years he would spend 8 to 10 hours a day in his small office where he would receive 30 to 40 visitors an hour. Cures aside, thousands more found spiritual healing and strength in the presence of this man of God with his simple and homey ways and boundless trust in St.

BLESSED ANDREW BESSETTE, C.S.C.

Joseph. His words were treasured and passed on to others. "Do not seek to be spared trials," he would say; "ask instead for the grace to bear them." To a quarreling husband and wife he said,"These quarrels are like a room with a draft through it. It takes two doors to make a draft, and if you close one of them it stops." He became so popular that four secretaries were answering some 80,000 letters annually.

Blasting for the basilica began in 1915. In 1924, the three hundredth anniversary of the naming of St. Joseph as Patron of Canada, 35,000 people were present for the blessing of the cornerstone by the Apostolic Delegate of Canada. Today it is one of the world's great churches.

JANUARY 7

1275

ST. RAYMOND OF PENAFORT, outstanding canonist, third master general of the Dominicans, a truly apostolic man. He joined the Friars Preachers at forty-seven after a distinguished career as professor and as archdeacon of Barcelona. He wanted his new superiors to give him a severe penance for the complacency he had sometimes taken in his teaching. Instead, they had him write a collection of cases of conscience to help confessors —the first of its kind. Under Gregory IX he compiled the five books of **Decretals,** the most authoritative collection of church law until the 1917 code.

As master general he put through a rule that a superior's voluntary resignation should be accepted if he had a good reason. And so, after only two years in office, he resigned because of his age; he was sixty-five, and would actually live to be one hundred. During the remaining years he devoted much apostolic effort to the Moors of Spain. He encouraged St. Thomas to write the **Summa contra Gentiles** and induced several Dominican houses to teach Arabic and Hebrew. He died on Epiphany, 1275.

312

St. Lucian of Antioch, martyr, who founded the Antiochene school of exegesis and did sound critical work on the Septuagint and on New Testament texts. Arius was his pupil. For a time he supported Paul of Samosata, but was evidently reconciled to the orthodox faith before his martyrdom at Nicomedia under Diocletian.

1131

St. Canute Lavard, the "Good," duke of southern Jutland and then king of the Wends, nephew of St. Canute, king of Denmark. He worked for justice and peace, spent much of his time fighting off Viking pirates, supported the missionary efforts of St. Vicelin, and was killed at the behest of a jealous uncle.

1309   *[Franciscan III O.]*

Bl. Angela of Foligno, a married woman suddenly converted at about the age of forty from a selfish and—by her account—sinful life to become a great mystic. Despite excruciating desolations and the death of her husband and sons, joy was her dominant characteristic. Her life is a good example of the harrowing temptations which can mark the higher stages of spiritual purification and of the way in which growth in holiness brings a corresponding realization of one's imperfections.

She became the center of a mixed group of Franciscan tertiaries. One Holy Thursday she said to a companion, "Let us go and look for Christ our Lord." They sold their veils to buy some food which they took to a hospital, where they washed the women's feet and the men's hands as they lay lonely and forsaken on their pallets. Bl. Angela is known principally through the visions she dictated to her confessor.

JANUARY 8 *

1366   *[O.Carm., O.C.D.]*

St. Peter Thomas, a Carmelite of contemplative disposition

O.SS.T. see Jan 22 for St. Vincent Pallotti.

and deep spirituality who spent much of his time on diplomatic missions for the pope. In 1359 he was sent to Constantinople as "Universal Legate to the Eastern Church" and the commander of a large body of troops. He died seven years later of wounds received in an assault on Alexandria.

1455

St. Lawrence Justinian, the first patriarch of Venice, serene and humble like his two modern successors, St. Pius X and Pope John XXIII. His life and teaching are best understood as a generous response to a religious experience he had at the age of nineteen: an apparition of a beautiful girl who called herself the wisdom of God. "Why do you seek rest for your mind in exterior things," she asked, "sometimes in this object and sometimes in that? What you are looking for can be found only in me. . . ." The vision left him with such fervor that he resolved to give himself single-mindedly to this one quest. He so cut back on things like sleep, drink, warmth, and bodily comfort that his mother, fearing for his health, tried to arrange a marriage. But instead Lawrence joined the Canons Regular of St. George at Venice. When the community stores perished in a fire he consoled a sorrowing brother, "Why be sad? We vowed poverty." His superiors moderated his bodily rigors but he was able to work on more interior attachments, such as human respect. To a friend who thought going out to beg with a sack would make Lawrence the object of ridicule he answered, "Let us go boldly in quest of scorn. We have done nothing if we have renounced the world only in word." To keep silent when unjustly blamed he would sometimes have to bite his tongue. But God granted him supernatural gifts of prayer, particularly at Mass, and much prudence.

He became superior general of the whole order and was bishop of Castello at fifty-three. When the patriarch of nearby Grado died, the pope joined the two territories and formed the patriarchate of Venice. He governed this see in a turbulent epoch with as much ease as his own community. His preaching and example constantly inculcated humility, the cross of

Christ, prayer, and works of charity. Besides sermons he left
fifteen treatises on the spiritual life and the apostolate. Holiness he saw as the progressive possession of the wisdom of God
obtained through love until a new creature is formed in the
image of Christ, and the apostolate he saw as nothing else than
the communication of this wisdom.

JANUARY 9 *

1622

Bl. Alix le Clercq, co-founder with St. Peter Fourier of the
Augustinian Canonesses Regular of the Congregation of Notre
Dame. She has a place after St. Angela Merici among those
who first organized communities of nuns for teaching. At nineteen she had the first of the striking dreams that became a feature of her life: she seemed to be approaching an altar; and
Our Lady—the **Notre Dame** in the title of the future order—
standing beside the altar, dressed in a strange religious habit,
beckoned her to come forward. At Mass a short time later, she
seemed to hear seductive dance music and to see the devil
directing a group of young people. This happened on three
successive Sundays. Without further delay she changed her way
of life and gave up dancing and the fancy clothes which had
meant so much to her. Her father as well as the pastor of a
nearby village, Peter Fourier—the future saint—wanted her to
enter a convent, but she said no. In another dream it came to
her that she was not to be a nun in any of the existing institutes. She felt she must found an "active" order. As a test
Father Fourier required her to find other girls of like purpose.
Soon she had four. At midnight Mass, Christmas 1597, in the
hamlet of Mattaincourt, Lorraine, all five dedicated themselves
to God and to serve their neighbor, especially the poor. Alix
was twenty-one. They decided their work would be to teach
young girls "to read and write and sew and, especially, to love
and serve." They would teach rich and poor free of charge "as
that is more pleasing to God."

---

*O. Carm. see Jan. 6 for St. Andrew Corsini.

The many obstacles Alix experienced in establishing the congregation gave her full opportunity to practice her maxim that "one act of humility is worth more than a thousand ecstasies." The two saintly founders did not always agree. Father Fourier did not have full confidence in Mother Alix, and eventually one of the other original five was made general superior. Bl. Alix was forty-six when she died. The Canonesses of the Congregation of Notre Dame flourished greatly and still exist today, mostly in Europe. In Germany alone, 2,000 of them were teaching when the great confiscation swept their monasteries away in 1803. Thirty years later the School Sisters of Notre Dame were established there to do what the Canonesses had formerly done. The work of Bl. Alix was also an inspiration to Bl. Marguerite Bourgeoys in founding the Congregation of Notre Dame at Montreal in the seventeenth century.

JANUARY 10

314
St. Miltiades, pope at the time Constantine gave peace to the Church.

395   *[O.S.B., O.C.S.O.]*
St. Gregory of Nyssa, the Cappadocian doctor who exercised a particularly profound influence on the spirituality of Eastern monasticism. A fervent Origenist, but a very original thinker, he is one of the most philosophic of the Greek Fathers and contributed heavily to the spiritual theology which was passed on to East and West through Pseudo-Dionysius.

He was raised by his sister St. Macrina—whose life he wrote—and by his brother St. Basil the Great, whom he calls "father and teacher." They groomed him for an ecclesiastical career but he married and became a rhetorician like his father. But after his wife's death he was persuaded by St. Gregory Nazianzen to enter a monastery; St. Basil also had his way and made him bishop of Nyssa.

His many writings belong almost entirely to the period of maturity after Basil's death. He was considered the leading theologian at the First Council of Constantinople. The Second Council of Nicaea would refer to him as "the father of the fathers." His **Catechetical Discourse** is particularly important as a compact and vital synthesis of patristic Christianity.

681

St. Agatho, pope, a Sicilian Greek. He was married for twenty years and occupied in business; then he became a monk. He served as treasurer of the Roman Church and at a very advanced age was made pope. In a dogmatic letter to the III Council of Constantinople, 680, he asserted the authority and infallibility of Rome and vindicated the Catholic faith against the "One-will heresy" with such dignity, energy, and learning that the council went on record to say, "Peter has spoken through Agatho."

1276

Bl. Gregory X, archdeacon of Liege, elected pope at the instance of St. Bonaventure. He called the II Council of Lyons as the best way to help the Holy Land and promote reunion with the Greeks. Since it had taken them three years to arrive at an election in his own case, he made it a rule that in the future no cardinal could leave the conclave before a pope had been chosen.

JANUARY 11

529

St. Theodosius, abbot, whose monastery at Cathismus near Bethlehem attracted so many disciples from various lands that the liturgy of the word was celebrated in three languages in separate churches, with everyone coming together after the gospel to complete the Eucharist in Greek. The community had a large guesthouse and three hospitals: for the aged, the sick, and the insane. Appointed cenobiarch by the patriarch of Jerusalem, Theodosius had responsibility for all the local monasteries, while St. Sabbas supervised the hermits. At ninety-five he traveled through Palestine strengthening the faithful against the "One-nature heresy" Emperor Anastasius was promoting. During a sermon in Jerusalem he cried out, "If anyone receives not the four councils as the four gospels, let him be anathema." He was banished, but a later emperor recalled him. He died at 105.

1208

Bl. Peter of Castelnau, Cistercian at Fontfroide, southern France, martyred while heading a papal missionary expedition to the Albigensians. St. Dominic began his preaching career as part of this band. Felled by a lance, Peter said to his assailant, "May God forgive you as fully as I do."

1729

Bl. Thomas of Cori, Italian Franciscan. His specialty was prayer, a habit he developed in childhood while tending sheep. As a priest he preferred the small, out-of-the-way friary at Civitella in the hills near Subiaco, where many extraordinary events were recorded about his prayer life and charity. As guardian he insisted that the divine office be said reverently and without haste. His saying was, "Unless the heart prays, the tongue only plays."

JANUARY 12

690

St. Benedict Biscop, abbot-founder of the twin monasteries of Wearmouth and Jarrow, one of the most attractive and practical churchmen of England's Anglo-Saxon period. His five trips to Rome, his love for the Scriptures, the liturgy, the see of Peter, the saints, and his enthusiasm for letters, art and architecture made his monasteries the cultural center of Northumbria and capable of producing St. Bede—who was entrusted to Biscop as a small boy and later became his appreciative biographer.

1167   [O. Cist., O.C.S.O.]

St. Aelred of Rievaulx, abbot and author, England's best known Cistercian. He combined unusual administrative ability and leadership with a wonderful capacity for divine and human love. His was the half-century in which monasticism attained its greatest ascendancy in the West and when the white robed monks of St. Bernard were replacing the Cluniacs in the lead role. Rievaulx had been founded only two years when Aelred arrived at the age of twenty-four, abandoning the court of King St. David of Scotland, where he was master of the household. Thirteen years later he was abbot of the monastery. He would soon have 300 choir monks and 500 brothers.

1700   [Canada, C.N.D.]

St. Marguerite Bourgeoys. In 1658 she opened Montreal's first school in a stable belonging to Maisonneuve, governor of Ville-Marie, as the settlement was then called. She founded the Congregation of Notre Dame, a teaching order which 300 years later numbered approximately 4,000 sisters. For half a century she was the leading feminine figure in the colony. Soon after her arrival from France, she worked to have the big cross restored on top of Mount Royal—Indians had destroyed the earlier one. Her last act was to offer her life for that of the novice mistress who was seriously ill.

1892   [O.S.M.]

St. Anthony Mary Pucci, Servite, a model pastor who spent nearly fifty years as parish priest of Viareggio, an Italian seaside resort.

JANUARY 13

368

ST. HILARY, bishop of Poitiers, pioneer doctor of the Latin
Church and principal opponent of Arianism in the West. His
work **On the Trinity**—written mostly during exile in the East—
is the best defense of the divinity and consubstantiality of the
Son. With St. Hilary, a generation before St. Ambrose, occidental
theology and exegesis came into their own. He introduced the
West to the theological treasurers of the Greek Fathers, helped
St. Martin of Tours inaugurate monasticism in Gaul, and introduced Latin hymnody—even writing hymns of his own—after
seeing how effectively the heretics used song to spread their
errors.

With him the Church in the West attained its first clear understanding of its necessary independence within a Christian
state. The faith begins to be in danger, he writes, as soon as
"definitions of the Lord's teaching are enacted by a human
judge, by the prince." Married and a convert from paganism, he
was well versed in philosophy and rhetoric. The quest for the
meaning of life led him to the Sacred Scriptures. "I found in
them," he writes, "this testimony of God the creator about himself: I am who am (Ex 3:14). . . . I was filled with admiration
at such a clear definition of God. . . . It is known that there
is nothing more characteristic of God than **to be**. . ."

Ca. 603

St. Kentigern or Mungo ("Darling"), bishop and founder
of Glasgow. His monastery became known as **Glasghu,** meaning
"dear family." St. Mungo's Cathedral, the finest building of
Glasgow, stands over his shrine.

1497   [*O.S.A., O.A.R.*]

Bl. Veronica of Binasco, Augustinian nun at Milan, a mystic
remarkable for her gift of tears and zeal for work. Keeping at

her tasks even in illness she would say, "I must work while I can, while I have time."

JANUARY 14

Ca. 260

St. Felix, a priest of Nola near Naples and the chief mainstay of that church in the Decian persecution. St. Augustine's treatise **On the Care of the Dead** was written to answer the question as to whether there was any spiritual advantage in being buried near this saint's tomb; for already in the fourth century St. Felix had a shrine with candles, miracles, and devotees claiming his special help.

1200   [*O. Cart.*]

Bl. Odo of Novara, Piedmontese Carthusian who became a chaplain to the Benedictine nuns at Tagliacozzo. As he lay dying he called out, "Wait for me, Lord, wait for me; I am coming with you." When those in the room asked to whom he was speaking he answered, "It is my king, whom I now see. I am standing in his presence." As if someone were offering him a hand he stood and, with arms out-stretched, died. He was nearly one hundred.

1237

St. Sava, abbot, archbishop, patron of the Serbs. He is the younger son of King Stephen I, who founded the independent Serbian state. Sava first established a monastery for the Serbs on Mt. Athos—it still exists today—and then returned with some monks to his own country where he built monasteries and became his people's first bishop.

1331   [*Franciscans*]

Bl. Odoric of Pordenone, energetic Franciscan missionary and prodigious traveler. In the early years of the fourteenth century he preached the Gospel in Turkey, Armenia, Persia, Ceylon, Java, Borneo, Japan, China, Tibet, and India; but he returned to northern Italy to die in his friary at Udine.

JANUARY 15

4th cent.
St. Paul of Thebes, whom St. Jerome popularized as the first Egyptian hermit.

6th cent.   [*O.S.B., O. Cist., O.C.S.O.*]
Sts. Maurus and Placidus, disciples of St. Benedict, who were entrusted to him for training in early youth and figured prominently in his miracles.

Ca. 570
Bl. Ita, Ida, or Mida, virgin, popular early Irish nun who established a convent at Killeedy in Limerick and conducted a school for small boys.

1648
Bl. Francis de Capillas, Spanish Dominican, first beatified martyr in China. He became a religious at seventeen and volunteered for the Philippine missions. He lived there in great austerity and then was sent on to China. He preached with much success until the Manchu dynasty came to power, and then he was put to death on a political charge.

1909   [*S.V.D.*]
Bl. Arnold Janssen, priest of the diocese of Muenster who was prepared for his role as founder of one of the Church's great missionary orders by parish work, assignments as teacher, diocesan director of the Apostleship of Prayer, and editor of a missionary publication. In

1875, when he was 37 and the Kulturkampf was at its height, he crossed the border into Holland and established at Steyl a seminary where German students could train for the missions. This was the beginning of the Society of the Divine Word—also called Steyler Missionaries—whose priests and brothers numbered 5,000 when the founder was beatified a hundred years later. Bl. Arnold also founded two feminine orders: the Holy Spirit Missionary Sisters to educate girls in missionary countries and the cloistered Sisters Servants of the Holy Spirit of Perpetual Adoration to pray for the missionaries and the missions.

JANUARY 16

430

St. Honoratus, founder of the famous abbey Lerins—today the island of Saint Honorat off the French Riviera. His monasticism provided for both solitary and community living. It is possible that St. Patrick spent some time under him. He was chosen archbishop of Arles.

Ca. 650

St. Fursey, disciple of St. Brendan and founder of monasteries in Ireland, England, and France. He is remembered especially for his visions of the spirit world and the after-life—accounts of which spread everywhere through St. Bede's **Ecclesiastical History.**

1127   [*O. Praem.*]

St. Godfrey of Kappenberg, Premonstratensian canon, one of St. Norbert's first and most enthusiastic disciples. He transformed his Kappenberg castle into an abbey and built a Norbertine convent in which his wife and sister became nuns, while he and his brother lived as canons. He died at thirty before reaching the priesthood.

BLESSED ARNOLD JANSSEN

1220 [*Franciscans*]

St. Berard and his four companions, **Sts. Peter, Odo, Accursio,** and **Adjutus**—the first Franciscan martyrs. St. Francis sent them west while he went to the Mohammedans in the east. They began in Spain, were banished to Morocco, and there kept preaching until they were beheaded. Hearing of their martyrdom St. Francis exclaimed, "Now I can truly say I have five brothers!" The career of these missionaries and the presence of their relics in the church of the Canons Regular of St. Augustine in Coimbra determined the Franciscan vocation of St. Anthony of Padua, then a canon at Coimbra.

JANUARY 17

356

ST. ANTHONY, abbot in Egypt, founder of Christian monasticism. His vocation began at eighteen or twenty. Bereft of both parents and left with the guardianship of a younger sister and the care of an estate, he often reflected that the apostles had left everything for Christ. Then one day in church he heard the gospel read: "If you wish to be perfect, go and sell what you own and give the money to the poor and you will have treasure in heaven; then come, follow me" (Mt 19:21). He disposed of his estate, keeping back only a small sum for his sister. But on hearing the further gospel admonition: "Do not worry about tomorrow" (Mt 6:34), he arranged to have a community of virgins look after her, gave everything away, and began to live as an ascetic near his own village. Manual labor, reading, and prayer became his chief occupation.

He gradually sought more remote solitudes. Disciples came —St. Athanasius was one of them—and eventually colonies of hermits formed. He made occasional appearances in Alexandria to strengthen the martyrs in times of persecution or to support

Athanasius against the Arians. Constantine wrote commending himself and his sons to Anthony's prayers. But the attentions of the great meant little to this man of God. "You must not be surprised," he told his monks, "if an emperor writes to us, for he is a man; but you should rather be surprised that God has written the law for mankind and has spoken to us through his son." He died on Mount Kolzim near the Red Sea in 356 at the age of 105. The following year St. Athanasius wrote his **Life.**

This most important document of the early period of monasticism was an immediate success. More than any other book it projected the ascetic ideal and peopled the desert with monks. St. Augustine's **Confessions** (8,6-8) witness to the decisive effect it had on him. Its most persuasive section is the famous instruction Anthony one day gave his brothers, urging them forward with reflections on the shortness of life compared to eternity and on the complete disproportion between present labors and the rewards of heaven. "We must further bear in mind," he told them, "that if we do not give these things up for virtue's sake, later we must still leave them behind. . . . Why not rather possess those things which we can take along with us—prudence, justice, temperance, fortitude, understanding, charity, love of the poor, faith in Christ, meekness, and hospitality?"

JANUARY 18

539

St. Gregory, bishop of Langres, France. On the death of his wife and after forty years as governor of Autun, he retired to live as a hermit; but the people brought him back to be their bishop. As civil ruler he had a reputation for strict justice, but now he distinguished himself by gentleness. St. Tetricus, his son, succeeded him as bishop; and his great-grandson is St. Gregory of Tours.

1270   [*O.P.*]

St. Margaret of Hungary, a Dominican nun who died at twenty-eight, and whose life has some of the extreme qualities of self-crucifixion exemplified in more recent times by St. Benedict Joseph Labre. Her father, King Bela IV of Hungary, committed her to a convent at the age of three to fulfill a promise he made should the Hungarian forces prove victorious.

At twelve she pronounced her vows in a Dominican convent her father built on an island in the Danube, the present Margaret Island near Budapest. Her reaction to the deference shown her royal person was to choose menial, exhausting and insanitary work, especially when someone was needed to perform the most lowly and difficult offices for the sick. She was particularly attractive, and Ottokar II of Bohemia wanted her in marriage. Her father was inclined to ask for a dispensation from her vows; but she threatened to mutilate her face, if the plans to remove her from the convent were not dropped.

1894

Bl. Agostina Pietrantoni, a Sister of Charity of St. Joan Antide-Thouret. She spent the seven years of her religious life nursing in the tuberculosis ward of the Santo Spiritu Hospital of Rome. She herself had contracted the disease but after a remarkable recovery asked to be reassigned to the same ward so that some other sister would not have to be exposed to the contagion.

Police action was sometimes necessary to quell the restless patients. "They are not bad," Sister Agostina would say, "they are suffering and need our compassion. Let us rather try to help them and pray for them." On Nov. 13, 1894, at the age of thirty she was stabbed to death by a former mental patient who had served as her assistant. An estimated 200,000 people took part in her funeral.

JANUARY 19 *

The Week of Prayer for Christian Unity begins today.

Ca. 389

St. Macarius the Egyptian, also called the Elder or the Great to distinguish him from Macarius of Alexandria, a contemporary ascetic of almost equal fame. Today's saint is the chief monastic organizer in the sandy wastelands of the Scete west of the Nile, the most remote of Egyptian deserts. There he spent sixty years. Renowned for his contemplation, asceticism, and spiritual direction, he attracted many disciples who lived as hermits. His sayings passed from mouth to mouth and many found their way into the later collections of the **Sayings of the Fathers,** which played such an important role in Eastern monasticism.

He was so highly esteemed that various writings, particularly sermons, began to circulate under his name. To a young man wanting to make a good start he said, "Go to the graveyard and upbraid the dead and then flatter them." When the disciple returned Macarius asked what answer had come from the graves. "None," was the reply. "Then, go," said Macarius, "and learn to be moved neither by praise nor blame." On prayer he taught: "There is no need to lose oneself in much speaking. It is enough to hold out one's hand and say: 'Lord as you know and will, have mercy.'"

Though he was one of the most strenuous ascetics — eating, for example, once a week—he told the story that God one day revealed to him that he had not yet attained the perfection of two married women who lived in a certain town. He went to see for himself and found two women who spoke no rash or idle words, lived in humility, patience and charity, sanctified their actions with prayer, and put up with the humors of their husbands. St. Macarius is mentioned in the canon of the Coptic and the Armenian mass.

S.J. Bl. James Salès and Bl. William Saultemouche (see Feb. 8), St. John Ogilvie (see March 10) as well as Bl. Melchior Grodecz and Bl. Stephen Pongracz (see Sept. 7) are included among the many Jesuits honored today.

1570 [*S.J.*]

Bl. Ignatius Azevedo and companions, Portugese and Spanish Jesuits who were on their way to the mission in Brazil when Huguenot pirates intercepted their ship near the Canary Islands. The religious were killed and thrown into the sea while the others on board were spared. Bl. Ignatius had already been in Brazil as official visitor and returned with so much enthusiasm for the missions that he inspired sixty-nine Europeans to volunteer. Thirty-nine of these were sailing with him. Their death occurred on July 15, but they are commemorated today along with numerous other Jesuit martyrs.

JANUARY 20

250

ST. FABIAN, pope for fourteen years, a martyr under Decius.

Ca. 300

ST. SEBASTIAN, a celebrated Roman martyr buried in the catacombs on the Appian Way. St. Ambrose reports that he was a native of Milan and suffered under Diocletian; but there is no reliable evidence that he was a soldier.

473

St. Euthymius the Great, abbot and bishop. This Armenian priest at the age of twenty-nine became a solitary near Jerusalem and a few years later withdrew to a more secluded spot near Jericho where a community of hermits gradually formed about him. His miracles and charity brought so many Arabs to the faith that the patriarch of Jerusalem ordained him bishop to care for them. Though his life was spent mostly in prayer, silence, and manual labor, he took a firm stand on the theological controversy of his day and brought many monks back from the "One-nature heresy" and even Empress Eudoxia herself. He guided his colony mostly through deputies with whom he would meet on Sundays. From the octave of Epiphany until Palm Sunday, he regularly withdrew further into solitude; and he sometimes took Sabbas—the future saint—with him. He died at the age of ninety-five. The preparation of the Byzantine Mass makes mention of him.

1095

St. Wulfstan, Benedictine monk and bishop of Worchester, the only Anglo-Saxon to retain a diocese after Lanfranc's reform in the wake of the Norman Conquest. Under him Worchester cathedral was rebuilt in grand style, but he was in tears as the old church was being pulled down. "We are destroying the work of saints," he lamented, for while the ancients were not so skilled in building they were famous in drawing people to God, "but we are famed for the neglect of souls and the piling up of stones."

JANUARY 21

Ca. 300

ST. AGNES, Rome's most popular virgin-martyr—though few details are known about her except that she was very young, about twelve or thirteen. Within a short time of her death a basilica was raised over her tomb by Emperor Constantine's daughter Constantina.

861

St. Meinrad, a priest of the Benedictine abbey of Reichenau who became a hermit **(Einsiedler)** in a solitary spot on the lower slopes of Mt. Etzel. The great abbey of Einsiedeln, Switzerland, was built on this site and took its name from the hermitage. St. Meinrad was murdered by two robbers to whom he had shown hospitality.

1642

St. Alban Roe, Benedictine, martyred for his priesthood under Charles I at the age of fifty-eight. He is remembered particularly for his invincible good temper during many years in prison, his spirit of prayer, and for the fact that during his priestly training at the English College in Douai he was dismissed for outspoken criticism of the way disciplinary infractions were handled by the superior. He was twenty-eight at the time.

He had embraced the Catholic faith during undergraduate days at Cambridge in consequence of his disconcerting attempt to convert a "papist" in St. Alban's prison. At thirty he became a monk at Dieulouard, Lorraine—a community now located at Ampleforth. After the Mass he was permitted to say on the day of his execution he blessed the people present and added, "When you see our arms stretched out and nailed to the city gates, imagine that we are giving you the same blessing as now." His companion in martyrdom, the **Bl. Thomas Reynolds,** a seventy-year old priest, was already on the hurdle when Father Alban came up, greeted him cheerfully and jokingly felt his pulse. At the gallows he gave the hangman something for a drink and told him in a merry mood to serve God, not to get drunk and to do his office well. He had no handkerchief to cover his eyes for he had given it away to a bystander. But he said he did not need one, because "the cause for which I die is so good that I am neither afraid nor ashamed to look on death, nor to be seen by those standing by." The two priests then gave one another absolution, and while they invoked the name of Jesus the cart was drawn from under them.

JANUARY 22

304

ST. VINCENT, deacon, martyred at Saragossa in 304, immovable under the cruelest tortures.

628

St. Anastasius, intrepid Persian martyr, popular in both East and West. Sacred images played a big part in his conversion to Christianity and stimulated his desire to imitate the martyrs. In turn, his own miraculous image at Rome was cited at the II Council of Nicaea as an argument against the Iconoclasts.

1850   [S.A.C.]

St. Vincent Pallotti, outstanding nineteenth century founder. His Society of the Catholic Apostolate established at Rome in 1835 and embracing clergy, religious, and laity, pioneered the effective insertion of laymen into the apostolate. St. Vincent's zeal was boundless; and he inspired others to practical action in such areas as night schools, agricultural institutes, and homes for girls, for the needy and aged. He organized retreats, missionary assistance, and the famous annual Epiphany week at the church of Sant' Andrea della Valle. Each day of that week the word of God is preached in a different language and the liturgy is celebrated in a different rite. The Pallottine Fathers—numbering more than 2,000 at the founder's canonization in 1963—grew out of the need for priests to be associated full-time with this multi-dimensional apostolate. Two congregations of sisters also bear his name.

Vincent was the third of the ten children of a prosperous grocer. As a schoolboy he made little progress until, at the suggestion of his mother and teachers, he made a novena to the Holy Spirit; after that his performance was outstanding. St. Caspar del Bufalo exercised a great influence over him; and Vincent in his turn was spiritual director of the Roman College and confessor at a half dozen seminaries in Rome. He had a singular devotion to Mary and to the poor. He would give his clothes away and come home half-dressed. Once he disguised himself as an old woman to reach the bedside of a man who threatened to shoot the first priest who came near. It is believed that the pleurisy of which he died at fifty-five was brought on when he gave his cloak away before a long, cold session in the confessional. The Romans spoke of him as a "second St. Philip Neri."

JANUARY 23

Ca. 250

St. Babylas, bishop of Antioch, martyr. He refused to let Philip the Arabian enter church on Easter until he had done penance for the murder of his predecessor, Emperor Gordian.

667

St. Ildephonse, honored as a doctor of the church in Spain, where his book in defense of the perpetual virginity of Mary deepened her devotion among the people and inspired writers and artists of later centuries. Among other contributions to the Mozarabic liturgy he is credited with a Mass in honor of Our Lady's Assumption. His book **On Famous Men** contains brief biographies of fourteen churchmen, all of them Spaniards except St. Gregory the Great. He was abbot of Agli near Toledo and then succeeded his uncle St. Eugenius as archbishop of that see.

1515

Bl. Paula Gambara-Costa, matron at Brescia, Franciscan tertiary in whose rule of life there was an entry to the effect that she would take a kindly view of her husband's faults and do what she could to keep them from coming to the notice of others. As it turned out she had much need of forbearance because of her husband's infidelity and his resentment at her charity to the poor, but in time she won him over.

1670

St. Charles of Sezze, Franciscan brother, who was dull at school, never getting beyond just learning to read and write, but so wise in the ways of God that cardinals at Rome found it profitable to talk to him.

JANUARY 24

1622

ST. FRANCIS DE SALES, bishop of Geneva, doctor, cofounder with St. Jane Frances de Chantal of the Visitation nuns. Unexcelled as a practical guide to holiness, he once wrote: "It is an error as well as a heresy to want to exclude the devout life from the military camp, the artisan's shop, or the married household. Wherever we are, we can and must aspire to a life of perfection." There are 400 known editions of his masterpiece, the **Introduction to the Devout Life**—itself simply an expansion of letters of direction written for the most part to a relative by marriage, Madame de Charmoisy. It was basic with him that "God is the God of the human heart" and that God draws us to Himself by that natural hunger everyone has to love Him above everything else.

The eldest of thirteen children and belonging to the Savoy nobility, he chose the priesthood despite his father's insistence on legal training and a secular career. During student days in Paris he began the file of examples from nature and his reading that he would later use so abundantly in his sermons and writings to illustrate truths about God and the soul. He was also prepared for his future work by an excruciating period of scrupulosity which even made him ill and from which he was suddenly freed when he prayed before the statue of our Lady and made a private vow of chastity. His literary career—he is now patron of journalists—began with a series of short monthly pamphlets distributed in the Calvinist district of Chablais for which he volunteered as a young priest. In time it became safe to preach more freely, and he succeeded in bringing most of the people back to the Catholic faith. He was ordained bishop at the age of thirty-five.

His second great work, the **Treatise on the Love of God,** took ten years to write. There are also 1,000 letters as well as the **Conferences**—community talks written up by the Visitation nuns. Pope John XXIII had St. Francis de Sales as his life-long model. In 1903, a year before his ordination, the future pope made this prophetic entry in his diary for today's feast:

"I spent today in the company of St. Francis de Sales, my gentlest of saints. What a magnificent figure of a man, priest and bishop. If I were like him, I would not mind even if they made me pope . . . I have read his life so many times. His counsels are so acceptable to my heart. By the light of his example I feel more inclined towards humility, gentleness and calm. My life, so the Lord tells me, must be a perfect copy of that of St. Francis de Sales if I wish it to bear good fruit. Nothing extraordinary in me or in my behaviour, except my way of doing ordinary things—'all ordinary things but done in no ordinary way.' A great burning love for Jesus Christ and his Church, unalterable serenity of mind, wonderful gentleness with my fellow men, that is all."

Various religious congregations have been founded under the patronage of St. Francis de Sales, among them the Missionaries of St. Francis de Sales, the Oblates of St. Francis de Sales, the Salesians of St. John Bosco, and the Sisters of St. Joseph.

JANUARY 25

Ca. 43

THE CONVERSION OF ST. PAUL. Jesus revealing himself to
Saul on the way to Damascus said, "I have appeared to you for
this reason: to appoint you as my servant and as witness of
this vision in which you have seen me and of others in which
I shall appear to you." From these private revelations St. Paul
emerged with an overpowering realization that Jesus of Nazareth was alive and that everything meaningful in heaven and
earth was summed up in him. "All I want is to know Christ
and the power of his resurrection and to share his sufferings
by reproducing the pattern of his death" (Phil 3:10).

For the Galatians he traced the course of his vocation from
the time of his conversion until his full acceptance as the
apostle of the gentiles: "You must have heard . . . how merciless I was in persecuting the church of God . . . Then God . . .
called me through his grace and chose to reveal his Son in me,
so that I might preach the Good News about him to the pagans. I did not stop to discuss this with any human being,
nor did I go up to Jerusalem to see those who were already
apostles before me, but I went off to Arabia at once and later
went straight back from there to Damascus. Even when after
three years I went up to Jerusalem to visit Cephas and stayed
with him for fifteen days, I did not see any of the other apostles; I only saw James, the brother of the Lord. . . . After that
I went to Syria and Cilicia. . . . It was not till fourteen years
had passed that I went up to Jerusalem again. . . . I went
there as the result of a revelation, and privately I laid before
the leading men the Good News as I proclaim it among the
pagans; I did so for fear the course I was adopting or had already adopted would not be allowed. . . . These leaders. . .
had nothing to add to the Good News as I preach it. . . . So,
James, Cephas and John, these leaders, these pillars, shook
hands with Barnabas and me as a sign of partnership: we were

to go to the pagans and they to the circumcised" (Gal 1:13-
2:9).

The Week of Prayer for Christian Unity ends today. Father
Paul Watson, founder of the Friars and Sisters of the Atonement, initiated this crusade of prayer as an Anglican in 1908.

1048
St. **Poppo,** abbot of Stavelot in Belgium and leader of a Benedictine reform which affected most of the monasteries of Lorraine.

JANUARY 26

1st cent.
STS. **TIMOTHY** and **TITUS,** bishops, disciples and companions of St. Paul. At Lystra on the second missionary journey Paul
selected Timothy, the son of a Jewish mother and a Greek father, to be his travel companion. As closest collaborator he was
so identified with Paul's apostolate that he is mentioned in
eleven of the fourteen Pauline epistles — in six of them as co-
sender. Titus was a gentile convert. He accompanied Paul to
the council at Jerusalem and was his envoy on several delicate
missions. The epistles to Timothy and Titus show them as St.
Paul's legates in Ephesus and Crete. He charges them particularly to preach sound doctrine and to preserve the deposit
of the faith.

404
St. **Paula,** Roman widow, mother of the saintly virgins Eustochium and Blesilla. For twenty years she presided over a sisterhood she founded near St. Jerome's monastery at Bethlehem.

12th cent.   [*O.S.B., O. Cist., O.C.S.O.*]
Sts. **Robert, Alberic,** and **Stephen Harding,** founders of Cit-

eaux in 1098 and in rapid succession its first three abbots. All were monks of Molesme who wanted a more literal observance of the rule of St. Benedict. European monasticism of every description was flourishing; but Citeaux in Burgundy projected an ascetic ideal of austere simplicity, hard work, and personal prayer that soon held first place in popular favor—especially after 1112 when St. Bernard arrived there with thirty companions. The white habit became a symbol of reform.

When St. Stephen Harding died there were 75 Cistercian abbeys—by the end of the century there were more than 500. Their many farms, often at some distance from the abbey, gave particular scope to brothers as a group distinct from the choir monks. The **Charter of Charity**—famous Cistercian organizational guidelines first drawn up by St. Stephen Harding—introduced two constitutional features which have since become an accepted part of monasticism: **general chapters,** to bring all the abbots together at regular intervals, and periodic **visitations** of every monastery by an outside abbot to interview the monks and take stock of religious observance.

JANUARY 27 *

1540

ST. ANGELA MERICI, foundress at Brescia, Italy, of the Ursulines, the first teaching order of women in the church. Orphaned at ten and raised by a well-to-do uncle she saw the need for catechetical instruction among the poor in her village. She inspired generous young women—many of them Franciscan tertiaries like herself—to help in this work.

Her project developed gradually, and what finally took form at Brescia when Angela was nearly sixty was something like a secular institute. The members lived at home—though they gathered for worship—and regularly went to various dwellings of the poor to give instruction. In this way they came into

---

*O.S.B., O. Cist., O.C.S.O. see Jan. 26 for Sts. Timothy and Titus.

close contact with entire families. It was one of Angela's favorite sayings that "disorder in society is the result of disorder in the home," and her objective was the rechristianization of family life—and thus of society—through the education of future wives and mothers.

On Nov. 25, 1535—now kept by thousands of Ursulines as their founding date—Angela and twenty-eight companions dedicated themselves to God under the patronage of St. Ursula. Their rule prescribed poverty, chastity, and obedience, but no habit—a black dress was recommended—no vows, enclosure or regular community life. These things were to come a few years after St. Angela's death, especially through the influence of St. Charles Borromeo, and were in turn modified in the course of the centuries to adapt St. Angela's ideal of service to the changing needs of the church. The first convent school for girls in North America was conducted by the Ursulines who arrived at Quebec in 1639 under Bl. Marie of the Incarnation.

1896 [*S.T.J.*]

Bl. Henry de Ossó y Cervelló, priest of the diocese of Terragona, Spain, seminary professor, preacher, writer, and founder of the Society of St. Teresa of Jesus. These catechetically oriented Teresian Sisters, founded in 1876 for the education of girls and the formation of Christian women, grew out of a group of school teachers to whom Bl. Henry gave spiritual as well as pedagogical direction.

Bl. Henry was an apostle of prayer, that "relationship of friendship" with God, which he along with his mentor, St. Teresa of Avila, saw as an indispensable means of knowing oneself, of living in truth and of growing in the love of God and of every virtue. Prayer was the source of his priestly joy, balance and strength, and he saw it as an effective means of changing the world. His book, entitled in Spanish "A Quarter of an Hour of Prayer," written when he was 33, went through fifteen printings before his death at 55 and through fifty more by the time of his beatification in 1979. By then, too, the Teresian Sisters throughout the world numbered some 2000 and had associated groups such as Teresian Youth, Teresian Laity, and Friends of Jesus. The founder also edited a monthly Teresian review and kept abreast of social questions affecting the apostolate. Hardly had Pope Leo XIII written **Rerum Novarum** before Bl. Henry followed with a social "Catechism for Workers and the Rich."

JANUARY 28 *

1274

ST. THOMAS AQUINAS, Dominican, author of the **Summa Theologiae,** patron of Catholic schools. His life and spirit are best characterized in the profession of faith he made when they brought him Holy Viaticum: "I am receiving You, O price of my soul's redemption. All my studies, my vigils, and my labors were for love of You. I have taught much and written much of the most Sacred Body of Jesus Christ. I have taught and written in the faith of Christ and of the Holy Roman Church, to whose judgment I offer and submit everything." He died on the way to the Second Council of Lyons, March 7, being only forty-nine or fifty years old.

His whole life had been spent in an atmosphere of prayer and study: from the age of six to fourteen with the Benedictines at Monte Cassino, then at the university of Naples where, despite frantic family opposition, he decided to join the recently formed Friars of St. Dominic, an order principally devoted to teaching and preaching. At Paris and Cologne—over a period of seven years—he was a special understudy to St. Albert the Great. He taught and preached at Paris, Orvieto, Rome, Viterbo, and Naples.

In one of his earliest writings, the much translated **On Being and Essence,** he shows himself already in possession of the insights regarding the act of existence which made his philosophy unique. Though he constantly wrote on controversial topics, there is a remarkable serenity in his work; for he made a point of not writing in the first person, thus avoiding the word 'I',

* *S.V.D. see Jan. 29 for Bl. Joseph Freindametz.*

BLESSED HENRY DE OSSO Y CERVELLO

and he never mentions contemporaries by name but simply
states the various opinions currently held on the matter under
discussion. Though in profound agreement with St. Augustine—
to whom he looked as his greatest teacher—he achieved a new
synthesis that went beyond mediaeval Augustinianism, and one
which subsequent ages have judged more in harmony with divine revelation and human reason. In the 650 years since his
canonization no other teacher has been so highly endorsed by
popes and councils, and he is the only doctor whom the II
Vatican Council specifically proposes as intellectual guide for
priesthood and university students.

JANUARY 29

ca. 570

St. Gildas, called the Wise, an important monastic figure
among the Britons in the sixth century. He was probably trained
in Wales under St. Illtud. The book he wrote on the Britons
is famous not only as the first history of that people but also
as a merciless expose of the vices of their ecclesiastical and
lay leaders. St. Gildas left the country and spent his last years
in Brittany.

While some do not take him seriously, others see in him the
spirit of apostolic reproof characteristic of Celtic monasticism.
He recalls how St. Basil righteously withstood the emperor despite a threat to his life. The book ends by reminding priests
that it is not enough merely to avoid personal sins; for according to the Scriptures, they will also be held responsible for the
sins of others unless they speak out fearlessly and are able to
say with St. Paul, "My conscience is clear as far as all of you
are concerned, for I have without faltering put before you the
whole of God's purpose."

1908

Bl. Joseph Freindametz, the first Society of the Divine Word missionary in China where he went at 28 and spent the remaining 28 years of his life, the first in Hong Kong and the next in southern Shantung. Ordained at 24 for the diocese of Brixen in Southern Tyrol, he applied for the foreign missions two years later and went to Steyl, Holland, where Bl. Arnold Janssen was founding his missionary society. The two were beatified together in 1975.

JANUARY 30 *

680

St. Bathildis, queen of France, nun. She was an English maiden sold as slave into the entourage of King Clovis II, whom she eventually married. Their three sons all became kings. As regent after her husband's death she forbade slave traffic and simony, promoted just taxation, and gave generous endowments to monasteries and churches. She founded the abbey of Corbie and the convent of Chelles. It was to this convent that she was sent when Ebroin, mayor of the palace, deprived her of power.

1640   *[Franciscan III O.]*

St. Hyacintha a Mariscotti, third order Franciscan nun at Viterbo, a remarkable instance of a religious who made a poor start, had a change of heart, slackened again, and finally after a second conversion reached a wonderful sanctity. When her parents married off her younger sister to a local noble, Hyacintha, deeply hurt at being passed over, became so disagreeable at home that she was practically forced into a convent.

For ten years she evaded the rule in every way possible until sickness and a stern rebuke from her confessor who beheld all the comforts she had accumulated in her room, brought on a period of fervor. But another serious illness was needed to

---

* *F.S.C. see Oct. 26 for Bl. Mutien Marie Wiaux.*

effect a lasting change. From then on her severity toward herself was excessive, though with others she showed much understanding and prudence. She became novice mistress and was instrumental in starting two lay confraternities to help the sick and needy in Viterbo. She died at fifty-five.

1710 [*C.O.*]

Bl. Sebastian Valfré, Oratorian in Turin, where he refused the archbishopric. In temperament, as well as in the quality and extent of his apostolate, he resembled St. Philip Neri. He is described as dying of punctuality; for hurrying to evening prayer, he arrived overheated, prayed in a cool room, and caught a chill. He was eighty.

JANUARY 31 *

1888

ST. JOHN BOSCO, educator and founder, he was an apostle of the printed word, worked miracles, read people's hearts, and had prophetic dreams.

The first dream, and one that would recur fifteen times at important moments in his life, gives an insight into his vocation and his special devotion to Mary. In an autobiography he wrote at the request of Pope Pius IX, he tells how he saw himself in a yard with a crowd of children, some playing and laughing, others swearing and using foul language. He began beating them and shouting to make them stop. Then a man in white told him to take care of all these boys. "You must win these friends of yours," he said, "not with cuffs and blows, but with gentleness and kindness." A beautiful lady next came forward, all in light. In place of the children there were now animals of all sorts. "Try to be humble and strong," she said, "and what you see happening to these animals is what you must do with my boys." As she spoke the wild animals be-

---

* *C.R.S.P. see Feb. 1 for St. Francis Xavier Bianchi.*

came gentle lambs playing contentedly around the Lady and her Son. When he told the dream next morning his mother said, "Giovanni will be a priest." He was nine at the time. Though poor and fatherless he was soon the center of a group of boys in his village.

His major work began at Turin the year of his priestly ordination when he met a poor orphan and decided to prepare him for Holy Communion. At the age of sixty, after training thousands of boys, he could not remember that he ever used direct punishment. Boys sensed at once that he loved them. He believed in friendliness, appreciation of effort, fostering a sense of responsibility, and removing occasions of disobedience— all in the presence of a loving, merciful God. Frequent confession and communion, thorough catechetical instruction, and training in the manual arts were all part of what became known as the Salesian Method; for he chose the gentle St. Francis de Sales as patron of the congregation he founded.

Already numbering well over twenty thousand priests and brothers, spread throughout the world and particularly numerous in South America, they form one of the largest orders in the church. With St. Mary Mazzarello he founded the Salesian Sisters, and for lay people he established a third order of Salesian Cooperators.

SAINT JOHN BOSCO

FEBRUARY 1

ca. 525

St. Brigid or **Bride,** who has been Ireland's most popular
feminine saint and in a sense the patroness of all the good
women born on Irish soil. She was abbess-foundress of Kildare.
Hers is believed to be the first community of nuns in Ireland.
Countless stories were told portraying her gaiety, driving energy,
and her charity to the poor—"What is mine is theirs," she
would say. As a model of Christian womanhood she was the
talk of the Irish wherever they went; and so she became popular in many places throughout Europe.

1220

Bl. Reginald of Orleans, the earliest of the Dominican saints
and blesseds. He died at thirty-seven, two years after meeting St.
Dominic. A one-time canon law professor at the University of
Paris, he was of invaluable help to St. Dominic in giving the
brotherhood its definitive form. According to a tradition in the
order, it was to Reginald that the Blessed Virgin made known
her wish that preaching brothers wear the white scapular of

friars instead of the rochet Dominic had worn as a canon.

1815

St. Francis Xavier Bianchi, Barnabite, superior, professor and apostle in Naples where thousands sought out his confessional. St. Alphonsus Liguori, having faced a similar conflict himself, helped him make up his mind to enter religion in spite of his father's opposition. His fame for performing miracles was widespread, especially because he foretold and then arrested the flow of lava from Vesuvius in 1804 and 1805.

1888

Bl. Anna Michelotti, who founded the Little Servants of the Sacred Heart of Jesus to care for the sick poor in their homes. She was lovingly initiated into this apostolate at 12 by visiting and tending the sick poor on the day of her First Communion, her mother leading the way. In her late teens and early twenties, bereft of family, she devoted herself totally to works of mercy and religion in her native Annecy, Savoy. At 27 the scene of her labors shifted to Turin, where in a special way she came under the influence of St. John Bosco. After four years she started her order, adding a fourth vow to serve the sick poor gratis, and she took the name Jane Frances of St. Mary of the Visitation. At 44 in very weak health she resigned her office and sought the lowest place. Bl. Anna died within a few months. When her sisters told her on January 31 that John Bosco had just died she said, "He, today. I, tomorrow. We will meet in heaven."

FEBRUARY 2

PRESENTATION OF OUR LORD. Originating in Jerusalem, this ancient feast is first mentioned by the pilgrim nun Egeria about the year 400. Speaking of Jerusalem she writes in her diary: "The fortieth day after Epiphany is celebrated here with the greatest solemnity. On that day there is a procession into the church of the Resurrection and all assemble there for the liturgy. . . . All the priests give sermons, and the bishops, too; and all preach on the gospel text describing how on the fortieth day Joseph and Mary took the Lord to the temple, and how Simeon and Anna the prophetess, the daughter of Phanuel, saw Him, and what words they spoke on seeing the Lord, and of the offering which his parents brought."

1640

St. Joan de Lestonnac, a widow who raised her four children and then turned to religious life, eventually founding the teaching order of Notre Dame of Bordeaux, also called the Company of Mary. Her own mother, sister of the essayist Montaigne, had tried to win Joan over to Calvinism as a young girl. She saw her order increase to thirty houses. Among the blessings she left to her order—which is still flourishing today—is the example of imperturbable patience under calumny and deposition.

1861

Bl. Theophane Venard, priest of the Paris Foreign Missions Society, beheaded at Hanoi at the age of thirty-one, the best known of the Vietnam martyrs. His fascinating letters, especially those written from a cage during his last two months, have inspired generations of French missionaries.

In a letter to his family he wrote: "Can you fancy me sitting quietly in the center of my wooden cage, borne by eight soldiers, in the midst of an immense crowd. . . . I heard some of them say, 'What a pretty boy that European is!' 'He is gay and bright, as if he were going to a feast!'" To his sister, a nun' "It is midnight. . . . About two feet from my cage a feeble oil lamp throws its flickering light on this sheet of Chinese paper. . . . According to all human probability, I shall be beheaded. . . . At this news, darling sister, you will shed tears, but they should be a joy!" To Bishop Theurel: "I should be very grateful if you could manage to send some remembrance of me to my family. My chalice was a family parting souvenir.

If my brother Eusebius could have it, he would be in seventh
heaven. . . ." To Eusebius he recalled how his vocation began
at their home village of St. Loup: "When, at the age of nine,
I took my pet goat to browse on the slopes of Bel-Air, I used
to devour the life and death of Venerable Charles Cornay, and
say to myself, 'And I, too, will go to Tonkin, and I too will be
a martyr!' "

FEBRUARY 3 *

ca. 316

ST. BLAISE, martyr, believed to be bishop of Sebaste, now
Sivas in central Turkey. Devotion to him as a healer of throats
developed in the East by the sixth century. He became particularly popular in Germany and France during the Middle Ages.

865

ST. ANSGAR, Benedictine, apostle of Denmark and Sweden,
first archbishop in Hamburg and Bremen, and papal legate for
the Scandinavian missions. He came as a young monk and
teacher from Corbie in Picardy to help found New Corbie, or
Corvey, in Westphalia—a monastery that was to be the cradle
of Christian civilization in northern Germany. He spent two
missionary periods in Denmark and Sweden, one of them after
his appointment as archbishop. A brilliant preacher and administrator, with many stories telling of his austerities and love
of the poor, he longed to become a martyr but died peacefully
at Bremen at the age of sixty-five. He made a permanent missionary contribution further south, particularly in Schleswig-
Holstein; but Sweden, where he was the first to preach the gospel, slipped back into paganism for another century and a half.

1305   [O.S.M.]

Bl. Joachim of Siena, son of the wealthy Piccolomini family,

---

*M.E.P. see Feb. 2 for Bl. Theophane Venard.

a Servite brother at fourteen. As a child he wanted to give so many things away that his father in jest said he would reduce the family to poverty. "But you told me yourself," the boy answered, "that what we give to the poor we give to Christ. Can we refuse him anything?" He loved to serve Mass and at times fells into ecstasy during the celebration but he could not be prevailed upon to become a priest. To avoid local acclaim he succeeded in being sent elsewhere, but the people of Siena insisted that their saint be brought back.

1840 [*O.S.A., O.A.R.*]
Bl. Stephen Bellesini, a native of Trent who became an Augustinian at sixteen just before the French Revolution and resumed community life as soon as it was legally possible. His was the uneventful but intensely apostolic life typical of a self-sacrificing priest. He served as novice master and finally became parish priest at Genazzano, Italy, where he was stricken at sixty-five while attending the sick during a cholera epidemic.

1838
Bl. Marie Rivier, who at 27 founded the Sisters of the Presentation of Mary to instruct poor girls. This was in France in 1796 just two years after the Reign of Terror shed so much blood to put an end to Christianity. In less than 10 years 20 schools were opened and from there the order spread to many other lands. At the beatification in 1982 the Presentation Sisters numbered nearly 3000. Mother Marie Rivier was 4 feet 3 inches tall and remarkable for her resourcefulness, tenacity, courage and joy. She died at 69.

FEBRUARY 4*

1590 [*O.P.*]
St. Catherine dei Ricci, a Dominican nun in Prato near Flor-

S.J.: among those honored today is also Bl. James Berthieu (see June 8). C.PP.S. see Aug. 20 for Bl. Mary de Mattias.

ence at thirteen, one of the most famous mystics. Among the more unusual phenomena were the spiritual "visits" she had with Rome's St. Philip Neri without leaving Prato, the stigmata which appeared in different ways to different observers, and the ring—always visible to herself—which our Lord placed on her finger on Easter Sunday, 1542, the first year she experienced Christ's passion. She was then twenty. Every week for the next twelve years, from Thursday noon until four on Friday afternoon, she witnessed the passion in a state of ecstasy broken only during the short time on Friday morning when she received Holy Communion. She would go through the same motions she saw Christ make. The convent was so disturbed by people who wanted to see for themselves, that Catherine, who had become prioress, asked all the sisters to pray that these ecstasies would stop. They lasted two more years.

An able administrator and psychologically very wholesome, she was never more content than when caring for the sick. She gave much spiritual advice in person and in letters of great charm. Death came at sixty-eight after a lengthy illness.

1612   [*Franciscans*]

St. Joseph of Leonessa in Umbria, Capuchin preacher and missionary. He was particularly devoted to the crucifix and generally held it while preaching. With crucifix in hand he underwent two cancer operations. It had been suggested that he be tied down; but he pointed to the crucifix, saying, "This is the strongest bond. It will hold me better than any cords."

As a young priest he spent two years as a volunteer missionary in Turkey. He ministered to Christians and particularly to galley slaves at Constantinople and—despite the death penalty—preached to the Moslems. He was imprisoned a second time as he was entering the royal palace to evangelize the Sultan himself. Condemned to death, he hung for three days suspended by hooks through one hand and one foot. Then he was unaccountably released.

1693 [*S.J.*]

St. John de Britto, Portuguese Jesuit missionary in southern India, where he identified with the culture and lived as a **guru.** The day before his martyrdom he wrote to his superior, "I await death with impatience. It has always been the object of my prayers."

FEBRUARY 5

Unknown date.

ST. AGATHA, virgin, martyred at Catania, and invoked by Sicilians for protection against the eruptions of Mt. Etna.

ca. 518

St. Avitus, a holy and learned bishop who succeeded his father in the see of Vienne. He was the mainstay of Catholic life in the territory occupied by the Arian Burgundians. An outspoken advocate of papal primacy and leader of the Romeward-looking bishops of France, he wrote, "If the pope of Rome is called into doubt, it is not a bishop but the episcopate itself that will be seen tottering." He won the leading Burgundians to the Catholic faith and made them the first Germanic nation to be attached to the Apostolic See. His eighty-six surviving letters are historically important.

1880

St. Josepha Rossello, foundress of the Daughters of Our Lady of Mercy. At sixteen she became a Franciscan tertiary. She spent the next ten years in works of charity and then she and three other young women offered themselves to the bishop of Savona, Italy, as a religious community to teach poor children, to care for abandoned girls in the diocese and to do all kinds of charity under the inspiration of divine compassion. She headed the congregation for forty years. By the time of her death on Dec.

7, 1880, there were sixty-eight convents. "Hands are made for work," she would say, "and the heart for God."

FEBRUARY 6

1597   [*Franciscans, S.J.*]

ST. PAUL MIKI and **COMPANIONS,** twenty-six Nagasaki martyrs, the first in the Far East to be canonized. Included are Paul Miki, a high-born Japanese Jesuit priest; two Jesuit brothers, also Japanese; six Franciscans, foreigners and mostly Spanish, and **St. Peter Baptist** as their leader; and seventeen Japanese and Korean lay persons—all Franciscan tertiaries, who were helping the priests in their work. Fastened to twenty-six crosses and raised aloft four feet apart in one long row, they continued to preach and sing. Each had his own executioner at his side ready with a spear and at a signal all were killed at the same moment. Among them, as intrepid as the rest, were three boys about thirteen years old who used to serve the friars' Masses: **St. Louis Ibarki, St. Anthony Deynan,** and **St. Thomas Kasaki.** It was then approximately fifty years since St. Francis Xavier had landed in Japan; and there were about 300,000 Catholics, only 100,000 less than today.

539

St. Vedast or **Vaast,** missionary bishop of Arras in northern France. As a young priest he helped prepare King Clovis for baptism.

ca. 690

St. Amand, abbot and regional bishop, apostle of Belgium and founder of its first monasteries. His headquarters were at Elnone, later called the Abbey of St. Amand. In time it became a purely Benedictine monastery, but in the beginning—as with many seventh century foundations in France—there was a combination of the rule of St. Benedict with elements from the rule of St. Columban.

1898

Bl. Maria Catherine Kasper, humble foundress at 31 of the Poor Handmaids of Jesus Christ. Her congregation grew out of the small group of young women who joined Catherine in visiting and tending the sick and caring for orphans in the small village of Dernbach, Germany. Clear-headed about the things of God, she governed the sisters with a warm, motherly heart until her death at 77, when their number was nearly 2000 and they had spread to many lands. "All our sisters must be saints," she would say, "but hidden saints." Her motto from the **Imitation of Christ** was, "Desire to be unknown and to be counted as nothing." Refusing the title of foundress she would say, "God's Holy Will must and shall happen in me, through me and for me."

FEBRUARY 7

1447 *[Franciscans]*

St. Colette, abbess-general and mystic, the nun who did more than any other in the 750 years of Poor Clare history to have the Primitive Rule observed, the rule which St. Clare herself wrote. When Colette began her work most of the monasteries were following the rule issued by Pope Urban IV, which permitted the sisters to have a fixed income.

At seventeen Colette lost both her parents and was left in the care of the abbot of Corbie in Picardy, where her father had been a carpenter. She tried the Beguines, the Benedictines, and the Poor Clares—in a space of less than two years—and then became a recluse. After four years, in response to the command of St. Francis in a vision, she set out to re-establish the Primitive Rule. She went to the anti-pope Peter de Luna, whom France was then acknowledging as Benedict XIII. He believed her, dispensed her from making a novitiate, received her into the Poor Clares, and made her abbess-general of any monasteries she could found or reform. She was then only twenty-five. In the next forty years she founded at least seventeen houses and reformed many others, also writing constitutions of her own.

Prayer was her great support. To be rapt in ecstasy after Communion was a normal occurrence. Fridays, kept free from all duties, she devoted entirely to the Passion, neither eating nor drinking. Asked what she considered the most painful thing that could happen to her she replied, "To pass a day without suffering anything for God." Today the majority of Poor Clare monasteries follow the Primitive Rule with its privilege of absolute poverty.

1812

Bl. Giles Mary, a rope-maker who became a Franciscan brother at Naples and spent his life as monastery porter showing compassion to the poor and sick. The more he gave away the more help seemed to flow in.

1871

Bl. Eugenia de Smet, foundress in Paris of the Helpers of the Holy Souls. By prayer, mortification, and work these sisters strive to give all possible help to the souls in purgatory. During a retreat at seventeen she made a firm resolution never to say "no" to God. She would later refer to this decision as her "conversion." The idea of founding such an order came to her as a spiritual experience on All Souls Day. She consulted the Curé of Ars and he told her to go ahead. The sisters help the sick, the poor and the abandoned.

FEBRUARY 8

1537

ST. JEROME EMILIANI, founder of the Somaschi, patron of

BLESSED MARY CATHERINE KASPER

orphans, a Venetian commander whose thoughts turned to the things of God during captivity in a dungeon. With his good resolutions crystalized by what seemed a miraculous escape, he entered the priesthood, founded an order at Somascha near Bergamo to care for orphans and the sick and also to educate clerics and the young. He died of a contagious disease he contracted while caring for the sick.

1124

St. Stephen Muret, abbot founder near Limoges of the Order of Grandmont, hermit-monks, similar in some ways to the Carthusians. He did not draw up a rule for he used to say that the Gospel of Christ is the only rule. The order flourished in France for over a century but became plagued with constitutional problems, particularly regarding the position of brothers.

1461

Bl. Anthony of Stroncone in Italy, Franciscan brother who strongly opposed the excesses of the heretical Fraticelli. For thirty years he lived practically on bread and water.

1593

Bl. James Salès, and **Bl. William Saultemouche,** Jesuit priest and brother killed by the Huguenots at Aubenas in southern France where Father Sales went in response to the Mayor's request for a series of sermons on the Catholic faith.

One night a mob gathered at the gate. The missionaries hurried to the church where the priest gave Holy Communion to his companion and consumed the remaining Hosts.

Father Sales defended the faith at length before a Calvinist court and when he refused to renounce articles of the faith, especially as regards the Eucharist, he was shot. Brother Saultemouche remained on the scene rather than take an opportunity to escape. They were martyred on February 7.

FEBRUARY 9

249

St. Apollonia, a martyr at Alexandria, whose dramatic death made her popular in the West. During the persecution of Emperor Philip this aged deaconess was seized and beaten. A large fire was kindled and she was given the opportunity of saving her life by pronouncing some impious words. She begged for a moment's delay and on being released eagerly jumped into the flames. St. Augustine believed her action was performed under special divine inspiration, for it would not otherwise have been lawful for her to hasten death in this way.

1910   [F.S.C.]

Bl. Michael Francis Febres Cordero, a Brother of the Christian Schools, scholar, poet and member of the Academy of Ecuador. He taught for over 40 of his 55 years, mostly in Quito, wrote text books that included one of the most successful Spanish grammars, and taught religion as his favorite subject, finding special joy in preparing boys for their first Communion. Deformed feet kept him from walking until he was five, at which time he also had an apparition of the Blessed Virgin.

Educated at home until the age of nine, he was one of the first to enroll in the Brothers' school at Cuenca in 1863, the year they came to Latin America. To offset his wish to become a brother, his parents sent him to the seminary to study for the priesthood; but in a matter of months violent headaches caused him to leave the seminary and he was free to return to the brothers' school. He entered the novitiate at thirteen, with his mother signing the permission in the father's absence. When the superior sent Br. Michael to Quito his father, not getting his own way about where his son should be, did not write to him for five years.

Br. Michael was in Rome in 1888 for the beatification of St. John Baptist de la Salle, the order's founder. He returned to Europe again in 1907 to help prepare teaching materials for the French brothers who were learning Spanish in order to work in Latin America, since anti-clericalism was forcing them out of France. He spent a year in Belgium and then was sent to Spain, where he died of pneumonia after experiencing some of the hardships of revolution and further anti-clericalism. On his premature death a day of national mourning was declared in Ecuador. In 1936, during the Spanish Revolution, the body of Br. Michael was returned with triumphal welcome to Quito.

FEBRUARY 10

547

ST. SCHOLASTICA, sister of St. Benedict. Consecrated a virgin while still very young, she would go each year to visit her brother and lodge at some distance in a house belonging to the monastery. St. Gregory's account of their last meeting is one of the best remembered stories in monastic history, for it showed the warmth of the divine and human love of this first 'Benedictine' nun and also served as a parable of the feminine approach.

The incident, as told by St. Gregory, occurred three days before Scholastica's death and a few weeks before that of St. Benedict. He went down the hill with several monks and spent the day with her. In the evening they ate together and continued their conversation until very late. "Please do not leave me tonight, brother," she pleaded, "let us keep on talking about the joys of heaven till morning." But the abbot felt he must return to the monastery for the night. So she prayed, and also shed some tears. Suddenly a fierce storm struck Cassino. "Leave now," she said, "if you can. When I asked you, you would not listen to me; so I turned to my God and He heard me." "We need not be surprised," observed St. Gregory, "that she proved mightier than her brother; she had been looking forward so long to this visit. Do we not read in St. John that God is love? Surely it is no more than right that her influence was greater than his, since hers was the greater love."

At her death St. Benedict had her buried at the abbey in the tomb he was readying for himself. "The bodies of these two," Gregory concludes, "were now to share a common resting place, just as in life their souls had always been one in God."

1164   [O. Praem.]
Bl. Hugh of Fosses, first companion of St. Norbert and his chief collaborator in establishing the Premonstratensians and in drawing up their rule. He is regarded as second father of the order. During his thirty-five years as abbot of Prémontré more than a hundred houses of white canons were founded.

1346
Bl. Clare of Rimini, who lived a frivolous life during her first marriage and during part of a second, until at the age of thirty-four she one day in church heard a voice, "Clare, try to say one Our Father and one Hail Mary for the glory of God, without thinking of other things." She enrolled as a third order Franciscan and went to extremes in her penances.

FEBRUARY 11*

OUR LADY OF LOURDES. On February 11, 1858, the Blessed Virgin appeared for the first time to Bernadette Soubirous in the recess of the Massabielle cliff near Lourdes, at the foot of the Pyrenees. Bernadette, then just fourteen, reported seeing a most beautiful woman, young and not taller than herself, dressed in white. A long rosary hung from her arm. She greeted Bernadette with a slight bow and seemed to invite her to pray. She passed the beads through her fingers as Bernadette recited the rosary.

On February 25th Bernadette was told, "Go, drink at the spring and wash in it." Perplexed, she started for the river Gave; but the maiden in white pointed to the floor of the cave. "I went there," Bernadette recounts, "but I only saw a little

*O.S.B., O.Cist., O.C.S.O. see Feb. 13 for St. Benedict of Aniane.

dirty water. I put my hand in but could not get enough to drink. I scratched and the water came, but muddy. Three times I threw it away, but the fourth time I could drink it." Some of the crowd made fun of Bernadette, whose face was daubed with mud; but by the end of the day water was running from the cave to the river. Within a week the spring was yielding what has since been its constant flow of 32,000 gallons a day.

On March 25, feast of the Annunciation, Bernadette asked the visitor her name and was told in the Lourdes dialect, "I am the Immaculate Conception,"—the dogma had been defined by Pope Pius IX four years previously. The eighteenth and last apparition took place on the feast of Our Lady of Mt. Carmel, July 16th, of the same year. Mary had made various requests of Bernadette: to pray for sinners, to do penance, to have processions there and a chapel built. Bernadette was the only one who ever saw the apparition or heard a voice. The ever increasing crowds, growing into thousands, saw only Bernadette in her states of ecstasy.

Cures occur during the processions and individual blessings with the Sacred Host as well as during the baths. Of the 5,000 cures reported in the first hundred years, fifty-eight were declared as certainly miraculous by the local bishop. But the blessings of Lourdes are primarily in the spiritual order, as in the case of St. Bernadette herself; for Mary told her in the third apparition, "I do not promise to make you happy in this life but in the next."

FEBRUARY 12

381

St. Meletius, bishop of Sebaste and then patriarch in the see of Antioch from which he was expelled several times by various emperors for not being an Arian. A few days after his arrival in Antioch, where Arian bishops had governed for nearly thirty years, a theological tournament was arranged by Emperor Constantius to sound out the new bishop. Several of the leading prelates were asked to expound the passage from **Proverbs** (8, 22), "The Lord created me at the beginning of his work"—a text the Arians understood as implying the creaturehood of the Word. First, George of Laodicea explained it in an Arian sense. Then Acacius of Caesarea gave it an interpretation bordering on the heretical. Meletius came third with a Catholic meaning, for he applied the text to the Incarnation.

He had only been in the city a month but already his meekness had won the hearts of the people. Though he suffered immediate exile, some of the Catholics, not satisfied with his orthodoxy, had another bishop ordained. Through a series of misunderstandings, which St. Basil tried in vain to dispel, it was this second Catholic bishop whom the two other great patriarchates of Alexandria and Rome recognized. The schism named after Meletius was still not resolved when he died in 381 while serving as president of the ecumenical Council of Constantinople. Earlier that year he had ordained St. John Chrysostom his deacon.

1237   [*O.P.*]
Bl. Jordan of Saxony, St. Dominic's first successor as master general. He exemplifies the academic dimension of this new order. He himself was an instructor in theology at Paris when he became interested in the friars through a student St. Dominic sent him. As a novice he attended the order's first general chapter, and at the next chapter he was chosen prior provincial of Lombardy. When scarcely two years in the order he was elected master general.

The Dominicans were the first religious order with a specifically academic mission and Bl. Jordan characterized their vocation as "living an upright life, learning, and teaching." His preaching attracted crowds of students to the order—St. Albert the Great being one of them. He governed for fifteen years.

His sayings became part of the Dominican lore. To one who wanted to know the best way to pray he said, "The way in which you can pray the best." Questioned whether it was better to read the Scriptures or to pray he said it was like asking whether it is better to eat or to drink. He lost his life in a shipwreck off the cost of Syria while on his way to Palestine. His biography of St. Dominic is one of the principal sources of information on the holy founder.

FEBRUARY 13

821

St. Benedict of Aniane, abbot-general in France. After St. Benedict and St. Gregory the Great no one has had more influence on the Benedictines, for he convinced Europe once and for all of the excellence of the Rule of St. Benedict; and he sketched the first outlines of the type of Benedictinism which Cluny would popularize throughout the later Middle Ages. His own enthusiasm for the Benedictine rule came only after three failures with monasticism of a more austere and solitary stamp.

After he had successfully founded or restored a dozen monasteries —over which he continued to rule as abbot—Louis the Pious commissioned him to reform all the abbeys of the kingdom of Aquitaine. When Louis ascended the imperial throne on the death of Charlemagne, he put Benedict at the head of all the monasteries of the realm. At Aachen, in 817, a synod was held for the abbots of the empire and legislation was passed to achieve a nationwide uniform observance. Benedict's monastery of Cornelimünster near Aachen was to be taken as a model, and every abbot was to send one or two promising monks there for training. This program soon collapsed along with the Carolingian empire.

The reform of St. Benedict of Aniane is best remembered for the usages and regulations he introduced over and above the Rule of St. Benedict, things that the new abbey of Cluny would adopt and make typical a century later: increased psalmody and ritual, centralization with exact uniformity, and a self-containment typified by the elimination of schools for outside students.

1308

Bl. James Capocci, Augustinian, archbishop of Naples, noted for his sanctity and the opinion that God had sent three teachers to enlighten the universal church: first, St. Paul the apostle, then St. Augustine, and in recent times Brother Thomas Aquinas. He made his studies at the University of Paris where he had as his teacher Giles of Rome, who in turn had been a student under St. Thomas.

FEBRUARY 14

869 and 885

STS. CYRIL—also called Constantine—and **METHODIUS,** co-patrons with St. Benedict of Europe, teachers of the Slavs and authors of their liturgy, the only brothers other than apostles who have a place to themselves in the universal Roman calendar. Greeks of Thessalonika with a speaking knowledge of Slavonic, they were sent by the emperor of Constantinople and by patriarch Photius to Moravia—now in central Czechoslovakia—where Duke Rastislav, who wanted to make his territory independent of the Franks and Germans, was looking for missionaries who could teach his people in the Slav tongue.

Constantine, who headed the mission, was a priest in his mid-thirties with a reputation as a brilliant philosopher. Methodius, an older brother, had become a monk and abbot after years as governor in a Slavonic sector of the empire. Before setting out for Moravia they constructed a Slavonic alphabet and trans-lated the gospels. Their work prospered. To obtain a bishop, a delegation went to Rome since Moravia was under its jurisdiction. There Constantine became a monk in a Greek monastery, took the name Cyril, and died fifty days later. Methodius was ordained a priest and, with permission to use the Slavonic liturgy, set out as papal legate to all the Slavs. In a matter of months he was back in Rome to be constituted archbishop in the long-defunct see of Sirmium—today Sremska Motrovica in Yugoslavia—with the whole of Pannonia and Moravia as his territory. He was directly subject to the Holy See. Resenting so much loss of territory, the Bavarian bishops made one difficulty after another. In addition, Duke Rastislav's successor preferred the Latin liturgy. St. Methodius was falsely accused, spent a period in exile, and was even imprisoned. The pope obtained his release, cleared him of the false charges, and reconfirmed—after a temporary withdrawal—the right to a vernacular liturgy.

St. Methodius spent the last of his sixteen years as bishop translating the remainder of the Bible into Slavonic and drawing up a code of church law. The two saints are specially venerated by Catholic Czechs, Slovaks, and Croatians, as well as by Orthodox Serbs and Bulgarians.

1613   [*O. SS. T.*]

St. John Baptist Garcias of Almadovar, theologian and local superior at Valdepeña, Spain, where he revitalized the Trinitarians by returning to the original rule. He reformed nineteen houses. His strict-living friars, who became known as the Discalced Trinitarians, pleased the people and attracted donations and vocations, but caused much hard feeling in the other houses. As it turned out, his was the only branch of the order that survived.

FEBRUARY 15

ca. 1045

St. Sigfrid, a bishop from England who worked in Norway

and Sweden. He is honored as apostle of Sweden and is credited with the conversion of King Olaf.

1682   [*S.J., S.C.J.*]

   Bl. Claude de la Colombière, Jesuit priest whose special mission it was to assure St. Margaret Mary Alacoque that her visions regarding the Sacred Heart were genuine. He was born near Lyons in 1641 and joined the Society of Jesus at seventeen. His preaching talent showed already in student days at Avignon. Selected to give the sermon on the occasion of St. Francis de Sales' canonization, he chose as his text the words from Samson's riddle, "Out of the strong came what is sweet." At thirty-three he took solemn vows and two months later became superior of the college at Paray-le-Monial in Burgundy. He stayed there less than two years, but long enough to give St. Margaret Mary Alacoque in the nearby Visitation convent the spiritual direction and encouragement she needed. He was next sent to England as court preacher to the Duchess of York, wife of the future King James II. Imprisoned on false charges in the Titus Oates scare, he was saved from martyrdom through the intervention of Louis XIV of France. Banished from England he died at forty-one in Paray-le-Monial.

   The theology of divine mercy prompting this early advocate of devotion to the Sacred Heart is forcefully expressed in a personal letter of direction to a nun in danger of death who was disturbed by the memory of her failures. "Rest assured," he writes, "that if I were as near rendering my account to God as you seem to be, it would be precisely the number and gravity of my sins that would serve to quicken my trust. Instead of being cast down by the realization of one's failures, to have a strong and boundless conviction of the Creator's goodness—that is a trust worthy of God. It seems to me that confidence inspired by innocence and purity of life does not give a very great glory to God. Is God's mercy able to do no more than save holy souls who have never offended him? Surely the trust that gives the Lord most honor is that of an errant sinner who is so convinced of God's boundless mercy that all his sins seem like a speck in comparison with that mercy."

FEBRUARY 16

1189

St. Gilbert of Sempringham, founder of the Gilbertines with their double monasteries, the only mediaeval order of English origin. The nuns followed the Rule of St. Benedict; and the priest chaplains, that of St. Augustine. He was the son of a Norman knight and an English mother. As a boy he was considered a weakling, being useless at knightly pursuits; yet when he died, worn out by austerities, he was just over one hundred.

1708

Bl. Francis de Laval, first bishop of the Diocese of Quebec, after Mexico the oldest diocese in North America. Of French nobility, he was a cleric at 8 and at 22 lost his father and two older brothers. His mother urged him to marry and manage the family patrimony, but he was by then a cleric by conviction. Ten years at the Jesuit school of La Flèche marked him deeply with love of virtue and zeal for the missions and the papacy. So he went on to major orders and at 24 was ordained a priest. For the next six years he showed himself a competent civil lord and a zealous churchman. At 31 he handed the patrimony over to a younger brother, renounced his position as Archdeacon of Évreux, and associated himself with the Hermitage at Caen, a pious group of priests and laymen intent on preaching, works of piety and holiness of life.

At 35 he was appointed Vicar Apostolic to New France. Gallicans dominated the French church in the seventeenth century. They objected to this appointment as an intrusion of Rome and dissuaded the French bishops from conferring the episcopal order on Laval. He was therefore ordained secretly by the papal nuncio in the exempt

Abbey of Saint-Germain-des-Prés in Paris. The following spring, April 1659, the new bishop sailed for his mission territory. It included today's Canada and most of the United States except the Atlantic colonies and California. Its total French population was hardly 2000. His vicariate was raised to a diocese in 1674.

Despite their unwillingness to support the officially constituted parishes and their objections to seminary tithes, the colonists revered and loved Bishop Laval. "I do not say he is a saint," wrote Bl. Marie of the Incarnation, "that would be saying too much; but I will truthfully say he lives like a saint and an apostle." He had the support of his clergy except for the Recollect Friars Governor Frontenac reintroduced into the colony to support more lenient moral views. The bishop resorted to excommunication to combat liquor trade with the natives. He fostered devotion to the Holy Family and to St. Anne. In 1663 he founded the Seminary of Quebec which he envisioned as the keystone of the apostolate throughout New France, being both the training center and a corporate body of the secular clergy.

In his early sixties poor health moved him to resign and he carefully picked his successor from France. But he would live on for more than twenty years, spent mostly at the seminary edifying all with his holiness of life and the patient with which he bore his greatest trial in the policy changes of his successor regarding the seminary—which has since evolved into Laval University.

FEBRUARY 17

13th and 14th cent.

THE SEVEN HOLY FOUNDERS of the Servite order. When these young Florentine cloth merchants left their families and possessions to begin a life of shared poverty in the district of Cafaggio outside the city wall, they had no idea of starting an order; there was only a common longing for a life in the spirit of the primitive church. They wore the grey habit of the Brothers of Penance, a lay fraternity to which they belonged, and devoted themselves to prayer, penance, and works of mercy. Before long, some of the group took up a solitary life on Monte Senario, twelve miles from Florence.

When the Dominican, Peter of Verona, the future saint and martyr, preached in Florence during advent and lent of 1244-45, the brothers helped him organize the lay Society of Mary, while he helped the brothers form a single religious community including both the hermits on Monte Senario and the apostolic group at Cafaggio. They called themselves Servants of Mary, as there was a chapel in honor of Mary at both places. The rule of St. Augustine was adopted and they also took the Dominican habit, but in black.

The motherhouse of the order today is the hermitage of Monte Senario while the generalate is the Priory of St. Marcellus in Rome. There are Servite nuns as well as a third order. The veneration of Mary under the title of Our Lady of Sorrows has, since the sixteenth century, become the characteristic devotion in Servite churches. In 1668 the friars obtained permission for the feast of Our Lady of Sorrows. The seven founders, canonized in 1888, are **Sts. Bonfilius, John Buonagiunta, Gerard Sostegni, Bartholomew Amidei, Benedict dell'Antella, Ricoverus Uguccione, and Alexis Falconieri.**

603

St. Fintan, abbot of Cloneenagh, a leading figure in Irish monasticism. He was hard on himself, living—it is said—on barley bread and muddy water; but towards others he was gentle and compassionate. St. Columba described him as having a ruddy face, gleaming eyes, and hair flecked with white.

FEBRUARY 18

449

St. Flavian, patriarch of Constantinople during four troubled years, the first to censure Eutyches. He withstood court intimidation and died in exile shortly after being deposed by Dioscorus of Alexandria in the "Robber Synod" at Ephesus. Two years later the Council of Chalcedon vindicated his memory, deposed Dioscorus, and condemned Eutyches. It was to St. Flavian that Pope St. Leo the Great sent the famous dogmatic letter, known as the **Tome,** containing an authoritative statement of Catholic faith regarding the two natures and unity of person in Christ.

1088

Bl. Marianus Scotus, Irish pilgrim who started off for Rome but got no farther than Regensburg in Bavaria. There he eventually founded the abbey of St. James, soon the center of a Benedictine congregation of Irish monasteries in southern Germany, the famous Schottenklöster of the twelfth and thirteenth centuries. Bl. Marianus is best remembered for his work as a copyist, the specialty to which he devoted so much time. Vienna Codex 1247 contains the Epistles of St. Paul in his beautiful hand with Latin and Irish glosses for the use of pilgrims.

1166

St. Theotonius, highly honored in Portugal, abbot of the Augustinian canons at Coimbra. One day as he was about to begin the Mass of the Blessed Mother, a message came from the Queen of Portugal to say that he should hurry through the Mass; but he sent work back that he was about to honor a sovereign greater than any on earth and that the queen was free to stay or to go.

FEBRUARY 19

441

St. Mesrop the Teacher, founder of Armenian Christian literature. After a good education, probably at Antioch, he became a monk. Ordained a priest by St. Isaac the Great, he undertook a missionary journey into the outer provinces of Armenia and returned convinced of the need for a written Armenian language. He invented a thirty-six letter alphabet and headed the small group, mostly young monks, whom St. Isaac commissioned to translate the Bible and various works of Greek and Syrian fathers. He helped found schools and monasteries, did missionary work among the Georgians and Albanians in the Caucasus region, and governed the Armenian church after the death of St. Isaac. The Armenian Mass invokes him as "Mesrop the Teacher."

1351 *[Franciscan III O.]*

St. Conrad of Piacenza, a devoted husband and father who eventually became a hermit. To flush out some game in a hunt he started a fire that did much harm. A poor woodsman was accused and was on the verge of being executed; so Conrad gave himself up. The damages he paid brought poverty, but gradually he and his wife began to appreciate the ideals of St. Francis. She joined the Poor Clares and he became a Franciscan tertiary. St. Conrad spent his last forty years as a solitary and counsellor in a cave at Noto, Sicily.

1468 *[O.S.M.]*

Bl. Elizabeth Picenardi, who formed a community of Servite tertiaries at Mantua. She was introduced to the practice of meditation by her mother.

FEBRUARY 20

304

Christians from Egypt martyred in Palestine, many of them at Tyre. Eusebius tells of instances he himself witnessed in which several relays of wild beasts would attack anyone except the intended victims—who were finally beheaded. One youth under twenty made a profound impression as he stood in one position without trembling, eyes raised and arms extended in the form of a cross, as the bears and leopards approached in all ferocity and then withdrew.

1894

Bl. Mary Henrietta Dominici, who at 31 was elected superior general in Turin of the Sisters of St. Anne and of Providence. Before accepting she asked the advice of St. Joseph Cottolengo's successor who said, "Put all your trust in God and then if you are not capable of governing you will at least have the humility to let yourself be removed from office." Six successive general chapters of this teaching order re-elected her, and she governed so well until her death at 64 that she can be considered the order's second founder. St. John Bosco had so much respect for the judgment of this exquisitely feminine and thoroughly spiritual nun that he sent her the proposed rules of his Daughters of Our Lady of Perpetual Help, asking her to "take away and add as you in your wisdom think fit." And he had her send some of her nuns to initiate his sisters in the ways of religious life.

Mother Mary Henrietta wrote an **Autobiography** and **Diary** at the command of her spiritual director and many of her letters also survive. Her words carried so much conviction because she first put them into practise herself. To one sister she wrote, "wish what God Wishes, as God wishes, and as long as He wishes." She urged another sister "to see God in one's superior and for his sake to obey promptly; to see God in the Rule and for his sake to observe it perfectly; to see God in one's office and for his sake to carry it out exactly; to see God in difficulties and ordeals and for his sake to bear them patiently; to see God in the inspirations of grace and for his sake to follow them generously and promptly." Death came through cancer. The doctor who treated her said, "I have seen many people die in the nearly 60 years of my practise; but I have never met such patience and resignation." Bl. Mary Dominici died on February 21.

FEBRUARY 21

1072

ST. PETER DAMIAN, monk, cardinal-bishop of Ostia, an indefatigable reformer in his own right and also in the service of a whole series of popes during the first phase of the Gregorian Reform. It was his pen, particularly the scathing denunciation of ignorance and vice among the clergy, that brought him to public attention, for he was a master of Latin style and a prolific writer.

He is usually taken as the classic medieval example of an extreme other-worldly emphasis. What he said of St. Romuald— the subject of his first book—could apply also to him, that he tried "to turn the entire world into a hermitage and make the whole multitude of the people associates of the monastic order." He could speak with such conviction about heaven because of his full experience of divine contemplation.

More than anything else he was a prophet crying out against everything within and without that can keep men "attached" to this world. The scourge or discipline was not his invention, but he encouraged it. Himself one of the most learned men of the eleventh century and even a poet of distinction, he evolved the theory of "holy simplicity," by which a person uses knowledge with complete detachment.

A native of Ravenna, after a short but successful career as a teacher, he became a priest and then joined the hermits founded twenty years earlier at Fonte Avellana by a disciple of St. Romuald. He was soon their prior—he would never call himself "abbot"—and reorganized their life combining the ideals of St. Romuald and St. Benedict, to produce a hermit-community structure wholly ordered towards contemplation. He would encourage his monks to exact observance saying, "We can never restore primitive discipline when once it is decayed. . . . Let us faithfully transmit to posterity the examples of virtue we have received from our forefathers." His works include letters, sermons, lives of saints, and many small treatises.

FEBRUARY 22

ST. PETER'S CHAIR, a feast celebrated in Rome as early as the fourth century. The Church on this day honors the ministry of service given to St. Peter of confirming his brothers in faith, feeding the lambs and sheep, binding and loosing. Christ also symbolized this ministry in a concrete way when he changed Simon's name to **Rock.**

1270

Bl. Isabel of France, sister of St. Louis, king of France, whose crusade she helped by paying the expenses of ten knights. As a young girl she experienced advanced states of prayer and embarked on the lifelong practice of penance and assistance to the poor. Queen Blanche, understanding her daughter, would coax Isabel to eat by promising gifts for the poor.

She resisted all suitors, including Conrad, son and heir of Emperor Frederick II. Pope Innocent IV urged her to accept this match for the advantage of Christian Europe, but she answered so humbly and wisely that the pope applauded her resolution to maintain perpetual virginity.

St. Bonaventure helped draw up the constitutions of the monastery of Poor Clares she founded near Paris. Isabel did not accept the role of abbess or even take vows, but retired to the convent, living outside the enclosure, where she could both pray and take care of the poor. Before Communion she would kneel down and ask pardon of the few servants she maintained.

1670

Bl. Joan Mary Bonomo, Benedictine nun at Bassano, Italy, mystic, a spiritual writer of merit. She had her first ecstasy at the time of profession.

FEBRUARY 23

ca. 166

ST. POLYCARP, bishop of Smyrna, apostolic teacher, burned at the stake. Ordered to revile Christ he answered, "For eighty-six years have I served Him, and He has done me no wrong, and how can I blaspheme my king who saved me?" The contemporary account of the martyrdom, his letter to the Philippians, and the letter St. Ignatius of Antioch wrote to him are among the most precious early Christian documents.

He is especially significant as a strong link between the teach- of the apostles and the fully documented theology of St. Irenaeus at Lyons in the year 200. For Irenaeus, as for Polycarp, apostolic tradition was the guarantee of sound doctrine. Writing to Florinus and rejecting his theological innovations, Irenaeus evokes childhood memories of Polycarp—whom Florinus also knew. "The presbyters before us," Irenaeus writes, "those who even had association with the apostles did not hand such teachings on to us. For while I was still a boy, I saw you in lower Asia with Polycarp. . . . I recall the events of that time better than what has happened recently . . . so that I can tell even the place where the blessed Polycarp sat and talked . . . his features, the discourses which he gave to the multitude, and how he reported his living with John and with the rest of the Apostles who had seen the Lord, and how he remembered their words, and what the things were which he heard from them about the Lord, and about his miracles and about his teaching, how Polycarp received them from eyewitnesses of 'the word of life,' and proclaimed them all in harmony with the Scriptures. These things even then I listened to . . . making notes of them not on paper but in my heart; and ever by the grace of God I turned them over in my mind. I can witness before God that, if that blessed and apostolic presbyter had heard any teachings like this, he would have cried out and stuffed his ears, and according to his custom would have said, 'O good God, to what times have you preserved me, that I should endure these things.'

He would have fled even from the place in which he was seated
or standing when he heard such words. And this can be made
clear from his epistles which he sent either to the neighboring
churches, to strengthen them, or to some of the brethren, to
exhort them and warn them."

FEBRUARY 24

616

St. Ethelbert, king of Kent, who received St. Augustine and
his monks into England in 597. The missionaries, St. Bede relates, had sent the king word "that they had come from Rome,
and brought a joyful message, which assured everlasting joys in
heaven to all who took advantage of it. . . . The King . . . ordered that they stay in the island where they had landed and
that they should be furnished with all necessaries, till he should
consider what to do with them. For he had heard of the Christian religion, having a Christian wife of the royal family of the
Franks, called Bertha. Her parents had allowed the marriage
upon condition that she should be permitted to practice her
religion with the bishop Luidhard, who was sent with her to
preserve her faith. Some days after, the king came into the
island, and sitting in the open air, ordered Augustine and his
companions to be brought into his presence. He had taken pre-
caution that they should not come to him in any house, lest
. . . if they were skilful in sorcery they might impose upon
him and so get the better of him. But they came furnished
with divine, not with magic, power, bearing a silver cross for
their banner and the image of our Lord and Saviour painted on
a board; and singing the litany they offered up their prayers
to the Lord for the eternal salvation both of themselves and of
those to whom they were come. When he had sat down, at the
king's command, and preached to him and his attendants the

word of life, the king answered as follows, 'Your words and promises are very fair, but as they are new to us, and of uncertain import, I cannot approve of them so far as to forsake that which I have so long followed with the whole English nation. But because you are come from far into my kingdom, and, as I conceive are desirous to impart to us those things which you believe to be true, and most beneficial, we will not molest you but rather have you as our guest and supply you with the necessary food. Nor do we forbid you to preach and gain as many as you can to your religion.' Accordingly he permitted them to reside in the city of Canterbury, which was the metropolis of all his dominion."

St. Bede goes on to tell how Ethelbert was baptized on Pentecost of the same year, with Pope St. Gregory sending him presents and reminding him how much Emperor Constantine had done for religion. Ethelbert built Saints Peter and Paul church in Canterbury, St. Paul's in London, and St. Andrew's in Rochester; and he helped St. Augustine obtain possession of an ancient Canterbury church—rededicated then as Christ Church Cathedral.

FEBRUARY 25

779

St. Walburga, Benedictine abbess of Heidenheim. Saints Winebald and Willibald were her brothers. Along with St. Lioba she came from England as a nun to help St. Boniface evangelize Germany. It was in the role of patroness against hunger and plague that she became so popular in Europe. By the ninth century "Walburga's Oil" had become a sacramental. It is a deposit on the stone slab near her relics at Eichstätt and still flows each year from Oct. 12 to Feb. 25.

806

St. Tarasius, patriarch of Constantinople, who presided over the second council of Nicaea in 787 and restored the veneration of sacred images. He was secretary for Queen Irene during her regency and was chosen patriarch while still a layman.

1131

Bl. Adelhelm, a Benedictine of St. Blaise in the Black Forest, who, about 1122, became the first abbot of Engelberg in Switzerland. He is remembered for his enterprise and his joyful trust in God amid the many difficulties that faced the new foundation.

1600

Bl. Sebastian Aparicio, pioneer colonist in Mexico, where he ended his days as a Franciscan credited with many miracles. The son of poor parents, he came to New Spain in his twenties. There he worked as a farmer, road builder, and trainer of young bulls—skills he also taught the Indians. He opened a delivery service in Puebla and then went into road construction. In 1542 he started building the highway that later reached Mexico City, a distance of 450 miles. He became wealthy, married at sixty, and when his young wife died he married a second time. When she also died he gave his wealth to the Poor Clares and at seventy-two became a Franciscan in Mexico City. He spent his last twenty years as begging brother for a large friary in Puebla.

FEBRUARY 26

1601

St. Anne Line, English martyr, a heroic example, along with her husband, of lay dedication in time of persecution. The daughter of ardent Calvinists, she became a Catholic during her teens and was disinherited. At nineteen she married a convert her own age who was soon arrested for attending Mass. He too was disinherited and died an exile in Flanders.

Anne was placed in charge of a house of refuge for priests which the Jesuit Father John Gerard opened in London. She managed everything: finances, housekeeping, contacts with guests, and strangers—"Mrs. Martha" the priests called her. She took vows of poverty, chastity, and obedience; and despite danger, ill health, and almost continual headaches, she possessed her soul in great peace.

The large crowd that gathered in the early morning on Candlemas Day 1601 aroused suspicions; and when the constables arrived, they found a room full of people and everything ready for Mass. Anne was arrested and received her death sentence with joy, for she had often told Father Gerard, "I naturally want more than anything else to die for Christ." To the crowd that gathered at Tyburn she said, "I am sentenced to die for harboring a Catholic priest; and so far am I from repenting for having so done that I wish, with all my soul, that where I have entertained one, I could have entertained a thousand." She then kissed the gallows, and kneeling down began to pray. She was in her mid-thirties.

1601

Bl. Mark Barkworth, martyr under Elizabeth I. An Oxford graduate, he became a Catholic at Douai, France, and a priest at the English seminary in Valladolid, Spain, where his enthusiasm for the Benedictine order caused a small tempest. On his way back to England he was received as a novice at the Spanish abbey of Hirache with the understanding that he could make profession at the hour of death if he had no opportunity to do so before.

Apprehended after a few months in England, he made a spirited defense and was condemned for treason. Managing to obtain a monastic habit, he was dressed as a Benedictine when he arrived at Tyburn along with his companion martyr, the

Jesuit, Venerable Roger Filcock. St. Anne Line had been executed earlier that day, and her body was still handing. Bl. Mark kissed the edge of her dress and hand saying, "Thou hast got the start on us sister, but we will follow thee as quickly as we may." He told the crowd that St. Augustine and his monks had preached the faith to their pagan ancestors. "And I come here to die", he said, "as a Catholic." It was in this way, at the age of twenty-nine, that he made his monastic profession, February 27, 1601.

FEBRUARY 27

1862   [*C.P.*]

St. Gabriel Possenti of Our Lady of Sorrows, Passionist; co-patron of Italian youth. In minor orders and almost ready for the priesthood, he died of consumption at Isola del Gran Sasso, Italy, three days before his twenty-fourth birthday. His cartoons of classmates at Spoleto College suggest the warm, aristocratic comraderie and keen mind that made him a class favorite and brought gold medals in general excellence and philosophy as well as the honor of giving the valedictory. But the day after graduation to the general surprise of Spoleto—for he seemed more interested in balls, theatre, and hunting—he set off for the novitiate. He was eighteen.

Two special traits come through from the personal notes found among his things and the pious letters he wrote to his family and friends: devotion to Our Lady of Sorrows and total self conquest through attention to little things. He is one of the saints who stressed Mary the most. "Reading through the lives of the saints," he wrote to his father, "I see how a great number of them, tepid and sinful though they once were, became saints because they had, by some practice of devotion, won the favor of this tender Queen, always ready to grant it to those who ask." He sent his favorite brother this advice: "When you feel inspired by her to make some sacrifice, make it at once with a good heart, and have no fear that Mary will be outdone in generosity."

The list of resolutions he wrote down for himself includes among many others: "**Faithfulness in little things** is the motto I will always follow in my efforts to reach holiness." "I will not say a word that might, in the least, turn to my praise." "I will not ask about anything through curiosity." "I will rejoice at the success of others." He ends with: "In giving me my vocation, God has bestowed upon me one of his best graces. I will give him in return the best that I have—the entire affection of my heart."

A long prayer he composed for his daily use contains this form of pleading: "What will you lose by giving me a deep love for You . . . ?" The saint endured violent temptations to blasphemy and unbelief. On his final night he experienced the darkness of the Cross and was assailed with lewd phantasies and temptations to conceit, but his last hour was one of deep peace as he clasped his favorite picture of Our Lady of Sorrows and invoked her name.

FEBRUARY 28

992

St. Oswald, a Dane by birth, who was brought up by his uncle, Archbishop Odo of Canterbury, received training in Benedictine monasticism at Fleury in France and then, as Bishop of Worcester and Archbishop of York, cooperated with Sts. Dunstan and Ethelwold in promoting monastic life and reforming the clergy of England. Of the seven abbeys he founded, Ramsey is the most famous. He died kneeling at his daily ritual of washing the feet of twelve wanderers or poor men who were fed at his table.

1360

Bl. Villana de Botti, or **Villana of Florence,** whose father, a rich Florentine merchant, thwarted her attempt to enter a convent and married her off instead. She then abandoned herself to a frivolous and idle life until one day, dressed for a ball, she gazed into a mirror to see how beautiful she was but saw instead a hideous form. When—according to the account of her life—two other mirrors returned the same image she took it to be the likeness of her sin-laden soul. Putting on the simplest of clothes, she went in tears to the Dominican church of Santa Maria Novella, made a full confession, and asked for help to begin a new way of life. In time she also became a Dominican tertiary.

Such was her care of the poor and reputation for holiness that after her death her body could not be buried for thirty days because of the crowds. When discouraged or depressed her husband would find strength by visiting the room where she died.

1890

Bl. Maria Repetto, the eldest of 11 children, became a Sister of Our Lady of Refuge in her native Genoa at 22 and during 60 more years, in the words of Pope John Paul II, "lived the great truth ... that Jesus must be contemplated, loved and served in the poor at all moments of our life." As portress she was known in Genoa as 'the holy nun,' always gracious and ready to help. St. Francis of Camporosso, whom the Genoese called 'the holy father' would send needy people of every sort to her. She read hearts, foretold the future, dispensed advice and material help, and had a reputation for powerful prayer. She loved St. Joseph and would answer requests by saying, "I will recommend you to St. Joseph. He will help you." Bl. Maria Repetto died January 5.

MARCH 1

6th cent.

St. Senan, Irish abbot on Scattery Island, remarkable for his hospitality and compassion. He pioneered the founding of monasteries along the coast and had a preference for islands where seclusion and natural beauty fostered contemplative prayer.

6th cent.

St. David, patron of Wales, where his great popularity in the later Middle Ages rested on a life written 500 years after his death—much of it improvised in order to make the see of St. David's (or Menevia) appear independent of Canterbury. He was probably a monk who helped give Welsh monasticism its emphasis on manual labor, fasting, and silence.

713

St. Swithbert, Benedictine missionary bishop, one of the twelve Anglo-Saxon monks who went with St. Willibrord to Frisia. His companions chose him as bishop and he was ordained by St. Wilfrid. He retired to the island of Kaiserwerth in the Rhine, where he established a monastery and where his relics are still preserved. The small island six miles from Düsseldorf was formerly known as Swithberth's Island.

1930

Bl. Brother Richard Erminio Pampuri, a physician who at 30 entered the Hospitaller Order of St. John of God and died after less than two years in vows. He was born at Trivolzio near Pavia, italy, and during student days was active in establishing a Catholic Action group and a Don Bosco club. His study of medicine was interrupted when he was conscripted during World War I and served in the medical corps at the front.

Daily Mass and Communion, membership in the Third Order of St. Francis and free service to the poor, helped him during his six years of medical practise preserve the dispositions he described in a letter to one of his sisters, a nun, "Pray that neither pride nor selfishness nor any other sinful passion will ever prevent me from seeing, treating and comforting the suffering Christ in my patients, always keeping alive the thought of how sweet and how fruitful the practise of my profession should appear to me."

MARCH 2

672

St. Chad, bishop of Lichfield, brother of St. Cedd. During one of St. Wilfrid's absences Chad was intruded as bishop of the Northumbrians; but Theodore, Archbishop of Canterbury, ruled that Wilfrid was the rightful bishop and that Chad's episcopal ordination was defective. When the saint willingly resigned the see saying that he had never thought himself worthy, Theodore was so impressed that he reordained him and made him bishop of the Mercians. Chad had the custom of travelling on foot;

but Theodore ordered him, in view of his age, to go on horseback.

1282 *St.*   [*Franciscan II O.*]

Bl. Agnes of Prague, daughter of the king of Bohemia, first cousin of St. Elizabeth of Hungary, and foundress of the first monastery of Poor Clares north of the Alps. She successfully evaded a whole series of engagements, the last—in her late twenties—with Emperor Frederick II. His escort arrived to bring her to Germany and her brother the king of Bohemia insisted that she go, but she appealed to the pope, maintaining that her consent had never been given and that it had long been her desire to become a nun. Frederick finally yielded. "I cannot take offense," he said, "if she prefers the King of Heaven to me." Her action caused such a stir among the aristocracy that a hundred girls followed her to the convent and wealthy ladies throughout Europe were inspired to found or enter monasteries of the Poor Clares.

She was a nun during forty-five years and served briefly as abbess at the pope's request. St. Clare spoke of her as her 'other self' and wrote four letters to her which still survive.

1606

St. Nicholas Owen, a Jesuit brother martyred under James I, a supberb carpenter and mason who for twenty-six years was employed principally in constructing hiding places for priests throughout England. Few, even of his own confreres, knew he was a Jesuit. Father John Gerard said of him, "I verily think no man can be said to have done more good of all those that labored in the English vineyard. For first, he was the immediate occasion of saving many hundreds of persons, both ecclesiastical and secular, and of the estates also of these seculars, which had been lost and forfeited many times over if the priests had been taken in their houses." Some of the saint's hiding places are still intact.

Apprehended and tortured on two earlier occasions, he was taken a third time and repeatedly tortured but only uttered the words "Jesus" and "Mary." On March 2 the rack literally tore him open and he died a few hours later.

MARCH 3

1033 or 1039

St. Cunegund, empress, who helped her husband St. Henry with affairs of state and governed his German territories in his absence. The royal couple secured such generous papal privileges for their own new diocese of Bamberg—whose cathedral and monastery they built—that it was popularly said that walls gave less protection than Cunegund's silk threads. After the emperor's death she became a nun in the convent of Kaufungen, which she founded; but she is buried with St. Henry in the Bamberg cathedral.

1713

Bl. Francis de Posadas, famous Dominican preacher at Cordoba, who was able to realize his vocation only after the death of his step-father. He avoided offices in his order and refused the bishoprics that were offered him but was always at the service of the poor.

1852

Bl. Teresa Verzeri, foundress at Bergamo of the Daughters of the Sacred Heart. Both in name and purpose her congregation was similar to the society founded by St. Madeleine Sophie Barat, and Teresa—deeply distrustful of herself as a foundress—went to Turin to discuss with St. Madeleine the possibility of amalgamating the two groups.

On her director's advice she three times entered the Benedictine convent at Bergamo and in obedience to him she three times withdrew — an experience which initiated her into religious life and taught her not to be over-concerned about what people might think or say. Immediately after her final departure she began giving religious instruction to girls. Her congregation grew out of the group that helped her in the work. Four of her sisters and her own mother joined the rapidly growing community.

MARCH 4

1484

ST. CASIMIR, son of the king of Poland. In his teens he led an army to the Hungarian border but turned back, refusing for reasons of conscience to cooperate further with his father's plans for a military take-over that would have put Casimir himself on the throne of Hungary. Austere, studious, and devout, he died of consumption at the age of twenty-three.

1021

St. Heribert, archbishop of Cologne and chancellor to Emperor Otto III, one of the most learned and zealous churchmen of his age. Typical of his entire ministry was the way he came on a cold December day, barefoot and poorly clad, to take possession of his diocese. His income he divided between the church and the poor, reserving a bare minimum for himself. Under the fine robes of office he always wore a hairshirt. He would seek out the sick and poor whether in their homes or hospitals, relieving them and washing their feet. He is remembered for the power of his prayer and is still invoked for rain.

1877

Bl. Placida Viel, second superior general in France of the Sisters of Mercy of the Christian Schools. When the foundress,

St. Mary Postel, was nearly eighty she recognized her successor in Placida—a shy novice of eighteen, a farmer's daughter—and gave her special opportunities for experience. Thirteen years later she was chosen superior. Both before and after her election she was often engaged in fund raising. A ruffian once struck her. "That is for me," she said with her habitual serenity and good humor, "and now what will you give for our building?"

During her thirty years in office the congregation grew from 150 sisters to over a thousand. "As long as no offense is given to God," was her characteristic proviso in every situation. She died at sixty-two.

MARCH 5

475

St. Gerasimus, abbot in Palestine, whose servere penances—among them going all of lent with no other food than the Holy Eucharist—were prompted by repentance for a period of heresy. As disciples increased he built a laura on the Jordan near Jericho with cells for seventy hermits and a common dwelling for the novices.

5th cent, or possibly later.

St. Kieran, venerated as bishop of Ossory.

1011

St. Willigis, archbishop of Mainz and chancellor of Germany, eminent churchman and statesman. A friend wrote of him, "His countenance remained ever unruffled, but even more remarkable was his inward peace. He spoke little but his few words carried more weight than many oaths from other people."

1734

St. John Joseph of the Cross, wonder-working Franciscan at Naples, where people would snip off bits of his habit as relics. In prayer and penance he was another Peter of Alcantara, to whose branch of the order he was attracted by the poverty and conversation of two friars who visited his home. He served as novice-master, superior, and provincial, though he tried repeatedly to be relieved from positions of authority and would have remained a deacon except for the decision of his superiors. At a time of crisis his prudence and reputation for holiness kept the Italian Alcantarines of Naples together, and under him as superior they were formed into a separate province.

He multiplied food, healed the sick, read people's thoughts — especially in confession — and experienced ecstasies and levitations. He died in his eightieth year on the day he had foretold. His tomb immediately became a place of pilgrimage.

MARCH 6

766

St. Chrodegang, the leading statesman and, after the death of St. Boniface, the foremost churchman in Frankland during the crucial years that laid foundations for the Holy Roman Empire in the West. He was chancellor under Charles Martel and continued to hold that office under Pepin, along with a new appointment — though still a layman — as bishop of Metz. He went on a diplomatic mission to Pope Stephen II and accompanied him on the historic trip to the Lombard king at Pavia and then on to France — the first time a pope crossed the alps — there in 754 negotiations were concluded that made the king of France a "Patrician" of the Romans. The leader of the Franks assumed the duty of protecting the patrimony of Peter — now practically transformed into the Papal States — since the Roman emperor in Constantinople was no longer able to do so.

Chrodegang was also the first in that northern region to adopt the pure Roman liturgy and use Gregorian Chant. He obliged his clergy to assist at choir office and live a common life according to a rule which he based on that of St. Benedict. Manual labor was obligatory and so was service in the kitchen. But as the clerics retained their own possessions, the difference of fortune between them was an obstacle to community life. Though St. Chrodegang's particular formula did not endure, he contributed to the development of canons regular and of cathedral chapters.

1311
Bl. Jordan of Pisa, outstanding Dominican orator at Florence. A contemporary of Dante, he also made his contribution to the creation of modern Italian by being one of the first great preachers to use the Tuscan dialect instead of Latin in his sermons. He would often begin to treat a subject in the morning in one church, continue it at noon in another, and finish it in the evening in a third, with the Florentines following him from church to church.

MARCH 7

203
STS. PERPETUA, FELICITY and **COMPANIONS,** five catechumens at Carthage baptized only after their arrest, and **St. Saturus** — probably their teacher — who voluntarily joined them in prison. Their martyrdom-narrative is the most famous in the early church and includes what is generally believed to be the authentic prison diary of St. Perpetua. When her pagan father, who was very attached to her, tried to weaken her resolve she said, "Do you see this vessel . . . ? Can it be called by any other name than what it is?" "No," he replied. "So also I cannot call myself by any other name than what I am, a Chris-

tian" She was twenty-two and had an infant son.

She records her joy on being permitted to keep the child with her: "I at once recovered my health, and my prison became a palace to me, and I would rather have been there than anywhere else." On the final day, after she had been tossed by a wild cow, she was able to encourage her brother and the catechumen Rusticus, present as spectators: "Stand fast in the faith, and love one another; and do not let our sufferings be a stumbling-block to you."

St. Felicity was a slave girl and also a mother, but her child was born in prison. The jailer, hearing her moan in childbirth, asked how she expected to face the wild beasts in the arena. "My sufferings here are my own," Felicity answered, "there, another will be in me, suffering for me as I for him."

974

St. John of Gorze, abbot, also called John of Vandières, who helped bring northern France out of the "Iron Age" following the collapse of the Carolingian empire. An old priest had inspired him with a love of the divine office, while a fervent community of nuns convinced him of the need for self-denial. With a companion he set about restoring Benedictine life in the abbey founded by St. Chrodegang at Gorce 200 years earlier and now fallen to ruin. The abbey soon flourished. From there the reform spread to nearby monasteries in Lorraine and during the next two centuries penetrated more than seventy abbeys.

MARCH 8

1550

ST. JOHN OF GOD, a Portuguese and a famous penitent; patron of hospitals, of nurses, and of the sick, founder of the Brothers Hospitalers. At about the age of forty, while tending sheep he was stung with remorse over his dissolute days in the army and decided to serve others in earnest. He started off for Moslem Africa to ransom captives and perhaps give his life for the faith; but the apostasy of a companion and the advice of a priest changed his mind. Instead he opened a religious goods shop in Granada. One day he was so moved by a sermon of St. John of Avila that he began acknowledging his sinfulness in public and went about the streets in such a wild state that he was eventually confined to an insane asylum for some months until John of Avila convinced him to desist from his extraordinary mode of penance and do something more helpful to himself and others.

Embarking on his new course right where he was he started to help take care of the other inmates. Next he rented a house where he could tend the abandoned sick; and for the remaining ten years his life was a prodigy of disinterested charity supported by humility, prayer, and self-denial. Helpers came, people opened their purses, and God worked miracles—such as the time he walked through flames unhurt carrying the sick to safety on his back.

The archbishop of Granada once questioned him about the complaint that he sheltered tramps and women of bad character. "The Son of Man came for sinners," the saint answered, "and we are bound to seek their conversion. I am unfaithful to my vocation because I neglect this, but I confess that I know of no bad person in my hospital except myself." He died at fifty-five. His followers drew up the rules of the order after his death and eventually took vows. St. John is invoked in the litany of the dying.

1866 or 1867

Bl. Simeon Berneux, vicar apostolic of Korea, six other members of the Paris Foreign Mission Society, and seventeen native Koreans, beatified from among the ten thousand put to death for their faith between 1866 and 1869.

MARCH 9*

1440

ST. FRANCES OF ROME, a much-loved, wonder-working Roman saint, a model wife and mother. She was a person of means with a keen sense of social responsibility, a mystic, and an inspirational leader who founded a Benedictine community of women—oblates without vows dedicated to the service of the poor. Married at twelve or thirteen, she was never known to have a quarrel with her husband, Lorenzo Ponziano, in their forty years of married life. Lorenzo took a sympathetic view of the devotions of his teen-age wife and of her personally nursing some of the worst cases in the Roman hospitals for which his family had responsibility. She disposed of her jewelry during a famine and could never do enough for the poor, but it was in her husband and children that she loved and served Christ in a special way. Her advice to the ladies she inspired was that a married woman must not forget she is a home-maker, and while it is praiseworthy for her to be devout "she must sometimes leave God at the altar to find him in her housework." Among her sorrows were the death of a nine year old son and a teenage daughter, her husband's banishment, and the plunder of family estates.

With a sister-in-law, who shared the same house, a beautiful friendship was knit once they discovered they also shared the same spiritual ideals. On her husband's death she took up residence with her Oblates of Tor de' Specchi—a named derived from a house she acquired for them a few years before, and where her followers still carry on her work. St. Frances is patroness of Benedictine oblates.

MARCH 10

1615

St. John Ogilvie, son of the Baron of Drum-na-Keith, and the

---

*O.F.M. Cap. II O. see May 9 for St. Catherine of Bologna.

only martyr of post-Reformation Scotland raised to the altar. He was brought up a Calvinist but during student days on the continent began to take a lively interest in religious controversy and the issues that divided his own relatives. Two Scripture texts particularly impressed his young mind: God "desires all men to be saved and to come to the knowledge of the truth" (1 Tm 2:4) and "Come to me all who labor and are heavy laden and I will give you rest" (Mt 11:28).

He was received into the Catholic Church at the Scots College in Louvain at the age of seventeen, became a Jesuit several years later and, after eleven years, a priest. He worked for three years in Austria and France, while pleading with his superiors to be sent to Scotland, especially as the leading Jesuits who had been there felt that because of the tightening of the penal laws further efforts were futile.

He traveled under the name of John Watson, sometimes as a cattle-dealer, sometimes as a soldier. By the time of his betrayal —only eleven months after his entry—his work was bearing fruit; but it was particularly the heroic constancy under torture and his vigorous defense at several trials that bolstered Catholic spirit in the land. He spent five months in prison and managed to smuggle out Latin accounts of what had happened. He was once kept awake for eight days in an attempt to make him reveal names of other Catholics. When tried in Glasgow he was asked if he had said Mass. "If this is a crime," he answered, "it should be proved not by my word but by witnesses." St. John Ogilvie was hanged at Glasgow.

MARCH 11

859

St. Eulogius, priest, ascetic, and popular preacher of Cordoba, bishop-elect of Toledo, promoter of Latin studies and Spain's outstanding martyr during the Moslem period. He is the central figure in a persecution that gave Cordoba some forty saints. He wrote up their lives and defended the martyrs against the censure of the collaborationist bishop of Seville who came to Cordoba as the emir's man and issued a proclamation to the effect that these Christians were suicides rather than martyrs.

Eulogius was able to show from church history that authentic martyrs were of several kinds; some did nothing aggressive, while others spontaneously came forward to proclaim Christ and denounce injustice and false worship; the current persecution had martyrs of both kinds. Perfectus, the earliest of the Cordoba group, had been tricked into committing the capital offense of denouncing Mohammed. Eulogius described the legal disabilities and harrassment under which the Christians lived and the blasphemies they heard when they came out of their corner of Cordoba. "Better to die now," he wrote, "than live such a burdensome, wretched life."

His own turn came toward the end of the persecution when he was arrested for harboring St. Lucretia, a Moslem girl who became a martyr. When the judge asked Eulogius why she was found in his house he answered, "She came to be instructed in the faith; and I could not send her away, for Christ has given me the office of teacher." And as Eulogius went on to denounce Mohammed he also was condemned. Told he could save his life by a single word he replied, "Oh, if you only knew what awaits us who adore Christ! If I could infuse into your heart what I feel in mine, you would not speak as you do but would hasten to despise worldly honors." On leaving the council chamber he was struck on the face. Turning, he said, "Strike this cheek too." His intimate friend Albar of Cordoba, a layman and the foremost example of Latin culture in Moslem Spain, wrote his biography.

Under leaders more accommodating and compromising than Eulogius the Christian community, though allowed to maintain its worship, gradually weakened and dissolved so that when Cordoba was reconquered by Spaniards from the north three-and-a-half centuries later few traces of living Christianity could be found.

MARCH 12 *

295

St. Maximilian, martyred at twenty-one, a third century conscientious objector. "I cannot enlist," he declared to the court, "for I am a Christian." When it was pointed out that there were Christians in the army he replied, "That is their business. I am also a Christian and I cannot serve." He was beheaded and his body was taken to Carthage for burial.

417

St. Innocent I, an energetic pope who helped spell out some of the implications of Roman primacy and did much to unify the worship and discipline of the Western church. He was particularly influential throughout the centuries because a number of his letters formed the nucleus of the earliest stratum of papal law in the standard collections.

It was a period of civil upheaval—Rome was sacked in 410, half way through his pontificate—and bishops throughout the West increasingly referred matters to the papacy for decision. In the Pelagian controversy two African councils asked the pope to approve their condemnation of the heresy. In reply, Innocent commended the African bishops for observing the ancient custom of not finalizing such matters without bringing them to the pope's attention, ". . . so that what has been rightly decided may be given the full weight of the authority of this see . . . " and then be passed on for the guidance of the Church throughout the world. St. Augustine, leader of the African bishops, on receiving the pope's reply said in a sermon (Sept. 23, 417): "The reports of two councils concerning this case were sent to the Apostolic See. From there replies have come; the case is closed (**causa finita est**)." These words of the great doctor were later popularized in the adage, "Rome has spoken; the case is closed."

It was to Pope Innocent that St. John Chrysostom appealed when deposed by an Eastern council. The pontiff demanded an-

---

other trial but the emperor would not agree. So after examining the case himself, the pope excommunicated the patriarch of Alexandria, ordered Chrysostom's restoration to Constantinople, and after Chrysostom's death would not re-establish communion until that saint's memory was vindicated.

MARCH 13

ca. 600

St. Leander, archbishop of Seville, apostlc of the Visigoths. For twenty years the leading churchman of Spain, he helped convert St. Hermenigild and his brother King Recared, and thus the Gothic nation from Arianism to the Catholic faith. Like St. Basil in Cappadocia, he belonged to a family of saints: his sister, Abbess Florentina, and his bishop-brothers Isidore and Fulgentius are all saints. Though 200 years apart, both families combatted Arianism, fostered studies, and took deep interest in monastic life.

On the early death of their parents, Leander became as a father to Isidore and supervised his education. For St. Florentina he wrote a letter on religious life, sometimes called the Rule of St. Leander. While on an embassy to Constantinople for Hermenigild he met St. Gregory the Great, made fast friends, and encouraged him to write the **Morals** or **On Job.** When Gregory as pope finally finished this work he sent it to Leander with a dedicatory letter. He contributed to the composition of the Visigothic liturgy which was then taking on its definite characteristics, and he probably deserves the principal credit for inaugurating at the third council of Toledo in 589 the new religious policy of making the councils a mixed gathering of princes, lords, and bishops. It was at that council that King Recared made his profession of faith and Leander delivered the closing address, in which he expressed the universal joy over the conversion of the Goths. "I send you the pallium," Pope Gregory wrote (IX, 121), "with the blessing of Peter, prince of the apostles. It is to be used only at holy Mass. In sending it I should earnestly admonish you on how you should live; but I say nothing, for your good deeds have anticipated my words." Spain honors him as a doctor of the Church.

MARCH 14

1915

Bl. Placid Riccardi, Benedictine priest of the Abbey of St. Paul-outside-the-walls, Rome, a spiritual director and pastor of outstanding prudence and meekness of heart. A monk at twenty and ordained a deacon just before the Italian troops took Rome in 1870, he was arrested for not presenting himself for military service and was sentenced for a year as a deserter, though he was released after six weeks in prison. He spent the next thirteen years in his monastery with such assignments as organist and vice-prefect of students, most of the following ten years as chaplain, confessor and abbatial vicar of a convent of Benedictine nuns in Amelia, and the last twenty—save for the final two years of illness—in charge of the historic abbey-shrine of Farfa, preaching, hearing confessions, and serving the poor.

"When I think of his humility," Cardinal Shuster his biographer wrote, "I like to compare it to a rock that keeps sinking to the bottom unless someone holds it up. . . . All were considered his superiors, he venerated everyone." He made a point of putting himself out for others. "He even obeys the dog," one of the brothers of his small Farfa community remarked. His biographer understood what this meant when Father Placid once asked him to enter by a back door so as not to disturb the dog sleeping on the front steps. He did, at times, come to the fore, as when he helped unmask a novice at St. Paul's whose pretended stigmata and visions had deceived the superiors; and he spent a brief period as novice master by special appointment of the Holy See.

His own novice master and future abbot, when asked the secret of Father Placid's holiness, replied, "From the very beginning of his novitiate until now, he has prayed much and he has prayed well; that is all." Mystic experiences were no part of his life; but penitential practices, such as the discipline, hair shirts and fasting, were; and his superiors had to moderate these just as they did his tendency to give everything away. There was little out of the ordinary about him until the miracles that followed his death. And such was the enthusiasm of the people in the hills about Farfa that when the body of their priest was brought back to them fifteen years after his death, it was twelve days before it could be entombed.

MARCH 15

1660   [*D.C.S.V.P., C.M.*]

St. Louise de Marillac, co-foundress with St. Vincent de Paul of the Daughters of Charity. When in 1960, three centuries after her death, she was declared patroness of those who do social work, — her order numbered 45,000 sisters — a figure which does not include the thousands of Sisters of Charity of various congregations who derive inspiration from her community.

Though she was loved by her father who belonged to the great house of Marillac she never knew her mother who gave birth to her out of wedlock. Deprived of family life she grew into a timid, melancholy child. Her marriage with Anthony le Gras was a happy one, but at thirty-four she was left a widow with one son who would cause her much concern.

She came increasingly under the influence of St. Vincent de Paul who discovered, along with her scruples and complexes, great generosity and a burning desire to love God and be of help to others; so he put her in charge of the young women he was organizing to care for the sick poor in their homes. Under him she trained the first recruits in her Paris home and drew up the original rules. Not wishing his group to come under the then standard requirement of enclosure, St. Vincent purposely avoided the externals of religious life. "Your convent," he told them, "will be the house of the sick; your cell, a rented room; your chapel, the parish church; your cloister, the streets of the city or the wards of the hospital; your enclosure, obedience; your grille, the fear of God; your veil, holy modesty." On her deathbed St. Louise pleaded with her sisters: "Be diligent in serving the poor. Love the poor, honor them, my children, as you would honor Christ himself."

1820   [*C.S.S.R.*]

St. Clement Mary Hofbauer, apostle and patron of Vienna, and called the second founder of the Redemptorists because of the impetus he gave to his congregation north of the Alps. The ninth child of a Moravian grazier and butcher, he was ordained at thirty-four. For twenty years he worked in a German parish in Warsaw; and during his last twelve he ministered in Vienna, particularly through the confessional. His penitents and friends, especially among the students, artists and writers—including some of the leading Romanticists—re-established the prestige of the Old Faith and were chiefly responsible for defeating the efforts made at the Council of Vienna to set up an independent German church.

MARCH 16

1940

Bl. Luigi Orione, founder, described by Pope John Paul II in the beatification homily as "one of the most eminent personalities of this

BLESSED LUIGI ORIONE

century... Entirely and joyfully the priest of Christ, he traveled all over Italy and Latin America dedicating his life to those in greatest suffering from misfortune, want, and human wickedness." "He had," the Pope said, "the character and heart of the Apostle Paul."

At 13 he went to the Franciscans but became seriously ill. St. John Bosco received him at the Turin Oratory where his confessor, Bl. Michael Rua, allowed him at 14 to make a private vow of chastity. Along with five companions he wanted to offer his life for the dying Don Bosco's recovery. Before novitiate he left the Salesians. Perhaps, like St. Paul, he was not one to build on other men's foundations. But his life's work would bear the deep imprint of his Turin days at the Oratory and the acquaintance he made with St. Joseph Cottolengo's "Little House of Divine Providence." "Little Cottolengo" is the name he gave one of his houses outside Buenos Aires. Like St. Joseph Cottolengo he would organize the various groups connected with his own "Little Work of Divine Providence" into religious communities. He started five: the Sons of Divine Providence comprising his priests, the Little Missionary Sisters of Charity, the Brothers of Divine Providence, and two rather contemplative communities: the Hermits of Divine Providence, of whom some were blind, and the Perpetual Adorers of the Blessed Sacrament, who because of their handicap are also called the Blind Sacramentine Sisters.

With charismatic reliance on Divine Providence he would respond to whatever need was before him: orphans, earthquake victims, troubled priests, anyone in distress. Starting as a seminarian in Tortona he welcomed poor boys to his room in the bell tower of the cathedral where he served as assistant sacristan to help pay his way. Still a seminarian he opened a home and school for orphans and when he was ordained, not yet 23, he continued to head the school and, gathering helpers, gradually extended his apostolate. "The secret and originality of Don Orione," according to Pope John Paul II, was that "he let himself be led only and always by the rigorous logic of love." "Our policy," Don Orione asserted, "is the great and divine charity which does good for all. Let our policy be that of the 'Our Father.' "

By nature fiery, strong-willed and impatient, he mellowed with the years, especially during his enormously successful three years, 1934-37, in South America. A year before his death he stated the essential program of his life: "to suffer, be silent, pray, love, crucify oneself and worship." Bl. Luigi died of a heart condition at Tortona on March 12, 1940, repeating the name of Jesus.

MARCH 17

ca. 460

ST. PATRICK, archbishop and apostle of Ireland. He was born, it seems, about 390 of Briton stock, probably in Wales. His father was a deacon. Patrick's faith became meaningful to him only after he was carried off as a captive and slave to Ireland at the age of sixteen. During six years of slavery he became a man of God. Of this first Irish period he wrote: "Every day I had to tend sheep, and many times a day I prayed. . . . I used to get up for prayer before daylight, through snow, through rain, and I felt no harm, and there was no sloth in me—as I now see, because the spirit within me was then fervent" **(Confession 16)**.

In response to the divine inspirations which began to direct his life he escaped and returned to his home; but in a dream he again heard the "voice of the Irish" saying, "Boy, come and walk among us once more!' **(Confession 23)** He evidently went to continental monasteries for training and was ordained a bishop by St. Germain of Auxerre. In thirty years of labor, mostly in the west and north, he and his co-workers converted Ireland.

His short autobiography or **Confession,** written in the warm personal style of St. Paul, combines humility and a sense of mission. He refused to accept gifts, and like St. Paul defended himself against false charges, was an enthusiastic promoter of consecrated virginity, and had a deep conviction of his personal call to the apostolate. "Regardless of danger I must make known the gift of God and everlasting consolation; without fear and frankly I must spread everywhere the name of God, so that after my decease I may leave a bequest to my brethren and sons whom I have baptized in the Lord—so many thousands of people" (**Confession** 14).

659

St. Gertrude, Benedictine abbess of Nivelles, daughter of Bl. Pepin of Landen and Bl. Ida, especially remembered for her hospitality. In Belgium, Holland, and the Rhineland travelers prayed to her for good lodgings, and gardeners, for plentiful crops. In some areas planting began on her feast, and fine weather on the seventeenth was taken as a good sign.

1620

Bl. John Sarkander, martyr of the seal of confession. He was pastor of Holleschau in Czechoslovakia, where his energy aroused Hussite opposition. Accused of complicity with Polish forces during a Protestant takeover, he was cruelly racked in an effort to obtain confessional information, and left to die in prison.

MARCH 18

386

ST. CYRIL, bishop of Jerusalem, doctor of the church, three times banished during the Arian controversy, principal author of the famous **Catecheses**—a profound yet simple series of twenty-four sermons on the creed, the **Our Father,** and the Easter sacraments. Possibly no other book serves so well to give an impression of the enduring quality of Catholic faith and practice.

Though the author does not use the word, he clearly teaches the doctrine of transubstantiation: "He once turned water into wine, in Cana of Galilee, and is it incredible that he should

have turned wine into blood? . . . what seems bread is not
bread, though bread by taste, but the body of Christ; and what
seems wine is not wine, though the taste will have it so, but
the blood of Christ . . ." (**Catecheses** 22).

1086

St. Anselm of Lucca, one of St. Gregory VII's most faithful
supporters against lay investiture. His uncle, Pope Alexander
II, nominated him bishop of Lucca and sent him to Germany
to receive the crozier and ring from Emperor Henry IV. But
Anselm, convinced that a secular power had no authority to
confer church offices, was unwilling to go through with the
ceremony.

Only after a new pope, Gregory VII, ordained him bishop
did St. Anselm finally submit to investiture; but it left him
with such an uneasy conscience that he abandoned his diocese
and became a Benedictine monk at Polirone. But the pope
sent him back to Lucca, and from then on he was in the thick
of the Gregorian reform. He said it would be better to have
no monks or canons than to have undisciplined ones.

1567

St. Salvator of Horta, Spanish Franciscan brother of great
austerity and humility. He healed so many with the sign of
the cross that his superiors kept moving him from place to
place to relieve the individual houses of the crowds that would
gather.

MARCH 19

SOLEMNITY OF ST. JOSEPH, foster father of Christ, husband
of Mary, protector of the universal Church, and patron of a happy death. By a mystery of Providence devotion to St. Joseph did

not flourish in the Middle Ages but was reserved for our day, though many saints, like Bernard of Clairvaux, praised his virtues and singular privileges.

In the fifteenth century St. Bernardine of Siena actively spread his cult; but it was particularly St. Teresa of Avila who popularized him in a lengthy passage of her autobiography. "I cannot call to mind," she writes, "that I have ever asked him at at any time for anything which he has not granted. . . . To other saints our Lord seems to have given grace to help men in some special necessity; but to this glorious saint, I know by experience, he has given grace to help us in all" (**Life** 6). Her first reformed convent was dedicated to St. Joseph.

Canada not only venerates him as principal patron but is the home of his principal shrine. Pope John XXIII inserted the name of St. Joseph into the Roman canon, placed the Second Vatican Council under his patronage, and in his talks often made allusions like this: "To learn to obey, to learn to keep silence, to speak, when need arises, with moderation and courtesy—this is what St. Joseph teaches us."

1289

Bl. John of Parma, seventh minister general of the Franciscans. He resigned his office when he felt he could no longer carry through the necessary reforms and nominated St. Bonaventure as his successor. A great lover of silence, he never indulged in idle speech; and when dying he admitted that he would have more to answer for in respect to his silence than his speech.

1497

Bl. Mark of Monte Gallo, whose wife became a Poor Clare and he a Franciscan. He promoted the **monti di pietâ** from which the poor could borrow without falling into the hands of usurers. In prayer he heard a voice, "Brother Mark, preach love," and this became his favorite theme as he tramped up and down Italy for forty years.

MARCH 20

579

St. Martin, archbishop of Braga in Portugal. He converted Galicia from Arianism and left some important spiritual writings.

687

St. Cuthbert, abbot-bishop of Lindisfarne, the "wonder-worker of Britain" whose tomb at Durham Cathedral was the favorite place of pilgrimage in the north of England until the Reformation. He combined the best traits of Celtic and Roman monasticism and helped implement the change-over to the Roman usages after the Synod of Whitby. When malcontents became abusive in discussion, he would rise with a placid look and dismiss the meeting until the following day. About being disturbed during sleep he said, "One cannot displease me by waking me out of my sleep but, on the contrary, gives me pleasure; for by rousing me from inactivity he enables me to do or think of something useful."

1286

Bl. Ambrose of Siena, student with St. Thomas under Albert the Great, Dominican orator, an ascetic with a deep longing for solitude yet much involved in public affairs. He died at sixty-five of overpreaching, breaking a blood vessel during a vehement denunciation of usury, and aggravating his condition the next morning when he took up his theme where he had left off.

1619

Bl. Hippolytus Galantini, Florentine layman who earned his living as a silk weaver, and from the age of twelve devoted himself to helping priests give religious instruction. He followed a regime of intense asceticism in his own home and established a group of catechists under a special rule. His Institute of

Christian Doctrine received papal approval and became a model for many similar lay groups in Italy. He introduced the custom of nocturnal adoration to counteract dangerous amusements.

MARCH 21°

1487

St. Nicholas of Flüe, father of a large family and prominent Swiss patriot in whom the contemplative and mystic life gradually gained ascendancy, but in a way that made it possible for him to exercise decisive influence at a crucial moment in his nation's history.

Though a man of peace and prayer, he helped defend his canton in two wars. Repeatedly he refused to be **landamman,** ruler of his canton, but was its representative at various conventions and served as magistrate and judge. His mother belonged to the "Friends of God," a pious society that cultivated strictness of life and constant meditation, particularly on the passion of Christ.

His eldest son, who did become **landamman,** described the saint's own prayer habits: "My father always retired at the same time as his children and servants, but every night I saw him get up again and heard him praying in his room until morning. Often too he would go in the silence of the night to the old church of St. Nicholas or some other holy place."

At the age of fifty Nicholas withdrew from his wife and family of ten—the youngest still a mere infant—and became a hermit. His countrymen finally persuaded him to abandon the remote solitude where a hunter discovered him and to occupy a cell and small chapel they built him on his own farm at Ranft. There he spent nineteen years, during which he took neither food nor drink, only Holy Communion—every other food inducing instant nausea. He now prayed from midnight to noon and in the afternoon gave advice, drawing on a knowledge

---

°*O.S.B., O.Cist., O.C.S.O. see July 11 for St. Benedict.*

which did not come from books, as he could neither read nor write.

When, in 1481, the delegates at the Conference of Stans were breaking up in a deadlock over the inclusion of two new cantons of Fribourg and Solothurn in the Swiss league, they stayed on one more day until the holy hermit could be consulted. The terms he suggested reconciled the differences and won unanimous approval. He died six years later. Today he is patron of Switzerland and venerated by countrymen of all faiths as a holy man and a patriot.

MARCH 22

457

St. Deogratias, archbishop of Carthage, whose concern for the distressed so won the hearts of the people during his three years as bishop that his body had to be buried by stealth to protect it from mutilation by relic seekers. When Genseric sacked Rome and returned to Africa with many captives, Deogratias sold church vessels and ornaments to redeem prisoners and reunite families. To meet the accommodations' crisis he turned over two of the largest churches and filled them with bedding.

1115

St. Ivo of Chartres, where he was bishop for twenty-five years, one of the leading theologians and churchmen of the latter phase of the Gregorian Reform. He is author of 25 sermons, 291 letters and two canonical collections. His clear insistence on the distinction between the election of a bishop— which was to be free and clerical—and the investiture of a bishop by a lay prince bore fruit in the Concordat of Worms several years after his death. He was ever imbued with the ideals of kindliness and mercy but was not one to compromise and he suffered imprisonment rather than condone an unlawful royal marriage.

1289

Bl. Peter of Siena, also known as Peter Tecelano and Peter the comb-maker. After the death of his wife he devoted all his time and money to help others, working at his trade by day and praying in various churches at night. He became a Franciscan teritary and eventually lived in a friary with a cell near the infirmary, where he continued his trade almost to the end. Even theologians came to consult him. To one who praised him he said, "You are raising too much wind for this poor dust."

MARCH 23

1606

ST. TORIBIO (or **Turibius**) **DE MOGROBEJO,** archbishop of Lima, the first New World saint. He was a Salamanca law professor who was put in charge of the inquisition at Granada and built up such a reputation for justice, moderation, strength of character, and apostolic spirit that, though not in sacred orders, he was chosen as the person must capable of remedying the lay and clerical scandals hindering the conversion of Peru.

For the next twenty-five years he went on foot through the immense territory, stretching 400 miles along the coast and deep into the mountains. He completed three pastoral visitations of the entire diocese, baptizing and confirming an estimated million people. After two years as archbishop he convoked the Third Council of Lima and promulgated decrees on catechetics, the sacraments, and church discipline that eventually gained acceptance through all of South America.

While his efforts on behalf of the Church and the poor were

often thwarted by those in power, his resolution and patience won out in the end. And he would remind his critics of Tertullian's remark that Christ said, "I am truth," not "I am custom." He founded the first seminary in the new world; and in Lima itself he was shepherd of such holy people as St. Rose of Lima, St. Martin de Porres, and Bl. John Massias. He learned the Quichua language and kept working on the Peruvian dialects until the age of sixty-eight, when death overtook him at Santa, north of Lima, during a pastoral visitation.

1702

St. Joseph Oriol, a miracle-working diocesan priest in Barcelona whose mortification, prayer, and apostolate of the confessional call to mind the more familiar figure of the Curé of Ars. He was not an extraordinary preacher, but his evangelical simplicity moved the hearers.

Seized with a desire for martyrdom, he once started off for Rome to volunteer for the missions. But at Marseilles he became sick. The Blessed Virgin appeared to him and told him his good intentions were accepted, but that he should return to Barcelona and care for the sick. He healed so many that his confessor forbade him to do any more miracles in the church because of the disturbance it caused. He foretold the day and hour of his death and prepared for the great moment by giving his few possessions away.

MARCH 24

1381

St. Catherine of Sweden, the holy daughter of a holy mother, for she was the fourth and favorite child of St. Bridget of Sweden. At eighteen she left her husband, with whom she had been living a life of continence, and went to Rome to visit her mother. Her husband died shortly after and she stayed on for twenty years, the inseparable companion of her mother's devotions, pilgrimages, and works of charity.

The other children also gathered in Rome to be with their mother at her death; and then all returned to Sweden where Catherine, as first abbess of the Bridgettines, directed the community at Vadstena according to the rule her mother drew up but never saw put into practise. Catherine soon returned to Rome for another five years to promote the cause of her mother's canonization. She died shortly after her return to Vadstena.

Never known to speak an unkind or impatient word, she prayed particularly that her community would be spared the ravages of detraction for, she said, both the tale-bearer and the one who listens carry the devil on their tongues.

1801 [*Franciscans*]

Bl. Didacus or **Diego of Cadiz,** Capuchin priest, popularly called the apostle of the Holy Trinity because of his devotion and ingenuity in making this sacred mystery the subject of his most fruitful sermons. Sometimes, when preaching on the love of God, he was seen to rise above the pulpit.

When churches were too small he spoke in the streets to crowds that stood spellbound for hours. He brought so much conviction and change of heart that the confessional was an integral part of his preaching. He avoided all presents and if obliged to accept something he immediately gave it to the poor.

MARCH 25

THE ANNUNCIATION OF THE LORD, marking the solemn moment at Nazareth when Mary, learning the will of God in her regard, gave her consent: "Let it be done to me according to your word." The tradition that Jesus was conceived and also died on March 25th is found in Hippolytus at the beginning of the third century. It may be that this is the earliest nativity feast and that it determined the dates of Christmas and of the birth of St. John the Baptist on June 24th. Mary is the model of all those who will "hear the word of God and keep it."

On this day martyrologies also commemorated the good thief whom our Lord canonized on the Cross: "Today you will be with me in paradise."

1586

St. Margaret Clitherow, glorious English martyr, a charming personality comparable in her way to St. Thomas More. A convert after marriage, she died at York in her early thirties for the crime of harbouring priests and attending Mass. She began each day with an hour and a half of prayer and meditation, confessed twice a week, and fasted four days a week. Her husband found two faults in her: she did not attend church with him — for which he was fined — and she fasted too much. Two weeks before her death the house was searched; altar furnishings were found, and she was taken into custody. To spare her children and servants the ordeal either of giving testimony that would condemn her to death or of lying, she would only answer, "Having made no offense, I need no trial": so she was pressed to death as the English law required for one who would not plead. She heard the sentence with serenity saying, "God be thanked. All that he shall send me is welcome. I am not worthy of so good a death as this."

On the eve of martyrdom she sewed her shroud and then spent the greater part of the night on her knees. To Agnes, a twelve-year-old daughter, she sent her shoes and stockings to signify that she should follow in her steps. Agnes became a nun at Louvain; and two of the martyr's sons, priests. Before the seven or eight hundred pounds were placed on her she prayed aloud for the pope, cardinals, clergy, Christian princes, and especially for Queen Elizabeth's return to the Catholic faith.

MARCH 26

391

St. Peter, bishop of Sebaste, brother of saints Basil the Great and Gregory of Nyssa. Their father died shortly after Peter's birth—he was the youngest of ten—and he was educated mostly by his oldest sister, St. Macrina. Peter succeeded Basil as head of the monastery the family established on the banks of the River Isis. As bishop he was a staunch opponent of Arianism and so endeared himself to his flock that within a few years of his death his anniversary was already a solemn commemoration.

ca. 651

St. Braulio, bishop of Saragossa, patron of Aragon, disciple of St. Isidore and probably the literary editor of Isidore's **Etymologies.** He was a most eloquent preacher, a keen controversialist, and a model of pastoral zeal. He became blind in his final years and spent the last day of his life reciting psalms. His forty-three surviving letters are an invaluable source of information on the relations of church and state in Visigothic Spain.

809

St. Ludger, bishop of Muenster, apostle of Westphalia. His gentleness, it is said, did more to attract the Saxons to Christ than Charlemagne's armies. Under the rule of St. Chrodegang he founded a monastery from which Muenster took its name. He was once summoned to the court of Charlemagne to answer a charge of indiscriminate almsgiving to the neglect of proper adornment of his churches. When a royal chamberlain came to call him one morning Ludger was at prayer and sent word that he would come as soon as he was finished. After a second and third messenger failed to hurry him the emperor became indignant, but Ludger explained that he believed the service of God was more important than the service of any man and that this had also been the emperor's mind when he appointed him bishop.

MARCH 27

ca. 718

St. Rupert. Not only was he the first abbot-bishop of Salzburg, Austria, but he actually founded the town, reclaiming the ancient **Jovavum** which had fallen into ruins, and he gave it its new name from the salt spring and the mines which he helped to develop. He established there the monastery of St. Peter, which he populated with Irish monks, and the convent of Nonnberg over which he set his niece, St. Erentrude, as abbess. In time both monasteries became Benedictine and still exist today, the oldest abbeys in Austria. St. Rupert and his monks evangelized the region and, along with the nuns, contributed greatly to its rich Christian civilization.

1178

Bl. Frowin, a Benedictine of St. Blaise in the Black Forest who became abbot of Engelberg in Switzerland. He strove to attach this new monastery to the Holy See and free it from secular control. He founded the monastic school and library, and was himself the chronicler of the abbey and an ascetical writer of distinction, doing much to establish the cultural traditions the monastery has kept to the present day.

1589

Bl. John Amias and **Bl. Robert Dalby.** Yorkshiremen and priests martyred under Elizabeth I. John Amias was a widower and a former cloth-dealer while Robert Dalby had been a minister of the new sect. Dr. Champney wrote: "I was myself an eye witness of the glorious combat of these holy men . . . and I returned home confirmed by the sight of their constancy and meekness in the Catholic faith. . . ."

MARCH 28

1414

Bl. Joan Mary de Maillé. A daughter of French aristocrats,
she began by helping the poor but finally went all the way and
became poor herself. Her heart was set on consecrated virginity;
and though she went along with the family marriage, she and
her husband agreed at the start to live in continence. Their
chateau near Tours was turned into an asylum for the poor of
the neighborhood, and they adopted three children. Her husband
died after sixteen years, and his family turned Joan out of his
house with the reproach that she persuaded him to such extensive almsgiving that the value of the estate had been reduced.

For a time she lived with her mother and there learned to
make medicines and salves. But, importuned by suitors, she
moved to Tours into a small house next to the church of St.
Martin. She assisted at the divine office and gave herself entirely to prayer, penance, and works of mercy. She became a
Franciscan tertiary and renounced in favor of the Carthusians
all she possessed—including her husband's chateau which had
been restored to her. She too lived on alms, slept where she
could—including pigsties and kennels—and shared the rejections
of the destitute.

For a long period she lived in a remote solitude and then
came back to Tours to occupy a room near a Franciscan church.
She found her growing reputation of holiness, healing, and
prophecy harder to bear than the contempt to which she had
become accustomed. With particular compassion she visited and
instructed prisoners and once obtained from the king of France
the freedom of all those imprisoned at Tours.

MARCH 29

1732

St. Lucy Filippini, who was left an orphan at an early age and soon joined forces with Bl. Rose Venerini in educating the poor girls at Montefiascone. Out of this association there developed the **Maestre Pie,** an institute of immense importance in the education of Italian women. In North America her group is known as the Religious Teachers Filippini. Her modesty, charity, intense conviction of the value of spiritual things, together with her courage and practical common sense, won all hearts. She would go out, rosary in hand, and collect girls for instruction. Schools multiplied rapidly. Sometimes, in the women's retreats she gave, her listeners would be so overcome with tears of repentance that they would beg her to stop, as they could stand no more. Though she spent only six months in Rome founding a school, she was already known throughout her district as "the holy teacher." She died on March 25.

1927

Bl. Joseph Moscati, physician of international standing, author of numerous scientific treatises, head doctor of a large Naples hospital complex. At his sudden death when only 46 the Neapolitans began speaking of him as the 'holy doctor.' A daily communicant who embraced his profession as an apostolate to the whole person, soul as well as body, he saw spiritual values as the true context of human life. "Beauty and the enchantment of life pass away," he said. "There only remains eternal love surviving in us. This is our hope and our religion, for God is love." In the autopsy room he placed a crucifix with the inscription "O death, I will be your death." He was not one to compartmentalize his faith or in any way to hide or compromise it. "Love the truth," he wrote for himself on October 22, 1922, "show yourself such as you are, without pretence, without fear, frankly. And if the truth costs you persecution, accept it. And if you should have to sacrifice yourself and your life for truth, be brave in sacrifice."

Doctor Moscati loved the poor whom he would serve gratis and visit in their hovels. He communicated warmth, kindness and hope as he passed through the hospital wards. At his beatification the words said of the Divine Healer were also applied to him, "He went about doing good." (Acts 10,38).

MARCH 30

ca. 649

St. John Climacus, monk and abbot on Mt. Sinai, of whom
very little is known other than his book, **The Ladder (klimax) to
Paradise,** which has become part of his name. This spiritual
classic synthesized in maxims and anecdotes the ascetic experience of three centuries of Eastern monasticism, much as
the **Imitation of Christ** would do for the **Devotio moderna** in
the fifteenth century. The **Ladder** is more salty than the **Imitation** and about twice as long. It also has a simpler format with
a ladder of thirty virtuous steps—one for each year of Christ's
hidden life. Renunciation is on the first rung; faith, hope, and
charity, on the thirtieth. Typical are sayings like these: "He
who says he loves God and is angry with his brother is like a
man who dreams he is running" (30, 27); "He who fondles a
lion often tames it, but he who coddles his body makes it still
wilder" (14, 6).

The history of the Jesus Prayer suggests that St. John Climacus may be the first to associate breathing with the repetition of
the name of Jesus when he writes, "**Hesychia** (silence) is an
incessant act of worship and a continual presence before God.
Unite the memory of Jesus with each breath; then you will understand the usefulness of **hesychia**" (27, 60-61).

1472

Bl. Amadeus IX, Duke of Savoy, who took such care to protect the poor in his law courts that people would say, "In the
rest of the world it is better to be rich, but in Savoy the beggars are favored and it goes hardest with the rich." He could
not refuse a request for alms and when out of money would
take off some of his clothes or give personal effects. To an ambassador who boasted of the hunting dogs his lord possessed,
Amadeus showed the tables of the poor. "It is with these,"
he said, "that I hunt for what is right and for the kingdom of
heaven."

1900

St. Leonard Murialdo, founder of the Pious Society of St. Joseph, one of Turin's social justice saints. As a young priest he devoted himself to the education of poor boys and directed the oratory of San Luigi which was offered to him by St. John Bosco. He helped organize Turin's first Catholic trade union and pioneered a whole range of projects such as homes for children, trade schools, and legislation to protect women and children in factories. He was also an energetic promoter of the Catholic press.

MARCH 31

1046

St. Guy, Benedictine abbot of Pomposa near Ferrara. He made a dramatic break with his milieu during a festival at Ravenna when, to the consternation of his parents, he stripped off his dressy clothes and gave them to a beggar. Donning the shabbiest things he could find he set off for Rome. In due course he became a hermit, a monk, abbot of St. Severus in Ravenna, and then of Pomposa, where his father and brother joined him. For two years he had St. Peter Damian give his monks lectures on Scripture. Under him Pomposa flourished exceedingly. He had a cell three miles from the abbey where he would go for periods of more intensive prayer and fasting. His Lents were particularly austere. Toward the end of his life he retired into solitude but died on his way to Piacenza where Emperor Henry III, who had heard of his sanctity and wisdom, summoned him for consultation.

1898

Bl. Marie-Eugenie Milleret de Brou, foundress at Paris of the semi-contemplative Congregation of the Assumption, devoted mainly to the Christian education of girls and characterized by the motto

"Orare et Educare" (Pray and Teach). She was born at Metz in 1817. Hers was a broken home, the father a free-thinker, a mother without deep religious convictions. After the death of her mother, a brother, and a sister, she was sent at 15 to another family, and then moved again to the home of some cousins in Paris. At 17 she was a sad, lonely teenager struggling over the meaning of life, when students, led by Frederick Ozanam, succeeded in starting the Notre Dame sermons with their Father Lacordaire as speaker. Six thousand packed his opening conference and returned to the Paris streets with a new vision of a religious transformation of society through Christ's Church. "My vocation," Marie-Eugenie would often repeat, "dates from Notre Dame." "Your words," she wrote to Father Lacordaire, "answered all my thoughts . . . gave me a new generosity, a faith that nothing was to shake. I was really converted and I had conceived the desire to give all my strength, or rather all my weakness, to this Church which alone, now, had in my eyes the secret and the power of good."

She came under the direction of the zealous and explosive Father Theodore Combalot, who told her of his desire to see an order combining teaching and prayer and dedicated to Our Lady of the Assumption. At 22 she began with three companions. She eventually broke with Father Combalot and in time would find much help from a more kindred spirit, the educator, Father Emmanuel d'Alzon, who was soon to found the Assumptionist Fathers.

At the time of her 'conversion' she wished she were a man so that she could take a leading part in the socio-religious transformation of society; but at her beatification in 1975 there were throughout the world 1800 sisters working under her inspiration to raise the cultural, moral and Christian level of education, sisters sharing in the single-mindedness of the purpose she expressed to Lacordaire: "To make Christ known, the liberator and king of the world—that is for me the beginning and the end of Christian education." Bl. Marie-Eugenie Milleret died at 81 on March 9.

APRIL 1

1132

St. Hugh, bishop of Grenoble, a contemplative bishop. During a long and fruitful apostolate, convinced of his unworthiness and harassed by blasphemous thoughts, he constantly yearned for solitude. At twenty-eight he seemed—to everyone but himself—the person best qualified to uphold clerical celibacy and to put down simony at Grenoble. He was ordained bishop at Rome by St. Gregory VII, but the pope had first to reassure him that his temptations to blasphemy were a special purification sent by God and did not make him unfit for the office.

But after two years as bishop, conscious only of his failures, he quietly withdrew, and became a monk at Chaise-Dieu. As soon as he was professed Pope Gregory sent him back to Grenoble and successive pontiffs kept him on the job for half a century. His virtues were such that he was canonized two years after his death. At times his sermons would have the congregation in tears. He gave St. Bruno the place called Chartreuse.

1194

St. Hugh, Cistercian abbot of Bonnevaux, nephew of the great St. Hugh of Genoble and like him, a man of prayer. He earned a place in history by negotiating peace between Pope Alexander III and Emperor Frederick Barbarossa in 1177.

1849

Bl. Louis Pavoni, an educator, founder of the Sons of Mary Immaculate of Brescia. In discipline he preferred gentleness to severity, saying that "rigorism keeps heaven empty." He died on April 1, 1849, during the tragic "Ten Days of Brescia", when the people tried to revolt against Austria. On a wet stormy day he led his boys out of the city. Standing on a hill overlooking Brescia and seeing the work of thirty years at the orphanage go up in flames, he felt the first of the heart spasms that would end his life in a few days.

APRIL 2

1507

ST. FRANCIS OF PAOLA, in Calabria; founder of the Minim Friars, a mendicant order with a rule taken mostly from St. Francis of Assisi. By a special vow the Minim's life becomes a perpetual lent with total abstinence from meat, eggs, and anything made of milk. Their motto is "Charity"; their fundamental virtue, humility; and their objective, to convert people to Christian life particularly by example. The Minims began as hermits.

At fifteen Francis became a solitary. Some disciples were attracted by his austere life and the cures he worked; but at twenty-five he understood that his call was to an active apostolate. He died in 1507 at the age of ninety-one. The last twenty-five years he spent in France, brought there by Louis XI, who had prevailed on the pope to send him the Calabrian wonder-worker. Francis prepared the king for death and by his advice at court was instrumental in restoring peace between France and Brittany, and between France and Spain. Minim superiors were called "correctors," a "corrector general" being the highest.

St. Francis of Paola is immensely popular in Latin lands, and because of the many miracles he worked in connection with the sea he was made patron of seafarers in 1943. His order flourished just before the Reformation and for more than a century after. Today the Minims are mostly in Italy.

APRIL 3

1253

St. Richard of Wyche, bishop of Chichester, model pastor. A brilliant scholar, he served as chancellor of Oxford before entering the priesthood at the age of forty-five. It took a papal threat of excommunication, before Henry III would allow him to take possession of the temporalities of Chichester. Richard refused to give ecclesiastical preferments to his relatives, saying that Christ gave the keys not to his cousin John, but to Peter, who was no relation. For his love of poverty he is often called "the English St. Francis.

1373

St. Andrew Corsini, whose undisciplined life was dramatically changed at fifteen by a scolding from his mother, followed by a prayerful visit to a Carmelite church. He soon became a Carmelite. At ordination he stole away to say his first Mass privately to avoid some of the fuss his wealthy family was making. When the canons of Fiesole chose him for bishop he hid, only to be discovered as the chapter was on the verge of another election. He proved to be one of those model bishops canonized by his own flock.

1875

Bl. Francis Coll, outstanding Dominican preacher, founder. The tenth and last child of a weaver, he lost his father at 3, entered a seminary at 10 and even at that age taught catechism and grammar in several homes to pay his way. He joined the Dominicans at 18 in Gerona, Spain. The sonorous voice of the future preacher earned him the office of cantor. The government closed and confiscated the Dominican houses in Spain just before Francis reached the priesthood, so he was ordained as an "exclaustrated religious" sponsored by the bishop of Vich. After ten years as assistant pastor he followed his great penchant for preaching and teamed up with St. Anthony Claret, who was a former fellow seminarian, and with several other priests. They obtained from Pope Pius IX faculties as Apostolic Missionaries. Francis spent the remaining 23 years of active priesthood preaching from town to town through all of the dioceses of Catalonia, traveling on foot, poorly clad, content with whatever was given him. In the face of massive ignorance, he developed within the devotional framework of the fifteen mysteries of the Rosary an intense but simple catechesis on the fundamental truths of the Faith. At the same time he served as moderator of the third order Dominicans of Spain. At Vich in 1856 he founded the third order Dominican sisters, called 'La Anunciata' after the first mystery of the Rosary, their purpose being to teach girls, especially the poor and uninstructed in rural areas. Their houses numbered 50 at their founder's death.

At the age of 57 while preaching he suffered a stroke. During a Calvary of six more years he gradually lost his mind and his sight. In a lucid interval he said, "If it is the Will of God that I should be blind, then, even if I could recover my sight by touching my eyes, I would not do it." In 1872, three years before his death, Spain's Dominicans were allowed to resume conventual life. Bl. Francis Coll should be seen as one of the principal figures in the continuity of the order during its 38-year black-out in mid-nineteenth century Spain.

APRIL 4

636

ST. ISIDORE, bishop of Seville, doctor of the Church, under whom the Spanish Church reached its peak development in the pre-Islamic period. He is sometimes called "schoolmaster of the Middle Ages," because his **Etymologies,** an encyclopedia of the rapidly disappearing classical learning, served as a favorite textbook until the sixteenth century. He was educated under the supervision of his older brother St. Leander. There is a story that he one day ran away from his hard taskmaster but returned with renewed determination after looking at the holes worn in rocks by the continual dripping of water.

In 633 he presided over the Council of Toledo. Among its canons was one ordering that a seminary be established in every diocese. He codified monastic law, and was probably the principal compiler of the books used in the Mozarabic Mass and divine office. He died in 636, as holy as he was learned. The canon of the Mozarabic liturgy mentions his name.

814

St. Plato, abbot on Mt. Olympus and later at Sakkudion near Constantinople, imprisoned for opposing the divorce and remarriage of Emperor Constantine Porphyrogenitus.

1589

St. Benedict the Black, a Franciscan brother, the son of a Negro slave in Sicily. As guardian and novice master he had a way of giving admonitions so that they were taken to heart without being resented. Such was his reputation for sanctity and miracles, that on his public appearances men and women would struggle to kiss his hand and snatch away bits of his habit. He is patron of the Negroes of North America and protector of Palermo.

APRIL 5

1419

ST. VINCENT FERRER, Dominican of Valencia, son of an English father and a Spanish mother, one of the most influential popular preachers of all times. Convinced that the second coming of Christ was imminent, he was able to make the four last things immediately real. He encouraged processions of flagellants and was followed throughout Europe by an army of penitents—sometimes reaching 10,000—who wanted to live under his direction. He had the gift of healing and brought large numbers of Jews and Moors to the Christian faith.

He played an unique role in the final phase of the Western Schism; for his sanctity and miracles seemed to shed an aura of divine approbation on the Avignon claimant, Peter de Luna ("Benedict XIII"), whom he supported. For a period Vincent was his confessor and advisor at Avignon; but in the course of time the saint came to see Peter's unwillingness to abdicate as the chief obstacle to the peace of the Church and so withdrew his support, leaving Peter practically without followers. A year later, during the Council of Constance Pope Martin V was elected. Vincent died soon after at Vannes, Brittany.

1095

St. Gerald, abbot-founder of the Benedictine monastery of Sauve-Majeure near Bordeaux. He instituted the practice of reciting the office of the dead for thirty days after a monk's death, and of giving his bread and wine to the poor for an entire year.

1574

St. Catherine, Augustinian Canoness at Palma on the island of Majorca, a saint who was granted extraordinary mystical graces but had also to endure violent molestations of the devil.

1744

Bl. Crescentia Höss, Franciscan at Kaufbeuren, Bavaria, daughter of a local weaver. She could not afford a dowry, but the Protestant mayor asked the sisters to receive her in return for a favor he did them in closing the noisy tavern next to the convent and giving it to the nuns. The tomb of this mystic is still popular today.

APRIL 6

912

Bl. Notker the Stammerer, musician, librarian, and guestmaster at the Abbey of St. Gall, described by his biographer as "weak in body but not in mind, stammering in tongue but not in intellect." He is the best known of a team of three—Ratpert and Tutilo are the others—who made their Benedictine monastery the principal oasis of culture for northern Europe at the beginning of the tenth century. He is particularly remembered for popularizing sequences—writing some thirty of his own—and for his work as chronicler.

1203

St. William of Eskill, canon regular who reformed monastic life in Denmark.

1252

St. Peter of Verona, Dominican defender of the faith in Northern Italy, the victim of conspiracy. His assassin became a saintly Dominican brother. As a young religious Peter was disgraced and banished on a false charge of entertaining women in his cell. One day while on his knees before a crucifix, praying over his unfair treatment, he heard our Lord say from the cross: "And I, Peter—what did I do to deserve my passion and death?"

1478

Bl. Catherine of Pallanza in Piedmont. At the age of fifteen she was so deeply touched by a sermon on the Passion that she resolved to consecrate herself totally to Christ. She withdrew alone to a mountain hermitage where in time other women joined her under the rule of St. Augustine.

APRIL 7

1719

ST. JOHN BAPTIST DE LA SALLE: patron of teachers; founder at Rheims of the Brothers of the Christian Schools, the oldest and most numerous congregation of teaching brothers. His originality did not consist in founding free schools—many had done that before—but in creating a body of trained laymen who would dedicate themselves by religious vows to teaching gratis and for life.

His congregation grew out of some side work he took on as a young priest in helping to train teachers in the local charity schools. His gifts as an educator and leader soon became apparent, and he saw it as God's will that he give himself completely to this work. To identify with the men he was training, he gave away his fortune—be belonged to the aristocracy—and lived in poverty. He made it a rule that no brother should ever become a priest nor should any priest be accepted into the congregation.

He opened the first teacher training school and revolutionized pedagogy by introducing the simultaneous classroom method in place of individual instruction. The brothers had countless difficulties to face, such as the storm raised by teachers who took fees; but the saint always set an example of trust in God and humility. He died on Good Friday, 1719, at the age of sixty-eight.

327

Sts. Jonas and **Barachisius,** Persian martyrs in the persecution of Sapor II, brothers who left their monastery at Beth-Iasa to bolster the courage of the Christians in prison. Their answers under questioning were so filled with wisdom that it was thought better to hold the trials at night away from the crowds. At one point Jonas said, "Judge whether it is not wiser to sow corn than to hoard it. Our life is seed, sown to rise again in the world to come, where it will be renewed by Christ in immortal life."

APRIL 8

ca. 558

St. Marculf or **Marcoul,** founder of the abbey of Nanteuil in Normandy. It was believed that a novena before the saint's relics gave the King of France the power to cure a lymphatic skin disease known as the King's Illness. As recently as 1825 King Charles X, after his coronation, ministered to some patients at the hospital of St. Marcoul in Rheims saying over each, "The king touches you; may God heal you."

1606

Bl. Julian of St. Augustine, Franciscan brother in Spain whose unusual devotions and mortifications made his superiors suspect he was unbalanced. They admitted him to profession only on the third try, after a period as a hermit had established the genuineness of his sanctity. He took his few hours of sleep in the open or leaning against a wall or in a confessional, and gained a reputation for a simple eloquence that went straight to the heart. But when the queen mother insisted on hearing him, he was so embarrassed that he could not speak a single word.

1816

St. **Julia Billiart,** co-foundress and superior of the Sisters of
Notre Dame of Namur in the chaotic period after the French
Revolution. She was prepared for the work by twenty-two years
as an invalid. Julia was past fifty and her congregation just
launched, when Father Enfantin asked her to join in a novena
for an intention he had. On the fifth day, the feast of the
Sacred Heart, he came to her and said: "Mother, if you have
any faith, take one step in honor of the Sacred Heart." She
got up at once, cured. A favorite expression, particularly impressive to those who came for religious instruction or advice during her illness, was, "How good the good God is!" She dedicated herself to Him by a vow of chastity at the age of fourteen.

APRIL 9

311

St. **Peter,** bishop of Alexandria, martyr. Such was his reputation that the Council of Ephesus, 130 years after his death,
used three of Peter's statements on the Incarnation. Of his
writings only a few fragments remain, the most important being
the fourteen **Penitential Canons** he drew up to guide his church
in practical conscience problems during an era of persecution.
His rules soon became a part of primitive Eastern church
law. Thus, those who had paid money so as not to be molested
were not required to do any penance, nor were those who had
fled even if others were arrested in their place. Those, however,
who pretended to apostatize or who sent pagans to sacrifice
in their place were required to do six months of penance. One
who yielded under torture or imprisonment and then had a
change of heart and again became a confessor was not to be
disquieted. Anyone who voluntarily came forward to denounce
himself was not to be disturbed even if his way of acting

brought persecution on others. Those who fell through want of courage without suffering either torture or imprisonment had to do penance for three years.

The compassionate quality of these and similar canons was a milestone in ancient penitential practice, but a more rigorous faction under Bishop Meletius took scandal and created a schism that would trouble the Egyptian church for several centuries.

1321

Bl. Thomas of Tolentino, Italian Franciscan and pioneer missionary in the East. He first went to Armenia, then to Persia, and was on his way to the Far East when his ship was driven onto Salsette Island near Bombay where, along with a layman and three Franciscan companions, he was beheaded by the Saracens on April 1.

APRIL 10

ca. 870

English monks and nuns martyred by Danish invaders. Among others are included the abbot and one hundred monks at Chertsey, abbot Hedda and his community at Peterborough, the monks of Bardney and Croyland, the nuns at Ely, and three anchorites at Thorney.

1460

Bl. Anthony Neyrot; martyr; a Dominican trained under St. Antoninus; captured by Saracen pirates and sold as a slave in Tunis, where he regained freedom but lost his faith reading the Koran. He repented, left his wife, resumed his habit and the recitation of the breviary, and boldly announced Christ to a large Moslem crowd in Tunis, before he was stoned and hacked to death.

1835

Bl. Magdalen di Canossa, foundress of the Daughters of Canossa. When her virtues were under discussion, Pius IX referred to a certain great man who "was humble enough to feed the poor at table with his own hands, but not humble enough to eat with them." Magdalen did both. As marchionness she had greatly impressed Napoleon during a stop at Canossa and so, at the age of thirty-four, she obtained from him an empty Augustinian convent at Verona, where with a few companions she began instructing poor girls.

"To make Jesus known to little children," was Magdalen's simplest way of stating her objective though nursing and adult instruction were not excluded. Her predilection for the dirtiest or most trying children is the reason why Canossian sisters today refer to a particularly difficult youngster as "one of mother foundress's children." As death approached she asked the sisters to help her kneel. Then she received Viaticum, joined in the prayers, and died with an exclamation of joy, leaning on the arms of Mother Annetta. Years before, when Annetta was just a girl, Magdalen had said to her, "One day you will be one of us and you will be there to help me when I die."

APRIL 11

1079

ST. STANISLAUS, bishop and principal patron of Cracow, martyred in 1079. He excommunicated Boleslaus II of Poland because of his scandals but paid for it with his life.

1608

Bl. George Gervase, Benedictine; a member of Drake's last expedition to the Indies, a convert to Catholicism, proto-martyr of Downside Abbey; executed under James I for his priesthood and loyalty to the Holy See. When the rope was placed about his neck, he stretched out his arms and sang the "**Suscipe me Domine** . . ." as at monastic profession.

1903

St. Gemma Galgani, virgin and mystic at Lucca. The special feature of her short life was internal and external identification with the Passion of Christ. The strange phenomena she experienced—visions, conversations with our Lord, the Blessed Virgin, angels and saints, the stigmata which appeared every Thursday and Friday for two years—all called attention to the complementary role of victim to which Christians are called in order to fill up the things that are wanting in the sufferings of Christ (Col 1:24). As a special victim she felt a kinship with Sts. Margaret Mary and Gabriel the Passionist both of whom had a part in her cure from an excruciating illness. She made several attempts to become a Passionist nun, but health stood in the way. She died of tuberculosis on Holy Saturday at the age of twenty-five.

1914

Also at Lucca, **Bl. Helen Guerra;** foundress of the Oblates of the Holy Spirit, better known as the Sisters of St. Zita, whose purpose is to foster devotion to the Holy Spirit and promote Christian education. She suffered calumny and deposition with great peace and, like St. Gemma, died on Holy Saturday.

APRIL 12

352

St. Julius I, pope for fifteen years, defender of St. Athanasius and of papal prerogatives. To the Eastern bishops who had intruded another bishop into Alexandria in place of Athanasius he wrote in the year 341: "It was a question of bishops and churches more than usually important since they, in times past, had the apostles themselves for rulers. Are you ignorant that the usual thing is to write first to us, and that thus justice may be rendered from here? Those then who, far from this, have acted in an arbitrary manner without reference to us would now like us to signify approval in a case where we have no knowledge. This is not as Paul commanded, nor as the tradition of the Fathers. This is a procedure wholly foreign and new. . . . I write what I write in the common interest, and what I write to you is what we have received from the blessed apostle Peter."

371

St. Zeno, of African origin, beloved bishop of Verona, who inspired his people to a life of strictest economy in order to provide relief after the battle of Adrianople. He established a convent for virgins even before St. Ambrose. Ninety-three of his sermons survive.

11th -13th cent.

The holy abbots of Cava. April 12 marks the death of **St. Alferius Pappacarbone,** who in 1011 retired with two companions to a deep cleft (la Cava) on Monte Finestre, three miles north of Salerno. Leo, the next abbot, was able to supply monks for a few neighboring monasteries. His successor, **St. Peter Pappacarbone,** nephew of the founder, had, like his uncle, trained at Cluny. Copying the Cluniac structure and customs he welded the Cava dependencies into a highly centralized Benedictine congregation. During his forty-three years as abbot he gave the habit to more than 3,000 monks and received forty abbeys and thirty-five priories from various bishops and princes.

To each monastery was attached the care of souls. With the spread of feudal economy 172 monasteries came under the order. Today's mention recalls, along with St. Alferius, the three other saints and eight blesseds who served as abbots of Cava during the three centuries in which it dominated the monasticism of

BLESSED HELEN GUERRA

southern Italy. The monastery still exists as a member of the Cassinese Federation and is an abbey-diocese with twenty-five parishes.

APRIL 13

655

ST. MARTIN I, the last martyr pope, fearless champion of orthodoxy, an enduring inspiration to succeeding pontiffs when harassed by pressures of every sort to compromise their teaching role in the Church. He was papal nuncio to Constantinople at the time of his election and knew what accepting the papacy would mean. Emperor Constans II had just issued a decree known as the **typos** forbidding all further debate on whether Christ had one or two wills, and ordering the deposition of the refractory bishops. Without delay the new pope called a council at the Lateran attended by 105 bishops, and presided in person over its five sessions. The Council condemned the "one-will heresy." The **typos** it denounced in these words: "Doubtless it is a great advantage to have no disputes in matters of faith, but the good must not be rejected with the bad, the doctrine of the fathers with that of heretics. Such conduct rather fosters than extinguishes disputes. Ceasing to defend the faith is no way to put down heresy. We have indeed to avoid evil and do good, but not to reject the good with the evil. We may indeed praise the good intentions of the **typos** but its terms we must reject. For they are altogether opposed to the spirit of the Catholic Church, which imposes silence indeed on error, but does not command truth and its opposite to be together asserted or denied."

Martin was taken as a prisoner to Constantinople, condemned for treason, publicly stripped of his pallium and most of his garments, dragged through the streets, and exiled to Kherson in the Crimea, where after two years he died of ill-usage and privations.

585

St. **Hermenegild,** martyr, son of King Leovigild and heir to the Visigothic throne. Converted by his Catholic wife and by St. Leander, he was ordered by his father to give up his dignities and possessions. He revolted and was defeated. A reconciliation took place; but when he refused to receive communion at Easter from an Arian bishop, his father in a fit of rage had him executed. His younger brother, Reccared, became the first Catholic king of Spain.

APRIL 14

1067

St. **Robert of Turlande,** Benedictine abbot. When a friend asked him for advice on how to expiate one's sins, Robert, who was then a young priest at Brioude, recommended the solitary life. His friend agreed provided he too would come along. Robert had just returned from a pilgrimage to Rome, seeking light on his own vocation and took this proposal as his answer. He became the founder and first abbot of Chaise-Dieu in Auvergne, which soon had several canonized saints and was the center of more than 100 priories in France alone.

1184

St. **Benezet** ("Little Benedict") the bridge builder; a patron of Avignon, where he was buried in the stone bridge he built over the Rhone as an act of public service. Untrained, small of stature, and poor, he seemed ill-suited for the task; but he acted in response to a vision. The Order of Bridge Builders, whose constitutions were approved five years after his death, regarded him as founder.

1433

Bl. **Lydwina of Schiedam** in Holland; a prodigy of patience in suffering; whose extraordinary life attracted so much attention that several biographies were written by contemporaries, including one by Thomas 'A Kempis. The Schiedam town council drew up a document in 1421 testifying of her that "within the past seven years she has used no food or drink at all nor does she take any now."

Though not formally canonized, she has been popularly identified as an example of expiatory suffering and invoked as patroness of the heroically afflicted. Before a skating accident at fifteen she differed little from other girls except for her vow of chastity. A rib was broken, complications set in, and she was reduced to an indescribable condition. Her pastor had her meditate on the passion and she recognized her vocation as victim with Christ. She became a willing sufferer and even added voluntary mortifications. Mystic experiences began when she was nearly thirty. During the last nineteen years she took no nourishment other than the Eucharist. She died on Easter Tuesday, being about fifty-three.

APRIL 15

1246

Bl. Peter Gonzales, Dominican preacher much esteemed by Spanish and Portuguese sailors whom he would visit on their ships. The turning point in his life was a Christmas day when, as a young, newly-appointed canon, dressed in all his finery, he was thrown from his horse into the mud while the crowd laughed. The incident opened his eyes to his own vanity. "If the world mocks me," he reflected, "I will mock the world."

1607

Bl. César de Bus, outstanding catechist and penitent, founder at Avignon in 1592 of the Fathers of Christian Doctrine, a congregation which still exists. God's principal instrument in bringing this well-

connected poet, painter, and pleasure-seeking adventurer to religious
seriousness at about the age of 30 was a simple, holy woman. She
would at times ask him to read to her from the lives of the saints. "God
is calling you," she said to him, "and you do not listen to him." He was
ordained at 38 and gave a religious instruction the first evening. Soon,
with a small band of priests he began to visit small towns to find the
uninstructed. He promoted family catechetics, reaching the children
with simple, lively explanations and engaging the adults in dialogue
instructions based on the Catechism of the Council of Trent. He
trained teachers and also founded a feminine order which was later
absorbed into the Ursulines. In a deep spirit of compunction he
accepted the blindness which afflicted him at 50 and continued to
give instruction and look after his religious congregations. "The Cross,"
he wrote, "will be my light."

At the beatification in 1975 Pope Paul VI recalled what an inspiration the catechetical work of St. Charles Borromeo had been to Bl.
César and quoted from a sermon in which St. Charles impressed on his
helpers the importance of their work: "Even if you had brought back
only one child to the Church . . . realize that your work would be of
great value! Christ had the whole world to redeem and for this
immense work he had only the short span of three years . . . And yet, of
this short space of time, what a considerable part he spent on the
Samaritan woman alone! Let this be the greatest stimulus for you."

1815

Bl. Leopold of Gaiche, near Perugia; Franciscan provincial
and papal missioner; celebrated preacher and confessor; founder
of the retreat house on Monte Luco near Spoleto. Strange phenomena accompanied his ministry, such as the gift of prophecy
or the crown of thorns that sometimes appeared above his head.
When Napoleon entered Rome, Leopold, already in his seventy-
fifth year, was imprisoned for refusing to take the required oath.

APRIL 16

665

St. Fructuosus; hermit; abbot; archbishop of Braga, Portugal.

He kept trying to get out of ruling others, but even in solitude
they came to him. He wrote a rule which admitted entire families into monastic life.

1783

St. Benedict Joseph Labre; pilgrim-beggar; a witness to voluntary poverty in its most abject form and to the virtue of religion, especially devotion to the Blessed Sacrament. The first
of fifteen children, he left home at eighteen to try the most
austere orders in France but gradually discovered that his vocation was to tramp through Europe from shrine to shrine,
penniless, living on handouts and thrown-away scraps, and
sleeping in the open. He became a Franciscan tertiary. Money
that came his way he would hand on to others. One benefactor
who thought Benedict passed his coin on because it was too
small belabored him with a stick, but Benedict said nothing.
He rarely spoke except to give or receive a charity.

He spent his last seven years at Rome, sleeping among the
He became known as "the saint of the Forty Hours." Towards
the end he slept in a poor man's hostel and always took the last
place in the soup line, often giving his portion to others. He
died on Wednesday of Holy Week, being picked up that morning from the steps of a church and taken to the home of a
butcher where he received the last sacraments. He was thirty-
five.

1879

St. Bernadette Soubirous, oldest child of a destitute miller.
She was fourteen, simple and uneducated, when the Immaculate Virgin began to appear to her at Lourdes. As a sister of
Notre Dame of Nevers her desire was to remain hidden and
forgotten, comparing herself to a broom: "Our Lady used me.
They have put me back in my corner. I am happy there and
remain there." She also died at 35.

APRIL 17

1680   [*U.S.A., Canada*]
Bl. Catherine or **Kateri Tekakwitha,** virgin, the first North American
Indian to be raised to the altar, remarkable for meekness, the spirit of
prayer and the penitential practises by which she united herself to
the passion of Christ. She died at 24 at the St. Francis Xavier Mission
on the south bank of the Lachine Rapids near Montreal, after only
five years as a Christian. Her mother, an Algonquin baptised at Three
Rivers, Quebec, was taken captive during an Iroquois raid and carried
off to what is now Auriesville, New York, St. Isaac Jogues' place of
martyrdom ten years before; and there she bore Catherine and one
son to a heathen Mohawk chief. At 4 Catherine lost her parents and
brother in a smallpox epidemic. Her own face was permanently
disfigured and her eyes left so pained by strong light that she would
shade her face with a blanket for the rest of her life.

She was raised by an uncle and for a time was passed from lodge to
lodge as no one wanted her. She resisted the several marriages
arranged by relatives, once running out of the lodge at the point
where the selected husband came to sit beside her. Eventually, when
at the age of 19 she received instruction and baptism, the Christian
faith and gospel virginity answered her deepest longings.

For over a year, as the only Christian in her lodge, she endured
continual mockery and abuse: 'The Christian' became her name, she
was lazy not going to the fields to work on Sunday, fun was made of
the Rosary. The priest who baptised her urged her to flee to the
Christian mission on the Rapids where, he said, she would have more
sweetness of peace in one day than in a year where she was. When
she escaped he sent this message, "Catherine Tekakwitha is going to
live at the Rapids. Will you kindly undertake to direct her? You will
soon know what a treasure we have sent you." She excelled in the
virtues and practises inculcated at her new home and with several
others wanted to live like the nuns at Montreal. Her new director
would write, "Every morning, winter and summer, she was in our
church at four o'clock... She remained several hours in succession in
prayer... Ordinarily she prayed only with her eyes and heart... All her

joy was to think upon Our Lord. If sometimes asked, 'Catherine, do you love our Lord? . . .,' 'O Father!, O Father!' she would say, and she could say no more. It is this love which made her renounce marriage to consecrate her virginity to Our Lord at the age of twenty."

Catherine was never strong, but death must also have been hastened by her merciless austerities. "I will love you in heaven," were her last words to Anastasia, the companion of her penances. At the point of dying she whispered, "Jesus, I love you." Miracles began at once, causing a great sensation throughout New France. "Pilgrimages are continually made to her tomb," a Jesuit at the mission wrote two years after her death, "and the savages, following her example, have become better Christians than they were."

APRIL 18

639

St. Laserian or **Molaisse,** who succeeded in establishing the Roman date of Easter in southern Ireland. He was ordained bishop of Leighlin by Pope Honorius I.

645

St. Richarius or **Riquier,** founder of the monastery of Centula —later called St. Riquier—in northwestern France. In the eighth century it housed 400 monks. The nearby town of Abbeville received its name from the abbey.

1176

St. Galdinus, cardinal-bishop and one of the principal patrons of Milan, supporter of Pope Alexander III during the schism promoted by Frederick Barbarossa. On his final day, though too weak to offer Mass, he delivered an impassioned sermon, lost consciousness in the pulpit, and died as Mass was ending.

1618 [*O.C.D.*]

Bl. Barbara Acarie, also known as Mary of the Incarnation, a mother and wife, who moved with equal grace among the destitute and the mighty, had the gift of mystic prayer as well as the hardihood to conduct a successful defence of her not-so-worthy husband in court. She took such pains with the religious education of her six children that she was asked if she intended them all to become religious. "I am training them to do God's will," she answered. All three daughters did in fact become Carmelites; and her sons remained men of staunch principles, one becoming a priest.

She is especially remembered for bringing the Discalced Carmelite nuns to France—St. Teresa appeared to her twice. While still married she trained women for Carmel and after her husband's death spent the last five years as Sister Mary of the Incarnation. She died on Easter Sunday.

APRIL 19

1012

St. Alphege, abbot of Bath, archbishop of Canterbury. He eliminated beggary from Winchester, where he was bishop for twenty-two years, and gave his life rather than burden his country with raising the huge sum of money the Danes demanded for his ransom. He is venerated as a martyr. To him the life of a lax religious seemed pointless, and he used to say it would have been better to remain in the world.

1054

St. Leo IX; an Alsatian who put an end to the "Iron Age" of the papacy and during six strenuous years launched the turbulent but glorious era that would later be called the Gregorian Reform in memory of Hildebrand, the future St. Gregory VII, whom Leo chose as his chief assistant. Though an appointee and close relative of Emperor Henry II, Leo saw the evils of papal subjection to princes. "I will go to Rome," he told the assembly that chose him at Worms, "and if, of their own accord the clergy and people elect me as their bishop I will yield to your desires; but, if not, I shall not regard myself as elected." His immediate successor, Victor II, would inaugurate the practise of having the cardinals elect the pope.

Leo made a visitation of a good part of Europe, holding synods in which married and simoniacal clergy were denounced and deposed. Though not a monk, this staunch defender of celibacy drew heavily on the support of the Benedictines, especially his favorite Cluniacs. He condemned Berengarius for denying the Real Presence, personally led an army against the Normans in southern Italy and was taken captive. A most tragic event, whose long-range consequences no one suspected, was the excommunication of Michael Cerularius, the provocative patriarch of Constantinople. The pope was already dead when his legates made their decision.

APRIL 20

709

St. Aldhelm, abbot of Malmesbury, bishop of Sherborne, the first Englishman to attain distinction as a scholar. Besides his extant Latin writings in prose and verse, he composed hymns and ballads in English for the instruction and edification of the poor.

1317 [*O.P.*]

St. Agnes, Dominican prioress at Montepulciano, mystic. She induced her well-to-do parents to allow her to go to a convent at the age of nine. By fifteen she was abbess at Procena. But the people of Montepulciano wanted to have their saint back and built her a convent which she aligned with the Dominican order. Among her many supernatural experiences it is recorded that just before the painful illness of her last years she was offered a chalice with the words: "Drink this chalice, spouse of Christ. The Lord Jesus drank it for you."

1419

Bl. Clare of Pisa. Her father was virtual head of the Republic of Pisa and so, despite a religious vocation, she was caught up in the family's social and political affairs. Engaged at seven, she used to slip her ring off during Mass. She was married for three years but was already a widow at fifteen. She stole off one night to the Poor Clares, but the next day her brothers stormed the convent and brought her home. Eventually she succeeded in establishing a strict branch of the Dominican sisters in a convent built by her father.

During a revolt one of her brothers fled to the convent door to escape a party of assassins who had already killed her father and two brothers. Judging it her duty to protect her community from the mob, she did not open; and her brother was slain on the spot. In later years, when the traitor's widow and daughters were in dire straits, she opened the convent doors to them.

APRIL 21

1109

ST. ANSELM, archbishop of Canterbury, doctor of the Church Born in Piedmont of Lombard and Burgundian parents, he became a monk at Bec, Normandy, at twenty-seven, succeeding Lanfranc as teacher and prior. It took much persuasion to make him abbot, while the archbishopric had practically to be forced on him.

Unlike Lanfranc, he was neither a statesman nor a diplomat; and his lack of sympathy with the needs and problems of ordinary life did not make for good understanding between church and state. But this most gentle saint did impress everyone as a true man of God possessed of such humility, control of temper, and personal charm that he disarmed even the most hardhearted men of affairs.

In the spirit of the Gregorian Reform he upheld the liberty of the church, preferring exile to compromise of any sort. An original and profound thinker, he is the one eleventh century theologian who is still read for his own sake. He gave genuine impetus to speculative thought and can with some right be called the "father of scholasticism." He described his approach as that of "faith seeking understanding"; another has characterized it as "theology written upon his knees."

ca. 185

St. Apollonius, Roman senator and martyr. A fairly reliable account of his defense before the senate has been preserved. It highlights in a simple way the moral ideals and straightforward theology which made Christianity so attractive to the pagan world. By way of an aside, Apollonius pointed out that it was no worse to die for the true God than to die of fever, dysentery, or some other cause.

1894   [*Franciscans*]

St. Conrad of Parzham; Capuchin brother who entered the order at thirty-one and spent forty years as porter at the Bavarian shrine of our Lady at Altötting, where the multitude of pilgrims offered endless opportunities for charity, patience, tact, and apostolic zeal. Contact with him left the deep impression that one was dealing with a man of God.

APRIL 22

ca. 174

St. Soter, pope. His contemporary, bishop Dionysius of Corinth, praised the Roman church for its tradition of generous alms to churches everywhere and added, "Your blessed bishop Soter has not only maintained this custom but has even increased it." Writing to Soter, Dionysius also expressed Corinth's respect for letters received from Rome: "Today we have observed the holy Lord's day in which we read your letter. Whenever we read it, we shall always be able to gain profit, just as we also do whenever we read the earlier letter written to us by Clement."

536

St. Agapetus I, pope for only eleven months but remembered for his firm stand on important issues in Rome, France, Carthage, and Constantinople. One of his first acts was to remove from the papal archives and publicly burn the documents Pope Boniface II had issued, five years previously, condemning the antipope Dioscorus. By this dramatic gesture Agapetus wished to repudiate the attempt of some of his immediate predecessors to appoint their own successors in the papal office—Pope Boniface had been such an appointee, while Dioscorus had been elected by a dissatisfied portion of the higher clergy.

At the request of the Ostrogoth king of Italy, Pope Agapetus went to Emperor Justinian and asked him—though without success—to call off the campaign of the Byzantine army to reconquer Italy. At Constantinople he found that Anthimus the patriarch—a protege of Empress Theodora—had been uncanonically transferred from his previous diocese and that he was of the monophysite party. The pope demanded his deposition and himself—the only instance of this in history—ordained the new patriarch, Mennas. Agapetus died in Constantinople a few weeks later. So applauded was his action on behalf of orthodoxy that he is also venerated as a saint in the Eastern Church.

APRIL 23

Unknown date
   ST. GEORGE, martyred at Lydda in Palestine before the reign of Constantine. In time, many legends were associated with his name, including the twelfth century account of him as a knight and dragon-slayer.

997   [*O.S.B.*]
   St. Adalbert; second bishop of Prague, whose short, agitated career—he was martyred at forty-one—gives heroic dimensions to the early days of this important diocese. Its territory included Bohemia, Silesia, Moravia, western Hungary, and lower Austria. Adalbert belonged to one of the strongest local families and had a passionate sense of his responsibilities. He was only twenty-six at the time of his appointment, and he entered Prague barefoot amid great rejoicing. He began at once to reform the semi-barbarous clergy and people, but after six years withdrew in discouragement.
   He had intended to go to the Holy Land but settled in a Benedictine monastery at Rome and took vows. Recalled to Prague he established Bohemia's first monks at Brevnov—soon a powerful religious center—and in a short time succeeded in founding at Meseritz the first permanent monastery in Poland. He was less successful with his faction-torn people and returned to his monastery in Rome. When the pope sent him back to Prague, he encountered greater opposition than ever and some of his kinsmen were massacred. For him further fruitful work in Prague was out of the question. So he set out on a missionary expedition to the pagans in Prussia, where he and his companions were killed after a week.

1262   [*Franciscans*]
   Bl. Giles of Assisi, the third and dearest of the early companions of St. Francis, a rustic, one of the "characters" of the order whose sayings were collected. "He who does not know

how to pray," he would say, "does not known God." For getting on with others he had this advice: "If you love, you will be loved. If you fear, you will be feared. If you serve, you will be served."

1458   [*O.S.A., O.A.R.*]
Bl. Helen of Udine, mother of a large family; Augustinian tertiary, in whose life there were many manifestations of the supernatural.

APRIL 24

1622
ST. FIDELIS OF SIGMARINGEN, Capuchin priest martyred in Switzerland. He first practised law and was known as the "poorman's lawyer." But as there was so much sordid dealing in the profession, he decided to become a Capuchin. He distributed half his goods to the poor and half for needy seminarians. At the same time he began to pray for two things: not to commit a single mortal sin and to die a martyr.

After some years of fruitful ministry, he was made superior of a group of Capuchin missionaries to the predominantly Zwinglian areas in the Grisons; and his martyr prayer was answered in a few months. Except for his crucifix, Bible, breviary, Capuchin rule and habit, he went in absolute poverty. The Congregation for the Evangelization of Peoples sponsored the Grison mission as one of its first acts. The official decree establishing the congregation was not published until June 22, 1622, two months after Fidelis met a glorious death, preaching the Gospel. He is considered the first martyr of this missionary arm of the Church, a model to be emulated through the centuries.

709
St. Wilfrid, abbot, bishop of York, chief spokesman for the

customs and discipline of the Roman Church at the Synod of Whitby in 664. He introduced the Rule of St. Benedict into his monastery at Ripon and did much to enhance the liturgy and spread the Roman Chant. A year after the Synod at the age of thirty, he was ordained a bishop but spent the greater part of the remaining forty-five years in exile because of jurisdictional disputes. In the meantime, however, he preached in Friesland and several parts of England, converting almost all of Sussex, where he also taught the people how to fish. He was the first English prelate to appeal a decision to the pope and he made three trips to Rome.

1868   [*R.G.S., C.J.M.*]

St. Mary Euphrasia Pelletier; foundress at Angers of the Good Shepherd Congregation, in which there were 2,067 sisters at the time of her death. Her contribution was centralization. St. John Eudes had founded the order 200 years before to provide for wayward girls and "fallen" women, but the houses were unconnected.

APRIL 25

ST. MARK evangelist; cousin of St. Barnabas; identical, apparently, with John Mark at whose mother's house the Christians were praying for St. Peter's release from prison (Acts 12:12). St. Paul considered Mark a quitter for turning back during the first missionary journey, but in later years found consolation in him as a helper and fellow prisoner. The apostolic tradition that makes Mark the interpreter and mouthpiece of St. Peter is supported by the vivid, eye-witness quality of Mark's gospel whenever Peter is present. It is sometimes called the "Gospel of St. Peter."

With the exception of St. Bede, none of the great fathers wrote commentaries on Mark. At that time he was regarded mostly as an abbreviator of Matthew, since almost the only passages found exclusively in Mark are the "ephatha" miracles (7:31-37), the curing of the blind man to whom men looked like trees walking (8:22-26), and the parable of the seed growing of itself (4:26-29). He is especially gifted as a story teller, sensitive to concrete detail. His purpose was to reveal to the pagan world the Good News that Jesus was the Son of God. A characteristic of his gospel is that Jesus tends to conceal his Messianic dignity until his trial and that He is recognized as Son of God only at his death.

Venice claims his body and venerates him as patron. His emblem, among the four beasts of Ezekiel, is the lion.

APRIL 26

ca. 860

St. Paschasius Radbertus, a foundling who became schoolmaster and abbot of Corbie in Picardy. A voluminous writer, he is author of the first speculative treatise on Transsubstantiation, although this word was not invented until the first half of the twelfth century, three hundred years after Radbertus; but he did use the word "substance" in his famous book **On the Body and Blood of the Lord.**

He taught that after the words of consecration, through a conversion of the **substance** of bread and wine, there is present on the altar the Eucharistic Body of Christ which is identical with his historical body. This ninth century theologian, who was not an Aristotelian nor much influenced by philosophy of any kind, uses the word "substance" to mean the reality that makes a thing what it is: so that after the consecration it is no longer true to say, "This is bread," but rather, as Jesus said, "This is my body."

1667

Bl. Peter (Pedro de San José) Betancour, a layman who did so much in Guatemala City to help orphans, children, beggars, the sick and travelers that he has the remarkable title, 'Mother of Guatemala.' An impoverished descendant of one of the Norman conquerors of the Canary Islands, he left the Islands as a young man, hoping to spread the Gospel in Guatemala. He arrived there destitute, and through personal experience learned what it was like to be homeless and to beg food in a bread line. For a time he worked in a textile factory where convict labor was also employed.

When he tried for the priesthood he soon found the studies beyond him. He joined the Franciscan third order, remaining a layman but wearing the habit. He started a hospital for the convalescent poor, an orphanage, a school, and an oratory. The organized co-workers he left behind became in time the Bethlehemite congregation caring for the sick. So sensitive was he to the feelings of the poor that he had Masses endowed to be said at a very early hour so that the poor would not miss Mass on account of their shabby clothes. Among the religious customs he started was that of gathering children on August 18 to sing the Seven Joys of the Franciscan Rosary, and that on Christmas Eve of imitating St. Joseph searching for lodging for Mary. Bl. Peter Betancour died in his forties.

APRIL 27 *

1236

Bl. Agnellus, a native of Pisa, founder and guardian at Paris, but remembered especially as the one St. Francis sent with eight companions to open the English province in 1224. In three months they established three houses, one of them at Oxford, where in 1229 Agnellus built a college for his many recruits and secured Robert Grosseteste, chancellor and most distinguished teacher at Oxford, as his first lecturer in theology. Grossteste remained on for six years — until his appointment as

---

* *S.J. see Dec. 21 for St. Peter Canisius.*

bishop of Lincoln—sufficient time for his interests in theology, science, and languages to give the college its characteristic orientation.

Oxford's rapid rise to fame as a university dates from the coming of the Franciscans, and their college continued to exercise enormous influence until the Reformation. Bl. Agnellus wished, like St. Francis, to remain a deacon; but he accepted priestly ordination in obedience to the general chapter. He died in his early forties.

1287

St. Zita; virgin; patroness of domestic help; a household servant whose goodness and miracles made her so popular that, within forty years of her death, Dante in the **Divine Comedy** was able to refer to her town of Lucca by simply mentioning "Holy Zita."

She entered a weaver's household as a maid at twelve and stayed on till her death, forty-eight years later. She attended daily Mass, gave food—often her own portion—to beggars, and put up with abuse from other servants who resented her being so religious. In time, however, they were won over by her genuine goodness; and she became the confidant of all, had charge of the children, and was put over the entire household by an irascible master whom she alone could manage. Stories were told of the miraculous way food multiplied, thus hiding her charities and protecting her from the master's rage. She had a special love for criminals sentenced to death, would visit them, and pray many hours for them.

1485

Bl. James of Bitetto, a Franciscan brother of Dalmatian origin who spent most of his life in southern Italy and who was remarkable for his gift of prayer. For years he was cook at the friary in Conversano; and as the flames suggested both the fires of hell and the burning love of God, he often fell into ecstasy during work.

APRIL 28

1841

ST. PETER CHANEL, the first martyr of Oceania. At his first Communion, he became aware of his missionary vocation. He nearly abandoned it, however, when studies became so tiresome that—bright as he was—he was on the verge of running away from school. But he prayed to Mary for help, held on, and entered the seminary at sixteen. Four years after ordination he joined the recently founded Marist Fathers and at thirty-three was deposited with a solitary companion on Futuna Island in the New Hebrides where he was totally dependent on the native chieftans until he was clubbed to death four years later. The entire island was converted within two years of his death. "He loves us," said one of his catechumens, "he does what he teaches. He forgives his enemies. His teaching is true."

1260   *[Franciscans III O.]*

Bl. Luchesio, whom Franciscans have traditionally honored as their first tertiary. Until his thirties, Luchesio was interested only in money and politics. But gradually, perhaps because of the death of his children, he became sensitive to the misery of others—especially the sick and prisoners—and gave away all his goods except a small plot he cultivated himself. St. Francis, wanting to form an association of people living a religious life in the world, gave Luchesio and his wife the habit and cord during one of his visits to Poggibonsi. His wife at first found it hard when Luchesio would give away the last scrap of food; but in time she, too, experienced some of the blessings of poverty.

1716   *[S.M.M.]*

St. Louis Mary Grignion de Montfort; a native of Brittany; whose short, tempestuous career gave the Church two religious orders and a new accent—possibly the strongest ever—on devotion to Mary. When he died at forty-three, the Daughters of

Wisdom consisted of four sisters, while the Company of Mary, now known as the Montfort Missionaries, had two priests and several brothers. Louis was a colorful and most effective home missioner.

At nineteen he took a vow to live only on alms. In a shabby cassock he practised such extreme poverty that beggars would offer handouts to him. To the proud austerity of Jansenism he opposed confident, expansive love of Mary.

During the canonization, Pope Pius XII pointed out that true Marian devotion consists essentially in union with Jesus under the guidance of Mary. While admitting that no individual set of practices could claim a monopoly, the pope commended particularly those attitudes which were the foundation of this saint's devotion to Mary: firm conviction regarding her powerful intercession, determination to imitate her virtues, and ardent love for Jesus and Mary. St. Louis is best known for his book, **The True Devotion to the Blessed Virgin Mary.**

APRIL 29

1380

ST. CATHERINE OF SIENA; doctor of the church; patroness of Italy; mystic and incomparable woman of action; heroine who, against overwhelming odds, persuaded Pope Gregory XI to leave Avignon and return to Rome.

The youngest of the twenty-five children of a prosperous Sienese wool-dyer, Catherine Benincasa had her first vision at six. Attracted to prayer and solitude she became a difficult teenager, resisting her mother in matters of amusement and dress, rejecting both marriage and religious life, but enamoured of consecrated virginity. At sixteen she became a Dominican tertiary and adopted their habit, but continued to live at home. For three years she left her room only for Mass and confession, and spoke to no one but her confessor. Her mortifications reached the point where she could manage on a spoonful of herbs and a few hours of sleep a day.

At nineteen, after the experience of Christ placing a ring on her finger—visible only to herself—she resumed normal family life, took her share of housework, and began to care for the sick and the poor. Soon she was the center of a motley band of men and women of all ages, professions, and classes—including scions of Siena's principal families—all attracted by the charm of Catherine's human and supernatural qualities. Gaiety, unconventionality, religious fervor, social involvement, disinterestedness, and loyalty to the church were the characteristics of this "club." Their concern, she wrote, was to remove hatred from man's heart and "bring him to peace with Christ crucified and with his neighbor." At twenty-eight she received the stigmata, which also remained invisible to others until after her death.

She had become all love for God and neighbor; ecstasies, peace missions, letters—some 400 remain—to help others and cure the ills of the church. Infused wisdom and the gift of exhortation were her special charisms. She took twenty-three of her company along on the three-month's historic embassy to Avignon. Reform she saw would come "not with war, but with peace and quiet, with the humble and continuous prayers, sweat and tears of the servants of God," and in communion with Christ's rightful representatives on earth. The pope she referred to as "the sweet Christ on earth." She urged the bishops to speak up. "I see the world spoilt," she wrote to the Cardinal of Ostia, "through refusal to speak out. Christ's spouse is pale." Her spiritual masterpiece, the **Dialogue of Divine Providence,** was dictated in ecstasy.

She died at Rome at the age of thirty-three, sealing her career with this offer of her life: "O eternal God, receive the sacrifice of my life for this mystical body of holy Church. I have nothing other to give but what you have given me. Take my heart, therefore, and press it to the face of this spouse."

APRIL 30 *

1572

ST. PIUS V, a bright and prayerful peasant boy from northern Italy who became a Dominican at fourteen, held important positions in his order, headed the Inquisition, and—supported by St. Charles Borromeo —was elected pope two years after the Council of Trent. His six-year pontificate, together with the longer period of consolidation under his successor Gregory XIII, translated into action the spirit and letter of the Council and gained for the Catholic Church the moral prestige to turn the Reformation tide in great sectors of Europe. Through an expanded and reform-conscious system of Roman congregations and papal nuncios, these two pontiffs gave church government the complexion it would keep until modern times.

Under Pius V, the Trent catechism was completed, and the breviary and missal revised. In Spain, it is true, his condemnation of bull fights went unheeded, but in papal territory prosecution of public vice was so relentless that people said Rome was becoming one big monastery. His politically ineffectual excommunication of Queen Elizabeth I in the bull **Regnans in excelsis** may be seen as the end of the medieval concept of a united christendom. The pope did, however, succeed in rallying sufficient Christian forces to break the Turkish advance at Lepanto in 1571. The Passion of Christ, to which he would devote all of Holy Week, was his special devotion and on his deathbed he was heard praying, "Lord, increase my sufferings, but increase my patience too."

1842

St. Joseph Cottolengo, a priest outstanding for his love of the poor and the afflicted. Seeing that Turin had no way of taking care of the destitute sick, he put his trust in divine Providence, hired five rooms and enlisted free help. Soon he was at the head of a veritable city with units for the distressed of every kind. He called it the Little House of Divine Providence.

---

*Canada, O.S.U. see May 1 for Marie of the Incarnation.

He kept no accounts, spent money as soon as it came, and convinced his volunteer staff—now formed into religious communities—that, like puppets moved by the hand of divine Providence, they would continue to do wonderful things if they responded "promptly and trustfully to the impulses from above." He also established several religious communities to share the work and assist the dying with their prayers. At the time of his canonization in 1934, the Turin hospital housed 9,000 patients.

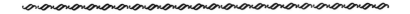

MAY 1*

ST. JOSEPH THE WORKER. By recalling the example of St. Joseph—and indirectly of Jesus—today's feast adds a Christian perspective to the first of May which was designated as a labor holiday by the 1889 International Socialist Congress.

Nothing could evoke more simply Our Lord's many years as a workman than the surprise in Nazareth when Christ began to teach and work miracles: "Is not this the carpenter, the Son of Mary?" (Mk. 6:3) and "Is not this the carpenter's son?" (Mt. 13:55). Pope Pius XI placed the church's struggle against atheistic communism under the patronage of St. Joseph, and Pope Pius XII established his Worker feast in 1955.

1672
Bl. Marie Guyart, Marie Martin, or **Marie of the Incarnation,** mystic, first superior of the Ursuline convent in Quebec, 'Mother of the Catholic Church in Canada,' as Pope John Paul II styled her in the beatification decree. Missionaries, first the Franciscan Recollects and then the Jesuits were on the scene before her, but hardly anyone else. There were, in fact, barely 250 Europeans in all of New France on

---

*O.H. see Mar. 1 for Bl. Richard Erminio Pampuri.

August 1, 1639, when the first six nuns landed at the village of Quebec: three ursulines to start a school for native and French girls and three Augustinian Hospitalières for the Hôtel Dieu. And it would be another twenty years before the country would have its first bishop in Bl. Francis de Laval.

Marie compiled dictionaries and catechisms in the Algonquin and Iroquois tongues but is what she wrote in French that makes her so significant today. Of an estimated 20,000 letters less than 300 survive. Fortunately, her son, who had become a benedictine priest in France, published some 220 letters, including especially the long, newsy ones she wrote him year after year. Shortly after her death he published her life, using mostly her own autobiographical writings, especially a book-length account she drew up at 54 at the request of her Jesuit confessor, Jerome Lalemant, brother of the martyr. A mystic of the first rank with a gift for writing, she is 'The Teresa of the New World' as the Pope in the beatification homily, quoting Bossuet, described her.

She was born at Tours in 1599, one of seven children of Florent Guyart, a master baker. At 14 she spoke to her parents about becoming a nun but they thought her too vivacious and arranged her marriage at 17 with Claude Martin, a stressful marriage which left her a widow at 19 with a son, Claude, of 6 months.

During the next 11 years there gradually came into her very capable hands the entire management of her brother-in-law's large cartage business involving deliveries throughout France and the handling of several dozen men. At 31 she entered the Ursulines at Tours, served as assistant novice mistress, mistress of the boarding school, and then at 39 left for Canada where she died at 72.

Her interior life was fairly normal until that day of grace at the age of 20—which she would refer to as her 'conversion'—when she was given an exact knowledge of every sin, fault, and imperfection since childhood, and saw herself immersed in blood, the Blood of Jesus shed for her sins. Regaining her senses she confessed her sins to the first priest, unconcerned about the fact that she was overheard. She found herself a changed person. She took that priest as her director, began to wear a hairshirt and do penance. Soon she made a vow of chastity. There would be visions of the Incarnation, of Christ putting her heart into his, and of the Trinity. Intimate union with the Incarnate Word became a normal state. She was interiorly directed where and when to become a nun and in the convent had two dreams, about a year apart, of the rugged land where she understood she was to build a house for Jesus and Mary. A voice finally told her the land was Canada.

Among interior crosses were the temptations to pride, blasphemy, and suicide that came shortly after her convent entry. During a half-dozen years in Canada there was "a revolt of her passions" in the form of strong negative feelings toward certain good people; but after praying to the Blessed Mother on the feast of the Assumption, 1647, "my aversion was changed into a cordial love for all those persons toward whom I experienced feelings of aversion and bitterness." But the most poignant trial was in leaving her son and his coming to the convent door and crying out "Give me back my mother!" Sisters, thinking her heartless, cried in her stead, while she suffered what she called "a living death," but with interior assurance that God would take care of her boy. Bl. Marie of the Incarnation died on April 30.

MAY 2

373

ST. ATHANASIUS, patriarch of Alexandria; doctor; the great champion of the divinity of Christ during the Arian crisis after the Council of Nicea, when the church—after enduring the emperors' persecutions—had to learn how to survive their protective embrace.

Athanasius received a good classical education, spent some time as disciple of St. Anthony the hermit, and had the advantage of being apprenticed as secretary to Alexander, the saintly bishop of Alexandria. He was about thirty and a deacon when he attended the Council of Nicea as his bishop's theologian. He succeeded to the patriarchate three years later and was already so spiritually and theologically mature that during the remaining forty-five years—seventeen of them spent in exile—he stood squarely by the doctrine of the Council of Nicea against overwhelming odds. His essential answer to Arians of every shade was: "This is not the faith of the Catholic Church; this is not the faith of the fathers."

Doctrinally he is important for a speculative presentation of the Church's teaching on the Blessed Trinity, particularly the generation of the divine Word as consubstantial (homo-ousios) with the Father. Though bearing his name, the Athanasian Creed was not written by him, for its original form was Latin.

The Arians, defeated at the Council, were successful at court. Athanasius was exiled by four different emperors. Under Constantine the Great he was sent to Trier. In 357 things were so bad that even in the West bishops had to condemn Athanasius if they wished to retain their sees. Pope Liberius refused and was banished.

Athanasius died at Alexandria eight years before the second ecumenical council would vindicate his holy memory. Of his many writings the pastoral letter of 367 is of special interest as listing for the first time the twenty-seven canonical books of the present New Testament.

1126

Bl. Conrad of Seltenbueren. About 1123 he founded the abbey of Engelberg, Switzerland, on his own property with Benedictine monks from the monastery of Muri near Basel. After obtaining powerful papal and imperial letters of exemption for his monastery, he entered the community as a brother. Sent to Zurich to defend the rights of the abbey, he was ambushed and killed.

MAY 3

STS. PHILIP and **JAMES,** apostles. At Bethsaida near the Sea of Galilee—the home of three, and possibly even six, of the apostles—Jesus invited Philip to follow him. In his enthusiasm Philip next day told Nathanael, "We have found him of whom Moses wrote, Jesus of Nazareth, the son of Joseph" (Jn 1:45). When some Greeks wanted to see Jesus they first approached Philip, who told Andrew; and the two of them brought the message to Jesus (Jn. 12:20-22). It was Philip, speaking for the others, who asked Our Lord to show them the Father, and they would be satisfied (Jn. 14:8).

The apostle James honored today is not the son of Zebedee but James the son of Alphaeus. The western practice has been to identify the son of Alphaeus with James 'the brother of the Lord', who was so prominent as bishop of Jerusalem, and also to ascribe the catholic epistle to him. Of this epistle Pope John XXIII, during a retreat (Nov. 23-27, 1948) ten years before his election, wrote: "Its five chapters are a wonderful summary of Christian life. The teaching about the exercise of charity, the right use of the tongue, the power of the man of faith, collaboration for peace, respect for others, the awful fate awaiting the rich, unjust, and hateful man, and finally the appeal for trust, hopefulness and prayer. . . . All this and more makes it an incomparable treasury of directives and exhortations, particularly and alarmingly applicable to those of us who are ecclesiastics, and also to lay folk at all times. One should learn it by heart and return to it from time to time to enjoy the heavenly doctrine line by line."

1314

Bl. Emily Bicchieri, a mystic and a highly successful superior, prioress of Dominican third order sisters in the convent her father built at Vercelli. She wanted her nuns to understand what religious life was all about and to realize that, if they did not strive to have the pure intention of doing everything for God's glory, they would be like people who go shopping without knowing where to get what they want or how much to pay.

MAY 4*

1345   [O.S.M.]

St. Peregrine Laziosi, a native of Forli in the Romagna, where he was an activist in the anti-papal party and during an uprising struck St. Philip Benizi, the pope's emissary, in the face. Philip's only reply was to turn the other cheek—an action which brought his assailant to immediate repentance and a complete reformation of life. Peregrine became a Servite like St. Philip and founded a house at Forli.

1505

Bl. Ladislas of Gielniow, popular patron in Poland and Lithuania, Franciscan provincial and outstanding missioner whose favorite topic was the passion of Christ. When a Tartar army of 70,000 descended on Poland in 1498 he counseled prayer and trust in God. Floods and bad weather—popularly attributed to the prayers of Bl. Ladislas—broke the invasion. Levitations were frequently recorded, including one during his last sermon before an immense crowd on Good Friday. He sank to the ground so exhausted that he had to be carried to the infirmary where he died a month later.

1535   [O. Cart.]

St. John Houghton and companions, and also the joint feast of the 200 canonized or beatified martyrs of England and Wales. The honor of being the first to die for the Catholic faith under Henry VIII goes to three Carthusian priors, **Sts. John Houghton, Augustine Webster,** and **Robert Lawrence,** along with **Bl. John Haile,** parish priest of Islesworth, and **St. Richard Reynolds,** a Brigettine monk, all executed at Tyburn, May 4, 1535. Looking out of his prison window that morning St. Thomas More—two months from his own death—saw them being tied to the hurdles. "Lo, dost thou not see, Meg," he said to his daughter, "that these blessed fathers be now going to their deaths as cheerfully as bridegrooms to their marriage."

---

*C.M.F. see May 8 for Mary, Mediatrix of All Graces.

The public records preserve this testimonial: "Robert Lawrence says that there is one Catholic Church of which the bishop of Rome is the head. Therefore he cannot believe that the king is supreme head of the Church." When Richard Reynolds was asked why he went against the opinion of so many lords and bishops and the parliament, he answered: "If you propose to maintain opinions by testimonies, mine will be far stronger than yours, because I have all the rest of christendom in my favor. I can even say I have all this kingdom in my favor, although the smaller part holds with you, for I am sure the larger part is at heart of my opinion, although outwardly, partly from fear and partly from hope, they profess to be of yours. As to the dead witnesses, I have in my favor all the general councils, all bishops, all historians, the holy doctors of the Church for the last fifteen hundred years, especially St. Ambrose, St. Jerome, St. Augustine, and St. Gregory."

MAY 5

449

St. Hilary, monk of Lerins; archbishop of Arles at the age of twenty-nine. He presided over councils, founded and reformed monasteries, kept vigilance over suffragan churches, and during spare hours worked with his hands to help the poor. In his zeal to improve things he removed a bishop on insufficient grounds and replaced another who seemed to be dying but actually recovered. On both accounts Pope St. Leo censured him, forbade him to appoint further bishops, and transferred the metropolitan dignity from Arles to Fréjus. St. Hilary died at forty-eight.

1038

St. Godehard, or **Gothard,** abbot of Niederaltaich, bishop of Hildesheim, restorer of many Benedictine monasteries—today's

Kremsmuenster and Niederaltaich among them. At sixty he
pleaded old age and unsuitability, but Emperor St. Henry insisted that he take over the diocese of Hildesheim. For the
next sixteen years he worked with so much zest that on the
purely material side he is today considered the greatest builder
in mediaeval Bavaria. He had a reputation of caring for the
homeless, but would not abide wandering monks or clerics.
He died on Ascension Day as eight choir boys singing lauds
in his sick chamber had just repeated the antiphon, "I ascend
to my father." The St. Gothard Pass apparently took its name
from a chapel built on the summit in his honor.

1836

Bl. Nunzio Sulprizio, whom misfortune, illness, and abuse
could fashion into a saint by the age of nineteen, thanks to
early religious training by a devout grandmother. He lost his
father, then his mother, then his grandmother, and at nine came
into the care of a blacksmith uncle who stopped the boy's education, overworked and underfed him, and beat him severely.
Soon Nunzio was lame with a festering foot and could walk only with
the help of a stick. At fifteen a wealthier and kinder uncle brought
him to Naples, where he received hospital care.

Ever cheerful, he consoled the other patients, shared his uncle's gifts with them, and carried on an effective apostolate.
Not content with the afflictions he already had, he added voluntary mortifications. When he seemed to be improving he began to study Latin with the priesthood in mind. He last words
were, "The Blessed Virgin! See how beautiful she is!"

MAY 6

1330

Bl. Bartholomew Pucci, a prominent citizen of Montepulciano,
Italy, who after raising a large family became a Franciscan. His

wife also made a vow of chastity. Superiors advanced him to the priesthood, disregarding his personal preference to remain a brother. Miracles, at times, supported his resolve never to deny a favor asked in the name of Christ. Seeing that he was looked on as a saint, he began to do things to make himself look foolish.

1857   [*S.D.B., F.M.A.*]

St. Dominic Savio, who died at fifteen of a lung condition after being a student at Turin under St. John Bosco for three years. He combined cheerfulness with a precocious seriousness in whatever concerned God. At seven, on his First Communion, he made these four resolutions: "I will often go to confession and will receive Communion as often as my confessor will allow. I will keep the feast days holy. Jesus and Mary shall be my friends. Death rather than sin." St. John Bosco preserved these resolutions in his biography of Dominic Savio, stating that the saintly boy often recalled them and made them his rule of life.

1870   [*O.S.M.*]

Bl. Clelia Barbieri, a foundress who died at twenty-three. From earliest childhood the faith meant everything to her and though she had little education herself she helped teach catechism. Under the guidance of the priests in her rural parish of Le Budrie near Bologna, she became the center of a group of young women who taught Christian doctrine to the poor children of the neighborhood, gave instruction in the rudiments of reading and writing, and cared for the sick. "We are so poor," she told her companions, "that no community could accept us. . . . And so let us start our own and then we can receive others." She was twenty-one when, with a group of three, she began community life under the patronage of Mary and St. Francis of Paola. They became known as the Minim Sisters of Our Lady of Sorrows.

Because of the early death of her father, Clelia from infancy grew up in such grinding poverty that her health had been weakened. She fell an easy victim to consumption. Her last days were especially remembered for the consolation she had when her favorite picture of Mary was brought from the parish church and for the deep impression she made when exhorting her sisters to mutual love, concord, and constancy in doing all for God and souls.

MAY 7

721

St. John of Beverley; monk at Whitby; bishop of Hexham; archbishop of York; founder of Beverley Abbey where he died. His shrine was a favorite pilgrim resort until the Reformation. St. Bede, who was ordained deacon and priest by him, tells of his miracles and holiness. He and St. Wilfrid were opponents in various jurisdictional disputes.

1728

Bl. Rose Venerini; outstanding teacher; foundress. As a girl she vowed to become a religious but on growing up gave in to many contrary attractions. "Lord, what can I do?" she would pray, "I haven't the strength. Unless you help me I can't break away." With the sudden death of her suitor the situation changed. She became a novice but left in a few months because her father's death required her to care for her mother. In the evenings she would gather women and girls in her home to say the rosary. Finding how little religious instruction many of them had, she began also to teach them.

Gradually her vocation became clear. In 1685, at the age of twenty-nine, with two companions she started a free school in her native Viterbo. With her gift for training others how to teach she was able to open similar schools elsewhere. The one she started at Montefiascone was continued along similar lines

by her protegee St. Lucy Filippini, foundress of the **Maestre
Pie.** She died at Rome leaving forty houses of her institute in
seventeen dioceses. Her group received papal approval only after her death. Today they are known as the Venerini Sisters.
Faithful to the method of their foundress, these sisters foster
frequent meetings with mothers in order to coordinate the school
with the family.

MAY 8

[*O.S.M., O.M.I., S.C.J., S.M.M.*]
Some dioceses and religious orders honor Mary on this day
under the title **Mediatrix of All Graces.** The II Vatican Council
presents Mary's mediating role as a consequence of her being
the Mother of Christ and, therefore, in the order of grace, our
mother—a maternity that began at the Annunciation and will
last without interruption until the number of the elect is fulfilled. "Therefore," says the document on the Church (N. 62).
"the Blessed Virgin is invoked by the Church under the titles
of Advocate, Auxiliatrix, Adjutrix, and Mediatrix. These, however, are to be so understood that they neither take away nor
add .anything to the dignity and efficacy of Christ the one
Mediator. . . . But, just as the priesthood of Christ is shared
in various ways both by sacred ministers and by the faithful
. . . so also the mediation of the Redeemer does not exclude
but rather gives rise among creatures to a manifold coopera-
tion which is but a sharing in this unique source. The Church
does not hesitate to profess the subordinate role of Mary. She
experiences it continuously and commends it to the faithful,
so that encouraged by this maternal help they may more closely
adhere to the Mediator and Redeemer."

303 or 305
St. Acacius, martyr at Byzantium (Constantinople) under Dio-

cletian. Constantine erected a church there in his honor. It was
nicknamed the "walnut" because built into its structure was a
walnut tree where the saint was suspended when being scourged.

550

St. Desideratus, one of three saintly brothers. After serving
King Clotaire as chief minister of state he was chosen bishop
of Bourges. He earned a reputation as peacemaker and wonder-
worker.

MAY 9

1443   [*O.Cart.*]
Bl. Nicholas Albergati, Carthusian cardinal. His principal
characteristic was holiness; but he is remembered especially as
the closest adviser and collaborator of Pope Eugene IV in the
struggle with the Council of Basel, when victory seemed assured
for the conciliar theory which maintained that the pope is subject to a council. It was only fifteen years since the Council
of Constance had deposed claimants to the papal throne, ended
the great schism, passed decrees setting the council over the
pope, and scheduled a council every ten years in perpetuity.
Emperor Sigismund supported Basel as he had Constance; bishops and theologians went along with the conciliarist mood
of the day; the pope stood almost alone; and to many it seemed
that even he had capitulated in 1433, reversing his earlier dis-
solution of Basel and accepting its acts as those of a legitimate
general council. Albergati too, in 1434, took the conciliarist
oath required of him and of three other papal legates at Basel
to the effect that the Council of Constance as well as every
other ecumenical council derives its power immediately from
God and that even the pope has to obey. How the cardinal understood the oath was shown in the preliminary debate. "I
hold," he said, "to the decisions of the Council of Constance

and of the Council of Basel as canonically assembled. I hold to these decrees in the way that the Church understands and admits them according to the teaching of the holy and ancient doctors.''

When Pope Eugene felt sufficiently secure to break with Basel and transfer the council elsewhere, it was Cardinal Albergati who opened it at Ferrara in 1438 and presided until the pope arrived. He served on the study commission with the Greeks preparatory to the 1439 declaration of union between East and West.

1463   [*Franciscans*]

St. Catherine of Bologna; Poor Clare abbess; mystic; writer, and artist. At fourteen she turned her back on court life and joined a new community of Franciscan tertiaries at Ferrara, serving in turn as baker, portress, and novice mistress. In time the group adopted the rule of St. Clare, Catherine being chiefly responsible for obtaining strict enclosure despite opposition from the citizens of Ferrara.

Harassed by temptations, including perplexity over the Real Presence, she was able to write a much translated and reprinted book on the seven weapons of the spiritual combat. Three rules she inculcated as novice mistress and later as abbess in Bologna were: speak well of others, practise constant humility, and do not meddle in the affairs of others. Some of her paintings survive, especially her illuminated breviary with its many miniatures. She is patroness of art.

MAY 10

603

St. Comgall, abbot-founder of Bangor, the largest and most famous monastery in ancient Ireland. He trained St. Columban, who brought Irish monasticism into France and Italy.

1459 [*O.P.*]

St. Antoninus; Dominican; best loved bishop of Florence. He served as superior in many houses, was skilled in theology and canon law, and assisted at all the sessions of the Council of Florence. He founded the convent of San Marco in Florence and had Fra Angelico—a one-time fellow novice—decorate it. Pope Eugene IV ordered him to accept the archbishopric of Florence, received the last sacraments from him, and died in his arms.

Antoninus—his small stature suggested the diminutive form of his name—simplified the episcopal household, keeping only a mule for transport. The animal was often sold to help the poor; but Florentines, who had grown fond of the archbishop's ways, kept buying it back for him. He had such a reputation for knowledge and prudence that Pope Nicholas V would not allow any of the archbishop's decisions to be appealed to Rome.

1569 [*O.H.*]

St. John of Avila; outstanding spiritual director; patron of the Spanish clergy. At his first mass instead of friends and relatives he invited the poor to a meal—his parents had already died leaving him sole heir of their wealth. He soon gave everything away and applied for the Mexican missions, but the government withheld permission because of his Jewish blood.

His priesthood spanned the troubled years from the early days of the Reformation until just after the Council of Trent—a time of crisis in Christian spirituality and in the priesthood. He made a specialty of both. With a sure grasp of essentials he was soon the leader of a group of priests dedicated to spiritual direction and solid priestly training. He initiated St. John of God and St. Francis Borgia into the ways of holiness, was a friend of St. Ignatius and spiritual adviser to St. Teresa of Avila, St. Peter Alcantara, and St. John of the Cross—as well as to Louis of Granada, who wrote his biography. Though he was imprisoned for two years by the Inquisition and had a book put on the Index, his true stature was recognized in his own time. Many referred to him simply as the "Master." He stressed the importance of a spiritual director but said he should be one person in a thousand. St. Francis de Sales quotes John of Avila with approval, but says the director should be one in ten thousand.

1796 [*C.M.*]

Bl. Peter René Roque; Vincentian priest; outspoken defender of religion during the French Revolution. He refused the Constitutional Oath, kept up his apostolate while in prison, and was guillotined at Vannes on March 1.

MAY 11

10th-12th cent. [*O.S.B., O.Cist., O.C.S.O.*]

The four holy abbots of Cluny **Sts. Odo, Mayeul, Odilo,** and **Hugh,** who between them governed for 175 years and brought their Burgundian abbey to a position of influence never equaled by any other monastery. At its zenith under St. Hugh there were throughout Europe nearly 1200 affiliated monasteries — many of them under the complete government of the abbot of Cluny — and over 300 monks at Cluny itself. It was the first example of a centralized religious order. Cluny was subject in both the temporal and spiritual order to the Holy See alone.

While not initiating the Gregorian Reform, the Cluniac Benedictines were the papacy's most loyal supporters in the struggle over lay investitute; and all five popes of the final fifty years of the conflict were monks, three of them Cluniacs. Symbolic of the stature of this "second Rome" beyond the Alps was the abbey church, 600 feet long, a masterpiece of Romanesque architecture and the largest church in Christendom until the sixteenth century when the new St. Peter's in Rome was of set purpose built a few feet longer.

1426 [O.S.M.]

Bl. Benincasa, miracle-working Servite who lived as a hermit on the mountain of Montagnata near Siena. He dispensed advice and healing through a small window.

1537

Bl. John Rochester and **Bl. James Walworth,** Carthusian martyrs. After the execution of St. John Houghton, prior of the London Charterhouse, the three monks who assumed government of the community also suffered: Humphrey Middlemore, William Exmew, and Sebastian Newdigate, all beatified. In an effort to break the community's resistance some of the more resolute monks—among whom are today's martyrs—were sent elsewhere and a Carthusian from Sheen, who had taken the Oath of Supremacy, was installed as prior. After two years of pressure, nineteen monks took the oath but ten others, three priests and seven brothers, remained firm. They were imprisoned at Marshalsea, tied to posts, and left to starve. For a time they were kept alive by the heroism of St. Thomas More's relative and foster daughter, Margaret Clement, who bribed the jailer, entered the prison disguised as a milkmaid, and put food in their mouths. But after Henry VIII expressed surprise that they were still alive, Margaret was refused further admission. No other group of religious in England was so clear-sighted and constant in their faith as these men of prayer.

MAY 12*

STS. NEREUS and **ACHILLEUS,** early Roman martyrs, soldiers who deserted after their conversion and suffered the penalty they were expected to inflict on others.

° *M.P.F. see March 29 for St. Lucy Filippini.*

ST. PANCRAS, martyr at Rome, probably under Diocletian. His cult became very popular in the sixth century.

403

St. Epiphanius, a Palestinian abbot and ascetic of great repute who became archbishop of Salamis in Cyprus. Though not a capable theologian, his readiness to express himself and to take sides makes him an interesting and important fourth century churchman. Uncovering heresies was his specialty. In one book he lists eighty of them. He sparked the Origenist controversy that embroiled St. Jerome and Rufinus. Without the local bishop's permission he ordained St. Jerome's brother in Jerusalem and had to take him back to Salamis. Despite his reputation for holiness, fear of Origenism made him, in extreme old age, an easy tool of the unscrupulous Theophilus of Alexandria in the plot to depose St. John Chrysostom. Epiphanius eventually recognized the intrigue, left before Chrysostom was condemned, and died on the way to Cyprus.

In one of his books he gives the creed of the church of Salamis which was taken over almost verbatim by the I Council of Constantinople in 381 at which he was present. The text soon became the baptismal creed of the Eastern Church. St. Jerome referred to him as "a last relic of ancient piety."

732

St. Germanus, patriarch of Constantinople. He condemned the "One Will heresy" and resolutely opposed the beginnings of iconoclasm. Emperor Leo III deposed him, and an iconoclast synod condemned him twenty years after his death; but before long the second Council of Nicea hailed him as the champion of orthodoxy and praised his holiness.

1328 [*O.S.M.*]

Bl. Francis Patrizzi, famous Servite preacher in Siena. Though he had foretold the day of his death, he went out to preach

that morning as he had been asked to do and collapsed on the
road.

MAY 13*

1028

St. Euthymius the Enlightener, who helped his father, St.
John the Iberian, found the famous — and still existing — monastery of Iviron on Mt. Athos. His main contribution — he gave
up being abbot to be freer for it — was translating Greek Fathers
into Iberian.

1834   [D.C.]

St. Andrew Fournet, co-founder of the Daughters of the Cross
and author of their rule. He was one of those zealous French
priests who risked their lives in the apostolate during the French
Revolution and contributed greatly to the nineteenth century
Catholic restoration by inspiring and guiding generous young
women to dedicate their lives to education and the care of the
neglected.

A book kept as a relic has this note in his childish handwriting. "This book belongs to Andrew Hubert Fournet, a good
boy, though he is not going to be a priest or a monk." Even
during studies in philosophy and law he seemed interested only
in having a good time. His mother tried to obtain a secretarial
position for him, but his handwriting was too poor. A change
came when he went to live with an uncle who was a poor and
holy priest. Another turning point was the off-hand remark of
a beggar when Andrew was pastor of Maillé and already doing
much to help the poor: "How can you say you have nothing
you can give when your table is glittering with silver!"

---

*S.N.D. see April 8 for St. Julia Billiart.

1881 [*F.M.A., S.D.B.*]

St. Mary Mazzarello, co-foundress with St. John Bosco of the Daughters of Our Lady Help of Christians, also called "Salesian Sisters," who do for girls what the Salesian priests and brothers do for boys. The vocation of this peasant girl of Mornese near Genoa developed gradually through a series of generous responses from early childhood: in the long walk to daily Mass and the youthful vow of virginity, in becoming a charter member at seventeen of a sodality with a rule of life, and in nursing an uncle and his family during an epidemic in which she contracted the illness that weakened her health and led her to take up dressmaking. With a sodality companion she opened a seamstress shop where local girls could be trained.

John Bosco visiting this shop in 1865, found its atmosphere of joy, work, and piety wholly suited to his dream of a congregation of sisters for educating girls. So at thirty-five, Mary found herself a mother superior with ten sodality members as the nucleus of a religious order. They occupied a building in her own village originally intended as a Salesian college. She died at forty-four as the order was spreading into South America. At her canonization in 1951, seventy years later, there were already 15,000 Salesian Sisters.

MAY 14

ST. MATTHIAS, apostle, chosen by lot to replace Judas. St. Peter's preliminary speech on eligibility stressed the apostles' role of witnessing to the resurrection of Christ. "One of those", he said, "who was of our company while the Lord Jesus moved among us, from the baptism of John until the day he was taken up from us, should be named as witness with us to his resurrection" (Acts 1:21-22). The relics of St. Matthias are venerated in the ancient Benedictine abbey of St. Matthias in Trier.

637

St. Carthach or **Mochuda,** author of a monastic rule and founder of the abbey and school at Lismore, so famous in Irish
history.

1043

St. Hallvard, patron of Oslo, a young Norwegian nobleman
who gave his life to protect a woman from pursuers.

1863

St. Michael Garicoïts, founder of the Priests of the Sacred
Heart of Betharram. His father, a Basque peasant in southern
France, considered the family too poor for Michael to become
a priest; but the boy's grandmother thought otherwise and with
the help of a priest friend found a way for Michael to work
his way through school. He served as curate, seminary professor, and then rector. To combat Jansenism and build up the
faith he spread devotion to the Sacred Heart, and finally founded
his missionary congregation modeled on the Jesuits.

MAY 15*

345   [*O.S.B., O.Cist., O.C.S.O.*]
   St. Pachomius, one of the principal founders of cenobitic
monasticism. St. Anthony, the first monk, lived as a hermit to
the end; and his followers, even when clustered around a master, lived on their own, coming together for the most part only
to partake in the Sunday liturgy.
   The community orientation Pachomius would give monasticism grew out of his first exposure to the loving concern of a
Christian community. With other young army conscripts he was
being taken down the Nile and at Luxor was shut up for the

O.D.N. see Feb. 2 for St. John de Lestonnac.
  C.P. see April 11 for St. Gemma Galgani.

night in the prison. The Christians of the area brought food and drink. He was told these kind people were Christians, men who bore the name of Christ and did good to everyone. There and then, according to the Egyptian accounts, Pachomius decided he too would bear Christ's name and serve and love all men.

When he embraced the ascetic ideal a few years later, he saw that community life could be a great help in the monk's search for holiness. His is the first known rule organizing such a fraternity. The future would belong to his type of monasticism, perpetuated in the East by St. Basil and in the West by St. Benedict. Writing 200 years after Pachomius, St. Benedict depends on him—even textually—on many points of community life; such as common ownership, obedience, punctuality, rank according to the time of entrance rather than age, keeping the scheduled times of prayer even during field labor or when on a journey, wearing the habit, gifts receivable only through the head of the monastery, not siding with one who has been corrected, the prior not taking a different line from the abbot, reporting that one has broken something, moderation in the amount of work assigned, and the passing along of an inventory list as the monks took weekly turns at various tasks.

Pachomius settled into his way of life at Tabennesi on the Nile north of Thebes during his twenties. Through manual labor and the various crafts he put his monasteries on a sound economic basis. His monks, as well as his communities of nuns, lived in monasteries housing thirty or forty and having their own superior, procurator, chapel, and refectory, while Pachomius served as a superior general.

1130 [*United States*]
  St. Isidore, patron of farmers and of Madrid, where he spent his life working on a farm. His wife, Mary, was as poor and as good as himself, and is also a saint.

MAY 16

ca. 577

St. Brendan, born at Tralee in Kerry, abbot-founder of Clonfert in Galway. He exercised great influence in his time, but his later fame rested chiefly on fabled sea voyages with fellow monks in search of the "Isles of the Blessed."

ca. 430 and 440   [*O.S.A., O.A.R.*]

Sts. Alypius and **Possidius,** associates of St. Augustine. Alypius, Augustine's closest companion, became bishop of Tagaste, their home town. Charming pages of St. Augustine's **Confessions** describe his friendship with Alypius and the influence they had on one another. Alypius was intelligent, earnest, and deeply loyal. About five years younger than Augustine, he was his student at Tagaste and Carthage and followed him into Manichaeism. Gladiatorial games were his one passion. As a lawyer he was incorruptible—fearless, too, in the face of threats. He found chastity no problem and kept Augustine from marrying by reminding him that marriage would put an end to their plan of some day searching for wisdom together in untroubled leisure. The opportunity did come at Milan, when, along with Augustine's brother Nebridius, they could devote themselves for a time to this quest. Present at Augustine's conversion, Alypius was baptized along with him by St. Ambrose. Back in Africa they co-operated closely as bishops, stood together against Donatists and Pelagians, and often wrote joint letters on church affairs. They also died about the same time.

St. Possidius, disciple, intimate friend and biographer of St. Augustine, became bishop of Calama in northern Africa.

1297   [*Franciscans*]

St. Margaret of Cortona, the Magdalen of the Franciscans, one of the great penitents of all time. A beautiful peasant girl but unloved by her stepmother, she eloped with a nobleman of Montepulciano in her early teens and was his mistress for nine years until his violent death. In the parish church she now openly confessed her sins and with a rope about her neck asked the forgiveness of all. From then on she mortified her body mercilessly to gain its mastery and to make atonement. She became a Franciscan tertiary, tended the sick, and counselled the many sinners who confided in her. St. Margaret passed through all the stages of prayer—including mystic experiences—and at the end lived alone, a contemplative with a consuming desire for solitude. She died at fifty, on February 22.

1657 [*S.J.*]

St. Andrew Bobola, Polish Jesuit who spent his whole life bringing the Orthodox—sometimes entire villages—into union with the Holy See. He was tortured and beheaded at Pinsk in White Russia.

MAY 17

816

St. Leo III, the pope who on Christmas, 800 A.D., crowned Charlemagne in St. Peter's, inaugurating the Holy Roman Empire of the West. The coronation took place at a moment when the pope needed the help of the Franks against Lombards and Saracens as well as against a murderous Roman faction that attacked him during the St. Mark's Day procession. There was already a long tradition of bishops wielding civil authority and of kings in control of Church affairs. The next thousand years would bring out all the advantages and deficiencies of this uneasy partnership. A few days before his coronation Charlemagne presided over a huge gathering of notables in the Vatican at which the pope himself was on trial—a sign of some of the things to come.

1592   [*Franciscans*]

St. Paschal Baylon. When designating a patron for Eucharistic congresses and confraternities of the Blessed Sacrament, Pope Leo XIII chose this Franciscan brother who spent most of his life as porter of various friaries in Spain and used his spare time kneeling in prayer before the Blessed Sacrament. His superiors once suggested that he become a priest; but like St. Francis, humility and reverence held him back. It was his delight to serve mass after mass, beginning early in the morning. At night he would stay behind in choir when the rest of the community had retired.

Of peasant stock, he was a shepherd until the age of twenty-four. He then entered a friary where St. Peter of Alcantara was carrying through his reform. Without schooling he taught himself to read and write, and as a friar made a scrap book, still preserved, of discarded odds and ends in which he jotted down in beautiful handwriting various prayers and reflections—some of his own composition—to nourish his devotion.

As porter he used many stratagems to secure delicacies for the sick and help for the poor. He had a reputation for miracles, but after his death they became so numerous that he was beatified within twenty-six years—even before St. Peter of Alcantara.

MAY 18

526

ST. JOHN I, martyr, the first pope to set foot in Constantinople. He went there at the head of a delegation sent by the Arian Goth, King Theodoric I. The purpose of this mission was to secure better treatment for the Arians in Constantinople—especially as Theodoric, during the thirty-three years of rule in Italy, generally allowed Catholics complete freedom. But in his final years Theodoric suspected treasonable coalition between the notables at Rome and Emperor Justin in Constantinople. He had Boethius executed and took Pope John prisoner at Ravenna. There he soon died of ill usage. Theodoric's death followed three months later, but not until he made the unprecedented move of appointing a new pope.

1161

St. Eric, king of Sweden and its principal patron until the Reformation. He gathered the ancient laws of the land into what became known as King Eric's Law. He was murdered after Mass by a conspirator in league with the Danish army.

1369 [*O.S.A., O.A.R.*]

Bl. William of Toulouse, Augustinian priest who did much to promote prayer for the Poor Souls.

1587 [*Franciscans*]

St. Felix of Cantalice; a Capuchin brother who spent his last forty years begging; one of the very popular figures in sixteenth century Rome. The city's children called him "Brother Deogratias," because his normal response to whatever happened was the ejaculation, "Thanks be to God!" He was a close friend of St. Philip Neri, and their usual greeting was to wish each other suffering for Christ's sake. He was known for his tender charity to the sick and poor, his gift of mystic prayer, his spiked metal shirt and his preference for living on bread, water, and leftovers. He died at seventy-two and soon had an abundance of miracles for his canonization.

MAY 19

988

St. Dunstan, abbot of Glastonbury and archbishop of Canterbury. He ranks among the greatest restorers of ecclesiastical and monastic life in England and by reason of his court activity under King Edgar has been called that nation's first "Prime Minister." Danish invasions and the annexation of monastic property by impoverished Saxon princes had long since closed every regular monastery in England, so that the semi-monastic community at Glastonbury, where Dunstan was brought up, was almost all that remained of the Benedictinism that flourished throughout the land at the time of St. Bede, two and-a-half centuries before. With Dunstan's appointment as abbot in his early thirties the regular observance of St. Benedict's Rule was begun anew.

Assisted chiefly by King Edgar and the monk-bishops Sts. Ethelwold and Oswald, he bequeathed to England at his death more than fifty fair-sized abbeys of men and women—all those great houses that would remain the focal point of monastic life until the Reformation 600 years later. Loved by his disciples and colleagues, he had a reputation for holiness, personality, and artistic skill. He made bells and excelled as goldsmith, illuminator, and musician.

1296

St. Celestine V, or **Peter of Morone,** a hermit who was pope for five months and then resigned. His austere life in the Abruzzi attracted disciples so that, almost despite himself, he founded a semi-solitary branch of Benedictines, eventually known as Celestines. The papacy had been vacant for two years when a message came—apparently from the saintly hermit on Mt. Morone—threatening the cardinals with divine vengeance if they did not act soon; and so they elected him. There was boundless joy among the people, as the choice of such an unworldly pope seemed to inaugurate a new era. He was about eighty, knew little of canon law, and was easily taken advantage of, especially by the king of Naples. Soon things were in hopeless confusion. He had a wooden hermitage built in the palace at Naples and was minded to turn church administration over to three cardinals but resigned instead. He assured the speedy election of his successor and returned to Mt. Morone; but the new pope, Boniface VIII, had him taken into custody lest he become a tool of an opposing party. He died at Anagni ten months later.

1303
St. Ivo Hélory, patron of laywers; a native of Brittany; ascetic; and judge in an ecclesiastical court. He later became a priest and a devoted pastor.

1291 and 1309   [*O.S.A., O.A.R.*]
Bl. Clement of Osimo and **Bl. Augustine Novello,** priors general of the Hermits of St. Augustine. Bl. Clement is called the second founder of the order for his revision of the constitutions. In this he was greatly helped by the brilliant Sicilian lawyer Matthew de Termini, who had become an Augustinian brother incognito under the name of Augustine Novello. When the friars had a law suit, he set forth the case so well that his identity was discovered.

MAY 20

1444
ST. BERNARDINE OF SIENA, Franciscan reformer and the most famous Italian preacher of his day. At twenty he organized a group of young men who took full charge of a Siena hospital where during a plague as many as twenty people were dying daily, unattended. Two years later he became a Franciscan and soon identified himself with the reform party known as the "Observants"—today the main body of the Friars Minor—as

distinct from the "Conventuals." Their growth in Italy from a few score to 4,000 during Bernardine's lifetime was due in good part to him. For a period he was their superior, but obtained papal permission to resign so that he might devote himself once again to his beloved preaching.

Schism, reform, and the Council of Basel kept the church in continual ferment over constitutional issues; but Bernardine's sermons dealt with topics of immediate concern to his hearers: repentance, the Passion, virtues, and the prevalent vices such as gambling, usury, discord, and ostentation. Bonfires of cartloads of "vanities" were a normal feature of his missions. With great fervor he fostered devotion to the Holy Name, to the Madonna, and to St. Joseph. He popularized the familiar "IHS" — Greek abbreviation for the name of Jesus. After sermons he would bless the people with a card on which this sacred monogram was emblazoned. He took to the streets when churches could no longer hold the crowds — one gathering was estimated at 30,000 — and would speak for three and four hours. His style was extremely simple, direct and colloquial, well seasoned with mirth and jokes. He made much use of a type of dialogue by question and answer in developing his argument.

Though he had a keen sense of social justice and preached against vice with apostolic freedom, he remained moderate on political topics and disapproved the practice of inveighing against the vices of ecclesiastics. He felt it was important to inculcate reverence and would arrange to speak to the clergy separately. He turned down three bishoprics. All Italy, he said, was already his diocese — all except the Kingdom of Naples, where he had not yet preached. He was on his way there when he died on Ascension Thursday, 1444.

1501

Bl. Columba of Rieti, Dominican tertiary, whose life in many ways resembles that of St. Catherine of Siena, to whom she was intensely devoted.

MAY 21

1170

St. Godric, lay hermit at Finchale under obedience to the prior of Durham. He began as a pedlar and then became a sea-faring merchant. A visit to Lindisfarne left him deeply impressed with the life of St. Cuthbert. After serveral pilgramages he settled at Finchale, where he spent sixty years in great austerity with a reputation for visions, prophecy, and friendship with wild animals. He foretold his own death and that of his bishop, also the martyrdom of St. Thomas Becket. Reginald, his contemporary biographer, preserved four sacred songs he heard Godric sing. They are the oldest examples of English verse whose musical setting has survived.

1861   [*O.M.I.*]

Bl. Charles Joseph Eugene De Mazenod, founder of the Oblates of Mary Immaculate, bishop of Marseilles. In 1808, when Rome and Pope Pius VII were in Napoleon's hands, this Provencal nobleman, aged twenty-six, entered St. Sulpice Seminary in Paris. "The state of abandonment in which I saw the Church was one of the causes determining me to enter the ecclesiastical life," he later wrote. "I was cut to the very depths of my soul to see the service of the altar being disdained now that the Church no longer had rich benefices to offer. . .Moreover, the Church was threatened with a new schism arising from Bonaparte's extravagant conception of a patriarchate in France independent of the Apostolic See."

He rejected the Gallican theses of one of his theology professors and asked for ordination from the bishop of Amiens rather than from Cardinal Maury of Paris who was more loyal to the Emperor than to the Pope. To his mother—who opposed his vocation—he wrote, "What God wants of me is that I devote myself in a special way to his service, so as to stir up the faith which is dying among the poor." He soon enlisted other priests to help with missions to the poor and most neglected and in 1816, when only thirty-three, founded his congregation. The clergy came next. "After sacred missions," he wrote in the Constitutions, "certainly the most excellent purpose of our order is the direction of major seminaries; for the missioners will labor in vain to snatch sinners from death if there are not priests in the parishes who are filled with the spirit of God."

As for his congregation, in a letter to his assistant he underlined some basics on which zeal and charity could build: "Do not cease to instill and to preach humility, abnegation and forgetfulness of self, contempt for the esteem of men. Let these virtues by forever the very foundation stone of our little society; once they are linked with a real zeal for the glory of God and the salvation of souls as well as a very tender and affectionate charity which is to be most sincere among us, they will make of our house a paradise on earth and will establish it more solidly than all possible regulations." From 1826, when the congregation received papal approval and its present name, special consecration to Mary became a characteristic of the order. Bishop De Mazenod retained his post as superior even after he succeeded his uncle as bishop of Marseilles.

The order, now so prominent in the world's missions, began to grow rapidly after 1841 when its first foreign house was opened. This was in Canada—beginning at Montreal—where missionary work has become so identified with the "Oblates" and where 100 years after the founder's death 2,000 of the congregation's 7,000 members were based. "Montreal," he wrote as the first Canadian missioners were on their way, "is perhaps nothing but the door which will lead the family to the conquest of souls in several lands. . . But I am thinking far ahead, and I am no prophet; however, I have always been a man of desires, and some of my wishes have been fulfilled." He died at seventy-eight.

MAY 22

1310

St. **Humility,** honored as a foundress of the Vallombrosan nuns. At fifteen her parents married her to a frivolous nobleman, but in the course of nine years she so inspired him with her ideals that—as their two children had died—they entered a double monastery in their home town of Faenza, near Ravenna. In search of greater austerity and recollection she became a Poor Clare, then a recluse at a Vallombrosan church. Her contemporaries were particularly impressed by her austerities, such as the habit of taking her short snatches of sleep in a kneeling posture, her head leaning against the wall. After twelve years the abbot general of Vallombrosa called on her to start a monastery for nuns of the order at Faenza. She died in Florence at her second foundation. Both of these communities still exist, though the order has only four convents, all in Italy.

1457   [*O.S.A., O.A.R.*]

St. **Rita of Cascia,** mystic of the cross, who because of her many miracles is venerated as "Saint of the Impossible." After the death of her husband and children she became an Augustinian nun at Cascia in Umbria. Within ten years after her death there was such devotion to her that her body was transferred and episodes of her holy life were depicted on her sarcophagus.

1538

Bl. **John Forest,** Franciscan provincial, chaplain and confessor to Catherine of Aragon, outspoken opponent of Henry VIII's divorce and author of a treatise against his pretentions to the primacy. Bl. John was burned at Smithfield after four years in prison.

1854   [*O. Carm.*]

St. Joachima de Mas y de Vedruna; devoted wife, mother of a large family; widow; foundress at Vich near Barcelona of the Carmelites of Charity, devoted to nursing and teaching. To her daughter Agnes who wished to become a nun, Joachima said, "No, God wants you to marry. Two of your sisters will be nuns." And so it was. St. Anthony Claret, as the bishop's delegate, received her religious vows.

MAY 23

1077

St. Leontius, a Greek of Constantinople who lived as a monk at Kiev and then became a missionary bishop at Rostov. He suffered so much from the heathens that he was venerated as a martyr and mentioned in the preparation of the Russian mass.

1173

St. Euphrosyne of Polotsk. Beside the Blessed Mother, only twelve women traditionally had a place in the Russian calendar and eleven of them were married. The nun Euphrosyne is the one exception. Though she was a recluse in her native town of Polotsk in White Russia, she travelled a good deal and was at Jerusalem when she died.

1764

St. John Baptist Rossi, Roman priest remembered particularly for his apostolate of the confessional and service to the neglected. Of a poor family, he received his education through the help of a benefactor. He practised indiscreet mortification and as a seminarian drove himself so hard that he had a complete breakdown and was stricken with epilepsy. But he was still ordained at twenty-three. For seventeen years distrust of self kept him from the confessional where, in fact, his special ministry lay. "I used often to wonder," he remarked to a friend, "what was the shortest road to heaven. It lies in guiding others there through the confessional. . . . What a power for good that can be." He would preach in marketplaces, hospitals, prisons—any place where the poor would congregate. He established a refuge for abandoned children and a hospice for the homeless. When he was made a canon he used the income to provide the church with an organ and a stipend for the organist. Though he inherited a house he gave it away, content with attic accommodations and the barest necessities. He died at sixty-six.

MAY 24

1153

St. David I, outstanding king of Scotland, the youngest of the six sons of queen St. Margaret. His just and Christian rule of thirty years consolidated Scotland's civil and ecclesiastical structures and brought the nation into the mainstream of European life. He established five bishoprics, including Aberdeen, and founded twelve important abbeys. His legacy to the Scots included the example of a holy death. The day before, he was urged to rest but answered, "Let me rather think about the things of God, so that my spirit may set out strengthened on its homeward journey. When I stand before God's tremendous judgment seat you will not be able to answer for me or defend me." So he continued to pray. He was buried at Dumfermline, an abbey founded by his parents.

1186

St. Nicetas of Pereaslav in Russia. The words of the lenten office, "Wash yourselves, make yourselves clean, . . . cease to do evil, learn to do good. . . ." changed him from an oppressive, much-hated tax collector into a vigorous ascetic. The robbers who murdered him thought the metal bands he wore for mortification were precious, so shiny were they from wear.

1636

Bl. John Prado, Spanish Franciscan, patron of the Morocco missions. He quietly bore the calumny which brought his removal from office. "God wills that I should suffer," he said. "May his will be done. The only thing that grieves me is the discredit it may bring upon our order and the scandal it may cause to the weak." At length his missionary desire was granted, and he was sent to Morocco, where his intrepid preaching was punished with forced labor in a tread mill and then with martyrdom.

MAY 25

735

ST. BEDE THE VENERABLE; Benedictine priest; doctor of the church; model of the saintly scholar-monk. His career began at seven under St. Benedict Biscop at the abbey of Wearmouth and Jarrow in Northumbria. "From that time," he writes, "I spent the whole of my life within that monastery, devoting all my efforts to the study of Scriptures; and amid the observances of monastic discipline and the daily charge of singing in the church, it has ever been my delight to learn, to teach, or write. . . . From the time of my ordination (at thirty) till my present fifty-ninth year I have endeavored, for my own use and that of the brethren, to make brief notes upon the Holy Scriptures either out of the works of the venerable fathers or in conformity with their thought."

His popularity rests especially on his **Ecclesiastical History of the English People.** In it, limpid style, serenity, humility, a judicious sense of historical truth, and the gift of story telling combine to produce a masterpiece, cherished by those who love unspoiled tales of saintliness and self-sacrifice. A deep piety, that never appears strained or put on, is the author's most characteristic trait; but critics continue to marvel particularly at his finished scholarship at a time when study was just beginning in England.

1085

ST. GREGORY VII, or Hildebrand, a native of Tuscany; Benedictine abbot of St. Paul-outside-the-walls, cardinal; chief adviser to five popes; key figure in what historians were to call by his name the "Gregorian Reform" — a seventy-five year struggle to recover for the church its essential freedom in papal elections and appointments to church offices. Clerical celibacy and simony were also issues, but secondary to lay investiture.

Emperors had often deposed popes, but Gregory was the first pope to claim or exercise the power of deposing an emperor. It was a time of pamphleteering and feverish study of ancient church law. Emperor Henry IV, at a low ebb in his fortunes, came to Canossa for the pope's absolution; but before long he seized Rome and, with the backing of most of the German bishops, set up an anti-pope. St. Gregory died in exile.

Forty years later the Concordat of Worms — the first concordat in history — worked out a compromise; but it did establish for all time Gregory's principle that ecclesiastical jurisdiction does not derive from secular power.

1607   [*O. Carm.*]

ST. MARY MAGDALEN DEI PAZZI, Carmelite mystic, novice mistress and superior at Florence, where she entered at sixteen and died at forty-one. She seems to have kept a place in the revised Roman calendar because she taught so effectively the value of suffering voluntarily accepted for love of Christ and the salvation of souls. "O Lord," she once prayed, "let me suffer or let me die, or rather, let me live on that I may suffer more."

1865   [*R.S.C.J.*]
   St. Madeleine Sophie Barat, foundress in France of the Society of the Sacred Heart. During her sixty-three years as superior she founded 105 houses for the education of girls. "Too much work," she said, "is a danger for an imperfect soul . . . but for one who loves our Lord, it is an abundant harvest."

MAY 26*

1595
   ST. PHILIP NERI, founder of the Oratorians. By doing the usual work open to a priest he so renewed the religious life of his milieu that he is called Rome's second apostle. He was a pious young Florentine working as an apprentice in Naples at a small business he was expecting to inherit when he had a religious experience which left him without interest in secular pursuits. He settled in Rome at twenty and lived in an attic for two years, an ascetic recluse except for a few hours of tutoring to pay for his keep. After studying philosophy and theology for three years, he sold his books and became a street-corner apostle. He had a way of getting others to help him care for the sick or accompany him in his favorite devotion to the seven churches. With infectious cordiality he would say, "Well, when are we going to start doing some good?" At twenty-eight while praying in the catacombs of St. Sebastian on the eve of Pentecost he seemed to experience a ball of fire lodge in his heart. Thereafter in his fervors his heart would often palpitate, enlarge, and give off warmth. Examination after death showed two ribs broken and arched, forming a large cavity over the heart. At thirty-five, on his confessor's advice, he finally became a priest.
   His Oratory grew out of the confessional where he was soon

*O.S.B., O.Cist., O.C.S.O. see May 25 for St. Gregory VII.

spending hours each day; he began organizing spiritual conferences and prayer sessions for his penitents. A big room or "Oratory" was built for these gatherings and the priests who helped were called "Oratorians." Baronius, the great historian and cardinal, was one of them. Philip started him off by insisting that he take church history as the subject of all his talks. Philip built the huge **Chiesa Nuova** and promoted confession, Holy Communion, and devotions.

He too became one of Rome's attractions with his joyous face and shabby cassock. There were stories of his tenderness with sinners in the confessional, how he read souls and worked miracles, how he played the clown when people came to have a look at a saint and the efforts he made to distract himself with jokes or light reading before Mass so that he could get through without falling into ecstasy. Death came on May 26th in the eightieth year, but he said Mass and heard confessions until the day before.

MAY 27

ca. 605

ST. AUGUSTINE, first archbishop of Canterbury, leader of the forty monks pope St. Gregory the Great sent from his own monastery at Rome in answer to an appeal from the English. On their way through France, hearing tales of English savagery, the missionaries lost courage and sent Augustine back to Rome urging the pope to call off the project, particularly as they did not know the Saxon tongue. But Gregory told them it was better not to begin a good work than to give it up once begun, and he encouraged them not to listen to wild talk but to put their trust in God and reflect that an eternal reward would crown their labors. They landed on the Island of Thanet early in the year 597.

Thanks to St. Bede, theirs is one of the best-known success stories in missionary history. On Thanet the monks were given the abandoned church of St. Martin, a relic of Roman days, and there, writes St. Bede, they "began to meet, to sing, to pray, to say mass, to preach and to baptize." Their apostolic spirit and simple community life, modeled on that of the early Church, made a deep impression. King Ethelbert was baptized on Pentecost of that year and a large number of his people on Christmas. Soon a hierarchy was established and the Anglo-Saxons were on the way to becoming a deeply Christian nation, firmly attached to Rome and the first stronghold of Benedictine monasticism.

St. Augustine was less fortunate in dealing with the already Christian Britons whom the pope had placed under his jurisdiction. He asked them to observe the Roman date of Easter, follow the Roman form of baptism, and help preach to the Anglo-Saxons; and for the rest they could follow their own customs. But at the crucial meeting they took it amiss that Augustine remained seated when they entered. Thinking him to be proud, they refused to recognize his authority. He shares with St. Gregory the title "Apostle of the English."

1820   [C.M.]
Bl. Francis Regis Clet, French Vincentian missionary martyred near Hankow at the age of seventy-two after nearly thirty years in China amid hardships of every kind, including much difficulty with the language. He was betrayed for a large reward and then abused and tortured for eight months.

MAY 28

576
St. Germanus, or **Germain,** abbot in Autun, bishop of Paris, noted for charity to beggars and fearless denunciation of vice at

the Merovingian court, where he placed King Charibert under excommunication. He built the church of the Holy Cross and St. Vincent in Paris—later renamed Saint-Germain-des-Prés— where he and several generations of the royal family were buried.

1541

Bl. Margaret Pole, niece of kings Edward IV and Richard III, martyr under Henry VIII, who at one time described her as the saintliest woman in England and had her as Princess Mary's governess. She supported Queen Catherine and opposed the marriage with Anne Boleyn. Her second son, Reginald—later Cardinal Pole—wrote a treatise against the king's claim to Church supremacy. Margaret was imprisoned but never given a trial. A servile parliament passed an act of attainder against her, and she was beheaded at the age of seventy.

1577

Bl. Bartholomea Bagnesi of Florence, an example of suffering heroically borne. Undernourished in childhood while in the care of a foster mother, she later had a complete breakdown when she learned of her father's plans for her marriage, for she had her heart set on following two older sisters into religion. The shock left her an invalid. She continued bedridden for forty-five years except for a short period after receiving the habit of a Dominican tertiary. Though she suffered complications of every sort, she was forgetful of self and exerted an effective apostolate among her visitors.

1645   [*Franciscan II O.*]

St. Mariana of Quito in Equador. Of Spanish descent, she vowed virginity as a young girl, practised merciless austerities, and died at the age of twenty-six, after publicly offering her life to stop an epidemic. She was a Franciscan tertiary and was permitted to take the three religious vows though she did not belong to any community.

MAY 29

ca. 347

St. Maximus, bishop of Trier, staunch defender of orthodoxy against the Arians and, for two years, host of St. Athanasius during his first exile. He was excommunicated along with St. Athanasius by the Arian bishops gathered at Philippopolis.

1252

St. Ferdinand III, king of Castile and Léon. He recovered important cities such as Cordoba, Cadiz, and Seville from the Muslims and founded the university of Salamanca and the cathedral of Burgos. He used to say that he feared the curse of an old woman more than the whole army of the Moors.

1876

Bl. Mary Rose Molas y Vallvé, intrepid foundress. At 16 she wanted to devote herself to hospital work in her home town of Reus, Spain, but her father refused. At 19, following the example of her mother—who would contract the disease and die—she selflessly served the stricken in a cholera epidemic. At 26, she left her home secretly and joined a group of pious women who served in the local hospital. They wore a habit but were not a church organization. She now became known as Sister Mary Rose and soon stood out as extremely capable, ready for any difficulty, tenacious, affable, affectionate, self-sacrificing and deeply spiritual.

After eight years she was sent with four companions to take over the troubled House of Charity in Tortosa which cared for 300 elderly, sick or destitute. In a matter of weeks she put the house in order. Then she opened a free school for the poor. In time the city council entrusted to her sisters the town hospital and school.

Convinced the sisters should become religious under Church authority, she eventually led a group of twelve to form a religious congregation in Tortosa. She was 42. The following year, 1858, they took the name Sisters of Our Lady of Consolation. When she died at 61 the sisters ran seven hospitals, 9 day and 2 boarding schools.

Among her deeds are recounted crossing the line of fire with some companions to ask a general to cease bombarding Reus, stopping a doctor from experimenting on foundlings in her hospital, rushing to the wounded in a railway accident, taking charge of lazarettos in time of plague, and long vigils or even whole nights spent in prayer. Her confessor and first biographer said that "her spirit was of steel as regards her own work and sorrows but was as delicate as that of a child before the sufferings of others." Mother Mary Rose died on June 11.

MAY 30

1431
St. Joan of Arc; second patroness of France; a unique saint who, under the influence of heavenly voices, intervened decisively in the political order of Europe and was burned as a heretic at the age of nineteen. At no other time since the breakdown of the Carolingian Empire did France come so close to losing her identity. It was Joan's mission to restore a soul to the nation.

The English, in league with the Duke of Burgundy, and at their peak of success in the Hundred Years War, were in settled possession of the greater part of present-day France. The parliament and the University of Paris had accepted England's ruler as legitimate king. Only the southwest held out; but its main stronghold, Orleans, was under siege and ready to fall.

Joan, a pious peasant girl at Domrémy in Lorraine, had, since the age of thirteen, been receiving minute instructions from her "voices" on what she must do to save France. At seventeen, dressed as a boy, she rode south through English territory for eleven days, gained audience with the rightful king, and soon led an expeditionary force which in eight days lifted the siege of Orleans.

She then went on to rout the English at Patay and in a mat-

ter of weeks was standing beside Charles VII at his coronation at Rheims deep in Burgundian territory. In her hands she
held the special standard she carried in battle bearing the
names "Jesus" and "Mary" and the image of two angels presenting the **Fleur-de-lis** to God the Father. All these events
she had foretold.

A year later she was taken by the Burgundians after a skirm-
ish at Compiègne, was sold to the English, and tried for heresy
by a church court packed with partisans of the English, including ten theologians from the University of Paris. The record of
her simple, unintimidated, and often shattering replies under
questioning is one of the treasures of hagiography and perhaps
the best example of the inspired answers Christ promised his
disciples under persecution. She died at the stake pronouncing
the name of Jesus.

Twenty-five years later her case was retried and she was pronounced innocent. Joan was declared a saint in 1920 and in the
same year France made her feast a national holiday.

1483 [*O.S.M.*]
Bl. James Bertoni, Servite priest at Faenza, where he died
with such a reputation of holiness that his father was granted
tax exemption and the status of burgher.

1527 [*Franciscan II O.*]
Bl. Baptista Varani, Poor Clare abbess at Camerino, a mystic
particularly devoted to the passion. She belonged to the ruling
family of Camerino and was slated for a brilliant marriage. For
three years she was all caught up in frivolities, except for a
meditation each Friday on the passion of Christ — something
she had promised as a child of ten after hearing a sermon by
Bl. Mark Montegallo. A sermon on the fear of God sobered
her again, and she gradually recognized her vocation to religious life and to close association with Christ in his sufferings.

Her writings continue to attract attention; and her revelations, **The Sufferings of the Agonizing Heart of Jesus,** helped spread devotion to the Sacred Heart.

MAY 31

THE VISITATION OF THE BLESSED VIRGIN MARY. The gospel account shows that this meeting of Mary and Elizabeth when both were with child was already the subject of much reverent reflection in the apostolic church; but the scene became increasingly popular as the setting for the **Magnificat** of vespers, the origin of a portion of the **Hail Mary,** and as one of the mysteries of the rosary. The feast was first observed in the thirteenth century by the Franciscans and extended to the Western church in the fourteenth.

812

St. William of Gellone, count of Toulouse, one of Charlemagne's favorite associates, also called William Shortnose, around whom—as the ideal of Christian knighthood—a whole cycle of chivalrous epic poetry developed. Sent to repulse the Saracens who were threatening southern France, he won their respect by his bravery, justice, and piety. He built a monastery at Gellone near Aniane and eventually left court to enter there as a brother.

1314

Bl. James of Venice. At seventeen this wealthy Venetian heir gave all his property to the poor and became a Dominican in his native town. He served as prior in several monasteries, had the gift of miracles and supernatural states of prayer, and was particularly devoted to the sick poor. After the Scriptures he found constant source of inspiration in the martyrology and lives of the saints. He remained cheerful and calm during four years of intense suffering from cancer and died at the age of eighty-two.

1583

Bl. Richard Thirkeld, already an old man at the time of his ordination, he prayed daily during eight years to be allowed to die for the faith. A night visit to a Catholic prisoner aroused suspicion, and he was arrested on the charge of being a priest. When condemned to death for treason he fell on his knees saying, "This is the day the Lord has made; let us rejoice in it and be glad." He died at London in the reign of Elizabeth I.

JUNE 1

ca. 165

ST. JUSTIN, martyr; a Palestinian Greek; the first Christian
apologist of whom some lengthy and important writings have
been preserved. A professional philosopher deeply imbued with
stoic and Platonic ideas, he discovered Christianity while still
in his prime and spent the rest of his life, possibly another
thirty years, traveling and disputing for Christ, dressed in
the philosopher's gown. He established a school at Rome and
was executed there under Marcus Aurelius.

St. Justin's special importance is his witness to second century practice and belief. He holds the four gospels as authoritative and is the first to quote them extensively. He is also the
first to describe the Sunday liturgy in all its essentials, and
he clearly attests belief in the Real Presence of Christ in the
Eucharist. His writings are the first to contrast Mary and Eve.
In St. Justin is portrayed the earliest notable encounter between
a thoroughly Christian mentality and professional Greek thought,
and he takes a positive view which he expressed in this way:
"The truths, which men in all lands have rightly spoken be-

long to us Christians. . . . All the writers, by means of the engrafted seed of the Word which was implanted in them, had a dim glimpse of the truth."

1396

St. Stephen; monk of Rostov in Russia, outstanding missionary who became bishop of Perm near the Ural Mountains, where he attracted heathens by the beauty and solemnity of divine worship. He gave people of Perm an alphabet and translated the liturgy and parts of the Bible for their use.

1617-1632

Two hundred and five beatified martyrs of Japan's second great persecution. All Christian teachers were ordered to leave, and death was the penalty for any Japanese who would have dealings with a priest. On June 1, 1617, **Bl. Alphonse Navarrette,** a Spanish Dominican, and **Bl. Ferdinand Ayalà,** a Spanish Augustinian, were beheaded along with a Japanese catechist **Bl. Leo Tanaka.**

JUNE 2

ca. 304

STS. MARCELLINUS and **PETER,** martyrs whose names are included in the Roman canon. Constantine buried his mother St. Helena in the church which he built over their grave. Marcellinus was a prominent Roman priest executed under Diocletian.

177

St. Pothinus, bishop of Lyons, and **companions,** whose martyrdom is recorded in **The Letter of the Churches of Vienne and Lyons** to the churches in Asia and Phrygia, a precious document that breathes the spirit of the apostolic Church and provides the earliest account of an organized Christian community in France. The martyrs were accused of incest and jeered as atheists and eaters of child's flesh. Their bodies were burned; and the ashes were scattered in the Rhone with the taunt, "Now let us see if they will rise again!" According to the theology of martyrdom expressed in the letter it was Christ, "the faithful and true martyr," who bore witness in these disciples.

Pothinus was ninety and already very weak; but his desire for martyrdom gave him strength, and "his soul," the text says, "was kept in him that through it Christ might triumph." When the governor questioned him as to who the god of the Christians might be, he answered, "If you are worthy, you will know." **St. Attalus** answered, "God has no name as a man has."

Sanctus under torture gave no other information than this one answer in Latin to every question, "I am a Christian." "This he confessed for name and for city and for race and for everything in succession, and the heathen heard no other word from him."

At the beginning some ten renounced their faith, but the steadfastness of the others and the bravery of some who voluntarily stepped forward brought renewed courage so that nearly all who had faltered won the martyr's crown.

1260
Bl. Sadoc and **companions,** a Dominican prior and his community, martyred by the Tartars at Sandomir in Poland.

JUNE 3

1885-87
ST. CHARLES LWANGA and **COMPANIONS,** Uganda martyrs

whose joy, courage, and straight-forward answers recall the "acts" of the early martyrs. Though there were others, both Anglican and Catholic, who died during the two-year persecution, twenty-two have been singled out for canonization. They were all recent converts, mostly young men between the ages of thirteen and thirty, attached to the court of King Mwanga. Some of the youthful martyrs had incurred the king's special wrath by resisting his unchaste advances.

On June 3, 1886, the Christians in Mwanga's entourage were burned at Namugongo. Thirteen of the saints were in this group, the leader among them being Charles Lwanga, twenty-four, who had charge of the king's pages and baptized four of them shortly before their execution. **St. Kizito,** thirteen, the youngest and a martyr for chastity, was one of these. On the way to execution he encouraged a crying companion—one who was eventually set free—with these words, "Say the **Our Father** and die like a man."

Within a year of the persecution the number of baptized among the Baganda rose from 200 to 500 and the catechumens from 800 to 3,000. In the decree of canonization Pope Paul VI hailed this joint martyrdom of Anglicans and Catholics as strengthening the hope of Christian unity.

545

St. Clothilde, queen, who helped bring her husband King Clovis to the Christian faith. She had much to suffer from the quarrels among her sons and in old age retired to Tours, where she died near the tomb of St. Martin.

7th cent.

St. Kevin, abbot-founder of the monastery of Glendalough and one of the principal patrons of Dublin.

1600   [O.H.]

Bl. John Grande, a Spaniard who stepped out of business at twenty-one, gave everything to the poor, and began to live as a hermit. Though others thought his life blameless, he became

particularly conscious of his sins and began to call himself
"El Grande Pecador" so that he is known in Spain today as
"John the Sinner." His vocation, however, was not to solitude
but to the service of the destitute—as he discovered after nursing two tramps he had found on the roadside and carried home
to his hut. He devoted the rest of his life to neglected prisoners
and the sick. A wealthy couple finally provided him with a hospital of his own which he affiliated with the Hospitalers of St.
John of God.

JUNE 4*

ca. 390

St. Optatus of Milevis in northern Africa, of whom little is
known beyond his remarkable treatise against Parmenian, the
first full-scale refutation of the Donatists. This sect was claiming to be the one true church and insisted on the rebaptism of
outsiders. Optatus pointed out that the true church is **catholica,**
or universal in extent; and how could the Donatists claim this,
huddled as they were in one small corner of Africa?

Regarding their claim to possess the "chair" he wrote: "We
must examine who first sat in the chair and where. . . . You
certainly know that to Peter in the City of Rome the episcopal
chair was first given. There Peter sat, head of all the apostles,
and for this reason he was called Cephas. In this one chair
all were to preserve their unity, and the other apostles were
not to stand up each for his own chair; for he would be a schismatic and a sinner who would set up another chair against this
one." Optatus then gives a list of the popes ending with Siricius, "our colleague with whom we and the whole world are
united by the communication of commendatory letters in the fel-
lowship of one communion." "Tell us," he concludes, "the origin of your chair, you who wish to claim the holy Church for

---

*O.P. see April 6 for St. Peter of Verona.

yourselves." Optatus also rejected the exaggerated importance Donatists gave the minister at baptism. "The sacraments," he wrote, "are holy of themselves and not through men."

1608 [*C.R.M.*]

St. Francis Caracciolo, formerly greatly honored as patron of Naples, where he won the hearts of the poor. He begged for them, constantly preached to them on the goodness of God, and after a few hours of sleep on a table or the altar steps would be waiting for them in the confessional the first thing in the morning. He entered the priesthood in fulfillment of a promise made at twenty-two to do so if he recovered from the leprosy-like disease that had brought him to death's door. With John Adorno he founded at Naples the Minor Clerks Regular, combining the contemplative life with the active ministry, particularly that of preaching missions and of giving spiritual care to the sick. The Clerks made a vow not to seek office of any kind and took turns, an hour each day, in adoration before the Blessed Sacrament.

JUNE 5

754

ST. BONIFACE, apostle of Germany, possibly the greatest missionary of the Middle Ages and, according to Christopher Dawson, the Englishman who has had the deepest influence on the history of Europe. He received his early training in a monastery at Exeter and then became a Benedictine monk and schoolmaster at Nursling, where he produced England's first Latin grammar. In 719, about the age of forty, he declined the office of abbot and with his heart on the German mission presented himself to Pope Gregory II, who changed his name from Winfrid to Boniface and gave him a general commission to preach to the heathens.

Such was his success in Frisia under St. Willibrord and in Hesse on his own that the pope called him back to Rome three years later, made him bishop with general jurisdiction over Germany, and gave him a letter of commendation to Charles Martel. With such civil and papal backing—the next pope would make him archbishop beyond the Rhine and papal legate in Frankland—and with the enthusiastic collaboration of a throng of Anglo-Saxon monks and nuns, many of them saints, he brought Christian faith and culture to large sectors of western Germany and gave the Church throughout the region its permanent structure. He founded new dioceses and headed them all with Anglo-Saxon bishops. He reorganized the church in Frankland, where a council had not been held in more than 80 years, and also attached this territory more closely to the Holy See. Only toward the end of his life did he establish a diocese for himself, selecting Mainz, when difficulties arose regarding Cologne which had been his first choice.

After providing himself with a worthy successor in his ccm-patriot St. Lull, Boniface, now an old man, returned again to the Frisian mission. At Dokkum, in present-day Holland, he was martyred along with 53 companions on the eve of Pentecost as he was preparing to confirm a large number of new converts. His body was taken to Fulda, his favorite abbey; and there at his tomb the bishops of West Germany gather for their meetings today.

JUNE 6

1134

ST. NORBERT, archbishop of Magdeburg, founder of the Premonstratensians, or Norbertines, canons regular under the rule of St. Augustine, who combine a monastic form of life with the active ministry. Norbert belonged to a noble family in Lorraine and, as a subdeacon in his early thirties, was attached to court as the emperor's almoner and was interested primarily in having a good time. But a close brush with death—he was thrown from a horse in a lightning storm—effected a sudden and total conversion. He became a priest, sold his property and gave everything away except a mule, forty silver marks, a missal, chalice, paten, and some vestments. A bishop had him try to reform a community of canons regular, but Norbert proved too strict for them. He then withdrew to the abandoned valley of Prémontré, near Laon in northern France, where in a matter of months he had forty companions, and on Christmas, 1121, they made profession of vows.

Appointed archbishop of Magdeburg by Emperor Lothair II, Norbert soon took a leading role in public affairs. The emperor wanted to make him chancellor, but the saint was worn out by labors and died at the age of fifty-three. By the next century the Norbertines had 500 abbeys. The order's characteristic emphasis on the Holy Eucharist derives from St. Norbert. There are also a few Norbertine nuns.

1840   [*F.M.S., S.M.*]

Bl. Marcellin Champagnat, founder of the Marist Brothers. As a seminarian at Genoble he showed a marked devotion to Mary, and along with Venerable John Colin belonged to a group of eleven students who were planning a missionary and teaching order in Mary's honor. Marcellin was particularly keen on including brothers in the congregation. He was not yet ordained a year when an experience with a dying boy totally uninstructed in the faith prompted him to found at once the brothers' sector of the society. He began with two zealous candidates. Seven years later he was released from parish ministry to give himself full-time to his growing fraternity. He was also a member of the Marist Fathers founded by John Colin, but the two branches did not fuse into one congregation.

At the time of their founder's beatification in 1955, the Marist Brothers numbered nearly 10,000. Above everything else he insisted on prayer and an intense spiritual life and often quoted the psalm verse, "Unless the Lord build the house, they labor in vain who build it."

JUNE 7

1626 *[O.C.D.]*

Bl. Anne of St. Bartholomew, Carmelite lay sister, favorite companion of St. Teresa of Avila on her journeys of foundation. Anne wrote of St. Teresa: "The day she died she could not speak. I changed all her linen, headdress and sleeves. She looked at herself quite satisfied to see herself so clean. Then turning her eyes on me she looked at me smilingly and showed her gratitude by signs." Bl. Anne was with the five Carmelites who introduced Teresa's reform into France and died at her own foundation in Antwerp, where some 20,000 showed their devotion to her before burial. She once pleaded her incompetence to govern others but heard this answer from Our Lord, "It is with straw that I light my fires."

1846

St. Anthony Gianelli, bishop of Bobbio, founder of the Sisters of St. Mary Dell' Orto, also called Gianelline, devoted to corporal service of their neighbor. His Oblates of St. Alphonsus, a society of priests dedicated to clerical training, did not survive. Poor, but bright, pious and hard-working, he reached the priesthood with the help of a benefactress. An outstanding preacher and spiritual father, he died at fifty-seven.

1889

Bl. Mary Teresa de Soubiran, foundress, in whose life the mystery of the cross—of success through failure—is starkly portrayed. After ten years as superior of a lay community with temporary vows, she longed for fuller consecration, and at twenty-nine founded at Toulouse the Society of Mary Auxiliatrix, devoted to perpetual adoration of the Blessed Sacrament and to works of charity—the first houses provided working girls with a home. Ten years later an ambitious assistant—who in fact was married and not validly a nun—had Mother Mary Teresa blamed for mismanagement, removed from office and expelled.

Back in the world she applied to several orders and at forty-two made profession as a Good Shepherd nun in Paris. She saw the spirit of her foundations ruined under the imposter superior general and died just a few months before things were set right. "All this," she wrote, "did not happen without extreme suffering. Only God can measure its depth and intensity, as only He knows the graces of faith, hope and love that flow from it. The great truth that God is all, and the rest nothing, becomes the life of the soul and upon it one can lean securely amid the incomprehensible mysteries of this world. . . . And would I have learned this without such cruel anguish? I do not think so."

JUNE 8*

ca. 560

St. Medard, bishop of Noyon. As patron of the grain harvest and vintage he is a favorite of the peasants of northern France, where his cult goes back to his death in the sixth century.

1236 and 1290   [O.P.]

Bl. Diana and **Bl. Cecilia,** first Dominican nuns in Bologna. Diana's dramatic vocation resembles that of St. Clare. She made a private vow of virginity under the tutelage of St. Dominic and, as there seemed little hope of family consent, ran away to a convent; but she was retrieved with such violence that she sustained a broken rib. On her second flight the family relented and eventually they helped build the convent on their own lands. Bl. Cecilia, believed to be the first Dominican nun,

---

*R. G. S. see Aug. 9 for Bl. Mary Droeste zu Vischering.

was brought from Rome to head the community and in her old age dictated graphic anecdotes about St. Dominic.

1625 [*O.SS.T.*]

St. Michael of the Saints, who became a Trinitarian in Barcelona at sixteen or eighteen and soon joined the reformed or "Discalced" branch of the order. He served as superior at Valladolid and died when only thirty-six with a reputation for miracles, ecstasies while saying Mass, and great devotion to the Blessed Sacrament.

1896

Bl. James Berthieu, French Jesuit martyred in Madagascar at fifty-seven during an anti-Christian and anti-French uprising. Taken right after Mass, he was accused of praying to God and leading others to do the same and of teaching that marriage could not be dissolved. His vestments and cross were removed. He was then stripped—retaining only the rosary on which he kept praying—and beaten to death.

In the 1870's when he arrived on the island—the fourth largest in the world—the Catholic mission was just being re-established after 200 years of neglect. Today the Malagasy Republic is fifty percent Christian and half of these are Catholic.

JUNE 9*

373

ST. EPHRAEM, doctor, most important of the Syrian Church fathers. When his native Nisibis in Mesopotamia was occupied by the Persians, he settled at Edessa in Roman territory. St. Jerome, a junior contemporary, made this entry in his book **On Illustrious Men:** "Ephraem, deacon of the church of Edessa, wrote many works in Syriac, and became so famous that his

---

*O.SS.T. see June 10 for Bl. Anne Mary Taigi.

writings are publicly read in some churches after the Sacred Scriptures. I have read in Greek a volume of his on the Holy Spirit, and though it was only a translation I recognized the sublime genius of the man." He is the greatest Syrian poet and contributed much to the use of hymns in the liturgy.

His many writings give abundant witness to the faith and practice of his church. Thus he speaks of Mary as being free of any taint of sin. In his testament he wants incense to be used for worship but not at his funeral and asks that Masses and prayers be offered on his behalf.

597

St. Columba or **Columcille,** apostle of Scotland. He was born in Donegal of blood royal and might have become a king of Ireland had he not preferred to be a monk and priest. Trained at Clonard, he founded several monasteries and churches, including Kells and Derry, and in 563 at the age of forty-two landed with twelve monks at Iona. This island—three miles long and one mile wide—of the Inner Hebrides on the southwest coast of Scotland would be the primatial seat of Celtic monasticism for Scotland, England, and parts of Ireland for the next two centuries and the point of origin in the missionary drive that christianized Scotland and Northumbria in one or two generations. Columba worked particularly among the Picts of the north. He died at Iona at seventy-six.

"Amid all his toils," writes St. Adamnan, his reliable biographer, "he appeared loving unto all, serene and holy, rejoicing in the joy of the Holy Spirit in his inmost heart."

Iona, with its monastery, cathedral, and tombs of saints and kings, was reputed the holiest ground in Scotland. Columba foretold the island's glory as well as its desolation when instead of monks' voices there would be the lowing of cattle, but he also prophesied that "ere the world come to an end Iona shall be as it was."

Dr. Samuel Johnson visiting the island 200 years after the Reformation observed, "That man is little to be envied . . . whose piety would not grow warmer among the ruins of Iona."

JUNE 10

1315

Bl. Henry of Treviso, day-laborer who secretly gave to the poor all he could spare beyond his subsistence; and when he became too old to support himself he lived on alms which he also shared with beggars, never keeping anything for the morrow. Daily he assisted at Mass and made his confession. Nothing could ever ruffle him. Children sometimes mocked the shabby, thick-set little man, with sunken eyes and long nose; but he never resented their treatment or made any reply. The Treviso notaries recorded 276 miracles within a few days of his death. The crowd broke into the cathedral during the night, and a wooden palisade had to be put up to protect the body. The instruments of penance he used were preserved in the cathedral, and the bishop wrote his biography.

1419   [*O.P.*]

Bl. John Dominic, Florentine Dominican, author, outstanding theologian, cardinal archbishop of Ragusa. As confessor and adviser of Pope Gregory XII, he worked effectively to heal the Western schism by encouraging the pontiff to resign. Fra Angelico painted his portrait and St. Antoninus, a disciple, wrote a short account of his life.

1837

Bl. Anne Mary Taigi; hard-working and devoted wife and mother; mystic. Her father was a spendthrift. At thirteen she went to work, first in a silk factory, then as a maid. At twenty she married Dominic Taigi, a Roman domestic servant much older than herself.

Her first attempt to open up her soul to a priest failed; but on the second try, shortly after the birth of the first of her seven children, she succeeded. She would regard this confession as her conversion. The priest, on his part, had been interiorly forewarned that this young lady was to be a saint. She at once gave up her attachment to dressy clothes, and in place of the amusements that had so attracted her she began to practise strict mortification—which her director had to moderate. She also joined the Trinitarian third order and attended Mass daily.

Along with ecstasies and the gift of prophecy she also had normal family problems, poor housing, a mother to nurse, a hot-headed husband whom she loved and served as Christ, and the peace to keep among a large family including a difficult daughter-in-law. The Blessed Virgin told her it was her vocation to show that holiness was to be practised in every walk of life.

Her husband at ninety-two was a witness at her beatification process. "It often happened," he said, "that upon my return home I found the house full of people. At once she would leave anyone who was there . . . a great lady or perhaps a cardinal . . . and would hasten to wait on me affectionately and attentively." Bl. Anne died on June 9, 1837.

JUNE 11

1st cent.

St. Barnabas, apostle, whose name is continually associated with that of St. Paul until the two parted just before the second missionary journey. It was he who introduced Paul to the apostles and vouched for the genuineness of his conversion (Acts 9:27). A decade later it was he again who went to Tarsus to find Paul, brought him back to Antioch and, for the space of a year, initiated him into the apostolate (Acts 11:25-26). They also attended the "council" at Jerusalem together (Acts 15:2).

Barnabas was a Jew of the tribe of Levi, a native of Cyprus. The **Acts of the Apostles** (11:24) describe him as a "good man, full of the Holy Spirit and of faith," and tell how he sold his estate and gave the money to the Apostles. After the Twelve and St. Paul he seems to be the most prominent person in the apostolic church. The **Epistle of St. Barnabas,** though a very early document, is not his work.

888

St. Rembert, Benedictine of Torhout near Bruges, biographer and missionary assistant of St. Ansgar and his successor as archbishop of Hamburg and Bremen. "Rembert," Ansgar admitted, "is more worthy to be archbishop than I am to be his deacon." The saint sold sacred vessels to buy back captives from the Norsemen and gave the horse he was riding to ransom a maiden taken by the Slavs.

1882

Bl. Paula Frassinetti, foundress at Genoa of the Sisters of St. Dorothy. Already from the age of twelve she had charge of the household. But she was sickly and went to live with her brother, Giuseppe, a holy priest often compared to the Curé of Ars. Poor health frustrated her attempts to join a religious order so she founded an institute of her own at the age of twenty-five. Its purpose was to educate girls, especially the poor. The Sisters of St. Dorothy number more than two thousand. Her brother founded the Sons of Mary Immaculate and his cause has also been introduced.

JUNE 12*

ca. 1080

St. Eskil, English missionary bishop in Sweden, where he was stoned to death for protesting a pagan festival.

1250   [*O. Cist., O.C.S.O.*]

St. Aleydis or **Alice,** Cistercian nun near Brussels. She contracted leprosy and had the great sorrow of being deprived of the Precious Blood through fear of contagion but was reassured by hearing these interior words, "Where there is part there also is the whole."

---

* *S.S.D. see June 11 for Bl. Paula Frassinetti.*

1299   [*Franciscan II O.*]
Bl. Yolande, or **Jolenta,** daughter of King Bela IV of Hungary
and niece of St. Elizabeth. She was happily married to Duke
Boleslas V of Poland, established several monasteries, and at
his death entered a Poor Clare community along with her widowed sister Bl. Cunegund and also a daughter. She later became
abbess at Gnesen, Poland, of a convent she founded.

1479   [*O.S.A., O.A.R.*]
St. John of Sahagun, Augustinian prior at Salamanca. Several
attempts were made on his life so outspoken was he against
oppression and other common forms of vice. It was thought that
the complications of which he died were the result of poisoning
by an adultress who was abandoned by her paramour in consequence of John's preaching.

1853   *C.S.S.*
Bl. Gaspar Bertoni, founder at Verona of the Stigmatine Fathers. He
was the close associate or spiritual director of a cluster of holy men
and women, a number of religious founders among them, such as Bl.
Charles Steeb, with whom Gaspar as a seminarian tended the sick and
battle-wounded. Ordained at 22, Gaspar within two years started a
Marian Oratory and before long his group could be credited with the
spiritual renewal of the Verona diocese. At 39 he gathered his priests
more closely under a rule based on that of the Jesuits. The Stigmatines
—a title derived from the place which served as their headquarters—
do priestly work of many kinds, with a strong emphasis on education.
Bl. Gaspar died at 75 after a great deal of illness born most patiently.

JUNE 13

1231
ST. ANTHONY OF PADUA, the prime example of a popular

saint. His cult began at Padua the day he died, with the people of the region in tumult over who would possess his body. His Tuesday devotions stem from his being buried on Tuesday, June 17, 1231. Pilgrimages to his tomb were organized with much solemnity and in less than a year the "Wonder-worker" saint was canonized. His popularity rests primarily on favors granted.

He is invoked as patron of the poor, of lovers, of marriage, of travelers. The alms given to the poor to obtain his intercession are called "St. Anthony's Bread." He is prayed to for lost articles and, as the apostle of charity, is called upon in every kind of need. He was one of the greatest preachers ever. Other saints took to the squares and streets when churches became too small; Anthony had need of the open fields. He died at thirty-six, worn out by preaching.

The certain facts of his life are few. Especially missing are genuine sayings, writings, and anecdotes that would portray his distinctive spirit. The several series of authentic sermons are not in the oratorical style but are more like outlines or collages of scholarly and religious commentaries on difficult biblical texts.

A native of Portugal, he became a canon regular in Lisbon at fifteen. Two years later he went to the house of studies maintained by the Augustinian Canons of Coimbra, where he spent eight years becoming expert particularly in Scripture, so that in declaring him a doctor in 1946 Pope Pius XII could call him **Doctor Evangelicus,** the "Gospel doctor."

He also concentrated on St. Augustine and later, as the first Franciscan theology teacher, gave the Friars Minor the first strong input of the Augustinian theology that was a characteristic of their early period.

Fired by the news of the friars' first martyrs—the five who went to Morocco and whom he may have met on their passage —he left his studies in 1220, became a Franciscan, and soon reached Morocco eager to preach and be a martyr. But illness intervened and on the return voyage a storm drove the ship to Sicily. In 1221 he attended the famous chapter of the "mats" at the Portiuncula and saw Brother Francis sitting at the feet of Brother Elias.

Anthony made no display of learning or talent and was assigned to a hermitage where he prayed and did domestic work. But his extraordinary gifts came to light when a scheduled speaker failed to arrive and the Portugese friar was asked to improvise for the occasion. And so the last ten of his eleven years as a friar were spent preaching in Italy and France and teaching the brothers theology. His last two years were passed mostly at Padua.

His pictures and statues give no hint of the penitential fever he was able to arouse in Lombardy or his boldness in denouncing vice, especially the pride, concupiscence, and avarice embodied in his pet social evils of usury and the exploitation of the poor.

JUNE 14

847

St. Methodius, patriarch of Constantinople, the first to celebrate the feast of Orthodoxy, a solemnity kept in the Byzantine rite on the first Sunday of Lent to foster veneration of the holy ikons of Christ and the saints.

The second council of Nicea in 787 had clearly distinguished between the cult of images and the true adoration reserved for God alone. The council defended the practice of lighting lamps and burning incense before the ikons of the saints, pointing out that honor paid to an image is really given to the personage it represents.

Methodius was a native of Sicily, who as a young man went to Constantinople in search of a government position. But a monk persuaded him to choose the monastic life instead. A staunch supporter of St. Nicephorus during the second iconoclast persecution, he spent seven years half-starved in a foul prison.

"If an image," he told Emperor Theophilus, "is so worth-
less in your eyes, how is it that while you condemn the image
of Christ you do not also condemn the veneration paid to images of yourself? Instead, you are continually having more of
them made." He was appointed patriarch on the death of the
last iconoclast emperor.

1046

Bl. Richard, abbot of St. Vannes in Verdun, close friend of
Emperor St. Henry, and leading figure in the eleventh century
restoration of Benedictine monasticism in Lorraine and northern
France, where he and his young associates caused twenty monasteries to flourish and thus did much to generate a climate
at the imperial court that could produce such churchmen as
pope St. Leo IX, who initiated the Gregorian reform.

Though some contemporaries blamed Richard for too sump-
tuous churches—St. Peter Damian pictured him in purgatory
laboring on a large construction engine—he did, in time of
famine, sell church ornaments to feed the poor. He labored for
peace in his own life, in his monasteries, and in the world at
large. He gave up a promising career as youthful dean of the
cathedral chapter of Reims and entered St. Vannes. But finding
the observance poor he went on to Cluny. After a few days,
however, abbot St. Odilo sent him back to Verdun, advising
him not to abandon but to revitalize his monastery.

He became abbot and governed during forty-two years, except
for the period when he gave in to his yearning for solitary contemplation and lived as a hermit; but after five years his monks
recalled him. He was an ardent promoter of the "Truce of God"
initiated by his contemporary, Abbot Oliva of Ripoll, who had
become bishop of Vich.

1138 [*O. Cist., O.C.S.O.*]

Bl. Gerard of Clairvaux, St. Bernard's favorite brother and
closest assistant. More interested in being a soldier, he was not
in the original band of thirty that accompanied Bernard to the

cloister, but he did come after a serious wound and long captivity taught him the emptiness of worldly glory.

JUNE 15

1601

St. Germaine Cousin, a deformed and sickly shepherd girl at Pibrac near Toulouse. Her life highlights some primary spiritual and Christian values for an age that questions the handicapped child's claim to life. Germaine's right hand was misshapen and paralysed at birth. She lost her mother, was unloved by her father, abused by a stepmother, and segregated from her healthy half-brothers and sisters.

But God favored her with supernatural patience and a charity that led her to share with beggars the scraps of food she received. During the long hours tending sheep, she learned so much in prayer that she was able to gather village children and speak to them of God. Neighbors gradually recognized her sanctity and shortly before her death at twenty-two her family began to treat her well. The many miracles at her tomb gave rise to an annual procession to the church of Pibrac.

1886

Bl. Aloysius Palazzolo, founder. The twelfth child of a wealthy Bergamo family, he became a secular priest at the age of twenty-two and soon began to work with the young of Bergamo especially the poor. With the help of a school teacher, Teresa Gabrieli, he established the Sisters of the Poor. In 1869 she took the usual three vows, along with a fourth to work unstintingly for the corporal and spiritual needs of poor girls. On the same day Aloysius brought in a deformed and totally abandoned orphan girl and expressed the **rationale** of his new order in these words: "I am looking for those who are rejected by others. When others help they do it better, but when others are unable to help then I will do all I can." During a retreat he resolved to give everything away and live in abjection like Christ. He turned his estate into an orphanage for boys and founded the Brothers of the Holy Family to carry on the work.

JUNE 16

1246 [*O. Cist., O.C.S.O.*]

St. Lutgarde, Cistercian mystic at Aywières near Brussels. She was favored with some marks of Christ's passion, particularly the sweat of blood. During prayer she seemed to see our Lord with her bodily eyes. When called away she would say, "Wait here, Lord Jesus, and I will come back as soon as I have finished." She undertook long fasts in reparation for the Albigensian heresy and joyfully accepted blindness during the last eleven years of her life as a God-sent means of total detachment from visible things.

1640

St. John Francis Regis, indefatigable Jesuit missioner in southeastern France. It is said that in his last four months he heard 10,000 confessions. He was then only forty-three and died of pleurisy, while continuing his scheduled mission. He would preach from farm to farm as well as to huge throngs.

"I have seen him," said one witness at his process, "stop in the middle of a forest to satisfy a crowd that wished to hear him. I have seen him stand all day on a heap of snow on a mountain instructing and preaching, and then spend the whole night hearing confessions."

He applied several times to be sent on the newly opened Canadian Jesuit mission. Appointments he would keep at any cost. Once he fell during a journey and broke his leg, but leaning on a stick and the shoulder of a companion he arrived at his destination and entered the confessional. After the day's work the leg was found to be healed.

The poor with all their needs were his special concern. His room was full of clothes, furniture, and odds and ends of all kinds which he collected for them. Among his penitents at Le Puy he organized a social program that included prison visitation, nursing, a granary for the poor, and a refuge for women.

People spoke of him as the "saint" in his lifetime, and his tomb at Louvesc high up in the mountains of the Ardèche soon became and has since remained one of the great pilgrimage centers of France. The future Curé of Ars, discouraged with his studies, made the sixty miles there on foot and attributed to this saint the realization of his own vocation to the priesthood.

St. John Francis Regis, during his nine-and-one-half years of priesthood, did more than anyone else in the Counter-reformation to restore the faith throughout the mountainous region of Viviers and Le Puy; and he continues to be the principal local inspiration for the area's staunch Catholicism. He died Dec. 31.

JUNE 17

1250

St. Teresa, daughter of King Sancho I of Portugal and honored along with her sisters, St. Mafalda and Sanchia. Teresa married the king of León; and Mafalda, the king of Castile; but both marriages were in time declared invalid because of too near ties of kinship. All three sisters did much to promote religious life and eventually identified themselves with the Cistercian order of nuns.

1435

Bl. Peter Gambacorta of Pisa, founder of the Poor Brothers of St. Jerome, a penitential monastic order. Peter supplemented his rule with quotations from St. Jerome. At one time there were forty-six monasteries, but in 1933 the numbers were so few that the Holy See suppressed the order.

1856

St. Emily de Vialar. At Gaillac in southern France she founded the Sisters of St. Joseph of the Apparition to care for the needy, especially the sick, and to educate children. She encountered much opposition from her father. He wanted her to marry and he found it troublesome to have the village sick and needy milling about the house during the fifteen years his daughter's apostolate was taking shape. But at the age of thirty-five Emily received a generous inheritance from her grandfather, Baron de Portal, physician to the king of France. With this she bought a large house and soon was able to pronounce religious vows along with seventeen companions.

Forty houses were established in her lifetime, including foundations in Africa, Asia, and Australia, as well as the first community of Catholic nuns established in Jerusalem in modern times.

After a particularly trying crisis she wrote, "I have had my lesson. A quiet trust in God is better than trying to safeguard material advantages." Her motherhouse was moved twice, ending in Marseilles under the saintly bishop de Mazenod. She died on August 24.

JUNE 18

1505

Bl. Ossana Andreasi, virgin, who directed a large household of brothers and their families and was remarkable for mystic experiences and an unobtrusive ascendancy over others by reason of her goodness, wisdom, and religious dedication. After an ecstasy at the age of five, she began to devote long periods to prayer and practiced strenuous self-denial. At eighteen our Lord placed a ring on her finger which she could always feel but never see; and later, for a period of five years, she experienced various incidents in Christ's passion.

She spent a large fortune in the service of the distressed and, according to the testimony of her closest friend, her day was not happy unless it included some service of mercy, whether nursing, giving alms, consoling or interceding for the unfortunate. So excellent was her practical judgment that the duke of Mantua, a relative, had her manage his household and the entire duchy during an absence. During her teens she enrolled in the third order of St. Dominic but did not make profession until thirty-five years later—shortly before her death.

1697

St. Gregory Barbarigo, bishop of Bergamo, cardinal, and finally bishop of Padua. He is remembered for his alms, support of seminary education, and generous help to leaders of the Orthodox Church. He set up a printing press with Greek, Hebrew, Syriac, Persian, and Slavonic type to prepare pamphlets for Christians under Moslem rule.

Pope John XXIII had him as a special model during seminary days and in 1960 granted him "equivalent canonization" by dispensing from the usual requirement of additional miracles beyond those already adduced in the process of beatification.

JUNE 19

1027

ST. ROMUALD, who as founder of Camaldoli initiated a vi-able form of eremetical life in the Western Church. He belonged to Ravenna's ducal family and on seeing his father duel and kill a man over some property entered the abbey of Sant' Apollinare-in-Classe at Ravenna. He was twenty. After only three years he obtained permission for a more solitary life and before long was embarked on his career of wandering hermit-reformer, founding numerous hermitages and monasteries throughout Italy.

Everywhere he urged contemplative prayer, using the triple formula of solitude, silence, and fasting. He gave much sound advice, composed a **Commentary on the Psalms,** foretold the future, and at one point, eager for preaching and martyrdom, obtained the pope's permission to proclaim the Gospel on the Hungarian mission.

He did not organize a congregation and only at the end of his life—though he actually died elsewhere—did he establish the hermitage of Camaldoli at the 3600 ft. level in the mountains of Tuscany overlooking Arezzo. Connected with the hermits and forming one family with them was a cenobitic monastery two miles away and a thousand feet lower. This community provided the organizational substructure for the hermitage by training novices, caring for the sick, the aged, the guests, and by handling financial and legal affairs. Profession was made according to the Rule of St. Benedict, and all were under the authority of one abbot. After Romuald's death the Camaldolese structure was codified and spread to many other houses.

Unknown date.

Sts. Gervase and **Protase,** venerated as Milan's first martyrs. St. Ambrose discovered their relics in the cemetery church of Sts. Nabor and Felix.

1341 [*O.S.M.*]

St. Juliana Falconieri, a Florentine, venerated by the Servite Third Order of nuns as foundress.

JUNE 20

1679

The martyrdom at London of five Jesuit priests; headed by **Bl. Thomas Whitebread,** the provincial; and **Bl. William Harcourt,** superior of the London district. They were accused by the professional perjurer, Titus Oates, as leading conspirators in the plot of the pope and the Jesuits to assassinate Charles II, put his brother—the future James II—on the throne, burn London, invade the land with foreign troops, and put the Protestants to the sword. The scare over the plot was engineered for political reasons but not by King Charles II—for he was sympathetic to the Catholic cause and would enter the church on his deathbed—but by ambitious party leaders, especially the Earl of Shaftesbury.

Shaftesbury took advantage of the anti-Jesuit animus of an influential group of Catholics who, like the Gallicans of France, were working for a type of national Catholic church and saw the Jesuits with their exemption and special vow of obedience to the pope as a great obstacle. For several decades they had been promoting expulsion of the Society from England. The leader of this faction during the twenty years previous to the Titus Oates Plot was Dr. John Sergeant, a priest and England's leading Catholic controversialist.

After the execution of five Jesuit priests when the mass hysteria in London was beginning to subside and people were saying the plot was a hoax, the much respected Dr. Sergeant and another priest gave testimony which helped propagate the opinion that it was a Jesuit maxim that kings could be killed. By means of the testimony of these priests, politicians interested in preventing the accession of James II, a Catholic, were able to rekindle the nation's fanaticism. Penal laws were again strictly enforced throughout the land, and many died without any reference to the plot.

In the three years 1678-1681, at least thirty-five were executed—eight of them Jesuits—and others died in prison. Thus

England's 150 years of martyrdom came to an end with St. Oliver Plunkett, Archbishop of Armagh, the last victim, executed July 11, 1681, charged with conspiring to bring in French and Irish troops for the Catholic rebellion.

JUNE 21

1591

ST. ALOYSIUS GONZAGA, Jesuit seminarian, patron of young men. His father had him train with miniature guns and march as a very small boy at the head of a platoon in military parade, but his mother's influence proved more decisive; and already at the age of nine, Aloysius had committed himself to a serious program of mortification. With some of the hottest blood of Europe coursing through his veins he became convinced that he was a twisted piece of iron that had to be twisted straight. With extraordinary toughness of character he held to his ideals and realized his vocation despite the impassioned appeals of a disconsolate father and a choice of brilliant civil or church careers.

At the age of seventeen he finally succeeded in renouncing his birthright. He transferred the marquisate of Castiglione in Lombardy to his nearest brother and entered the Society of Jesus. His hope was to work as a priest on the foreign missions. But the plague of 1591 struck him down after he had spent himself caring for the sick in Rome.

When St. Robert Bellarmine, his confessor, assured him it was possible for a person to go straight to heaven at the moment of death without any purgatory, Aloysius fell into an ecstasy in which he learned he would die on the octave of Corpus Christi. He recited the **Te Deum** in gratitude. Bellarmine was of the opinion that in his twenty-three years Aloysius had never committed a mortal sin.

A deathbed incident gives an insight into his spirit and motivation: he kept brushing off his headcap and finally explained to his attendants as he looked on the crucifix, "He didn't have one on when he died." The saint's role as a model of purity is a recognition of his spirit of mortification and the guard he kept over his senses in a lust-ridden court environment.

JUNE 22

431

ST. PAULINUS, bishop of Nola near Naples, poet, zealous pastor, friend of Sts. Augustine and Jerome. Three days before he died, two visiting bishops standing at his bedside celebrated the divine Mysteries with him. Of his many writings only thirty-two poems, some letters, and a few fragments remain.

1535

STS. JOHN FISHER, bishop of Rochester, and **THOMAS MORE,** chancellor of England, beheaded for the Catholic faith under Henry VIII. While little is known about **St. Alban,** England's first martyr, whose feast is also celebrated today, the lives of these glorious sixteenth century martyrs are an integral part of English history. It is hard to read the story of their resistance to injustice without feeling enthusiasm for personal integrity and quiet, humble strength of character. "Not that I condemn other men's conscience," Fisher said, "their conscience may save them, and mine must save me."

John Fisher, a merchant's son, became identified with Cambridge University. He went there at fourteen and without any exertion beyond scholarhip, priestly zeal, and devotion to duty, was chancellor at thirty-five. He was appointed bishop of Rochester the same year. At forty-eight he began the study of Greek, and Hebrew at fifty-one; and he had these subjects re-introduced at Cambridge. With his personal collection he also laid the foundation of the university library.

He wrote the first refutation of Lutheranism, was Catherine

of Aragon's strongest support, and ended his court defense of the validity of her marriage by recalling that John the Baptist had lost his life for a like cause. Both he and Thomas More refused the oath of succession and the Act of Supremacy. He was named cardinal a month before his death.

At 5:00 in the morning of June 22, he received word that he would die that day. He took two more hours of sound sleep. For comfort he carried the New Testament with him to the scaffold. He was sixty-six.

Thomas More was beheaded two weeks later, July 6. He was fifty-seven, twice-married, the father of four, one of the most balanced and attractive public figures in history. Not only was he a saint, an incomparable lawyer, parliamentarian, and minister of state, but also a complete human being as husband, father and friend. A barrister's son, he spent two years at Oxford, was admitted to the bar at twenty-three and to parliament at twenty-fix. He married at twenty-seven.

While studying law he lived with the London Carthusians during four years, deliberating over his vocation. He left the charterhouse with the life-long habits of rising at 2:00 a.m. and studying until 7:00, of saying the little office and hearing mass daily, of taking the discipline on Fridays and wearing a hair shirt. He wrote much, including the **Utopia;** and while in prison produced his best spiritual book, **The Dialogue of Comfort against Tribulation.** Few episodes can be more inspiring than the court trial at which he was condemned. "I die," he said at the scaffold, "the king's good servant, but God's first."

JUNE 23

679

St. Etheldreda or **Audrey,** queen of Northumbria, foundress and abbess of Ely, one of the most popular Anglo-Saxon saints both because of the miracles at the shrine where her body lay incorrupt and because, though twice married for the sake of family connections, she lived in continence and became almost a symbol of the appeal and validity of the monastic way of life. King Anna of the East Angles was her father; saints Sexburga, Ethelburga, and Withburga were her sisters.

1213

Bl. Mary of Oignies in Belgium, mystic, who persuaded her husband to live in perpetual continence and to turn their home into a hospital for lepers. Her friend Cardinal James de Vitry, an objective reporter, wrote of her: "For a long time she could not look at a crucifix or speak of the Passion or even hear others speak of it, without becoming faint."

1860   [*S.D.B., F.M.A.*]

St. Joseph Cafasso, secular priest who taught moral theology at the Institute of St. Francis in Turin and then became its director. There some sixty young priests would receive practical initiation into the ministry. He trained St. John Bosco, a priest from his own home town and only four years younger than himself, was his spiritual director, and persuaded him to devote himself to the training of boys.

Joseph Cafasso considered worldiness the priest's worst enemy. He was small and somewhat deformed in body, but of kindly, serene, and gay countenance, and, says St. John Bosco, possessed undisturbed tranquility. He would give priests this advice about confession: "Our Lord wants us to be loving and full of mercy, to be fatherly towards all who come to us without reference to who they are or what they have done. If we repel anyone, if any soul is lost through our fault, we shall be held to account."

His work with prisoners caught the imagination of Turin, for he accompanied sixty criminals to execution and none died impenitent. Though he called them his "hanged saints" and asked them to pray for him, he held that the best way to prepare for a happy death was an upright life, detachment from the world, and love of Christ crucified.

JUNE 24

THE BIRTH OF ST. JOHN THE BAPTIST, Precursor of our Lord. "John" means "the graciousness of God," and the Canticle of Zechariah traditionally used at the church's morning prayer expresses God's graciousness in keeping his promises by sending this child to announce the rising Sun come to visit us from on high (Lk 1:78). As the last of the Old Testament prophets, John appeared in the desert of Judah dressed, like Elijah, in camel's hair, alerting the nation that the Messiah had arrived. He urged everyone to penitence and to undergo a ceremonial washing in preparation for the Messiah's washing, the baptism in the Spirit and fire (Mt 3:1-12).

The scene of John's activity on the Jordan was near to the flourishing Qumran community. During his ministrations their buildings would often have been in view. He himself was not a member of a community but a solitary herald. Though he had disciples, it was not his purpose to form them into a community but to lead them to Christ. "He must become more and more," he told them; "I must become less and less" (Jn 3:30). St. Augustine explains how appropriate it is that at this feast the days begin to grow shorter while six months later, at the birth of Christ, they increase once again.

483

Sts. Felix and **Cyprian,** bishops, and many other martyrs, victims of the cruelty of the Arian Huneric, king of the Vandals, who drove Catholics into the Sahara Desert by the hundreds; where they perished of exhaustion, ill usage, and thirst.

JUNE 25 *

8th cent.
St. Adalbert, a Benedictine of English origin, companion of

---

*O. Cart. see June 26 for St. Anthelm.

St. Willibrord on the Frisian missions. The center of his activity was Egmond, where the Dutch abbey of St. Adalbert stands today.

1142

St. William of Vercelli, founder in southern Italy of several monasteries devoted to asceticism, solitude, and preaching. His abbey of Monte-Vergine has endured to the present day. At its peak influence in the late Middle Ages it was the center of ninety Benedictine houses.

1160

Bl. John of Spain, founder of the charterhouse of Reposoir near Lake Geneva. He compiled constitutions for the Carthusian nuns.

1471

Bl. John Soreth, a forerunner of St. Teresa of Avila. For twenty years prior general of the Carmelites, he became so tanned and weathered during his constant trips throughout Europe that he was known to the common people as "the black one." By incorporating several groups of Dutch Beguines, he founded the Carmelite nuns and gave them the unrelaxed rule along with special bylaws. He also promulgated new constitutions for the friars, stressed the life of prayer, and encouraged the foundation of houses of stricter observance to restore religious life after the ravages of the Black Death.

JUNE 26

925

St. Pelagius or **Pelayo,** boy martyr still famous throughout Spain. Held as hostage at Cordova, he refused to save his life by accepting Mohammed. Hroswitha, abbess of Gandersheim in Germany, wrote a long Latin poem about him later in the same century.

1178

St. **Anthelm,** first Carthusian minister general, bishop of Belley, near Lyons. A frivolous but generous priest, he gained a sense of his true vocation through contact with the Carthusians; and at thirty-three he was chosen prior of the Grande Chartreuse. He repaired buildings damaged by an avalanche, called a general chapter, and brought the various charterhouses under the central authority of his monastery. When the opportunity came he resigned from office but soon was prior at Portes, where the monks had accumulated too many stores: so he made free distribution to the needy.

He helped rally the religious in France, Spain, and even England to support Pope Alexander III against the emperor's antipope. Ordered to accept the bishopric of Belley, where celibacy was a big issue, he gave a two-year warning and then deprived the married clergy of their appointments. Such was his prestige that the pope named him legate to England in the Thomas Becket affair, though Anthelm was unable to go. The fever of which he died came on as he was distributing food during a famine. He had so endeared himself to his people that the town of Belley was for a time called Anthelmopolis.

1794 [*C.M.*]

Bl. **Madeleine Fontaine** and **three companions,** Sisters of Charity of St. Vincent de Paul, martyred at Cambrai during the French Revolution. Condemned as "pious counter-revolutionaries," they approached the guillotine singing the **Ave Maris Stella.**

JUNE 27

444

ST. **CYRIL,** patriarch of Alexandria; doctor; vehement champion of Mary's title "Mother of God"; leading theologian and president at the Council of Ephesus, where Nestorius, patriarch of Constantinople, was condemned for teaching that the divinity and humanity were so separate in Christ that Mary should be called "Christ-bearer" only. The council—a tangle of papal, imperial, and patriarchal authorities—was marred by Cyril's deposing Nestorius in the very first session before the arrival of the patriarch of Antioch who was the emperor's appointee as president of the council. Pope Celestine I had, however, already passed judgment on the controversy and commissioned Cyril to remove Nestorius from his see if he did not recant.

Ephesus marks a stage toward the more complete formulations of the Council of Chalcedon twenty years later, in which the orthodox dogma of one Person in two natures was clearly taught. It is unfortunate that the earlier, still fluid terminology permitted Cyril to speak of one **physis** (nature) in Christ, a circumstance which agitators and heretics later exploited to lead Egypt and other churches into the one-nature position. Referring to this confusion over the word "nature," Pope Paul VI, speaking to the Armenian Catholicos Vasken I during a visit to Rome in 1970 asked, "Has not the time come to clear up once and for all such misunderstandings inherited from the past . . . ?"

1232

Bl. Benvenuto of Gubbio, an unlettered soldier St. Francis accepted among the friars. At his own request he was allowed to care for lepers, and he always remained cheerful and courteous as he tended the most repulsive cases for the love of Christ.

1345   [O.S.M.]

Bl. Thomas Corsini, miracle-working Servite brother at Orvieto, Italy.

JUNE 28

ca. 202

ST. IRENAEUS, bishop of Lyons, the most important theologian of the second century. Through him, as Eusebius put it a century later, "The sound and orthodox faith of the apostolic tradition has come to us in writing." He was a disciple of St. Polycarp in Asia Minor and then went to France as a missionary, thus becoming a witness for both East and West. He learned to speak Celtic but wrote in Greek. As a delegate of the church of Lyons he made at least one stay in Rome and, on a later occasion, interceded with the pope on behalf of the Christians of Asia Minor.

His great work **Adversus haereses** — preserved only in Latin — put an end to gnosticism as a force in the Church. Appealing to tradition against the gnostics, he wrote a famous passage about Rome, though its proper translation is debatable in the absence of the original Greek. "As it would take too long," he said, "to transcribe here the succession of bishops of all the churches, we will consider the greatest and most ancient, known by all, founded and established at Rome by the two very glorious apostles Peter and Paul. . . . With this church, because of its more important position the entire Church — that is the faithful everywhere — must agree, in which the tradition which has come from the apostles has always been preserved in every place" (**Adversus haereses** 3:3,3). The feast of St. Irenaeus falls the day before that of Sts. Peter and Paul.

1847

St. Vincentia Gerosa, co-foundress with St. Bartholomea Capitanio of the Sisters of Charity of Lovere, near Brescia, an institute closely modeled on the Sisters of Charity of St. Vincent de Paul. While Bartholomea's special vocation was teaching, hers was tending the sick. She used to say, "A person who does not know the Crucified One knows nothing. But to know Him is to know everything." Their congregation has enjoyed remarkable growth and is spread throughout the world.

JUNE 29

ca. 67

STS. PETER and **PAUL,** apostles. The earliest evidence shows that Rome commemorated her two martyr-apostles in a joint feast on June 29th. Each received an extensive commission from Christ, and the ancient Church saw Rome as the repository of their ministry as well as of their relics. About no other apostles is there so much New Testament information.

St. Peter (St. **"Rock"** in English) always heads the list of the twelve and is their spokesman on the most solemn occasions. The Church throughout the centuries venerated him as God's fisherman, bearer of the primacy, vicar of Christ, foundation and bond of the church, model of repentant sinners, protector and universal patron.

St. Paul, the incomparable missionary and author of the earliest New Testament writings, has exerted an unsurpassed influence on Christianity, particularly in the transition from Judaism to Christianity and in spelling out the personal, communal, and cosmic dimensions of the mystery of Christ. His favorite expression "In Christ," which occurs some fifty times, sums up his theology and apostolate. While becoming all things to all men, he did not adulterate the Gospel but could in all confidence and warmth of personal love urge his converts, "Take me for your model, as I take Christ" (1 Cor 11:1).

JUNE 30 *

64

THE PROTOMARTYRS OF ROME. The feast of Sts. Peter and Paul is followed by a joint feast of Rome's first martyrs. In July, 64 A.D., a fire broke out near the great circus, raged for six days and seven nights, and then blazed up afresh for three more

---

*Franciscans III O. see July 1 for Bl. Raymond Lull.

days, till two-thirds of Rome lay in smoldering ruins. Nero's easy mood over the fire helped spread the rumor that it was his doing. Tacitus tells how the emperor then laid the blame on the Christians and had them rounded up and executed in an orgy of cruelty at a public festival held at night in his gardens. Some, smeared with pitch, served as torches to provide illumination.

1095

St. Ladislaus, king of Hungary, second only to St. Stephen I in the civil and ecclesiastical history of the nation. He established the diocese of Zagreb.

1139

St. Otto, chancellor to Emperor Henry IV and his appointee as bishop of Bamberg in the thick of the investiture struggle. Otto delayed until he was able to receive episcopal ordination from the pope himself. He was so upright that both emperor and pope trusted him; and under Henry V the Concordat of Worms was concluded through his mediation. Despite political preoccupations he took personal care of his diocese, made two highly successful missionary expeditions into what is now northwest Poland, and founded more than twenty monasteries.

1646

Bl. Philip Powell, Benedictine martyred under Charles I. He studied law in London under the future monk and spiritual author, Augustine Baker. When the jailer brought news of the day of execution, Father Philip asked for a glass of sack in which to drink his health. On the scaffold he said it was the happiest day of his life and that he suffered for no other reason than being a priest and a monk.

JULY 1

ca. 446

St. Shenute, or **Shenoudi,** after St. Pachomius the most power-ful organizer of Egyptian monasticism, and the only prominent early writer in the Coptic language. He is credited with intro-ducing public religious vows.

551

St. Gall, bishop of Clermont, whose meekness under insult completely disarmed his opponents. He took particular care in training his nephew, St. Gregory of Tours.

1316

Bl. Raymond Lull, mystic; tireless traveler and prolific writer; a native of Majorca whose missionary zeal made him one of the most determined proponents of Islamic Studies in the Middle Ages. At thirty he was converted to a life of total seriousness through a vision—five times repeated—of Christ hanging on the cross.

After providing for his wife and children, he directed his rest-

less talents and enthusiasms to the conversion of the Moors. He
did not enter the priesthood. The Franciscans venerate him as
a member of their third order. He immersed himself in the language and thought of the Moors, tried to interest important
people in establishing centers of Moslem learning, and for a
time taught Arabic metaphysics at the University of Paris.

His search for a common ground showed that Christians,
Jews, and Moslems could agree on the notion of God and on a
few of His most basic attributes. These common notions he
worked into an ingenius system that became known as Lull's
Art. Its purpose was to show the interconnection and unity of
all the sciences and arts, and ultimately to convince unbelievers
of the truth of the Blessed Trinity and the Incarnation. He went
to preach the Gospel in Tunisia, was twice deported, and—according to one account—died a martyr on his third attempt.

JULY 2*

862

St. Swithun, bishop of Winchester, spiritual adviser to King
Ethelwulf, remembered for his charity and humility. At his
own request he was buried in the churchyard where his grave
would be exposed to rain and trodden underfoot by those who
passed by.

1616   [S.J.]

St. Bernardino Realino, Jesuit, outstanding director of souls.
He graduated in law at Bologna but left the town after a violent argument in which he wounded his opponent. He served
as mayor in several towns, showing real ability in handling men
and business affairs, but at the age of thirty-four became a
Jesuit. He is now identified with Lecce in Apulia, where he
spent forty-two years as a priest. He founded its college and

*S. J. St. Francis Regis is also celebrated today (see June 16).

built a church; but spiritual guidance, particularly in the confessional, soon became his chief occupation. The supernatural in the form of cures, visions, and prophecies marked his old age; and for two and-a-half centuries after his death, phials of his blood were seen to liquify.

The Society of Jesus honors several other members along with St. Bernardino. Included are **Bl. Julian Maunoir** (died January 28, 1683), whose dramatic missions during forty-three years renewed the faith throughout Brittany; and **St. Francis Jerome** (died May 11, 1716), who is still venerated as an apostle of Naples. Bl. Julian experienced a burning thirst for souls at Communion during his ordination retreat and heard our Lord say, "I labored, I wept, I suffered, I died for them." Julian would do the same. St. Francis Jerome as a young priest was attracted by the possibility of making a new attempt to enter Japan and reopen that mission, but his superior told him to take the kingdom of Naples as his Japan. Not satisfied with the crowds that thronged his pulpit and confessional, he ranged through prisons, galleys, and hospitals, preached in the streets and sought sinners out in their own haunts. He was popularly credited with reconciling 400 hardened sinners annually.

JULY 3

ST. THOMAS, apostle, whose belief accentuates the reality of the bodily resurrection and serves as an encouragement to faith—"Blessed are they who have not seen and have believed." (Jn 20:29). There is a very ancient tradition that St. Thomas preached the Gospel in southern India.

ca. 400
    St. Heliodorus, intimate friend of St. Jerome. In a letter **Ad**

Heliodorum, treasured by early ascetics as a manifesto of their principles, St. Jerome rebukes this disciple for not coming along into the desert of Chalcis. Later, when Heliodorus was bishop of Altinum in Aquileia, Jerome was able to refer to him as a model pastor and thanked him for money and supplies for translating the Bible.

458

St. Anatolius, patriarch of Constantinople during the Council of Chalcedon when his see took its most decisive steps to establish itself as the leading bishopric of the East. Pope St. Leo I, while commending Anatolius for his zeal in opposing the "One-nature heresy," reminded him that "a Catholic, especially if he be a priest of the Lord, should avoid the corruption of ambition just as he avoids the taint of error." The pope was referring to measures passed in the fifteenth session of the Council of Chalcedon whereby Constantinople was accorded the position of honor immediately after Rome and received extensive patriarchal territory and jurisdiction as well as the right of accepting appeals from anywhere in the orient. The papal legates did not assist at that session and Pope Leo refused to sanction the legislation. Canon 3 of the Council of Constantinople seventy-five years earlier had given Constantinople the first place of honor after Rome; but the popes had taken no cognizance of the provision, continuing to follow the Council of Nicea, which recognized Alexandria as the second ranking see.

JULY 4

1336

ST. ELIZABETH (or Isabella) OF PORTUGAL, daughter of King Peter III of Aragon, wife of King Denis of Portugal, and named after her great-aunt, St. Elizabeth of Hungary. A peacemaker, she is credited with stopping or adverting at least five armed conflicts among her immediate relatives on the thrones of Portugal and Spain—twice it was her son Alfonso rebelling against his father. She raised her husband's illegitimate children, nursed him devotedly in his last illness, and brought him to a holy death. Then as a Franciscan tertiary she settled near the Poor Clare monastery she had established in Coimbra. But she died at Estremoz, Portugal, where she arrived in the wake of her son's army on her final mission of peace. Though she succeeded in reconciling him and her nephew, the king of Castile, the journey and summer heat proved too much for her feeble body.

ca. 740

St. Andrew of Crete, archbishop of Gortyna in Crete, one of the principal hymnographers of the oriental church. He inaugurated a type of penitential hymn or Great Canon still in use. He is also remembered for his sermons.

973

St. Ulric, bishop of Augsburg, apparently the first person solemnly canonized by a pope. The bull issued by John XV is dated 993. He made a point of visiting a hospital every afternoon and daily washed the feet of twelve of the poor and gave them alms.

1091

Bl. William of Hirsau, the outstanding promoter of monasticism in Germany during the eleventh century. As abbot of the recently restored Hirsau in Wurtemburg he adopted the Cluniac observances—though without Cluny's centralization of authority—and composed a set of **Customs** which spread to many monasteries in northern Europe. He was one of Pope Gregory VII's chief supporters against Emperor Henry IV.

The emperor sent Bishop Werner of Strassburg to destroy Hirsau, but before he could fulfil his mission death overtook him—a sudden event that deeply impressed the people as an act of divine justice. On his deathbed William gave the monks this exhortation: "Continue unto death in unshakeable fidelity to the unity of the Church and in submission to the Apostolic See."

1315 [*O.S.M.*]

Bl. Ubald Adimari, Florentine Ghibelline leader notorious for his dissolute life. Converted by St. Philip Benizi, he became a Servite and spent the remainder of his life on Monte Senario, a model of penitence.

JULY 5

1539

ST. ANTHONY ZACCARIA, founder in 1530 of the Clerks Regular of St. Paul, also called Barnabites after the church of St. Barnabas in Milan that served as headquarters. Their purpose was to revive divine worship and Christian life by faithful ministry of the sacraments and frequent preaching. They strove to proclaim the Gospel with special reference to the epistles of St. Paul. Under the direction of St. Anthony, Countess Louisa Torelli founded the Angelicals of St. Paul, a feminine congregation devoted to the rescue of girls. Anthony Zaccaria began as a doctor but soon felt the call to heal souls as well. He died at thirty-six. Today the Barnabites are primarily engaged in education.

ca. 1000

St. Athanasius, the first to organize monasticism on Mt. Athos. Though Athos had for generations been a favorite resort for hermits, it still had no real monasteries until the emperor made Athanasius superior of the solitaries in the area. There was a good deal of resentment among the hermits when in 961 he began to build his monastery and church and lay out a harbor. He himself had no desire to govern others, having left an earlier monastery in Asia Minor to avoid becoming abbot.

He adopted the laura system, thus leaving a good measure of solitude; and a number of monasteries founded in his lifetime have continued to exist until today, including his first, now called St. Athanasius or simply Laura, situated on the east side of the 6700 ft. mountain. In all he ruled over fifty-eight monasteries. He was killed along with five of his monks when the keystone of the vault of the church on which they were working fell.

For the past thousand years the Holy Mountain has been the center of Greek monasticism. In 1927 this thirty-five mile peninsula, comprising twenty voting monasteries, was organized into a self-governing department of Greece. Before the Russian revolution there were 9,000 monks in residence, the majority from Russia; now there are between one and two thousand.

JULY 6

1902

ST. MARY GORETTI, martyred for purity when just under the age of twelve, five weeks after her first Communion. The assault took place one afternoon in her home at Ferriere di Conca near Nettuno, thirty-one miles from Rome. A neighboring peasant boy of eighteen, Alessandro Serenelli, enraged at her resistance, stabbed her several times. "No," she said, "God does not wish it! It is a sin. You would go to hell for it", adding that she would rather die than commit such a sin. Taken to the hospital, she lived another twenty-four hours. Maria not only forgave Alessandro before she died but also remembered him in heaven. He was sentenced to thirty years of hard labor, and for a long time remained surly, brutal, and unrepentant. Then a sudden change came over him, which he attributed to a dream or vision in which Mary gathered some flowers and offered them to him. On his release after twenty-seven years, he remarked that "some crimes can never be fully paid for." His first act was to visit Mary's mother to ask her forgiveness. He spent his last years as a Franciscan tertiary at a Capuchin house at Macerata, and died in 1970.

Mary's mother was present at the canonization in 1950. The church has given St. Mary Goretti a place in the universal calendar as a modern St. Agnes.

1922

Bl. Maria Teresa Ledóchowska, a foundress who devoted her exceptional talents to the evangelization of Africa and the abolition of slavery, especially through the apostolate of the press, and who was referred to as 'Mother' by a whole generation of missionaries and their African congregations.

At 26, urged by Cardinal Lavigerie, of Algiers and Carthage, who was mounting an all-out attack on slavery, she began the **Echo of Africa,** a magazine published in many languages. In 1894 at 31, she founded the Missionary Sisters of St. Peter Claver under the jurisdiction of the Congregation for the Propagation of the Faith of which her uncle, Cardinal Ledóchowski, was prefect. She traveled throughout Europe giving talks, set up printing establishments, wrote articles and countless letters to help the missions, and directed her institute with prudence and much love until her premature death in Rome at 59.

Maria Teresa came of a remarkable family. She had a Polish father, a Swiss mother, Austrian citizenship, and the title of Countess. Her cardinal uncle while Archbishop of Gnesen-Posen was the champion of Polish resistance to the Kulturkampf. Her brother Wladimir Ledóchowski was Jesuit General from 1915 to 1942 and her sister Ursula founded the Sisters of the Sacred Heart of Jesus in the Death Agony.

JULY 7

705

St. Hedda, monk of Whitby, bishop of Winchester, famous

BLESSED MARIA TERESA LEDOCHOWSKA

for his miracles. The men of Essex used to take dust from his tomb and stir it in water, making a healing drink for man and beast. Within twenty-five years of the saint's death Bede was able to report that a large pit had been dug out in this way.

ca. 787

St. Willibald, Benedictine, relative of St. Boniface, who appointed him the first bishop of Eichstaett. His monastic life began at five. At twenty he left England on a pilgrimage with his father and brother. His father died at Lucca and his brother stopped at Rome; but Willibald continued on, the first recorded English pilgrim to the Holy Land. The memories of his ten-year journey produced the earliest travel book by an Anglo-Saxon. He eventually came to St. Benedict's shrine at Monte Cassino where, after a break of 150 years, community life had just been restored by Abbot Petronax. Drawing on his experience of English monasticism Willibald helped instruct the monks on how things were done in a large, flourishing monastery. Within a generation Monte Cassino was a model abbey. Willibald stayed only ten years, for the pope sent him to Germany to help St. Boniface. There he labored for another half century. He founded a double monastery at Heidenheim, where his brother St. Winebald ruled over the monks and his sister, St. Walburga, over the nuns.

1591

Bl. Roger Dickenson, hanged at Winchester for being a priest; and **Bl. Ralph Milner,** executed for assisting him. Milner, a convert, was a farmer and the father of eight. He could have saved his life by making a visit to the local parish church. Seven women were also sentenced to death for allowing Bl. Roger to celebrate mass in their houses, but they were reprieved at once. They then asked to be allowed to die with their pastor but were only returned to prison.

JULY 8

303

St. Procopius, outstanding ascetic, the first martyr in Palestine under Diocletian. When asked to offer sacrifice to the emperor he answered in the words of Homer, "It is not good to have several masters; let there be one chief, one king."

1153   [*O. Cist., O.C.S.O.*]

Bl. Eugene III, the first Cistercian pope. He gave up an important position in the diocese of Pisa to enter St. Bernard's community at Clairvaux. Back in Italy at the head of a colony of monks he repeopled the ancient abbey of St. Anastasius at Tre Fontane, Rome, and was still its abbot when the cardinals chose him pope. St. Bernard wrote the ascetical treatise **De Consideratione** for his benefit and reminded him that in former days the apostles "let down their nets for a draught, not of silver and gold, but of souls." Pope Eugene's sanctity gave him an ascendancy over men and an equanimity in the most varied international and domestic affairs. He issued three bulls making special provisions for lepers.

1900   [*Franciscans*]

Bl. Gregory Grassi, vicar apostolic in China, and twenty-eight companions attached to the Franciscan missions in Shansi and Honan, beatified in 1946. Of an estimated 30,000 Catholics killed in the Boxer Rebellion some 3,000 have been put forward for canonization. Today's martyrs include six Franciscan friars, three of them bishops; eleven laymen, mostly Chinese; five Chinese seminarians; seven European sisters, Franciscan Missionaries of Mary. The sisters were between the age of twenty-five and thirty-five. When Bishop Grassi urged the nuns to disguise themselves and escape, they showed no particular eagerness. "Do not stop us from dying with you," they said.

"If we are not brave enough, God will give us the strength."
When their turn came they knelt down and sang the **Te Deum.**

JULY 9

1572 *[Franciscans, O.P., O. Praem.]*

The Martyrs of Gorkum, seventeen priests and two brothers
canonized in 1867. Illegally taken prisoners when the town of
Gorkum, in Holland, surrendered to Calvinist raiders, they
were first given the option of saving their lives by denying
the Real Presence and the primacy of the pope and then were
hanged in a deserted monastery near Briel. One priest of good
observance defected, while two others whose lives had been
unedifying remained steadfast in the faith. The group includes
the Franciscan guardian, **St. Nicholas Pieck,** and ten of his
friars, three secular priests, two Premonstratensians, an Augustinian canon, and a Dominican. A Franciscan priest, the
Dane **St. Willalde,** was ninety years old.

1794 *[O.S.U.]*

During the French Revolution, thirty-two nuns of four different orders martyred at Orange in southeastern France and
beatified in 1925. They were mostly Ursulines (sixteen) and
Perpetual Adorers of the Blessed Sacrament (thirteen) from Bol-
lène, who refused the republican oath of liberty and equality.
During their nine months in prison they organized into a community with a superior, had several hours of religious exercises a day beginning at 7:00 in the morning, and exemplified
the apostolate of the beatitudes within the prison. They were
finally executed singly or in small groups during the space
of three weeks in July, 1794, on the charge of trying to destroy
the republic through fanaticism and superstition. The Benedictine, **Bl. Mary Rose Deloye,** was the first.

At each day's guillotining the dwindling survivors would recite the prayers for the dying and then sing the **Te Deum**. **Bl. Pelagia Bès,** a Perpetual Adoration sister, on hearing her sentence passed around a box of sweets which she said "are for my wedding." The group also included two Cistercian nuns.

JULY 10

1073 and 1074

Sts. Anthony and **Theodosius,** abbots of the Caves, Russia's most famous monastery. Anthony, its founder, a hermit type, after a stay at Mt. Athos, tried various Russian monasteries and then settled in a cave on the wooded cliff at Kiev beside the Dnieper. Others joined him and dug small caves for themselves as well as larger ones for community functions. Anthony moved on and founded another monastery near Chernigov but returned to the Caves, where he died at ninety-three.

In the meantime Theodosius had become abbot. Though he came of a wealthy family he used to dress like the serfs and worked with them in the fields. He learned baking so that he could make altar breads and then as a young man joined the monks at the Caves. He was abbot forty-two years and is considered the father of the Russian style of cenobitic monasticism, with its particular blend of action and contemplation. He enlarged the buildings and adopted the rule of St. Theodore the Studite.

Along with prayer and mortification he stressed corporal and spiritual works of mercy. He built a hospital and a hospice— in the nineteenth century the abbey could accommodate 20,000 pilgrims—sent a cartload of food to prisons on Saturdays, rebuked the mighty, directed consciences, took his share of manual labor, for two years fed and nursed an invalid monk, and delivered homilies that became a part of Russia's spiritual heritage.

Best remembered among his many sayings is the question he put when listening to the minstrels in the hall of the ruler of Kiev. "Sir," he said, "will it sound the same in the life to come?" Thirty-four years after his death he was canonized by the bishops of the Kiev province, thus becoming Russia's second saint.

1727 [*Franciscans*]

St. Veronica Giuliani, Capuchin abbess at Citta di Castello, Italy, novice-mistress for thirty-four years, a mystic who also had the stigmata.

1860

Bl. Emmanuel Ruiz, Bl. Francis Masabki and **nine companions,** martyrs at Damascus, selected for beatification from several thousand Christians put to death in Lebanon and Syria by Moslem bands who were outraged over the religious toleration clause the Turkish government accepted at the Congress of Paris after the Crimean War.

Father Ruiz was slain in church where he had gone to consume the Blessed Sacrament. As his blood was dripping over the altar some of his assailants ran to the bells and pulled the ropes, yelling, "Come! Mass has begun, the priest is waiting!" He and seven of his companions were Franciscans, mostly from Spain, while Francis Masabki and his two younger brothers were Maronite laymen.

JULY 11

ca. 547

St. Benedict, abbot, the great legislator of Western monasticism, patron of Europe along with Sts. Cyril and Methodius. Scripture aside, probably no other book has had such a deep influence on the Latin church as the **Rule** of St. Benedict. Pope Pius XII called him the "Father of Europe" and in the light of history challenged anyone to deny Benedict this title.

When he was about twenty—approximately the year 500— Benedict broke off his studies at Rome to pursue religious ideals. He lived first in a small village and then for three years as hermit-monk in a cliff cave at Subiaco, convinced that the true meaning of life was to be found in the search for God rather than in student revelry or worldly success. Such divine blessing crowned his search that when Gregory the Great, fifty years after Benedict's death, set about recounting in the **Dialogues** the marvellous things he had heard about local saints, he devoted the entire second book to Benedict of Nursia, the outstanding miracle-worker of the century and a true father of the poor.

Disciples were attracted to the young hermit and leading Roman families sent him their sons for training. Soon he had twelve small communities. Then to avoid the jealousy of a local priest, he handed the direction of the colony over to others and began a new monastery at Monte Cassino. At the same time he abandoned the cluster idea in favor of a single closely knit monastic family according to a rule which he was now able to finalize.

About one tenth of this **Rule** is Sacred Scripture, with the book of **Psalms**—which the monks were required to memorize as the staple of community prayer—quoted almost as frequently as all the other Scriptures combined. He draws heavily on earlier monastic authors, touching up and weaving together, but never quoting them by name. Only St. Basil, the father of Eastern monasticism, is mentioned. His genius for selecting and improving is probably best seen in relation to the uneven and enigmatic **Rule of the Master.**

St. Benedict's most characteristic stresses are on a very personal love of Christ and on discretion. Throughout the **Rule** he blends broad principles with concrete applications to guarantee and maximize the advantages community life can offer a well-motivated but otherwise quite ordinary Christian who is "truly seeking God." The abbot, always remembering human frailty, should order all things "in such a way that the strong have something to strive after and the weak nothing at which to take alarm."

In 1964, when Pope Paul VI declared St. Benedict patron of Europe, there were some 12,000 Benedictine monks and nearly twice that number of sisters, in addition to 13,000 Cistercians and Trappist monks and nuns, living under his **Rule**. Most monasteries also have lay Oblates of St. Benedict, resembling a third order. The **Rule** of St. Benedict has been printed in over 2,000 editions.

JULY 12

ca. 1002

St. John the Iberian, abbot, a native of Georgia on the Black Sea. With his son, St. Euthymius, and a brother-in-law he founded Iviron on Mt. Athos for his fellow Iberians. The monastery still exists; though it is now occupied by Greeks.

1073

St. John Gualbert, abbot, founder of the Vallombrosan Benedictines. He entered the abbey of St. Miniato in his native Florence but left to get away from simony and to find a greater poverty and silence. He chose Vallombrosa, a wooded valley in the hills sixteen miles from Florence. From Camaldoli, which he had visited, he borrowed the idea of having brothers to take care of external affairs and whatever manual labor would be required outside the enclosure. He was strong on silence but also on apostolic speech.

His monasteries, of which there were nine by the time of his death, were veritable fortresses in the battle against simony. He denounced the simoniac bishop of Florence and to force his deposition allowed his monk Peter—Bl. Peter Igneus, the future cardinal—to undergo trial by fire, and he mobilized his monks to campaign throughout Tuscany against the sale of church offices and the disregard of clerical celibacy. With Sts. Romuald and Peter Damian he forms a trio of prophetic semi-hermit monks who caught the popular imagination and generated in Italy the climate that made possible the Gregorian Reform.

1598   *[Franciscans]*

St. John Jones, a Welsh Franciscan sent on the English mission at his own request. Charged with treason for returning to England after being ordained overseas, he replied, "If this is a crime I must own myself guilty; for I am a priest and came over into England to gain as many souls as I could to Christ."

1679   *[Franciscans]*

St. John Wall, Franciscan, martyred August 22nd at Worcester, where he had ministered to the Catholics for twenty-two years. In prison he wrote of his trial: "I was not . . . troubled with any disturbing thoughts, for I was then of the same mind as by God's grace I ever shall be, esteeming judge and jury the best friends to me that ever I had in my life. I was so present with myself, while the judge pronounced sentence, that I am the same time offered myself to God."

JULY 13

1024

ST. HENRY II, duke of Bavaria and emperor from 1002 until 1024. He was an energetic and conscientious ruler in the days just prior to the Gregorian Reform, when the head of the empire also controlled the German church, particularly the appointment of bishops and abbots. He founded the diocese of Bamberg and restored many bishoprics. Along with his consort St.

Cunegund he was an ardent promoter of monastic life and was named patron of Benedictine lay oblates by St. Pius X. He is one of the few rulers with a place in the universal Roman calendar; Sts. Louis of France, Stephen of Hungary, and Wenceslaus of Bohemia are the others.

ca. 700

St. Mildred, first abbess of Minster-in-Thanet, one of the most popular saints in mediaeval England. In 1937, Benedictine nuns from Eichstaett, Germany, restored monastic life on Thanet, thus recalling their own Anglo-Saxon origins and repaying a debt of nearly twelve hundred years.

1435 *[Franciscan III O. Nuns]*

Bl. Angelina of Marsciano, foundress of a congregation of third order Franciscan nuns. At fifteen she was married to the Count of Civitella; but he died within two years, so she took the habit of a Franciscan tertiary and converted her castle in the Abruzzi into a home for devout and apostolic young women.

So successful was she in persuading girls in the area to choose the state of virginity that she was denounced as a sorceress and a Manichee. When only twenty she became abbess of her first enclosed convent at Foligno. She founded thirteen more before her death and insisted that the communities remain small, with never more than twelve sisters to a house.

JULY 14

1614

ST. CAMILLUS OF LELLIS, founder of the Ministers of the Sick, an order of nursing priests and brothers now known as Camillians. As a youth of seventeen this six-and-a-half foot giant set off with the Venetian army to fight the Turks, but an ulcerous leg soon disabled him. He was admitted into the hospital of

San Giacomo in Rome as a patient and servant but was dismissed for card-playing.

Gambling was his besetting sin, bringing both destitution and shame; but at twenty-five he broke the habit for good, began to practice penance and gave himself in earnest to serve the sick at San Giacomo. Twice he tried to become a Capuchin, but his leg worsened, and he had to leave. A rupture would also bother him the rest of his life, but he now recognized that his vocation was with the sick.

He became hospital superintendent and with the approval of his confessor, St. Philip Neri, entered the priesthood so that he would have more to give to the sick. He organized a group of helpers who took a vow to serve the sick, including the plague-stricken. Once a pest-ridden galley came to Naples but was not allowed into port; so the Camillians boarded the ship. Two died of the infection, to become the order's first martyrs of charity.

When Camillus could no longer walk, he would drag himself from bed to bed to see if there was anything the patients wanted. He died at sixty-four, leaving 330 professed; another 170 had already laid down their lives before him. With St. John of God he is patron of the sick, of hospitals, and of those who nurse the infirm.

1298

Bl. James of Voragine, archbishop of Genoa, author of the **Golden Legends,** the most popular lives of the saints ever written. The literary **genre** of these semi-factual accounts is that of parables on how wonderfully God and creation respond to holiness.

1610   [*Franciscans*]

St. Francis Solano, Spanish Franciscan who spent his last twenty-one years in South America. The ship that brought him from Panama ran aground off Peru, but he refused to abandon the Negro slaves who could not get into the life boats. He already had them under instruction and succeeded in baptizing many, before part of the ship broke away and some were drowned. The others he encouraged for three days until the storm abated and rescue came. He died at Lima with a reputation for miracles. "May God be glorified," was his favorite expression; and he had the habit of singing with a lute before the altar of Our Lady.

JULY 15

1274

ST. BONAVENTURE, outstanding Franciscan theologian, the minister general whose influence over the order was so profound that he is called its second founder. It was his mission to give theological expression to the Franciscan ideal and through wise constitutions and seventeen years of firm, apostolic leadership to stabilize the life-style of the exuberant young order, avoiding the extremes of both the lax and the "spiritual" parties. "The perfection of a religious man," he reminded all his friars, "is to do common things in a perfect manner. Constant fidelity in small things is great and heroic virtue."

He fostered higher studies and showed in theory and by personal example how learning fits in with gospel simplicity. "The way to God," he wrote, "consists especially in two things: in a perfect knowledge of Christ by faith, and a perfect imitation of him through sharing in his cross."

He was probably about four and still in his native Bagnorea near Viterbo when St. Francis came and—as Bonaventure relates in his **Life of St. Francis**—cured him of a mortal illness. He joined the friars in his youth, was sent to Paris for his studies, and then taught there. He helped St. Thomas defend the mendicant orders; for there was such jealously and opposition at the university that papal intervention was needed before the two could receive their doctorates, though both had already produced their monumental commentaries on the **Sen-**

tences of Peter Lombard. Bonaventure was then thirty-five. That same year he was chosen minister general, and from then until his death at fifty-three was the dominant churchman in the West.

The evening **Angelus** grew out of decisions of his general chapters directing the friars to ring their church bells at sundown, to recite the **Hail Mary** three times in honor of the Incarnation, and to spread the devotion among the people. It was partly through his intervention at Viterbo in 1271 that Bl. Gregory X was elected pope after a three-year vacancy. He refused the archbishopric of York but under obedience to Gregory X became bishop of Albano and cardinal. He had the chief role in preparing the agenda for the II Council of Lyons, was prominent in the discussions with the Greeks, and delivered the homily celebrating the union of the churches of East and West. The pope administered the anointing of the sick when Bonaventure fell ill, and the council as a body attended his funeral. He is the "Seraphic Doctor." Love of God, prayer, and contemplation were his great preoccupations. "Prayer," he wrote, "is the source and origin of every upward progress that has God for goal." And again, "Contemplation demands the greatest simplicity, and the greatest simplicity demands the greatest poverty."

JULY 16

OUR LADY OF MT. CARMEL, patronal feast of the Carmelites and the title by which their churches and monasteries are commonly dedicated to Mary. The most striking feature of the Palestine coast is the wooded promontory, called Carmel—meaning "garden" in Hebrew—rising 1800 feet above the Bay of Haifa. Known as the "sacred cape" in Egyptian geographical lists, it was an ideal place for worship and the favorite retreat for the prophet Elijah.

The Carmelites took their origin from the hermits who migrated there when the crusaders made the holy mountain safe for Christians. Carmel had an oratory dedicated to the Blessed Virgin; and as the hermits developed into a mendicant order in the thirteenth century, dedication to Mary was kept as one of their most characteristic features. This devotion they spread in subsequent centuries especially by associating lay people with themselves by means of the brown scapular of the order.

1015

St. Vladimir, grand prince of Kiev, venerated as apostle of Russia. Converted at the age of thirty-two, he gave up five wives, married the daughter of Emperor Basil II of Constantinople and promoted Christianity with humble faith and a generous, upright life. His feast is kept on July 15.

1848

St. Mary Magdalen Postel, foundress of the Sisters of the Christian Schools of Mercy. By the age of eighteen she had taken a private vow of virginity and started a school for girls. During the French Revolution she was authorized to keep the Blessed Sacrament in her home and minister Viaticum to the dying.

She was already over fifty when it became possible to begin a religious congregation in France. She expressed her apostolate in this way: "I want to teach the young and inspire them with the love of God and a liking for work. I want to help the poor and relieve some of their misery."

JULY 17

ca. 398

St. Marcellina, who inspired her younger brother, St. Ambrose, with a love of virtue. He reported the sermon Pope

Liberius delivered in 353, when he consecrated her a virgin. St. Ambrose spoke so often and so convincingly on holy virginity that some mothers in Milan kept their daughters away from his sermons.

1242   [O.P.]

Bl. Ceslaus, Silesian nobleman, brother of St. Hyacinth and provincial of the Dominicans in Poland. The successful resistance to the Mongol army at Wroclaw in 1240 was attributed to his prayers.

1794   [O. Carm., O.C.D.]

Sixteen Carmelite nuns of Compiègne, beatified in 1906. When contemplative nuns were driven from their convents, the Compiègne Carmelites dressed in secular clothes and divided into four groups. By taking up quarters near each other they were able to carry on something of their way of life, but after several years they were arrested. They then called the mayor and before a notary public made a formal retraction of the official oath they had taken four years earlier and about whose lawfulness Catholics were divided. At Paris, dressed once again in their religious habits, they were sentenced for making themselves "enemies of the people by conspiring against sovereign rule." They filled the hour-long ride to the guillotine with choir chants and the prayers for the dying; and as each mounted the scaffold she sang the short psalm 117, "Praise the Lord all you nations."

1851   [S.J.C.]

Bl. Anne Mary Javouhey, foundress of the Congregation of St. Joseph of Cluny. As a young girl during the French Revolution her help to priests reached the point of heroism. At a secret Mass in her home she vowed chastity and promised to devote her life to help the poor and to educate children.

After two unsuccessful attempts to enter existing orders, she opened a school with three of her sisters and soon, with five more companions, started a religious congregation. She was twenty-seven. Mother Javouhey is best remembered for her work in Guiana, where the French government once entrusted to her personal supervision the emancipation of 500 Negro slaves.

JULY 18

ca. 390

St. Pambo, well-known desert father, disciple of St. Anthony, remembered especially for silence and for his wise sayings, many of which passed into the collections of desert lore.

His story became a standard illustration for the scripture verse, "If any man offend not in word, the same is a perfect man" (Jas 3:2). Socrates in his **Church History** tells how Pambo, being illiterate, went to another monk to be taught a psalm. Psalm 39 was selected. When Pambo heard the first verse, "I said, I will guard my ways that I may not sin with my tongue," he went off without waiting for anything further, thinking this would be enough if he could master it. A half year later his tutor reproved him for not coming back for more, but Pambo said he was still working on that first verse. Much later, asked again about his project, he replied, "I have scarcely succeeded in accomplishing it during nineteen years."

1123

St. Bruno, bishop of Segni, Italy, outstanding Scripture scholar of his age and a staunch supporter of Pope St. Gregory VII. He defended the Catholic doctrine on the Eucharist against Berengarius at the Roman Council of 1079. Leaving his diocese he became a monk at Monte Cassino and then abbot, but Pope Pascal II had him return to his bishopric.

1482

Bl. Simon of Lipnicza, Franciscan provincial in Poland, a famous preacher. He was just graduated from Cracow University, when a mission by St. John Capistran attracted him to the friars. Like St. Francis he went to the Holy Land in quest of martyrdom, but the gift of his life was accepted in his own country as a victim of the epidemic of 1482 in which he had served the sick with unstinting devotion.

JULY 19

379

St. Macrina, one of the best examples of the good influence of an older sister. The eldest of ten, she deserves much of the credit for her three brothers who became bishops and saints: Basil the Great, Gregory of Nyssa, and Peter of Sebastea.

Macrina's mother taught her to read. At twelve she became engaged; but the young man died and so she gave up the idea of marriage and devoted herself to the family, especially as her father died about the time Peter was born. To Peter, as Gregory of Nyssa says, she was a mother, father, teacher, and guide. When Basil came home somewhat conceited after his higher studies in Constantinople and Athens, she gradually weaned him away from wordly pursuits. After all the children were settled, she and her mother started a religious community on one of the family estates. She is called Macrina the Younger to distinguish her from her grandmother, St. Macrina the Elder.

449

St. Arsenius, a desert father remembered especially for his gift of tears and a number of his sayings. This highly educated Roman became an ascetic in Egypt at the age of forty and lived there until his death at ninety-five. He once said: "After talking I always have something to repent, but I have never been sorry for having kept silence." Though he actually died peacefully in a spirit of deep trust, he once gave this answer to someone who asked if he feared to die: "I am very much afraid, and this fear has never left me from the time I first came into these deserts."

1679

St. John William Plessington, about forty years of age, executed near Chester for his priesthood during the Titus Oates scare in the reign of Charles I. His speech at the scaffold was printed; at one point he said: "I have deserved a worse death; for though I have been a true and faithful subject of my King, I have been a grievous sinner against God. Thieves and robbers that rob on highways would have served God in a greater perfection than I have done had they received so many favours and graces from Him as I have. . . ."

JULY 20

After 850 B.C.   [*O. Carm., O.C.D.*]

The Prophet Elijah, whose feast is kept by the Carmelites. After Moses, who appears along with him at the Transfiguration, he is the prophet most frequently mentioned in the New Testament. It was Elijah's Mission (1 Kings 17-19)—his name means "Yahweh is my God"—to challenge almost single-handed the Baal worship which King Ahab brought from Tyre. Elijah foretold the drought, confounded the priests of Baal on Mt. Carmel in an ordeal by fire, and ushered in the rain. He multiplied bread and oil for the poor widow and raised her son to life. Nourished by the miraculous bread, he made the 300-mile flight to Mt. Sinai. As the biblical account (2 Kings 2:11-13) has him taken up in a whirlwind and does not mention his death, it was popularly believed that he would return; and therefore, some questioned John the Baptist if he were Elijah (Jn 1:21);

and others saw him in Jesus (Mt. 16:14).

833

St. Ansegisus, abbot, restorer of the great French abbeys of Luxeuil and Fontenelle—the latter with its important scriptorium and library. His compilation of Carolingian laws long remained in use.

1900

Bl. Ignatius Mangin and **companions,** martyrs in the Boxer Rebellion. Of some 5,000 Catholics who were killed in the Vicariate Apostolic of Southern Chihli, four French Jesuits and 52 native Chinese were beatified in 1956.

JULY 21

1619

ST. LAWRENCE OF BRINDISI, the foremost Capuchin when that order did so much to preserve and renew the Catholic faith during the early years of the counter-Reformation. He became a friar at sixteen, studied at Padua, and soon earned a reputation as a preacher. With Bl. Benedict Urbino he went north to found friaries and combat militant Protestantism. They began by ministering to the plague-stricken and soon established the houses which grew into the Bohemian, Austrian, and Styrian provinces.

St. Lawrence played a momentary but dramatic role in halting the advance of the Turks under Mohammed III. As chief chaplain to the out-numbered and discouraged Christian forces, with crucifix raised aloft, he rode before them to victory at Szekesfehervar in 1601.

The following year, still in his early forties, he was chosen to head the order. He governed the 9,000 Capuchins with energy and charity, balancing the rigor of primitive observance with the needs of the apostolate; but he refused re-election three years later.

Pope, princes, and townsmen used his diplomatic services; for people easily recognized in him a true man of God. He welded the Catholic League in 1610, made peace between Savoy and Spain in 1614, and, despite his waning energies, went to Spain on behalf of the citizens of Naples—he had escaped dressed as a Walloon soldier—and, finding King Philip III in Lisbon he prevailed on him to remove the tyrannical Duke of Osuna from the post of Viceroy in Naples. He died soon after in Lisbon on his sixtieth birthday, July 22, 1619.

It is especially his works, ten large volumes, over half of them sermons and only recently published, that are giving him prominence today, and have earned him the title 'Doctor of the Church!'

1400

Bl. Oddino of Fossano in Piedmont, secular priest who could never do enough for the poor. His bishop had to order him to include meat in his diet and to take enough out of the church revenues to provide for his minimum necessities. He turned his house into a shelter for the destitute, directed a guild that cared for the sick, had a free hospital founded in Fossano, and died of the plague contracted while tending the sick. He was a Franciscan tertiary.

JULY 22

ST. MARY MAGDALEN, or Mary of Magdala in Galilee, who stood beside the cross of Jesus, assisted at his burial, found the empty tomb, and was the first to behold the risen Christ. She was one of the women who followed Jesus and ministered to his needs—he had cured her of a serious illness, described as seven devils by St. Luke. The gospels do not warrant her identification with the penitent woman who anointed the feet of Jesus nor with Mary, the sister of Martha and Lazarus.

668

St. Wandrille, abbot-founder of the famous monastery of Fontenelle—now called St. Wandrille—in Normandy. While still young he and his wife separated in order to enter religion. Attracted by the ascetic ideal St. Columban had popularized in France, Wandrille left court and gained personal experience first as a solitary and then in the communities of Bobbio and Romain-Moûtier under the rules of St. Columban and St. Benedict. Combining observances from both he founded his own ascetic fraternity at Fontenelle, which soon flourished as a missionary and cultural center. His essential message to his brothers was that "a man must be ready to ascend ever higher through humility."

1679

St. Philip Evans, Jesuit, and **St. John Lloyd,** imprisoned at Cardiff after the scare over the Oates "plot" and martyred for their priesthood. Father Evans was playing tennis when the under-sheriff brought news that the execution was set for the following day. He did not return to his cell till the game was finished, and he spent part of the remaining time playing the harp and conversing with friends who came to say farewell. At the gallows he spoke to the people in English and Welsh. Father Lloyd, a secular priest, made no long speech because, as he said, "I never was a good speaker in my life."

JULY 23

1373

ST. BRIDGET, patron of Sweden; mystic; foundress of the Bridgettines. Today the Bridgettines are only nuns, but originally each monastery had a small number of monks who were subject to the abbess and cared for the spiritual needs of the sisters.

Daughter of the governor of Upland in Sweden, Bridget married at about fourteen, became the mother of eight, and lost her husband in her early forties.

In response to recurring visions and revelations that began at seven, Bridget foretold the future, fearlessly denounced vice, and —except for pilgrimages—spent her last twenty-five years in Rome obtaining approval for her new order, and giving advice as coming from God on the burning issues of church and state, including the return of the papacy from Avignon.

Her favorite children were Catherine, who is also a saint; and Charles who, to his mother's consternation, became infatuated with Queen Joanna of Naples and was on the verge of an unlawful marriage when he suddenly became ill and died. St. Bridget was canonized eighteen years after her death.

Hers is a classic case of private revelations. Many blamed the Western schism on the pope's return to Rome and considered it reprehensible that those in authority should give credence to the visions of pious women like Bridget and Catherine of Siena. The councils of Constance and Basel took up the question. Several centuries later, the canonist who would become Pope Benedict XIV said of St. Bridget's and similar revelations: "Even though many of these revelations have been approved, we cannot and ought not give them the assent of Catholic faith, but only that of human faith, when the rules of prudence present them as probable and worthy of pious credence."

Today there are several autonomous Bridgettine monasteries as well as a new branch founded in 1911 by Elizabeth Hesselblad. This group has re-occupied the original site of Vadstena and works for Sweden's return to the Catholic faith.

1292 *[Franciscan II O.]*

Bl. Cunegund or **Kinga,** daughter of King Bela IV of Hungary and wife of King Boleslaus V of Poland. They lived together in good works and continence, and after his death she became a Poor Clare in a convent she had founded at Sandeck.

JULY 24*

1015

Sts. Boris and **Gleb,** martyrs, sons of St. Vladimir of Kiev, especially honored in the Russian church as "passion-bearers" or innocent men who repudiate violence. An elder brother contrived their murder, and they quietly accepted suffering and death. Boris had soldiers ready to fight; but he said, "It is better for me to die alone than to be the occasion of death to many." He is patron of Moscow.

1503   *[Franciscan II O.]*

Bl. Louise of Savoy, widow, abbess of the Poor Clares at Orobe, Switzerland, daughter of Bl. Amedeus, Duke of Savoy. At eighteen she married Hugh of Châlons, who shared her ideals and co-operated in her charities and pious designs. She had a poor-box to which anyone who used unbecoming language had to make a forfeit. Of balls that took place at her court she used to say—like St. Francis de Sales after her—that they were like mushrooms:"The best are not worth much." After her husband's death she became a nun. As abbess she made a particular point of taking good care of the Franciscans who passed by and always considered their presence a special blessing.

1594

St. John Boste, martyred near Durham under Elizabeth I. A fellow at Oxford, he became a Catholic, was ordained overseas, and for years was one of the priests most sought-after by friends and enemies. A renegade made a sacrilegious confession and Communion, and then betrayed him. He was racked so severely that he became a permanent cripple.

At the scaffold he said the **Angelus** with a verse and **Hail Mary** on each of the bottom three steps. At the top, with the rope about his neck, he began a sermon but was stopped. As

---

*O. Carm. see June 5 for Bl. John Soreth.

the executioner was dismembering him he regained consciousness and was heard to say, "Jesus forgive thee."

JULY 25

ST. JAMES THE GREATER, apostle, a Galilean of Bethsaida, called with John his brother while mending their fishing nets with their father Zebedee (Mt 4:21). Our Lord named them "sons of thunder" (Mk 3:17), possibly because of their impetuous temperament. It was they who asked for fire from heaven to strike the inhospitable Samaritans (Lk 9:54), and their mother requested a place for them on either side of Jesus in his kingdom (Mt. 20:21). Christ gave them special treatment: with Peter they were present at the raising of the daughter of Jairus (Mk 5: 37), at the transfiguration (Mt 17:1), and during the agony in the garden (Mt 26:37). James is usually named third in the list of apostles. He was beheaded by Herod Agrippa in the year 42.

The later accounts that he brought the Gospel to Spain are without foundation. In the eighth century the belief spread that a star revealed his relics in Spain, and in time his shrine at Compostela rivaled Rome as a place of pilgrimage.

ca. 408

St. Olympias, deaconness of Constantinople, friend and support of St. John Chrysostom. Through loyalty to him she suffered exile, poverty, and the dispersal of her religious community. She belonged to one of the great families of Constantinople but lost both parents and was raised by Theodosia, a pious relative of Sts. Basil and Gregory Nazianzen.

Wealthy, beautiful, spirited, and religious, she, at eighteen, married the prefect of the city. To mark the occasion St. Gregory Nazianzen sent the bride some advice in the form of a poem, the earliest Christian "mirror for women." Her husband soon died and, when Emperor Theodosius wanted her to remarry, she put him off with the remark that if God wanted her to live as a wife He would not have taken her husband.

Still in her twenties, she was consecrated a deaconess by Archbishop Nectarius and built a convent next to the cathredal where, with a group of holy widows and virgins, she gave herself to prayer and kept a hospital and orphanage.

She was so open-handed with her wealth that St. John Chrysostom once said: "I praise your good will, but you must give alms in the right way. If you give to those who already have enough it is as though you poured your wealth into the sea. You have dedicated your possessions to the poor . . . so you are only a steward. . . . Limit your gifts according to the need of the one who asks. In this way you will be able to help a greater number." St. Olympias died when not yet fifty, a year after St. John Chrysostom.

JULY 26

STS. JOACHIM and **ANNE,** parents of the Blessed Virgin. Their names are not given in the authentic gospels but in the influential, through apocryphal, **Protogospel of James** written about 165. In the sixth century Justinian dedicated a shrine to St. Anne at Constantinople. The cult of St. Joachim began in the East about two centuries later.

1641

Bl. William Ward, a Westmorland priest martyred under Charles I. He began his ministry at forty and spent twenty of the next thirty-three years in prison. "In all the time I knew this holy man," a priest acquaintance testified, "I could never hear him relate any passage or speak of any subject, but it either began or ended with a memory of Almighty God's service, if his whole speech were not upon that theme." At the Tyburn scaffold he gave forty shillings for distribution among poor Catholics, half a crown to the hangman, and a florin to the hurdle driver.

1833

St. Bartholomea Capitanio, foundress with St. Vincentia Gerosa of the Sisters of Charity of Lovere, a village in the Brescian Alps. She died when only twenty-six. At sixteen, unable to obtain parental approval for entering religion, she nevertheless made a vow of chastity. With a teacher's certificate and an exceptional gift for inspiring others, she was soon the center of a group of women devoted to catechetical instruction and to helping in every kind of need. She would go into the tavern to bring her drunken and abusive father home, but had the consolation of winning him back to a good life. After his holy death she bought a small house next to a hospital which her group was operating, and there the congregation was launched in 1832. When she died of consumption the following year, St. Vincentia Gerosa took over the leadership of the community. Three hundred of the saint's letters have been published, along with two volumes of spiritual notes.

JULY 27*

432

St. Celestine I, pope for ten years, remembered especially for his vigorous assertion of papal authority during the Nestorian controversy in which Constantinople, Alexandria, and Antioch, the three principal sees of the East were involved. At the Council of Ephesus the priest Philip, one of his legates, made this assertion: "There is no doubt, and in fact it has always been understood, that the holy and most blessed Peter, prince and head of the apostles, pillar of faith and foundation of the Catholic church, received the keys of the kingdom from our Lord Jesus Christ . . . , who, even to this time and for ever, lives

---

*C.M., D.C.S.V.P. see Dec. 30 for St. Catherine Labouré.

and judges in his successors."

Celestine sent St. Germain of Auxerre to put down the Pelagian heresy in England and wrote a long letter to the bishops of France regarding St. Augustine, his recently deceased friend, whom he calls one of the "best teachers." He defended him against the Semi-Pelagians, among whom St. John Cassian was the most aggressive.

459

St. Simeon, called the Stylite, initiator of a most extraordinary form of asceticism and apostolate. At thirteen this Cilician shepherd was deeply impressed at hearing the beatitudes, especially, "Blessed are those who mourn. . . . Blessed are the pure of heart." He joined a monastery, outdid everyone in mortifications, and then became a hermit. His holiness and gift of healing attracted crowds, and to escape he began living on top of a column. Twice a day he would speak to the people below. His first pillar was ten ft., his last—on which he spent twenty years —rose more than sixty feet into the air. The top was about six feet in diameter, had a railing but no roof or seat.

The practices which impressed his contemporaries most were his taking neither food nor drink during the whole of lent for at least twenty six years and his posture, for even during sleep he would stand erect or just lean. To discover whether this lifestyle was prompted by vain glory the local bishops and abbots ordered him off his pillar. When he showed complete readiness to obey, the order was withdrawn. Gentle and kind to all, he was consulted by emperors and high churchmen and idolized by heathens as well as Christians. From Antioch his fame gradually spread throughout the empire. He is called The Elder because 150 years later there was another St. Simeon Stylite.

1737   [*Franciscan II O.*]

Bl. Mary Magdalen Martinengo, Capuchin novice mistress and abbess at Brescia, a mystic with special devotion to the crowning of thorns.

JULY 28

ca. 199

St. Victor I, a pope of African origin, and the first, according to St. Jerome, to celebrate the Sacred Mysteries in Latin. He excommunicated the churches that followed the Asia Minor custom of celebrating Easter on the fourteenth day of the Babylonian-Jewish month of Nisan without paying any regard as to whether it was Sunday or some other day of the week. This action—the earliest recorded instance of a move by the Roman church to regulate universal church affairs—seemed over-severe to many bishops, including St. Irenaeus of Lyons who reminded the pope that in the past apostolic and holy men had differed about Easter without breaking the bonds of charity and peace.

ca. 433

St. John Cassian, abbot, author of the first and possibly the most successful "summa" of spiritual theology in the West. Monastic trappings aside, the outlines of the problems of the spiritual life as given by Cassian have, with few exceptions, remained identical down to contemporary times. And he is still readable today. He has a way of opening profound discussions with concrete observations like this: "Many, who have abandoned with contempt large fortunes, enormous sums of gold and silver and magnificent estates, let themselves, a little later, be troubled about an eraser, a stylus, a needle, or a reed to write with."

Using Scripture, psychological insight and spiritual discernment he synthesizes the monastic experience of the East on such subject as prayer, discretion, purity of heart, or the eight capital sins—slightly modified by St. Gregory the Great to make the standard seven.

Theologically Cassian's weakness was to overstress free will to the prejudice of grace in the soul's initial stance toward faith and goodness of life—Semi-Pelagianism it will be called in modern times—but during the Middle Ages it was named "Massilianism," after Cassian's town of Marseilles. Though aware of this error St. Benedict saw such worth in Cassian that twice in the **Rule** he mentions the **Institutes** and **Conferences** as typical and ideal matter for public and private reading.

Cassian was most probably born in Rumania. He received religious training in a monastery at Bethlehem, spent ten years familiarizing himself with Egyptian monasticism, received deacon's orders from St. John Chrysostom at Constantinople, was in Rome for ten years, became a priest, and settled at Marseilles about 415, where he opened two monasteries, one for men and one for women.

ca. 565

St. Samson, abbot and bishop, one of the greatest Welsh missionaries. A pupil of St. Illtud, he became monk and abbot on Caldey Island, and is credited with monastic foundations in Ireland and Cornwall, and finally in Brittany where he died.

JULY 29

ST. MARTHA, who in her solicitude to show hospitality to Jesus complained that her sister Mary sat listening to him instead of helping with the work. "Martha, Martha," Jesus said to her, "you are anxious and troubled about many things. One thing is needful. Mary has chosen the better portion, which shall not be taken away." Our Lord loved the two sisters and their brother Lazarus; but the Roman calendar commemorates only Martha, who was traditionally seen as typifying the active life.

1030

St. Olaf II, king, youthful hero of Norway's independence and patron saint of the nation. Son of a royal chieftain, he spent his youth as a Viking pirate, was baptized in Rouen at eighteen and then fought for King Ethelred of England against Canute of Denmark. Returning home, he cast off the overlordship of the Danes and Swedes and at the age of twenty succeeded in uniting Norway under his own rule.

He fought under the sign of the cross, extended the policy of forced conversion, and imported missionaries from England. He was king for thirteen years until opposition to his stern measures and Canute's success in England made it easy for Denmark to reassert its claims. Olaf fled to Russia but returned to Norway with a few Swedish troops, only to be slain at Stiklestad. His cult was immediate. Norway's greatest church, St. Olaf, was built over his tomb. This shrine made Nidaros, today known as Trondheim, the civil and ecclesiastical center of mediaeval Norway.

1099

Bl. Urban II, grand prior of Cluny, pope for eleven years. He is particularly remembered as the enthusiastic initiator of the first crusade and a firm proponent of the Gregorian Reform. St. Bruno, who had once been his teacher at Rheims, was called from the solitude of the Grand Chartreuse to be on hand as the pope's favorite counsellor.

JULY 30

ca. 450

ST. PETER, archbishop of Ravenna, whose sermons earned him the title **CHRYSOLOGUS** ("golden words") and also the distinction of being a doctor of the Church. The 183 surviving homilies are short—fifteen minutes would be a maximum. Ravenna was then capital of the empire in the West; and Galla Placidia, noted for her building activity, was regent while St. Peter was archbishop.

Of no other doctor of the Church does so little biographical detail survive. The only piece of correspondence that remains has to do with the heretic Eutyches, who wrote from Constantinople to the principal bishops of the world defending his position. Peter replied: "On everything, honorable brother, my advice is that you obediently heed what the most blessed pope of the city of Rome has written; because blessed Peter who lives and presides in his own see proffers the truth of faith to those who seek it. For, in the interests of peace and of faith, we cannot carry on a judicial inquiry in matters of faith without the consent of the bishop of Rome."

1860 [*C.M.*]

St. Justin de Jacobis, Italian Vincentian, bishop, first prefect and vicar apostolic in Ethiopia. Today's Catholic Church there may be traced to his humility, tact, and holiness during years of bitter persecution. He established a seminary at Guala from which fifteen native priests were ordained in the year 1852.

1942

Bl. Leopold Mandić of Castelnovo, diminutive Croatian Capuchin whose normal routine at Padua during his last 33 years—he died at 76—was to celebrate an early Mass and then sit in the confessional and remain there practically the entire day. Pope Paul VI in the beatification address eulogized him: "so humble, so serene, so absorbed as to appear almost ecstatic in an interior vision of his own of the invisible presence of God . . . He is a weak, popular but authentic image of Jesus . . . 'Come to me, all you that labor and are burdened. I will give you rest.' . . . He became holy," the pope continued, "mainly in the exercise of the Sacrament of Penance . . . He calls priests to a ministry of such vital importance . . . And he reminds the faithful whether fervent, half-hearted, or indifferent, what a providential and

BLESSED LEOPOLD MANDIC, O.F.M. CAP.

ineffable service individual and auricular confession still is today." Bl. Leopold's other great apostolate was Church unity, especially reunion of the Eastern Churches of the Slav peoples, for which he offered himself unconditionally as a victim.

JULY 31

1556

ST. IGNATIUS LOYOLA, founder of the Jesuits and patron of retreats. The short military career of this eleventh and last child of the Basque lord of Loyola ended when a canon ball fractured his thigh. The bones were badly set and had to be rebroken. He was thirty. In the long convalescence, he could find nothing else to read except a life of Christ and a volume on the lives of the saints; and so a new world now opened up before him as he realized the emptiness of earthly ambition. God's greater glory—**ad maiorem Dei gloriam**—would be his goal.

A vision of the Blessed Mother holding the child Jesus greatly encouraged him. He vowed chastity and set off for the abbey and shrine of Our Lady of Montserrat near Barcelona. There he made a three-day confession and after an all-night vigil gave his knightly apparel to a beggar.

He spent the next eleven months at Manresa, a few miles from the abbey, helping in a hospital and doing penance. He suffered from scruples but also experienced consolations and had a favorite cave where he would pray in solitude. During these months of initiation into the ways of God, he put together the substance of his **Spiritual Exercises,** a handbook for making a permanent choice of Christ during the course of a month's retreat.

After an apostolic episode in Palestine he spent eleven years in study, having to begin with the rudiments of Latin. At the age of forty-three he earned the degree of Master of Arts at the

University of Paris. At Montmartre, on the feast of the Assumption that same year of 1534, Ignatius and six companions— St. Francis Xavier and Bl. Peter Favre among them—took vows of poverty and chastity and bound themselves to preach the gospel in the Holy Land or, failing this, to put themselves at the service of the Holy Father. Pope Paul III took a special interest in them and permitted some to become priests. After ordination Ignatius postponed his first Mass for more than a year.

Eventually the group formed into a religious order, but without the customary requirement of praying the divine office together in choir. Obedience was stressed, authority centralized, and a forth vow of special obedience to the Holy Father was added.

In 1541 Ignatius was elected first superior general. His fifteen remaining years he spent in Rome directing the "Company of Jesus" as they called themselves. According to the pope's original plan their number would be limited to sixty, but when Ignatius died there were nearly a thousand. Today they are the largest order of men centralized under a single authority.

AUGUST 1*

1787

ST. ALPHONSUS LIGOURI, bishop of St. Agatha of the Goths near Naples, doctor, founder of the Congregation of the Most Holy Redeemer for preaching missions especially in neglected country regions. The growth of the Redemptorists, with their characteristic parish missions, the translation into many languages of such devotional books as **The Glories of Mary, Visits to the Blessed Sacrament, The Way of the Cross,** and the spread of devotion to Our Lady of Perpetual Help, bear witness to the immense influence St. Alphonsus has had on Catholic piety in the nineteenth and the first half of the twentieth century.

He was above all a missioner burning with a zeal for souls. During most of his ninety years he had a vow not to waste a moment of time. He opposed Jansenist rigorism and constantly stressed the loving mercy of God and the help of Mary. He urged frequent Communion, wanted priests to show great compassion and gentleness in the confessional, and insisted that homilies be simple—in line with his own admission that he had

---

*S.S.S., S.M. *see Aug. 3 for St. Peter Julian Eymard.*

never preached a sermon which the simplest person could not understand.

He first came to the attention of moral theologians through a letter in which he showed that cursing the dead would not normally be a serious sin because it was done with so little real intent; and so priests would not need special faculties to absolve the sin even in dioceses where bishops, in an effort to stamp the vice out, had restricted confessors' powers by making it a "reserved" sin.

He wrote his famous **Moral Theology** to prepare his young missioners for hearing confessions. This prodigious compilation and evaluation of the opinions of earlier authors won for St. Alphonsus papal approbation as a safe guide in confessional practice.

The life of this ardent saint is filled with an abundance of dramatic detail, from his admission to the bar at Naples when only sixteen to his expulsion from his congregation at the age of 83. He is patron of confessors and moralists.

984

St. Ethelwold, Benedictine at Glastonbury under St. Dunstan; abbot of Abingdon; bishop of Winchester, who worked with St. Dunstan and St. Oswald to restore English monasticism.

AUGUST 2

371

ST. EUSEBIUS, first bishop of Vercelli and, according to St. Ambrose, the first in the West to live under a rule in community with his clergy. He may thus be considered the founder of canons regular. At the Council of Milan in 355 he was one of the three bishops who, though threatened with death, refused to sign the condemnation of St. Athanasius. Instead, Eusebius laid a copy of the Nicene Creed on the table and insisted that everyone sign it before taking up the case against Athanasius. Tumult ensued. He was exiled but later returned to combat Arianism, along with St. Hilary.

1190 [*O.P.*]

Bl. Joan of Aza, mother of St. Dominic, a woman of striking beauty and great spirituality.

ca. 1215 [*Franciscans*]

The Portiuncula, primarily a Franciscan feast commemorating the dedication of St. Mary of the Angels or Portiuncula, the small chapel St. Francis repaired and where he received his vocation, founded his order, vested St. Clare, held general chapters and died. The Portiuncula indulgence which made that church so famous, according to the 1968 norms, may be gained on August 2 in any parish church.

1546 [*S.J.*]

Bl. Peter Favre, or **Faber,** of Savoy, the first companion of St. Ignatius and the first to make the **Exercises** under his direction. It was he that celebrated Mass at Montmartre when the seven first Jesuits took their vows in 1534. "I used to be constantly agitated," he wrote, "and blown about by varying winds, proposing to myself one day to get married and other days to qualify as a physician or lawyer or school teacher or doctor of theology or just a plain priest." Of himself and his Paris University roommate, the future St. Francis Xavier, he said, "We hampered . . . ourselves gravely—or at least I did— by refusing to admit that the cross of Christ had any claim to a place in our studies, either at the beginning or in the middle or at the end."

"Favre," wrote Simon Rodriguez, also one of the original seven, "had a rare and delightful sweetness and charm which I have known in no one else to the same degree. . . . His amiability, his charm of talk, inclined all those in his company to the love of God." He attracted St. Peter Canisius and St. Francis Borgia to the new order.

In an unecumenical epoch he gave his fellow Jesuit, James Laynez, this guidance: "In the first place it is necessary that anyone who desires to be serviceable to heretics of the present age should hold them in great affection and love them very truly, putting out of his heart all thoughts and feelings that tend to their discredit. The next thing he must do is to win their good-will and love by friendly intercourse and converse on matters about which there is no difference between us, taking care to avoid all controversial subjects that lead to bickering and mutual recrimination. The things that unite us ought to be the first ground of our approach, not the things that keep us apart."

The gentle spirit that won all hearts is shown by this characteristic entry in his spiritual diary, after a porter refused him admission: "So I had to stay outside, and it came into my mind that many times I had admitted vain thoughts and evil imaginings into my soul while refusing entry to Jesus who was knocking at the door. . . . I prayed for myself and for the porter that the Lord would not make us wait long in purgatory before admitting us to heaven." He died at forty.

AUGUST 3

448

St. Germain, a civil ruler who became bishop of Auxerre. He studied and practised law at Rome, and then was sent back to his native Auxerre as military governor of northwestern Gaul. Though married and not a cleric, he was chosen bishop and for thirty years was the leading churchman in France. It was probably at his monastery that St. Patrick received his training and by him that Patrick was ordained bishop. He made two missions to England, went to the highest Roman authorities in Gaul to plead for tax relief on behalf of his people, and died at Ravenna on another mission of mercy.

1323

Bl. Augustine Gazotich, Dominican, bishop of Zagreb and then of Nocera, founder of several Dominican houses; an effective reformer. To spur his friars on he used to remind them of the words of his patron, St. Augustine: "As I have hardly ever seen better men than those living a holy life in monasteries, so I have never seen worse than those in monasteries who do not live as they should."

1868

St. Peter Julian Eymard, founder, canonized by Pope John, who called him "the great friend of the Eucharist." At eighteen he entered the novitiate of the Oblates of Mary Immaculate at Marseilles, but his health broke down. He became a priest of the diocese of Grenoble and then joined the Marists.

"One idea haunted me," he said, explaining the further development of his vocation. "It was that Jesus in the Blessed Sacrament had no religious order to glorify this mystery of love, an order whose sole object was entire consecration to Its service."

In 1856 at Paris with the approval of the Archbishop and of his Marist superior general, he founded his first community of Priests of the Blessed Sacrament, who would recite the divine office in choir and perform the various duties of the priestly ministry with perpetual adoration and devotion to the Blessed Sacrament as their primary work. Two years later he founded the Servants of the Blessed Sacrament, a feminine branch. He also established the Priests' Eucharistic League, whose members pledge themselves to spend a weekly hour of adoration. For the laity he organized the Archconfraternity of the Blessed Sacrament. He died on August 1, 1868. At the time of his canonization in 1962 his congregation had 1500 priests and brothers.

AUGUST 4

1859

ST. JOHN VIANNEY, Curé of Ars, patron of parish priests, one of the best known modern saints. "If you want the whole diocese to be converted," he once told his bishop, "then all the parish priests must become saints." His life was the best example of what one holy priest can do.

He was the fourth of six children of a peasant family in Dardilly. With only a few months of formal schooling in childhood, he began at eighteen to receive private tutoring from the pastor of a neighboring parish in preparation for the seminary.

Studies were hard. As his Latin was hopeless, the major seminary at Lyons dismissed him; but his old tutor, convinced of his piety and spiritual prudence, gave him a private course in theology from a French manual. He was ordained at twenty-nine. In less than three years he was sent to Ars, a village of 230 people about twenty-five miles north of Lyons.

His approach to the apostolate was the Gospel formula of prayer and fasting to which he added tireless work. He ate barely enough to keep alive—for the first six years it was mostly boiled potatoes—and when there was no other duty he would be in church. When asked if the Curé's sermons were long one informant answered, "Yes, long ones . . . There are some who say there is no hell. But he believed in it."

Ars had for some time been just a mission of a neighboring parish, and the few who came to church were mostly elderly women. Gradually the pastor's influence was felt. Sunday work, drunkenness, and dancing stopped. In ten years the town was transformed, and stories of remarkable conversions and cures had begun to attract outsiders. He could foresee the future and read people's thoughts. Saints and sinners came for advice. Daily for the next thirty years there were generally some 300 visitors waiting to go to confession or have some contact with the Curé. A special booking office in Lyons issued tickets that were good for a week, because a person could not be sure of seeing the Curé and returning home in less time than that. A regular coach ran between Ars and the nearest station for Paris.

He would come out of his rectory at about one in the morning, walk the thirty yards to the church and ring the **Angelus** as a signal that he was ready for confessions. At seven he would offer Mass. His thanksgiving over, he would return to the confessional, emerging at eleven to give a catechism instruction, and then go to his dinner which took fifteen minutes.

After a visit to the sick he would return to the confessional, coming out again for evening prayer. He then retired to his rectory and shut himself in for three or four hours of sleep. He died in Ars at 73. When the priest brought viaticum the dying saint murmured, "It is sad to receive Holy Communion the last time."

AUGUST 5

DEDICATION OF THE BASILICA OF ST. MARY MAJOR, the world's largest church devoted to Mary and the principal Roman memorial to her title "Mother of God" **(Theotokos)**, which had just been vindicated at the Council of Ephesus in 431. To mark the occasion Pope St. Sixtus III had the old Liberian basilica restored and about the year 435 dedicated it to the Blessed Mother. The magnificent triumphal arch with its mosaic date from that time.

642

St. Oswald, king of Northumbria, who was responsible for bringing in St. Aidan and monks from Iona to evangelize his territory. Before the battle in which he defeated the pagan Cadwalla, he had a huge wooden cross erected and then addressed these words to his small, outnumbered army: "Let us all kneel down and together ask the almighty, living and true

God to defend us in his mercy against this proud and cruel enemy; for God knows that we undertake this war for the just safety of our people." St. Bede tells of the miracles still worked in his day by the wood of this cross.

Nine years later Oswald died in battle against the pagan King Penda. Seeing himself hopelessly hemmed in, he offered his last prayer for the souls of his soldiers, giving rise to the proverb: "'O God, be merciful to their souls,' as Oswald said when he fell."

1367

Bl. John Colombini, founder of a society of brothers devoted to penance and charity, especially the care of the sick. John's conversion came through reading the lives of the saints when his wife thrust a book in his hands after he had fallen into a temper because dinner was not ready on time. His order, called, "Jesuats," and not to be confused with "Jesuits," lasted 300 years.

AUGUST 6

TRANSFIGURATION OF THE LORD. The transfiguration may have occurred during one of the nights Jesus passed in prayer. Peter, James, and John were with him as they would also be in Gethsemane when his humanity was crushed by interior agony. On both occasions the apostles were heavy with sleep. The transfiguration is a preview of the resurrection, and the gospels connect the two events: Moses and Elijah spoke with Jesus about his passion; furthermore the disciples were told not to say anything until after the resurrection.

There is also a close parallel with the revelation on Sinai: the mountain, the glory, the cloud, the tents, the voice from heaven, and Moses himself. On the mount of transfiguration the law and the prophets bear witness to Jesus, in whom dwells the fullness of the divinity corporeally. The whole scene is meant to animate the apostles and later Christians to an entire acceptance of the new revelation. "This is my beloved son, with whom I am well pleased; listen to him" (Mt 17:5).

523

St. Hormisdas, widower and archdeacon of the Roman Church, pope from 514 to 523, and the father of Pope St. Silverius. More than 100 of his letters remain. He is particularly remembered for the famous **Formula of Hormisdas,** a profession of faith the Eastern bishops were required to sign in concluding the schism caused by Acacius of Constantinople, who had tried to conciliate the Monophysites. Stressing the primary importance of correct faith, the "formula" states that in virtue of Christ's promise to Peter, "the Catholic religion has always been preserved without blemish by the Apostolic See . . . in which there is the entire, true and perfect solidity of the Christian religion."

AUGUST 7

258

ST. SIXTUS II and **COMPANIONS,** the pope mentioned in the Roman canon who was martyred along with four or possible six, of his seven deacons. The other deacon, St. Lawrence, suffered four days later. In the rebaptism controversy Sixtus upheld the position of his predecessor, Stephen I, that heretics were not to be rebaptized. But Sixtus was more mild and did not excommunicate the opposing churches. Schism was thus averted and the practise of rebaptizing was gradually abandoned.

1547

ST. CAJETAN, principal founder of the Clerks Regular, better known as Theatines—a name deriving from Theate, the diocese of Peter Carafa, the first superior and future Pope Paul IV. St. Cajetan is one of those most responsible for the beginnings of genuine church reform during the first years of the Protestant Reformation.

The son of a Venetian count, he studied law at Padua and took an administrative post under Pope Julius II. A reversal of fortune helped him become serious about the spiritual life. He reached the priesthood at thirty-six, just a year before Luther nailed up his 95 theses.

Seven years later, with three other priests, he started the Clerks Regular, clerics engaged in the ministry but bound by solemn religious vows and dedicated to high standards of asceticism and pastoral ministry. They rejected benefices and, without begging, would depend on the voluntary donations sent by God's Providence. "Seek first the kingdom of God" was the motto on their coat of arms. In his last illness, when advised by his doctors to exchange his boards for a mattress, Cajetan replied, "My Saviour died on a cross—allow me at least to die on wood."

Among the pious practises traditionally fostered by the Theatines is the so-called "heroic act" of renouncing all one's merits and suffrages in favour of the souls in purgatory.

ca. 1308   [*O. Carm., O.C.D.*]
   St. Albert Trapani, Sicilian Carmelite, noted for his preaching and work with the Jews.

1638   [*Franciscans*]
   Bl. Agathangelo and **Bl. Cassian,** French Capuchins martyred after trying for five years to initiate reunion with the Copts in Egypt and Ethiopia.

AUGUST 8

1221
   St. Dominic, founder of the Dominicans. Their official title,

"Order of Preachers," states accurately what Dominic had in mind: a world-wide order dedicated to promoting, on a community basis, the things that would make good preachers: holiness, asceticism, deep study and sound doctrine, familiarity with the spirit of the times and also its errors, and the full disciplined use of gifts of temperament and other talents. He was an innovator because preaching until then belonged almost exclusively to prelates.

Born at Calaroga, Spain, he took after his mother, Bl. Joan of Aza, in completeness of character and personal charm. He became a Canon Regular of St. Augustine at about 16 and was superior at 31. Except for two trips across Europe in the company of his bishop to make marriage arrangements for the son of the king of Castile, Dominic led a retired life of prayer and study until 1205, when he and his bishop offered themselves to Pope Innocent III for mission work in Russia. But the pope sent them instead to help convert the Albigenses in southern France. Dominic was 35. He would have only 16 more years.

A saint of clear vision, energy and deep personal prayer, he saw at once that those already on the mission were ineffective because their life-style was too rich and soft. His preachers would live on alms, carry books but no money, and offer the Albigenses and ascetic ideal equal to that of their own austere leaders. The first Dominicans were women: a convent he established in 1206 at Prouille, consisting of Albigensian converts who by prayer, asceticism, and the instruction of young women would form an auxiliary corps. Today the feminine branches far outnumber the friars.

In 1215, after ten years of preaching, Dominic organized his companions into an order under the rule of St. Augustine. Giving universities a special priority he dispersed his preaching brothers throughout Europe. Five years later he held the first general chapter and drew up the constitutions. When he died, the following year, there were already sixty-one houses. The Dominican motto is: "to contemplate and to share with others the fruits of contemplation."

AUGUST 9

1091

St. Altman, bishop of Passau, apostolic delegate in Germany during the thick of the conflict between Emperor Henry IV and Pope Gregory VII. When Bishop Altman read out the pope's decree against simony and married priests, the anti-celibacy clergy raised a tumult. The saint died in exile.

An early biographer says that when Altman became bishop many churches were of wood and so were the priests, but he built stone churches and inspired priests with solid, noble ideals.

1242

Bl. John of Salerno, superior — though the youngest — of a band of thirteen friars St. Dominic sent to preach in Tuscany. After two moves they settled at Santa Maria Novella in Florence.

1899

Bl. Mary Droeste zu Vischering, sometimes called a second Margaret Mary because it was her private revelations that prompted Pope Leo XIII to write the encyclical **Annum Sacrum,** May 25, 1899, and to consecrate the human race to the Sacred Heart on June 10th of that year. The encyclical urged bishops to foster Sacred Heart devotion and ended with the Act of Consecration which has been used ever since and is now specially indulgenced for public recitation on the Feast of Christ the King.

Daughter of two leading German Catholic families, Mary had such poor health that she was unable to enter religion in her late teens but instead made a vow of chastity and began to follow a regime of prayer and works of mercy while living at home. On a hospital visit she one day noticed a girl sick and apparently neglected because of her bad reputation. She took the girl in her arms and in that embrace recognized her call to help these girls.

Marvelously, her health now began to improve and so at 24 she joined the Good Shepherd Nuns, received the name Mary of the

BLESSED MARIA DROESTE ZU VISCHERING

Divine Heart, and was professed in the convent of her native city of Muenster, where for several years she would have charge of the girls. She was then sent to Portugal, where at 30 she was appointed superior in Oporto. Soon a spinal condition developed which gradually invalided her. Mary Droeste zu Vischering died at 35 after the first vespers of the Feast of the Sacred Heart, just three days before the Holy Father consecrated the human race to the Sacred Heart.

AUGUST 10

258

ST. LAWRENCE, deacon of the Roman Church under St. Sixtus II, after Sts. Peter and Paul the most famous Roman martyr. Prudentius, about 400 A.D., ascribes the conversion of Rome to his prayers and tells of the crowds at the church of St. Lawrence and the many answers to their prayers. In the fourth century he not only had a feast but also a vigil.

There has been much debate over the circumstances of his martyrdom. As he died in the persecution of Valerian in 258 he must have been beheaded. Very possibly, burning on the grid-iron was the torture to which he was first exposed.

824

St. Nicetas, abbot on Mt. Olympus, who allowed the other abbots to talk him into receiving Communion from the iconoclast patriarch intruded into Constantinople by Emperor Leo the Armenian. Recognizing his mistake he went back and publicly retracted, saying that he would never abandon the tradition of the fathers regarding sacred images. He spent the next six years, half-starved, in a dungeon; finally, under a new emperor, he was able to retire to a hermitage.

1740

St. Theophilus of Corte in Corsica. The only son of an aristocratic family, he ran away at fifteen to join the Capuchins; but his parents brought him back. Two years later he became a Franciscan of the Observance. He had the gift of miracles and touched hardened sinners in his sermons. When called to Rome to give evidence for the beatification of his close friend Bl. Thomas of Cori, he made such an impression that the bishop of Nicotera, who was in charge of that case, remarked, "I have been questioning one saint about another saint." When he was laid out for burial so many people took pieces of his habit as relics that his cassock had to be replaced before burial.

AUGUST 11

1253

ST. CLARE, foundress of the Poor Clares, identified with St. Francis and his ideal of evangelical poverty. She put herself under his direction after hearing one of his lenten sermons and on Palm Sunday secretly left home—she was 18—to keep a midnight appointment at the Portiuncula, where Francis with some friars led her to the chapel, cut off her hair, received her religious promises, gave her the sackcloth habit and cord of his order, and handed her over to some Benedictine nuns until he founded his convent at San Damiano. All Assisi was aroused. Then Agnes, Clare's fifteen year-old sister, stole away and joined her. Eventually her own mother and another sister put themselves under her rule.

The nuns observed a continual fast, ate no meat, spoke only when charity or necessity required, wore nothing on their feet, observed the night and day rhythm of choir office, and lived within the enclosure. While spared the rigors of the friars' apostolate, the nuns would make their contribution by a more penitential way of life. Though the gaiety of the Poor Clares is proverbial, they remain the most penitential of the large orders of nuns.

St. Clare is best understood as the feminine version of the spirit of St. Francis: love of God and of all creation, devotion to the humanity of Christ and especially his passion, humility, detachment, simplicity, and enthusiasm—all combining to make her more, rather than less, human.

Clare, in her rule, called herself the "little plant" of St. Francis. No one else understood him so well or upheld his ideals so faithfully. In the matter of poverty she won over, and in a sense subdued, three of the great popes of the century. When Gregory IX offered to dispense her from the vow of strict poverty she replied, "Holy Father, absolve me from my sins but not from the obligation of following our Lord." She died in 1253 at the age of sixty and was canonized two years later.

AUGUST 12

304

St. Euplius, deacon at Catania in Sicily who gave himself up as a Christian and, contrary to the edict of Diocletian, had in his possession a copy of the gospels. After three months in prison he was asked if he still had the forbidden writings.

"I do," was the reply.

"Where are they?"

"Within me."

"If you still have them," the governor continued, "bring them here."

"They are within me," Euplus repeated and showed by a gesture that he knew them by heart. He was then ordered to be tortured until he would sacrifice, but he remained firm and was beheaded.

1689   [*O.SS.T.*]

Bl. Innocent XI, resolute reformer, pope from 1676 to 1689. At forty-nine he became a priest and bishop, although he had been a cardinal since the age of thirty-three. He was apprenticed in the family bank in Genoa at fifteen but became a lawyer and gained a reputation for honesty, fearlessness, and love of the poor.

Before accepting the papacy he required that the cardinals agree to complete the reform of the Council of Trent, uphold the freedom of the Church in the Gallican controversy, and defend Christendom against the Turks. He condemned the quietism of Molinos and inculcated frequent and even daily Communion provided there was no herding, and due attention was given to preparation and reverence. He censured sixty-five propositions gathered from various moralists and directed the General of the Jesuits to urge the universities of the order to support the more probable opinions in moral theology.

Such was the pope's reputation for holiness that his cause was taken up at once; though Gallicanism remained so strong that he was beatified only in 1956.

ca. 1350   [*O.S.A., O.A.R.*]

Bl. John of Rieti, brother of Bl. Lucy of Amelia, Augustinian friar, remembered for service to others, contemplative prayer, and gift of tears.

AUGUST 13

235

STS. PONTIAN and **HIPPOLYTUS,** martyrs buried in Rome on August 13 and already in the fourth century honored on the same day. Pontian was pope from 230 to 235. Hippolytus the martyr is very probably the same as Hippolytus the ecclesiastical writer, a person of rigorist tendencies who sharply criticised Pope St. Callistus on doctrinal and personal grounds and headed an opposition party as antipope. His **Apostolic Tradition** is the best source book on second and third century Roman liturgy and church order. It contains the oldest example of a Roman canon —the one now used with some modifications as the second Eucharistic Prayer.

662
St. Maximus the Confessor; greatest Greek theologian of the seventh century; author of some ninety major treatises; a truly heroic figure whose ascetical works are still read. He resigned his post as secretary to Emperor Heraclius to become a monk at Scutari in Albania. He spent his last twenty-five years opposing the "one-will heresy" and succeeded in obtaining its solemn condemnation at Rome by the Second Lateran Synod in 649. Rome he described as "that apostolic see which has received universal and supreme dominion, authority and power of binding and loosing over all the holy churches of God." Emperor Constans II seized both Maximus and Pope St. Martin I, tried them in Constantinople and had them banished. At eighty-two Maximus was again brought to Constantinople and condemned. His tongue and right hand—so often used to teach two wills in Christ—were cut off. He died soon after in exile.

1862 [*F.S.C.*]
St. Benildus Romançon, a brother of the Christian Schools, whose vocation and joy it was to teach religion. He had charge of the brothers' school at Billom and then at Saugues, France. "Brother Benildus was a fine teacher," a pupil testified," a bit strict but always fair. He would encourage the backward ones, and made us work hard." "I live for the apostolate," he wrote," . . . if I die teaching religion, I die at my proper task."

AUGUST 14

1480

Bl. Anthony Primaldi and his fellow townsmen, who suffered martyrdom when the Turks captured Otranto in southern Italy. The band was offered liberty if they would embrace Islam. Anthony Primaldi, an old artisan, bolstered their courage with words such as these: "We have fought for our city and our lives. Now we must fight for our souls and for Jesus Christ. He died for us. We must die for him."

1941   [*Franciscans*]

St. Maximilian Kolbe, Polish Conventual Franciscan, who gave his life at forty-seven by voluntarily replacing a younger man—the father of a family—in the starvation bunker of the Nazi concentration camp of Auschwitz. On the vigil of the Assumption, still conscious after fourteen days, he was dispatched by a lethal injection, realizing in this way the martyrdom he had chosen at the age of ten during a childhood crisis when the Blessed Virgin appeared with a white crown of purity and a gold crown of martyrdom and asked him to make a choice. He took both.

Becoming a friar in Poland at sixteen, he passed through a period of intense scruples, contracted tuberculosis during priesthood studies in Rome, and there—as a means of counteracting anti-Catholic influences in society and of keeping untarnished the high ideals of youthful friars—established the Militia of the Immaculate, apostles who would convert and sanctify souls through the mediation of Mary. Over his prie-dieu he kept the picture of some saint to whom Mary had appeared.

The life of this sickly but indefatigable worker illustrates one of his favorite sayings that "good is more contagious than evil." By 1939 his monthly review **Knight of the Immaculate** reached a circulation of one million and his headquarters,

SAINT MAXIMILLIAN KOLBE, O.F.M. CONV.

Niepokalanow near Warsaw, with its 700 Franciscans, was the largest religious house in the Catholic world. He also established a Marian Center in Japan and India. "Sanctity," he told his friars, "is not a luxury, but a simple duty. It is one of Christ's first principles: 'Be perfect as your heavenly Father is perfect.'"

AUGUST 15

ASSUMPTION OF THE BLESSED VIRGIN MARY, principal feast of Our Lady and the patronal day of churches dedicated to Mary without any further title.

On Nov. 1, 1950, Pope Pius XII solemnly proclaimed as a divinely revealed truth "that the Immaculate Mother of God, the ever-virgin Mary, on the completion of her earthly life, was assumed body and soul into heaven."

By the fifth century, August fifteenth was kept at Jerusalem as the Commemoration of the Mother of God. In the sixth century the feast of Mary's Falling Asleep spread throughout the East. Finally in the eighth century the day was celebrated as the Assumption of the Blessed Virgin Mary.

The encyclical **Munificentissimus Deus,** before defining the dogma, reviewed the increasing awareness of this truth over the centuries, recalled the words of Holy Scripture which the fathers and theologians used to support their considerations and underlined this dogma's harmony with many other truths of the faith, such as Christ's resurrection and our own.

But the strongest reason derived from the more than 1000 years of explicit faith and practice of the Church and the practically unanimous affirmative replies which Pope Pius XII had received from every diocese in the world to the two questions which he put to the bishops: "Do you judge that the bodily assumption of the Blessed Virgin can be proposed and defined as a dogma of faith? Do you, with your clergy and people, desire it?" The definition is a practical expression of the belief that the Spirit of Truth dwells in the Church directing it to an ever more perfect knowledge of revealed doctrine.

3rd-4th cent.

St. Tarcissus, who was attacked by a Roman mob while carrying the Blessed Sacrament and gave up his life rather than allow the Eucharist to be profaned.

AUGUST 16

1038

ST. STEPHEN, king, who welded the Magyars into a nation and laid the foundation of Christian Hungary. As a boy he was baptized together with his father Geza, and at twenty married Gisela of Bavaria, sister of the future Emperor St. Henry II. At twenty-two he succeeded his father as chieftain of the Magyars. Three years later, on Christmas A.D. 1000, he was blessed as the first king of Hungary, receiving the title from Pope Sylvester II, who also sent him the now famous crown.

Stephen used foreign missionaries to Christianize the country, particularly the Benedictines of the newly-founded abbey of Pannonhalma. By the time of his death—he governed forty years—Hungary was transformed from tribal status into a feudal kingdom of Western stamp, with two archbishops, eight bishops, and five abbeys. Stephen had a law requiring everyone except religious and churchmen to marry, and he forbade the union of Christians and pagans. Many stories are told of his charity to beggars, including the incident when he gave alms in disguise, was knocked down, and had his purse stolen.

1243

Bl. Lawrence Loricatus, for thirty-three years a recluse near

St. Benedict's cave at Subiaco, Italy. In youth he killed a man, and though it was an accident he practised severe penances all his life. He is called "Loricatus" from the sharp-pointed coat of mail he wore next to his skin.

ca. 1378

St. Roch, protector in time of pestilence and patron of invalids. He was a native of Montpellier but is also greatly venerated in Italy, where he served the plague-stricken. His most famous shrine is in Venice, where his relics were kept.

AUGUST 17*

1257   [*O.P.*]

St. Hyacinth, a canon of Cracow who joined St. Dominic at Rome. He labored with so much success among his people that he is venerated as an apostle of the Slavs and a patron of Poland.

1308   [*O.S.A., O.A.R.*]

St. Clare of Montefalco, Italy, Augustinian abbess, a mystic especially devoted to the Passion.

1736

Bl. Joan Delanoue, a patron for the selfish; foundress of the Sisters of St. Anne of Providence of Saumur to care for the poor, sick, and neglected. The youngest of twelve children, she inherited at twenty-five a small shop at Saumur, France, where her parents catered especially to pilgrims on their way to a nearby shrine. With a younger niece, Joan took the business over. She began to keep the shop open on Sundays and discontinued her mother's practice of giving alms to beggars. She

---

*O. Cist, O.C.S.O. see Aug. 19 for St. John Eudes.

would send her niece to buy food just before meal-time so that it would not be a lie when she told beggars she had nothing.

One day, however, she gave free lodging to an old lady, a visionary, thought by some to be mental. Her first visit left Joan so spiritually disturbed that she consulted a priest, closed her business on Sundays, and gradually began to perform acts of penance.

On the visionary's next visit Joan realized that her vocation was not shopkeeping but the service of the poor in response to Christ's words, "I was hungry . . . , thirsty . . . , a stranger . . . , naked . . . , a prisoner . . ." (Mt 25: 36-37). She began by giving away her best dress. Soon she was rewarded with a deep spiritual experience of three days' duration in which she foresaw her congregation.

At thirty-two she closed her shop and for the next thirty-eight years would rather give than receive. The Providence House she eventually built at Saumur could accommodate 300 sick and neglected.

AUGUST 18

330

St. Helen, empress, an inn-keeper's daughter who won the heart of Constantius Chlorus but was set aside in favor of a more political marriage when Constantius became Caesar. Nevertheless her son Constantine the Great held her in such esteem that he had her proclaimed empress. Helen was then in her sixties and not yet a Christian.

Baptized after the agreement of toleration at Milan, she remained an important religious figure for the next seventeen years. She is remembered for her devout life and the churches she built at Rome, Constantinople, Bethlehem, and on the Mount of Olives. Eusebius, the principal reporter of the discovery of the true Cross, does not mention her part in it; but St. Ambrose, later in the same century, does. The year 330 A.D. is the last on which her name appears on coins.

1230   [*O.P.*]

Bl. Mannes, an older brother of St. Dominic and one of the original group of Dominicans that adopted the rule of St. Augustine in 1216 and made profession the following year. Prayerful and prudent, Mannes rendered particular service as director of the order's nuns at Prouille and Madrid.

1906

Bl. Ezechiel Moreno Díaz, Spanish Augustinian Recollect, who was ordained in the Philippines, served there for 15 years, returned to Spain for a time as prior in Navarre and then led a mission to Colombia where he opened a house in Bogota. From the age of 46 till his death at 58 he served in Colombia as a bishop, the last 10 in the diocese of Pasto. When this model pastor offered to resign because of serious illness, Pope Leo XIII said, "Return to Pasto. The world has need of bishops like you."

AUGUST 19

1680

ST. JOHN EUDES, founder in Normandy of the Congregation of Jesus and Mary—Eudists—to train priests, and of the Sisters of Our Lady of Charity—parent body of the Good Shepherd nuns—to provide a home for wayward girls.

John Eudes joined de Bérulle's Oratory at twenty-two and became most effective in the pulpit and the confessional. "The preacher," he used to say, "beats the bushes but the confessor catches the birds." Devoted as he was to giving missions, he saw the even greater need for a congregation to train holy priests.

The first celebration of the feast of the Sacred Heart took place under his direction in the seminary chapel at Rennes, three years before St. Margaret Mary had her first revelation. He composed the office and Mass himself. He was also the first to institute the feast of the Holy Heart of Mary. His best remembered saying is that to celebrate Mass properly would require three eternities: one to prepare, one to offer the Mass, and one for thanksgiving.

640

St. Bertulf, abbot of Bobbio, northern Italy, in 628 when Pope Honorius I withdrew that monastery from the jurisdiction of the local bishop—the first recorded instance of the monastic exemption that would eventually become the rule.

1157   [*O. Cist., O.C.S.O.*]

Bl. Guerricus, Cistercian author. He was sent by St. Bernard to be the first abbot of Igny in the diocese of Reims.

1297   [*Franciscans*]

St. Louis of Anjou, youthful saint who resigned his right to the Kingdom of Naples to become a Franciscan. "Jesus Christ," he said, "is my kingdom. If I possess him alone I shall have all things. If I have him not I lose all." Forced to accept the bishopric of Toulouse, he pronounced his religious vows on Christmas Eve, was ordained bishop five days later, and died within a few months at the age of twenty-three.

1348   [*O.S.B.*]

Bl. Bernard Tolomei, abbot, a Sienese lawyer and public servant turned hermit, who founded the Olivetan congregation of Benedictines and died of contagion while caring for the plague stricken.

BLESSED EZECHIEL MORENO DIAZ

AUGUST 20

1153

ST. BERNARD, abbot of Clairvaux, doctor, leading churchman of the twelfth century and principal promoter of Cistercian monasticism. At twenty-two he persuaded thirty of his relatives and friends to come along with him and enter the abbey of Citeaux in Burgundy. There St. Stephen Harding was implementing a reform whose watchword was exact observance of the Rule of St. Benedict, with particular emphasis on simplicity, self-support through manual labor, and the atmosphere of silence that would be conducive to reading and prayer.

Citeaux, founded a short time before, had been without novices for several years. Bernard's arrival triggered an unprecedented release of monastic energy. In three years he was sent out at the head of a colony of thirteen. They settled at Clairvaux in the diocese of Langres.

As a leader, writer, preacher, and saint he was irresistible. He personally founded 68 monasteries and still had 700 monks left in his own. Clairvaux became the spiritual center of Europe. At one time St. Bernard had among his former monks the pope, the archbishop of York, several cardinals, and numerous bishops. When he died at sixty-three there were 339 houses in the Cistercian complex.

For years on end he had to be active in public affairs, and his lament at being torn away from the peace of the cloister was the genuine cry of a contemplative soul. He won a good part of Europe to Innocent II and preached the Second Crusade.

At the Council of Sens he read out his list of heretical propositions gathered from Abelard's writings and asked him either to defend the propositions, amend them, or deny they were his. Abelard, though he was the one who had asked for the public debate, stammered, "I will not answer the Cistercian. I appeal from the Council to the See of Rome," and then walked out of the cathedral.

Bernard was canonized twenty-one years after his death. His

brothers Guy, Gerard, and Nivard, and his sister Humbeline are listed among the Blessed. The warm and personal spiritual writings of this doctor of divine love have exerted much influence on Franciscan and later schools of piety, and were recommended by Pope Pius XI as particularly suitable novitiate reading.

1866

Bl. Mary de Mattias, foundress in Italy of the Sisters Adorers of the Precious Blood, who are also devoted to teaching. By the time of her beatification in 1950 there were 400 houses spread throughout the world. She became aware of a special divine call at the age of seventeen during a mission by St. Caspar del Bufalo. "Calvary," she once said, "is the school of good manners."

AUGUST 21

1914

ST. PIUS X; bishop of Mantua; patriarch of Venice; pope of the Holy Eucharist and the catechism. He was the second among the ten children of the village postman in Riese, Venetia. He spent seventeen years in parish work and then became chancellor of Treviso and spiritual director at the seminary. Only slack or complaining seminarians could disturb his habitual calm.

During eleven years as pope it was his one aim "to restore all things in Christ." He fostered priestly holiness and catechetical instruction, encouraged early, frequent and even daily Communion, reformed the breviary and calendar, restored church music, reorganized the Roman curia, undertook codification of Canon Law, condemned Modernism, founded the Biblical Institute and Biblical Commission, and handled the religious crisis of France in such a way that the papacy gained a free

SAINT PIUS X

hand there in the appointment of bishops.

But his greatest achievement was personal holiness, transparent goodness, and simplicity. He loved to call himself a "country priest" and did not follow the practice of conferring titles of nobility on his relatives, particularly the three sisters who came to take dinner with him once a week. When the heraldic commission asked what title to give them he said, "Call them the sisters of the pope." In his last will he wrote: "I was born poor, I have lived poor, I wish to die poor."

When once asked what was the basis of his policy, he put his hand on the crucifix and said: "Here is my policy." "God will provide," was the motto always on his lips. Pius X died on August 20, 1914, a few weeks after the outbreak of World War I.

ca. 479

St. Sidonius Apollinaris; statesman; poet; panegyrist; son-in-law of Emperor Avitus; bishop of Clermont. His 147 letters are an important source of information on fifth century Gaul.

AUGUST 22 *

THE QUEENSHIP OF MARY, observed on the octave day of the Assumption, just as the fifth Glorious Mystery of the Rosary follows the fourth. Mary's title of "Queen" or an equivalent form like "Our Lady," "Empress," or "Mistress" is one of her earliest; and already during apostolic times there is a suggestion of it in Elizabeth's salutation the "Mother of My Lord" (Lk 1:43).

Today's feast recalls Mary's dignity as an intimate, voluntary co-operator with her Son in every step of his redemptive mission, and underlines her loving initiative and resourcefulness as the Mother of Mercy. Pope Pius XII consecrated the world to the Immaculate Heart of Mary, Mother and Queen, on October

---

* *M.E.P. see Sept. 26 for Korean Martyrs.*

31, 1942, and instituted the feast of the Queenship of Mary in 1954.

1679

St. John Kemble, martyr under Charles II, a gentle saint who is particularly attractive because of his detachment and freedom of soul which increased with age. He had served on the English-Welsh mission for fifty-three years when the Titus Oates "Plot" provided an excuse for a general round-up of priests. Urged to hide himself, he answered, "According to the course of nature I have but a few years to live. It will be an advantage to suffer for my religion, and therefore I will not abscond."

He was condemned as a seminary priest—for he had been trained abroad—and was executed at Hereford in his eighty-first year. When the under-sheriff came to bring him to the scaffold he asked for time to finish his prayers, to smoke a pipe of tobacco, and to have a drink. His first miracle was on behalf of the daughter of the man who had denounced and arrested him.

AUGUST 23

1617

ST. ROSE OF LIMA; patroness of the New World, of South America and of Peru; daughter of a conquistador; the first saint in the Americas to be canonized. From early childhood she chose St. Catherine of Siena as her model. Like Catherine she received mystic graces, practised extraordinary mortifications, and promised virginity. Not permitted to enter a cloister, she became a Dominican tertiary at twenty, and lived at home in as much seclusion as she could manage—having a hermitage in her garden. But she also kept a room where she tended destitute elderly people.

During the long illness that carried her off at thirty-one she would often pray: "Lord, increase my sufferings—and with them increase your love in my heart." Huge crowds hindered the funeral for several days until a private burial was contrived in the Dominican church.

1285 [*O.S.M.*]

St. Philip Benizi, Florentine, principal propagator of the Servites in Italy and the one who codified the rules and constitutions of the order. He graduated in medicine from Padua, practised for one year, and then became a brother in the newly founded Order of the Servants of Mary. Four years later the superiors insisted that he become a priest, and at the age of thirty-four he was elected superior general. He had a remarkable gift for drawing others to a life of holiness. Thus, there are seven blesseds and one saint among the men he attracted.

After the death of Clement IV there was a strong rumor that Philip was being seriously considered for the papacy, so he went into a mountain cave where he hid for three months until the election was over. His parting words on handing over the generalate were: "Love one another! Love one another!"

On his deathbed he asked for his "book." Eager hands offered him the Bible, the breviary, the rosary. But blessed Ubald knew the book from which St. Philip learned his wisdom and handed him the crucifix. On it he fixed his calm eyes until he died. He was fifty-three.

AUGUST 24

ST. BARTHOLOMEW, apostle, whose name is found in the lists of the apostles, but nowhere else in the New Testament. Since the ninth century he was commonly thought to be the

same as Nathanael, of whom Our Lord said, "Behold an Israel-
ite in whom their is no guile" (Jn 1:47). Earlier fathers—St. Augustine and St. Gregory—did not identify them, and many
moderns do not consider Nathanael one of the Twelve.

1826

St. Joan Antide-Thouret, foundress of a congregation engaged
in welfare work and education and today known as the Sisters
of Charity of St. Joan Antide-Thouret. She was the fifth child
of a large family near Besançon and in her early twenties entered a Paris house of the Sisters of Charity of St. Vincent de
Paul, but the Revolution dispersed the community before Joan
could take vows. The vicar general of Besançon waved aside
her objections against founding her own school and community:
"Courage, virtue and trust in God are what is required, and it
seems to me that you have these three qualities."

The order quickly spread to Switzerland, Savoy, and Naples;
but the time came when she would no longer be received in her
own motherhouse because the Bishop of Besançon, a convinced
Gallican, withdrew the houses in his diocese from the congregation. She spent the remaining years founding convents in Italy.

1865

St. Mary Michael Desmaisières, foundress in Spain of the
Handmaids of the Blessed Sacrament, who work for women of
the streets and the unprotected. She was Viscountess of Sor-
balán, resisted various marriage plans, and stayed for some
years with her brother while he was Spanish ambassador at
Paris and Brussels. All the while she was laying the foundation
for her future work by daily Communion, work with the needy,
and such mortifications as instruments of penance under her
fine clothes. She died of cholera in Valencia, where she went to
nurse during an epidemic.

AUGUST 25

1270

ST. LOUIS IX of France, a ruler who won the love and deep loyalty of officials as well as subjects. He spent six brave years as an unsuccessful crusader in Egypt and Palestine and died a victim of typhus in Tunis at the age of fifty-six, as he was starting off on a second crusade. Within months numerous miracles were reported, and he was canonized twenty-seven years later.

The **Life of St. Louis,** a masterpiece of anecdote by the fellow crusader Jean de Joinville, was so popular that the saint's words and example became a part of the household wisdom of Christian France. Preachers would repeat maxims of the king, such as his advice to Joinville not to contradict anyone unless silence would be sinful; and every mother knew how Queen Blanche, half English and half Spanish, had taught Louis as a child to believe in God and love Him, and how she impressed on his young mind that it was better to die than commit a mortal sin. Louis in turn had eleven children and was fond of telling them bed-time stories about good and bad kings. He had a high regard for religious life and is patron of Franciscan tertiaries.

Next to his personal example the saint's greatest achievement was in jurisprudence. With him cases coming before the king or parliament began to be recorded, and an attempt was made to write up customary law. He published his own list of impartial yet very human directives for judges and officers of the realm. His own rule lasted forty-four years.

1648

St. Joseph Calasanctius, founder of the Piarist Fathers, a teaching order of priests. After studying law he turned to theology and became a successful priest and vicar general in the diocese of Urgel, Spain. But in response to a mysterious call he gave up his benefices, distributed much of his inheritance, and went to Rome, where his vocation as an educator gradually unfolded.

He began with the Confraternity of Christian Doctrine, but soon he became convinced that a free religious school for the poor was the most pressing need. As none of the organizations he approached would undertake such a project he realized it was God's will that he should go ahead on his own. Three other priests joined him and within a week they had 100 pupils. He was then forty-one.

During forty more years he saw his work flourish. Then came his 10-year way of the cross as the 500-member order was torn asunder by an ambitious newcomer who gained influence with the Holy See. The saint was set aside and the congregation practically ruined—though it was restored twenty years later. He counseled obedience and found strength in the words of Job, "The Lord gave and the Lord has taken away; blessed be the name of the Lord" (Job 1:21). St. Joseph Calasanctius is the patron of Christian schools.

AUGUST 26*

1838   [D.C.]

St. Joan Elizabeth Bichier des Ages, foundress with St. Andrew Fournet of the Daughters of the Cross, also called the Sisters of St. Andrew, a congregation which grew from one of those clusters of heroic young women who did so much to make up for the lack of priests during the French Revolution. A treasured relic from that period is a small picture of Our Lady of Help with these words on the back: "I, Joan Elizabeth Mary Lucy Bichier, today dedicate and consecrate myself to Jesus and Mary forever. May 5, 1797." She was twenty-four.

Devout Catholics would not patronize the "constitutional" priest in the parish, but each evening Joan gathered the farmers and their wives for prayers, hymns, and spiritual reading. She

---

*C.P. see Sept. 6 for Bl. Dominic Barberi.

then came under the influence of a priest who held services in a barn at Maillé. This was St. Andrew Fournet. He eventually sent her away for a few months' novitiate and then made her a mother superior.

The small band, which included some of Joan's closest companions, would devote itself to works of charity and teaching. They hoped to join one of the established orders when better times returned, but within twenty-five years they already had sixty convents of their own.

In founding the Basque house at Igon, Joan met another priest and future saint, Michael Garicoïts. She encouraged him so much in founding the Priests of the Sacred Heart of Betharram that he was able to say: "It's all the good sister's doing. I had only to do what she told me." The two were canonized together in 1947.

1897

St. Teresa of Jesus Jornet e Ibars, foundress at Barbastro in Spain of the Little Sisters of the Abandoned Aged. As a small girl she would bring poor people to her peasant home and her parents would feed them. She became a teacher but soon felt a strong attraction to religious life. Circumstances and a temporary skin condition kept her from entering the convents of her choice so she returned to teaching. But in 1873, when she was thirty, Father Saturninus Lopez Novoa made her the center of a projected community that would care for neglected elderly people. Ten women took the habit at the same time. When St. Teresa was canonized in 1974 there were over 3,000 members.

"The Little Sisters," Pope Paul remarked in the canonization address, "have been and are the witnesses of the emptiness that often afflicts the old. They have been chosen to fill that emptiness with warmth and human affection. They have been chosen by God to reaffirm the sacredness of human life and to underline the truth that man is a child of God and can never be regarded only as a tool of cold utilitarianism."

AUGUST 27*

387

ST. MONICA, model Christian mother, wife and widow. A few days before her death she said to Augustine: "Son, nothing in this world now affords me delight. I do not know what there is left for me to do or why I am still here. There was only one thing for which I wanted to live a little longer, and that was to see you a Catholic Christian before I died. God has granted me this in superabundance, for I see that you are now his total servant and have despised all earthly happiness" (**Confessions** 9, 10). Some years earlier she had the consolation of seeing her husband, Patricius, enter the church before his death.

As her name shows, Monica was of African Berber stock. Saint though she was, and often favored with divine illumination during prayer, she did not always know the best way to help her brilliant but erring son. She urged him to marry and almost had her way. Once she begged a bishop to talk to him, but the bishop realized that Augustine was not yet ready to listen. As Monica kept pleading and broke into tears the bishop lost patience but assured her, "It is impossible that the son of these tears should perish" (**Confessions** 3, 12). She accepted this answer as coming from heaven and kept on praying.

In Carthage, while she was in a chapel of St. Cyprian, Augustine slipped away and sailed to Rome without her. She followed him as far as Milan, where she loved St. Ambrose as an angel of God come to help her son; and she readily gave up some of the North African devotions of which Ambrose disapproved, such as Saturday fasts and the wine and cakes she brought to church on martyrs' feasts. She took part in the dialogues at Cassiciacum, which were published as some of St. Augustine's earliest works. Asked whether a person who has what he wants is happy, she answered, "Yes, provided he wants what is good."

Death overtook her at Ostia, Italy, where the whole of

---

*Sch.P. see Aug. 25 for St. Joseph Calasanctius.

Augustine's party was waiting for a ship back to Africa. At one time Monica had been much concerned about being buried next to her husband, but now she said, "Nothing is far from God and there is no fear that he will not know where to raise me up at the end of time." Augustine marveled at the way God had put her mind at rest on the matter. "Lay this body anywhere," she said, "this only I ask of you, that you remember me at the altar of the Lord wherever you may be" (**Confessions** 9, 11).

AUGUST 28

430

ST. AUGUSTINE, bishop of Hippo, doctor, author of the Confessions and more than 100 other books. probably the best-known and most influential Christian since St. Paul. He was born in 354 at Tagaste, now Souk-Ahras, Algeria. His parents saved to give him the best education and sent him to Carthage for his final two or three years. There, at seventeen, he already had a son by a woman with whom he would live for thirteen years. St. Monica's admonitions on purity seemed womanish to him. Her faith, too, he abandoned—though he was only a catechumen—to join the semi-Christian Manichees.

One of the turning points in his life was reading Cicero's **Hortensius** at the age of nineteen, for it inflamed him with an intense and abiding desire for true wisdom. So he turned to the Scriptures to see what they had to offer, but soon gave them up as inferior to Cicero. Then, in Tagaste, Carthage, Rome, and Milan he taught rhetoric—that combination of classics and oratory to which Roman students devoted their last years of higher education. Gregarious and a natural leader with a remarkable capacity for friendship, he became the center of a group of intellectuals who at one time were thinking of forming a commune. For nine years he was connected with the

Manichees. Then came a period when he thought sceptics were probably the wisest men.

Such was his state of mind on arriving at Milan in his thirtieth year. There he met St. Ambrose. "I came to love him," Augustine wrote, "for his kindness towards me. . . . I attended carefully when he preached. . . . Opening my heart to learn how eloquently he spoke, I came to feel, though only gradually, how truly he spoke. . . . I began to see that the Catholic faith . . . could be maintained on reasonable grounds" (**Confessions** 5, 13-14).

Augustine began to appreciate Scripture and again became a catechumen. Neo-Platonism, by teaching him to reflect on his own mental processes, showed him a way out of materialism. He also came to see evil as an absence of good rather than as the positive thing the Manichees made it. But a moral problem remained. "Lord," he would pray, "give me chastity, but not yet" (**Confessions** 8, 7). Then came the dramatic experience in the garden, the child's voice bidding him "take up and read," and his conversion—for he now found himself with the strength to observe Christ's law. He was baptized at thirty-two, became a priest four years later, and was a bishop at forty.

Until his death at seventy-five he preached and wrote on every current theological question. His church in north Africa was a beacon to the Catholic world. No other Latin Father wrote so much. He was so human and his theology so biblical that succeeding generations continued to find him relevant. His answer to the Donatists of Africa, **"securus judicat orbis terrarum"** — "the whole world (the whole church) judges safely" — shattered Newman's **Via Media** theory and led him in turn to the Church universal (**Apologia** ch. 3).

Augustine gathered his followers into a monastic community, and at Hippo he wrote a rule valued especially for its brevity, discretion, and emphasis on charity. It is observed by Augustinians, Dominicans, and more than 150 other institutes of men and women in the Church today.

AUGUST 29

THE MARTYRDOM OF ST. JOHN THE BAPTIST. In the words of Jesus, John was "a light burning and shining" (Jn 5:35), a herald of truth. His baptism and preaching bore testimony to Christ, to the moral law, and to the need for repentance. His death witnessed in a particular way to the integrity of marriage and to the dignity of the human person who speaks out fearlessly for what is right. The marriage of Herod Antipas was both incestuous and adulterous, for Herodias was also his niece.

Herod's birthday party, with its lust, gluttony, human respect, ambition, hatred, and cruelty, set the stage for the final act of the last and greatest of the Old Testament prophets. Josephus tells how the Jews believed that the destruction of Herod's army was God's punishment for the murder of John. "John", he adds, "was a good man who commanded the Jews to exercise virtue, both in doing right towards one another and in piety towards God, and so to come to baptism."

1628

Bl. Richard Herst, a recusant Lancashire farmer executed for murder under Charles I despite all the evidence. He left six young children and a seventh still unborn. When the hangman was fumbling with the rope he called up: "Tom, I think I must come up and help thee." There is still preserved this note he sent to his confessor: "Although my flesh is timorous and fearful, I yet find a great comfort in spirit in casting myself upon my sweet Saviour with a most fervent love, when I consider what He has done and suffered for me; and my greatest desire is to suffer with Him. And I had rather choose to die a thousand deaths than to possess a kingdom and live in mortal sin. . . ."

AUGUST 30

1588

St. Margaret Ward and **Bl. John Roche,** executed in London under Elizabeth I for helping Father William Watson escape from Bridewell prison. Margaret was flogged and hung up by the wrists, the tips of her toes barely touching the ground. At the trial, though threatened with more torture, she would not reveal the whereabouts of the priest. Promised liberty if she would ask the Queen's pardon and attend church, the saint replied that she was in no way sorry for having saved the priest; and as for going to the prescribed church, she was convinced it was unlawful; and she was ready, if she had them, to lay down many lives for the sake of God and her conscience.

On the same day three other lay people were executed for relieving priests — **Bl. Edward Shelley, Bl. Richard Martin,** and **Ven. Richard Flower.** There was also **Bl. Richard Leigh,** who was martyred for his priesthood. They sang on the way to Tyburn but were not allowed to address the crowd.

1604

Bl. Juvenal Ancina, Oratorian, bishop of Saluzzo in Piedmont. In his twenties he occupied the chair of medicine at Turin, treated the poor free of charge, and had chess and the writing of poetry as hobbies. Though he was regularly in the presence of the dying and a frequent attendant at funerals, the young doctor, listening one day to the chanting of the **Dies Irae,** was overwhelmed by the realization that after death comes judgment.

He seriously thought of becoming a Carthusian, but St. Philip Neri pursuaded him to enter his Oratory instead. Ordained at thirty-six, he wrought marvels in Naples and Rome. One of his practical measures was a deposit with a barber to whom he would send anyone with unkempt hair or beard.

He ran off for five months while three bishoprics stood empty, but several years later the pope ordered him to accept the see of Saluzzo. Before long he was poisoned by a friar whom he had rebuked for scandalous living.

AUGUST 31 *

651
St. Aidan, Irish monk of Iona, first bishop of Lindisfarne, the leader of the missionaries responsible for bringing Christianity to most of northern England. Whatever gifts he received from the rich he passed on at once to the poor.

The monk who preceded him on this mission failed completely and on returning to Iona laid the blame on the character of the English. But Aidan spoke up in chapter. "Brother," he said, "I think you were too rigorous . . . and that you did not follow the Apostle's rule of first giving them the milk of milder doctrine until little by little . . . they were able to understand the more perfect mysteries and fulfil the greater commandments." The community, impressed by Aidan's discretion, sent him instead.

For seventeen years he traveled continually, always on foot, and wherever he saw people he turned aside and spoke to them about the faith. "He was," writes St. Bede, "a bishop inspired with a passionate love of goodness, but at the same time a man of remarkable gentleness and moderation."

661
St. Finan, Irish monk of Iona, St. Aidan's immediate successor as bishop of Lindisfarne, a staunch supporter of Celtic observances. He baptized Penda, leader of the Middle English, and Sigebert, king of the East Saxons. At Lindisfarne he built a cathedral of wood thatched with sea grass.

---

* *C.O. see Aug. 30 for Bl. John Juvenal Ancina.*

1315   [*O.S.M.*]

Bl. Andrew Dotti of Borgo San Sepolcro in Tuscany. He became a Servite after hearing St. Philip Benizi speak on the text, "Whoever does not renounce all that he has cannot be my disciple" (Lk 14:33). An outstanding preacher, he retired at sixty to spend his last days as a hermit.

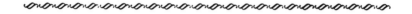

SEPTEMBER 1

1367   [*O.S.M.*]
Bl. Joan Soderini, Servite in Florence, close associate of St. Juliana Falconieri and her successor as prioress. As a young nun she gave herself to tasks others avoided, and endeared herself to her community by her even temper and cheerfulness.

1490   [*Franciscans*]
St. Beatrice da Silva, sister of Bl. Amadeus of Portugal, foundress of the Conceptionist Nuns. She left court and turned to religious life after a jealous queen, listening to gossip, put her in prison. During forty years she lived in secular dress at a Cistercian monastery in Toledo, and then founded her own community which soon after her death aligned with the Poor Clares and today forms a branch of that order.

1770   [*O. Carm., O.C.D.*]
St. Theresa Margaret Redi, popular Carmelite miracle-worker in Florence, where her body remains incorrupt. During five years—she died at twenty-three—she used the opportunities

cloistered life offered for serving others, especially the sick of her community. She was intensely devoted to the Sacred Heart.

1855 [C.M.]

Bl. Gabra Michael, dissident Ethiopian monk reconciled to the Holy See by Bl. Justin de Jacobis. He directed the college established by Bl. Justin and helped him translate a book of moral theology into Amharic and compose a catechism. He was scourged and condemned to death, but at the pleading of the English ambassador and other notables was reprieved. The sentence was changed to life imprisonment.

On March 28th, exhausted by illness, harsh treatment, and age, he died on the roadside as he was dragging his chains along in the retinue of the Ethiopian king. He is venerated as a martyr.

SEPTEMBER 2

1792 [*Franciscans, C.J.M.*]

The Paris or **September Martyrs,** a group of 191, beatified in 1926, victims of the prison massacres Sept. 2-3, 1792. In the previous month there was such fear of rebellion and foreign invasion that the municipalities were authorized to round up all suspects, including the priests who had declined the constitutional oath—which meant nearly all the bishops and half of the lower clergy. A number were taken into custody. In Paris several religious houses were converted into prisons for clergy.

On Sept. 2 the rumor spread that Verdun had surrendered and that the prisoners were planning an uprising. Mobs stormed the Parish jails and killed more than a thousand prisoners, including also common criminals. The priests were asked whether they had taken the oath. If they said, "No," they were killed on the spot. It is believed that not a single priest saved his life by a lie. "I do not understand," M. Violette who was in charge of the executions at the Vaugirard section reported the following morning, "They seemed happy; they went to death as to a wedding." The oath consisted in a promise to uphold liberty, equality, and the Civil Constitution of the Clergy with its complete subjection of Church authority to civil structures.

The martyrs include the Archbishop of Arles, **Bl. John du Lau,** and two other bishops, 113 secular priests—Canadian-born **Bl. André Grasset de Saint-Sauveur** among them—twenty-four disbanded Jesuits, twelve Sulpicians, five laymen, and a number of clerics and religious of various orders including **Bl. Augustine Chevreux,** superior general of the Maurist Benedictines, and **Bl. John Francis Burté,** superior of a large Franciscan house in Paris.

SEPTEMBER 3

605

ST. GREGORY I, doctor; father of the mediaeval papacy, a principal founder of Christian Europe. This incomparable pastor is called "the Great" because of his contribution in the areas of moral and ascetical theology, chant—which even bears his name—and liturgy, ecclesiastical administration, monasticism, evangelization, and the social mission of the church.

The 854 extant chancery letters, spanning his fourteen year pontificate, are so many masterpieces of Christian wisdom and jurisprudence, each characteristically Gregorian in the way it situates the business at hand within the broader context of the Gospel and the common good. No other pope has supplied canonists and moralists with so many enduring formulas. He brought to the papacy all that was best in the Roman tradition of law, respect for rights, courtesy, and order.

Belonging to a Roman family that had already supplied two popes—St. Felix III was his great-great grandfather—he was educated for a career in law and administration. Already in his thirties he was prefect of Rome with responsibility for finances, food, defence, and policing; but after a year he turned the family house on the Coelian Hill into a monastery dedicated to St. Andrew and became a simple monk. He also established six more monasteries on his estates in Sicily.

Four years later he was ordained a deacon and sent as papal representative to the emperor at Constantinople. There he spent seven years, and after a period back in Rome as one of the city's seven deacons, was made pope by popular choice.

He maintained the primacy of Rome, censured the patriarch of Constantinople for assuming the title "ecumenical patriarch" and, for his part, chose "Servant of the servants of God" — a title popes have kept ever since. In default of any other effective authority he became the **de facto** ruler of Rome and negotiated directly with the Lombard invaders. He appointed competent administrators of the vast papal patrimony, carefully checked their reports, cared for the poor, ransomed captives, and rebuilt ruined churches.

The first monk to become pope, he understood monasticism from within, gave it an official place in the ecclesiastical structure, saw its missionary possibilities, and sent forty of his own monks to evangelize the English. His legislation kept monasteries under local bishops but guaranteed their independence in elections, the use of personnel, and finances. Except for him nothing would be known of the life of St. Benedict, whose rule he recommended so highly.

The pope's **Pastoral Rule,** intended as a handbook for bishops, still remains irreplaceable reading for those engaged in the care of souls, which Gregory calls "the art of arts."

SEPTEMBER 4

5th cent.

St. Poemen, abbot, Egyptian desert father, many of whose sayings became classic. To a monk who was blaming the devil for his troubles he said, "It is always the devil who is blamed. I say it is self-will." Another was worried over blasphemous thoughts, but in his case Poemen saw that the suggestion did come from satan. So he told the monk to answer in this way: "Let your blasphemy fall on you. It is not mine, for my heart detests it." About tale-bearing he said, "There could be no poorer evidence than scandalous stories told by a monk."

543

St. Caesarius, monk at Lerins and for forty years bishop of Arles. He is Gaul's outstanding churchman of the sixth century and the one mainly responsible for the Council of Orange, 529, which ended the Semi-Pelagian controversy.

He wrote a monastic rule for a convent of nuns under his sister, St. Caesaria. He is sometimes ranked first among the popular orators of the early Latin church. His sermons were frequent, simple, and short; and he expected priests to read the entire Bible four times a year and also to preach. "A man," he said, "worships that on which his mind is intent during prayer. Whoever in his prayers thinks of public affairs or of the house he is building, worships them rather than God." He died August 28.

1252   [Franciscan III O.]

St. Rose of Viterbo, youthful Franciscan tertiary greatly honored in her native town.

SEPTEMBER 5

ca. 700

St. Bertin, a monk sent from Luxeuil to help St. Omer. He became abbot of a monastery—later named after him—on the island of Sithiu. Besides evangelizing the Pas-de-Calais, St.

Bertin and his monks took the lead in draining the surrounding swamp and showed the people how to build solid houses. His emblem is a boat.

1905

Bl. Maria Assunta Pallotta, a missionary sister whose special attraction is the ordinariness of her religious life and the reassurance it offers fervent nuns whose convent life would resemble hers except for her trip to China and early death at twenty-six. She was a hard-working, devout child of extremely poor parents in Picena, Italy. Her education went little beyond learning to read and write; but she helped teach catechism, developed early a habit of prayer, and had a special love of Mary. She was nearly twenty before her parents could spare her and consented to her becoming a nun.

She entered the Roman house of the Franciscan Missionaries of Mary, a congregation that had recently been established in Madras, India. This order's objectives had a particular appeal for her: poverty according to the ideals of St. Francis, daily exposition and adoration of the Blessed Sacrament, missionary work, and the offering of oneself as a victim for the Church and the salvation of souls.

Maria, determined to be a saint and do God's will in everything, passed the first five years in various convents of Italy helping in domestic, infirmary, and catechetical work. She spent her final year in Shansi province of northern China, cooking and severely tried by scruples. She died in a typhus epidemic on April 7, 1905.

The several pages of resolutions found among her writings begin with this one, "I came to the convent to become a saint. What good will it do to live long if I do not attain my goal?" She had an intense sense of union with Christ through her vows of poverty, chastity, and obedience and in the short letter in which she volunteered for the missions and made known her wish to care for the lepers she three times expressed the thought "if Jesus wills."

The day after her perpetual vows she wrote to her parents,

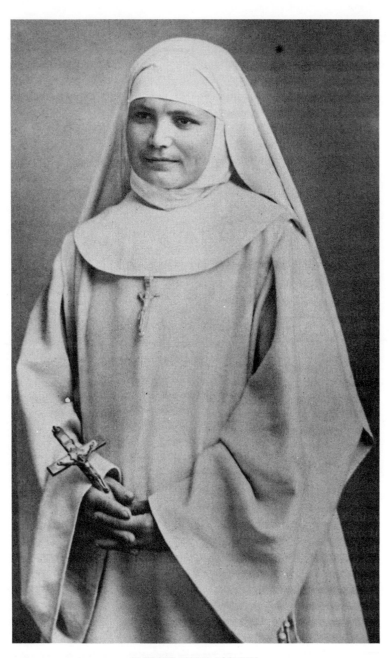

BLESSED MARIA ASSUNTA

"Yesterday I offered myself as a victim for the Church, and I asked God to make me die on the spot if I were ever to commit the smallest voluntary fault."

Her goodness and the mysterious perfume that filled her room twenty minutes before her death and lasted for two full days moved others to ask her assistance, and God answered with miracles.

Known by their habit as "White Franciscans," her Franciscan Missionaries of Mary already have eight sisters beatified.

SEPTEMBER 6

1230

Bl. Bertrand of Garrigues, a secular priest who worked with St. Dominic on the Albigensian mission and was one of the six who made up the first Dominican community. He helped found the house near the University of Paris as well as the monastery in Bologna. When the order was divided into eight provinces in 1221, the territory of Provence was entrusted to him.

1491 [*O.S.M.*]

Bl. Bonaventure Tornielli, also called Bonaventure of Forli, vicar provincial of the Servites, a late vocation and outstanding preacher. He died on Holy Thursday at Udine, where he had just finished the lenten sermons.

1588

Bl. William Hartley and **Bl. John Hewett,** priests; and **Bl. Robert Sutton,** a schoolmaster, martyrs in London under Elizabeth I. An eyewitness, William Naylor, wrote of Bl. Robert Sutton: ". . . the sheriff promised to procure his pardon if he would but pronounce absolutely the word **all;** for he would that he should acknowledge the queen to be supreme head in

all causes without any restriction; but he would acknowledge her to be supreme head in all causes temporal; but for that he would not pronounce the word **all** without any restriction, he was executed. This I heard and saw."

1849

Bl. Dominic Barberi, who was Passionist provincial in southern Italy and then opened the first Passionist monastery in England. His saintliness wrought many conversions despite his unattractive, even ugly, appearance which made him the object of ridicule and persecution. He received John Henry Newman and three others of the Oxford Movement into the Catholic Church. He died on August 27.

SEPTEMBER 7

363

Sts. Juventinus and **Maximinus,** officers in the imperial guard, beheaded at Antioch for their outspoken condemnation of the persecution under Julian the Apostate. A sermon of St. John Chrysostom a generation later shows their popularity in Antioch and witnesses to the faith and practice of the church as regards the cult of martyrs. "Let us," he says, "visit them frequently. Let us touch their shrine and embrace their relics with confidence, so that we may obtain some blessing from them. For just as soldiers showing to the king the wounds they received in his battles, speak with confidence, so they, by a humble representation of their past sufferings for Christ, obtain whatever they ask of the king of heaven."

ca. 560

St. Cloud, grandson of Clovis and St. Clotilde. When he was eight his two brothers were murdered, but he escaped. Instead of trying to recover the kingdom, he became a priest and hermit-preacher at Nogent on the Seine, a site now known as St. Cloud. He died at thirty-six.

1619

Three priests and influential educators tortured and martyred at Kosice in Slovakia by a band of soldiers under a Calvinist leader. They are the diocesan priest, **Bl. Mark Crisin,** a Croatian, and two Jesuits, **Bl. Stephen Pongracz,** a Hungarian, and **Bl. Melchior Grodecz,** a Czech.

1644

Bl. John Duckett, a secular priest, and **Bl. Ralph Corby,** a Jesuit, martyred together for their priesthood at Tyburn under Charles I. The Corbys show how a family could treasure the faith in time of persecution. Bl. Ralph's father became a Jesuit brother and brought his own father—who was then 100—back to the Church. The martyr's two brothers also joined the Jesuits, while his mother and two sisters entered Benedictine convents in Ghent and Brussels.

SEPTEMBER 8

BIRTHDAY OF THE BLESSED VIRGIN MARY, a feast introduced in the East in the sixth century and in the West during the seventh. Fulfilment of prophecy and universal joy are the themes of today's celebration.

701

St. Sergius I, pope, born in Sicily but of Syrian stock. The times were so troubled that he was able to assume office only after submitting to extortion. He is particularly remembered for sanctioning in the West the four feasts of Our Lady observed in the East: today's feast along with the Purification, the An-

nunciation, and Mary's Falling Asleep. Despite personal danger
he refused to sanction the council held in the Trullo at Constantinople, 692—which the Greeks consider ecumenical. Among
its objectionable canons were some that universalized the Greek
discipline regarding marriage and clerical celibacy, and gave
Constantinople a position equal to Rome in church affairs,
though second in dignity. He intervened on behalf of St. Wilfrid, consecrated St. Willibrord bishop for the Friesland mission,
and—though nothing came of it—asked Abbot Coelfrid of Wearmouth and Jarrow to send St. Bede to Rome, as the pope had
need of learned advisers.

ca. 725

St. Corbinian, apostle of Bavaria. He began as a hermit near
Melun, but the fame of his holiness made solitude more and
more difficult. Pope St. Gregory II sent him as a missionary
bishop into Bavaria.

1694

Bl. Bernard of Offida, Italian Capuchin brother noted for
his wisdom and miracles and particularly gifted in settling
family quarrels. He died at ninety.

SEPTEMBER 9 *

ca. 556

St. Kieran, abbot-founder of the famous Irish monastery and
school of Clonmacnois on the Shannon.

1654   [*United States, S.J.*]

St. Peter Claver, Spanish Jesuit, the slave's saint. While
studying at Majorca he volunteered for the missions at the
prompting of another saint, Alfonso Rodriguez, the brother

°C.S.Sp. see Sept. 11 for Jacques Désiré Laval.

porter at the college. Alfonso urged him to go to the Indies to save the countless perishing souls.

Peter landed at Cartagena in present-day Columbia, one of the principal slave markets of the New World. There, after his ordination in 1616 at the age of thirty-five, he became the friend, doctor, apostle, and champion of the slaves, taking over the work of Father Alonso de Sandoval, author of two books that alerted the world to the horrors of the slave trade.

Peter met every slave ship with medicines—on a "normal" crossing from Africa a third of the captives had already died —biscuits, brandy, lemons, and whatever else could be gathered from house to house. So appalling was the condition of the human cargo—half crazy through fear, hunger, confinement, and disease—that Father de Sandoval would turn pale and break into a cold sweat on hearing that another slave ship was about to arrive.

Father Claver had with him a band of Negro interpreters who knew the various dialects. He would say, "We must speak to them with our hands before we try to speak to them with our lips." The slaves understood him best, when he kissed their festering wounds.

His love made it possible for them to believe in the love of Christ, and he would insist that they learn this prayer: "Jesus Christ, Son of God, you will be my father and my mother and all my good. I love you much. I am sorry for having sinned against you. I love you very much." In thirty-eight years he baptized some 300,000. He would sign himself "Slave of the slaves for ever."

SEPTEMBER 10

1305   [*O.S.A., O.A.R.*]

St. Nicholas of Tolentino, an Augustinian who after his ordination made a resolution to preach every day. He spent his last thirty years at Tolentino in central Italy, where he died with a great reputation for miracles and apostolic zeal. "Say nothing of this," was his usual comment after a miracle; "give thanks to God not to me; I am only an earthen vessel, a poor sinner."

1617-1632

Of the thousands of Japanese who died for their faith, the twenty-six canonized saints are celebrated on Feb. 6—St. Paul Miki and companions. Another 205 are beatified. Fifty-two of these blesseds suffered Sept. 10, 1622, at Nagasaki. Included are Japanese, Koreans, and Europeans, nine of them Jesuits, eight Dominicans, and three Franciscans. Entire families were beatified.

Most of the ecclesiastics and the men who kept house for them were tied to stakes and large fires lit around them at a distance of some twenty-five feet. When the heat was seen to gain too quickly on its victims, the fires were damped down. Some victims succumbed in a few hours, others lingered till the next morning. Two wavered and begged for mercy—not apostatizing but only asking for an easier and quicker death, which was denied them.

The English skipper, Richard Cocks, told of seeing about twenty-five martyred at Kioto: "Among them little children five or six years old burned in their mother's arms, crying out, 'Jesus, receive our souls.'"

1641

St. Ambrose Barlow, a Benedictine executed under Charles I after twenty-four years of priestly ministry in England. He was the fourth of fourteen children and went abroad for his studies. An acquaintance wrote that he was so "mild, witty, and cheerful in his conversation, that of all men that ever I knew he seemed to me the most likely to represent the spirit of Sir

Thomas More. . . . Neither did I ever see him moved at all upon occasions of wrongs, slanders, or threats . . . but as one insensible of wrong, or free from choler, he entertained them with a jest, and passed over them with a smile or a nod."

SEPTEMBER 11

1840 [*C.M.*]

Bl. John Gabriel Perboyre, French martyr in China. A sermon he heard at fifteen inspired him with the missionary ideal. He joined the Vincentians and spent the first twelve years after ordination successively as teacher, seminary rector, and assistant novice-master, asking at intervals to be sent to China, as stories of persecution kept coming in from there.

He arrived on the mission in 1835 and was taken prisoner four years later. For a whole year he endured fearsome tortures, because he refused to trample on the cross or betray his companions. Four Chinese characters meaning "Teacher of a false religion" were branded on his face. He was finally strangled along with five common criminals.

In consequence of his execution the British Government insisted on a clause in the Treaty of Nanking, 1842, stipulating that any foreign missionary who was arrested should not be dealt with by Chinese authorities but be handed over to the nearest consul of his own nation—preferential treatment which would have the long-range effect of identifying Christianity with imperialism in China.

1864

Bl. Jacques Désiré Laval, the Peter Claver of Mauritius and the first Holy Spirit priest raised to the altar. After training in Paris he worked as a doctor in a small village in his native Normandy. "He is the only educated person that goes to Mass," the people would say; but in time he too stopped. Remorse and deep conversion followed. He decided to be a priest, explaining to his brother "Once I am a priest I will be able to do more good." After three seminary years he was ordained at the age of 35. For two years he was pastor of tiny Pinterville, Normandy, and then with his bishop's permission followed Bishop Collier to the island of Mauritius, which had nine priests but none working with the 80,000 Negroes scattered through the island, all of them former slaves or their descendants. Father Laval would spend his remaining 23 years of priesthood giving himself to evangelize his "dear Blacks" and help them in every other way he could. He was one of the first members of Father Libermann's missionary Society of the Immaculate Heart of Mary and he made his final vows after the merger with the Holy Spirit Fathers, whose official title then became Congregation of the Holy Spirit under the Protection of the Immaculate Heart of Mary. Francis Libermann described Father Laval as a "saint who always says he does nothing." When not needed elsewhere he would be praying before the Blessed Sacrament. One hour on his knees was his normal preparation for Mass, and a half-hour of silence his thanksgiving. At 52 he had a stroke while hearing confessions, but he lived and worked eight more years. Near the end he wrote to his superior, "My great fear and worry is that in some time it may be impossible for me to say holy Mass, the only consolation that remains to me." Bl. Jacques Laval died September 9.

SEPTEMBER 12*

453

St. Pulcheria, upright, capable and wholly orthodox, probably the most important of the theologically-minded empresses of Constantinople. Her return to power in 450 made the Council of Chalcedon possible. In 414, when only fifteen, she was named empress and also regent for her younger brother Theodosius II. After his marriage she was gradually ousted by a new empress with Nestorian sympathies.

---

*O. Cist., O.C.S.O. see Sept. 14 for St. Peter of Tarantaise.

But Theodosius died in 450, and Pulcheria again became ruler. She married the elderly senator Marcian—on condition that she could keep her vow of virginity—and together they summoned the Council of Chalcedon. She died three years later. Pope St. Leo I had several times requested her assistance in settling ecclesiastical affairs and the council hailed her as "Guardian of the faith," and a "second St. Helen."

1617

Bl. Victoria Fornari-Strata, who married at seventeen, was left a widow at twenty-five, and after settling her six children —five of whom became religious—founded the Blue Nuns of Genoa. During a period of uncertainty as to whether to re-marry in view of her own needs and those of her young family, she had a vision of the Blessed Virgin and heard these words: "My child Victoria, be brave and confident, for it is my wish to take both the mother and the children under my protection. I will care for your household. Live quietly and without worry-ing. All I ask is that you trust yourself to me and from now on devote yourself to the love of God above all things." She made a vow of chastity and gave her whole time to God, her children, and the poor.

At forty-two with ten companions she founded her contempla-tive community, devoted to Mary's Annunciation and hidden life at Nazareth. One of the order's charities is to make vest-ments and altar linens for poor churches.

SEPTEMBER 13*

407

ST. JOHN CHRYSOSTOM, archbishop of Constantinople; doc-tor; the most read and best loved of the Greek fathers, and in terms of the writings which have survived he is their most proli-

---

O.C.D. see Sept. 20 for Bl. Mary of Jesus López de Rivas.

fic writer. No other father in the East or West explained Scripture for the people so thoroughly and practically.

He was devoutly raised at Antioch by his mother, Anthusa. "What women there are among the Christians," his instructor exclaimed on learning that John's mother had remained a widow since the age of twenty. This teacher was probably the pagan Libanius, the greatest rhetorician of the day.

As a priest John would excel even his tutor in audience rapport. At sermons that could last two hours, the throng in Antioch's largest church hung on his words, often with enthusiastic cheers. In this city of a quarter or half million, the military headquarters of the East, and frequent residence of the emperor, John preached for twelve years; and when the court needed a bishop that would give Constantinople prestige, he was kidnapped and carried off secretly to avoid a popular uprising.

Since the time of his baptism in young manhood his one interest had been the spiritual life. During his twenties he spent six years as a monk—two of them as a solitary in a mountain cave above Antioch. There he memorized the New Testament, fasted and cut down on sleep until deteriorating health forced him back to the city.

The high ideals set forth in his most famous book, **The Priesthood,** guided him as priest and bishop. He removed unworthy clerics and bishops from office, spoke out plainly against vice, and defended the poor and oppressed.

No other father excels him as a moralist; and the most attractive part of his sermons is the section—generally at the end —in which he inveighs against some common vice, such as anger, pride, ostentation, lust, or avarice.

Empress Eudoxia and a cluster of court ladies interpreted some of the bishop's blunt words as aimed at themselves. The unscrupulous patriarch of Alexandria, Theophilus, took advantage of this hatred in high places, had the saint condemned by a synod of bishops and banished by Emperor Arcadius. John spent three years in exile at Cucusus, Armenia, but still remained too influential, especially through his letters—236 are extant—written to encourage his adherents. So he was marched off in a gruelling trek to a more remote spot on the Black Sea but died of exhaustion on the way and was buried at Comana in Pontus. He was about fifty-two.

Pope Innocent I, defending John's cause, refused communion with the bishop who was intruded in his place. In 438, thirty-one years later, Empress St. Pulcheria and Emperor Theodusius II, atoning for the sin of their parents, marched in the triumphal procession that received the saint's body back into Constantinople.

The name "Chrysostom" (golden-mouth) was first given him in the sixth century. He is patron of preachers.

SEPTEMBER 14

EXALTATION OF THE HOLY CROSS. The Church today venerates the true cross and celebrates the double anniversary of the finding of the cross in September 326 and the dedication of the churches Constantine built on the sites of the Holy Sepulchre and of Calvary. Egeria, visiting Jerusalem at the end of the fourth century, mentions the veneration on Good Friday and the week-long celebration in September.

Though St. Paul frequently refers to the cross in a figurative and devotional way, the symbol was seldom used during the first three centuries. But after Constantine's victory under the sign of the cross, it soon became the favorite and most characteristic Christian symbol. The emperor used it on his standard, shields, and coins and had it sculptured on a triumphal column in Rome. He also abolished crucifixion as a death penalty.

St. Cyril, bishop of Jerusalem from 350 to 387, says the cross "has been distributed fragment by fragment and has already nearly filled the world." With the relics devotion also spread. AT a later date today's celebration came to include the triumphal return of the cross to Jerusalem in 630, when Emperor Heraclius recaptured it from the Persians.

1175

St. Peter, archbishop of Tarentaise in Savoy, a Cistercian at twelve and first abbot of Tamié at thirty. After thirteen years of apostolic reform in his archdiocese he disappeared, and was found a year later serving as a brother in a Cistercian abbey of Switzerland. Ordered back to his see, he effectively supported Pope Alexander III against Emperor Frederick Barbarossa. Because of his charity and healing powers, he was venerated as a saint even before his death. His canonization took place within seventeen years.

ca. 1313

St. Notburga, virgin, popular in the Tyrol as patroness of poor peasants and hired servants. Her whole life was spent in the household of Count Henry of Rattenberg, except for the short period when she was dismissed for giving left-overs to the poor instead of the pigs.

SEPTEMBER 15

OUR LADY OF SORROWS. Simeon's prophecy that the Child was set for the rise and fall of many and that a sword would pierce Mary's soul concludes with the words, "that out of many hearts thought may be revealed" (Lk 2:35). Through the centuries saints have meditated on the Passion and on Mary's intimate role at the foot of the cross. She exemplifies the place of suffering in the lives of those nearest to Christ and is invoked in a special way as the compassionate mother and comforter of the afflicted.

Her sorrows were variously listed. Seven became the most popular number. Commonly included are: the prophecy of Simeon, flight into Egypt, loss of Jesus in the temple, way of the cross, crucifixion, the taking down from the cross, and burial.

In the fifteenth century, confraternities of the Seven Sorrows greatly popularized the devotion. This is the patronal feast of the Servite Order.

1510

St. Catherine of Genoa, mystic, heroic servant of the sick and poor. This lay woman was the inspiration behind the Oratory of Divine Love, a lay-clerical fraternity that began in Genoa and spread through Italy, giving the Church St. Cajetan and some of the principal leaders of Catholic renewal during the first years of the Reformation.

At sixteen she was the pawn in a political marriage to an unfaithful husband. She spent the next five years pining away and five more trying to forget her distress in a whirl of frivolities.

Conversion came suddenly at twenty-six, after prayer to St. Benedict. While kneeling for a blessing she was overcome by a great love of God and a realization of her own unworthiness. "No more world! No more sin!" she kept repeating to herself. After a vision of Christ carrying his cross, she made a general confession and became a daily communicant. By this time her husband had squandered his wealth, and she was able to bring him around to a better life. The two of them, living in continence, spent the next twenty-five years caring for the sick. Her spiritual sayings were soon collected and became very popular.

SEPTEMBER 16

253 and 258

ST. CORNELIUS, pope, and **ST. CYPRIAN,** bishop of Carthage, martyrs honored at Rome on the same day as early as the fourth century. **Cornelius** was pope from 251 to 253 and, with Cyprian's help, withstood the Novatian schism.

Cyprian was a professional rhetorician converted in his forties and chosen bishop within three or four years. Despite his inexperience he was the leading Latin churchman and theologian of his day. A man of action, dedicated to his flock, sympathetic yet firm and conscious of his authority, he showed a keen sense of the need to act in concert with other bishops as well as with the clergy and laity of his own diocese. His interesting letters, concerned as they often are with local problems and personal faults, give the best insight into mid-third century Church affairs. They are among the finest examples of the way a bishop can teach and reprove in the name of the Gospel. Cyprian's denial, however, of the validity of baptism conferred by heretics and his rejection of the authority of Pope Stephen I on this point mar an otherwise magnificent ecclesiology.

The re-baptism controversy preserved the record of Pope Stephen, bishop of Rome, exercising supervision over the whole Church and claiming this authority as successor of St. Peter. To Cyprian he laid down the principle: "No innovation is to be introduced, but let that be preserved which tradition has handed down." And it was Rome's tradition to recognize the validity of baptism conferred by heretics.

Firmillian, bishop of Caesarea, wrote to St. Cyprian, "I am justly indignant . . . at the manifest stupidity of Stephen. Though he so glories in the position of his episcopate and contends that he has the succession from Peter on whom the foundations of the Church were established, he introduces many other rocks and sets up the new structures of many other churches since by his authority he maintains that they too have baptism" (Cyprian, **Letter** 75). Cyprian did not yield, but the Roman position eventually prevailed and today provides a sacramental basis for much contemporary ecumenism.

ca. 432

St. Ninian, English bishop, apostle of Galloway, first missionary in Scotland of whom there is historical record.

921

St. Ludmila, martyr, who with her husband, a convert of St. Methodius, built the first Christian church in Bohemia. She had a decisive part in training her grandson, King St. Wenceslaus.

SEPTEMBER 17

1621

ST. ROBERT BELLARMINE, Jesuit cardinal whose **Controversies,** in four volumes, made him the leading Catholic apologist of the counter-reformation. The work went through twenty printings in his own lifetime and remained popular for three centuries. He was a nephew of Pope Marcellus II and became a Jesuit as he was turning eighteen.

Despite poor health during most of his sixty-eight years, he seemed to have energy and talent for everything: studies, teaching, the pulpit, writing, spiritual direction, administration, and —during four years as Archbishop of Capua—pastoral care. He was so short that he had to stand on a stool in the Louvain pulpit to be properly seen. His special talent for being practical is shown by such varied publications as a Hebrew grammar, two very successful catechisms, and—just a few months before his death—a book **On the Art of Dying Well.**

He became Vatican librarian and during fifteen years was the foremost cardinal in the Curia. He had a leading part in the Galileo affair and it fell to him, in 1616, to inform Galileo of the Holy Office decision that the Copernican theory could not be held. He expressed his mind the previous year when he wrote: "If there were a real proof . . . that the sun does not go around the earth but the earth round the sun, then we should have to proceed with great circumspection in explaining passages of Scripture which appear to teach the contrary, and admit that we did not understand these passages, rather than declare something as false which is proved to be true. But as for myself I shall not believe there are such proofs until they are shown to me" (Letter to Foscarini, Apr. 12, 1615).

379
St. Satyrus, a lawyer who administered the temporalities of the diocese of Milan for St. Ambrose, his younger brother.

1179   [*O.S.B.*]
St. Hildegard, first great German mystic, a Benedictine abbess remarkable for her visions and the freedom with which she reproved the mighty in the name of God. Confided to the care of Bl. Jutta at seven, Hildegard took the veil at fifteen. She transferred her community to Rupertsberg near Bingen and made a foundation at Eibingen. Her famous book **Scivias** is the product of twenty-six visions dictated to the monk Volmar.

1214   [*O. Carm, O.C.D.*]
St. Albert, Augustinian Canon, bishop of Vercelli and then —because of his saintliness and diplomatic ability—patriarch of Jerusalem. He worked tirelessly to keep peace between the Franks and Saracens until he was assasinated by a disgruntled official whom he had deposed. He is best remembered as the author of the primitive Carmelite rule, a short document of sixteen chapters regulating the contemplative life of the hermits on Mt. Carmel.

1224   [*Franciscans*]
Commemoration of the impression of the stigmata on St. Francis of Assisi while on retreat on Mount Alvernia—the most famous instance of this mystic phenomenon.

SEPTEMBER 18

1645 [*O.P.*]
St. John Masias, Spanish Dominican brother at Lima, Peru, where he served as porter and cared for the sick and needy. He trained the priory donkey to make the rounds alone and receive food and clothing for the poor.

1663 [*Franciscans*]
St. Joseph of Cupertino, Franciscan, outstanding among modern saints as the one who seemed to give least promise for the apostolic ministry but worked the most miracles once he was a priest. He was a dull, clumsy, and hot-tempered child. His widowed mother looked on him as a nuisance. He apprenticed as a shoe-maker but without success. The conventual Franciscans refused him admission, and the Capuchins dismissed him after eight months. He was finally accepted as a servant by the Conventuals and given the habit as a member of the third order.

Mildness, humility, and penances gradually earned him the good will of his confreres. He became a choir religious and, despite hopeless difficulties with studies, was ordained a priest. From then on his life was one long succession of ecstasies, miracles of healing, and supernatural events on a scale not paralleled in the authenticated life of any other saint. He is particularly famous for his levitations.

Anything that could remind him of God might put him into ecstasy. So absorbed was he in the things of God that he could mistake a passing woman for Our Lady or a fellow friar for St. Francis or St. Anthony. His superiors kept moving him from one friary to another, but the crowds would find out where he was. For thirty-five years he was not allowed to celebrate Mass in public.

He would constantly urge people to pray. "Pray!" he would say, "pray! If you are troubled with dryness or distractions, just say an **Our Father.** Then you make both vocal and mental prayer."

SEPTEMBER 19

ca. 305

ST. JANUARIUS, bishop of Benevento, martyr, patron of Naples. No further details of his life are known; but he has a place in the universal calendar because of the celebrity of the liquefaction of his blood, which occurs in the Cathedral of Naples eighteen times each year near his feasts. While the people pray — particularly a privileged group of poor women known as the "aunts of St. Januarius" — the priest turns the four inch glass phial up and down in the sight of the onlookers until the dark mass liquefies.

Various thermal experiments and spectroscopic analyses have been made; but the phenomenon, which goes back to the fourteenth century, continues to elude natural explanation.

690

St. Theodore of Canterbury, "the first archbishop," says St. Bede, "whom all the English church obeyed." He held synods, promulgated canons, and transformed a missionary church into a well-established ecclesiastical province that lasted until the Reformation. He was a sixty-six year old Greek monk from Tarsus living in Rome and not yet a subdeacon, when Pope Vitalian promoted him to orders and sent him to England.

1591   [*O.S.A., O.A.R.*]

Bl. Alphonsus de Orozco, Spanish Augustinian mystic, author of devotional works, outstanding preacher, and confessor. Each year he produced a book on the Blessed Mother.

1852

St. Emily De Rodat, foundress in France of the Congregation of the Holy Family of Villefranche. After the Revolution she helped the poor, taught catechism, and tried to join three different orders, but finally started her own to meet the need for a free school in her home town. The congregation grew rapidly and widened its scope to include charitable works of all kinds as well as a number of contemplative houses.

Her secretary objected to the respectful way Mother Emily answered abusive letters. "Don't you know," she replied, "that . . . anyone is entitled to walk over us?" She had strong temptations against faith and hope but was also able to say, "I was bored only once in all my life, and that was when I had turned away from God."

SEPTEMBER 20

1246

St. Michael, Duke of Chernigov, and **St. Theodore** his companion, military heroes during the thirteenth century Tartar invasions when the Russian Church gained its earliest martyrs. Michael at first showed cowardice by abandoning Kiev, but returned voluntarily and went into the Tartar camp to draw their attack away from the common people. He resisted every inducement to deny the faith, or betray his nation. To protect his people against reprisals he did not attempt to escape, but was tortured and finally beheaded.

1640

Bl. Mary of Jesus López de Rivas, about whom St. Teresa wrote to her Discalced Carmelites in Toledo, "I am sending you a postulant with a dowry of five thousand ducats, but I assure you her character is such that I would willingly give fifty thousand for her." And she told the nuns that if they sent her away because of her poor health she would receive her at Avila. Teresa, at 62, then wrote to this novice of 17, whom she had not actually seen, to thank her for the dowry. Only a fragment of the letter remains and it begins mysteriously, "I know that our Lord has revealed the same thing to you as He did to me but His Majesty desires that you should be aware that I know of it too. Remember, you must render your Bridegroom no small service among these nuns."

Except for the five months she spent on a new foundation, Mary of Jesus lived 63 years of cloistered life in Toledo, serving eight times as novice mistress. Prioress at 31, she was deposed during her second term through calumny, and for twenty years until the truth was made known she bore the disgrace with much patience, thankful for the opportunity to suffer unjustly with Christ. Again she was made prioress and then novice mistress, an office in which she died at 80. Characteristic of her mystic life was its intimate harmony with the feasts and seasons of the Church Year. As a very old and infirm nun she would take her place near the choir grill and from there join in the singing of Mass with remarkable zest. Bl. Mary of Jesus died on September 13, 1640.

1866   [*Franciscans*]
St. Francis Camporosso, Capuchin begging brother at Genoa. He was a particularly familiar figure in the dockyards where he answered questions people put to him about their relatives overseas.

SEPTEMBER 21

ST. MATTHEW, also called Levi, apostle and evangelist, the publican who left the toll house when Jesus said, "Follow me" (Mk 2:14). Of his later life nothing is known for certain. His was the favorite gospel of the early church, especially because it lent itself so well to liturgical reading and preaching, grouping,

as it does, most of Christ's teaching into five long discourses—
the "sermon on the mount" being the first—each ending with
the words, "and it happened when Jesus had finished. . . ."

Composed primarily for Jewish Christians living in Palestine,
it is preeminently the gospel of the "Kingdom"—the word is
mentioned fifty-one times—and of the Church. It teaches that
Jesus is the promised Messiah, the Lord of the World, and that
the destiny of Israel is being fulfilled in the small remnant of
Jews who formed the nucleus of the Christian church.

Only this gospel gives the text in which Jesus confers upon
Peter the power of the keys and calls him the foundation rock
of the church (16:18-20). Only Matthew tells of Peter walking
on the water beside Jesus (14:28-31) and of Peter's paying the
temple tax for them both (17:24-27). Comparison with Mark
shows how careful Matthew's gospel is to bring out the dignity
of Christ and the apostles. It ends with majestic words that are
characteristically appropriate for solemn proclamation in church:
"Be assured I am with you always to the end of time" (28:20).

SEPTEMBER 22*

3rd cent.
ST. MAURICE and **COMPANIONS,** soldiers martyred in Switzerland. There was great devotion to them in the Middle Ages in
consequence of an unreliable fifth century account that described
them as an entire legion of 6,000 Christians recruited in upper
Egypt (the Theban Legion), who refused to a man to take part
in public sacrifices, and gave their lives for Christ.

1770
Bl. Ignatius Balocco of Santhia, Capuchin who died in Turin
at ninety-one with a reputation for miracles. At seven he lost
his father and came under the care of a holy priest. In time he
too became a priest, and being especially attracted by the ideal

---

*O.S.A. in the United States and Canada see Nov. 25 for St. Thomas Villanova.

of religious obedience, joined the Capuchins at thirty.

He was particularly remembered as sacristan, novicemaster, and military chaplain, and was in much demand for confession and spiritual conferences. His ideal of practical service was shown in his always looking for the menial jobs, and by the incident of the Congo missionary who wrote to his former novicemaster asking prayers because it seemed that eye trouble would force him to leave the Congo. Father Ignatius prayed that the ailment might be transferred to himself, since he was of little use. The missionary's sight recovered; but the novice-master had to be relieved of his position—his eyes becoming so bad that he could not read, though eventually he recovered with the help of doctors in Turin. He bore the infirmities of old age with great joy and made a point of showing religious obedience to the one who took care of him. He foretold the day of his death.

SEPTEMBER 23

704

St. Adamnan, native of Donegal, ninth abbot of Iona, author of a life of St. Columba. After a visit to Wearmouth and Jarrow, he became convinced that some of the Celtic peculiarities should be abandoned; and he succeeded in having Easter observed on the Roman date in many churches of Ireland, but not in his own monastery. At the Council of Birr he persuaded the assembly that women should not take part in warfare and that women and children should not be killed or taken prisoners. The decision is known as "Adamnan's Law."

1087

Bl. Victor III, the pope who succeeded St. Gregory VII. It was a year before his election took place and another year before he finally accepted. After that he lived only four months;

and as Rome was in the hands of an anti-pope, he stayed at Monte Cassino, where he was once abbot. Under him the monastery had fluorished in discipline, learning and art, and grew to 200 monks.

1520

Bl. Helen Duglioli of Bologna, who was widowed after thirty years of virtuous and happy married life, and devoted the time that remained to works of charity. The common people of Bologna spontaneously proclaimed her a saint.

1637

Bl. Lawrence (Lorenzo) Ruiz. For his 1981 pastoral visit to Eastern Asia Pope John Paul II chose Manila as the place for the first beatification outside Rome. Some two million faithful attended. Raised to the altar were 16 Nagasaki martyrs, the majority Japanese and all of them Dominican priests or their associates. They suffered between 1633 and 1637. Included was the first Filipino martyr, Bl. Lawrence Ruiz. He was the young father of a family, a calligrapher, the son of a Chinese father and a Tagala mother, and a member of the Dominican Rosary fraternity in Binondo, now part of Manila.

Being involved in what seemed to be a crime, he was actually fleeing the Philippines, but the ship he boarded was secretly taking a group of Dominican missionaries to Japan. He decided to remain with them. When taken captive and offered freedom he chose fearful torture and death, saying to his executioners, "I am a Christian and I shall die for God. For Him I would give many thousands of lives if I had them."

SEPTEMBER 24

1046

St. Gerard, Benedictine; first bishop of Csanad; martyr; an apostle of Hungary. While abbot of St. George in Venice, he started on a pilgrimage to the Holy Land; but King St. Stephen begged him to remain in Hungary to work among the Magyars and to tutor his son, Emeric, the future saint. Through hatred of his faith, a band of assasins fell upon him as he was crossing the Danube at Buda. His body was later brought back to Venice, where he is highly venerated as the city's first martyr.

1054

Bl. Herman the Cripple, Benedictine, an amazing example of mastery over handicaps. Though an invalid from birth, this fifteenth child of the count of Altshausen lived forty-one fruitful years, mostly in the abbey of Reichenau on Lake Constance. He could speak and write only with difficulty, and could not move from side to side without help. Yet he mastered the learning of his time, wrote a world chronicle, left treatises on mathematics and astronomy—one had to do with the construction and use of the astrolabe—and earned a broad reputation as a teacher and sympathetic counselor.

He is particularly remembered, however, as probably author of two of the most beautiful anthems in honor of Mary, the **Alma Redemptoris Mater** and the **Salve Regina** ("Hail Holy Queen"). He was entrusted to the monastery at the age of seven and admitted to profession at thirty.

1721

St. Pacifico Divini of San Severino near Ancona, Italy, a Franciscan who, after ten years of fruitful priestly ministry, fell sick—and for thirty-three more years carried on the apostolate of suffering, being deaf, blind, and almost a cripple. He even added a hair shirt, the discipline, and a program of fasting which the superiors had to moderate. Ecstasies, especially at Mass, were frequent; and he had the gifts of prophecy and miracles.

SEPTEMBER 25

716

St. Ceolfrid, Benedictine, coadjutor of St. Benedict Biscop in establishing the twofold monastery of Wearmouth and Jarrow where he was abbot for thirty-five years. His ideal of monastic observance and scholarship is best seen in St. Bede whom he trained. When an epidemic carried off all the other monks of Jarrow, these two sang the divine office alone until a new community could be formed.

Bede describes him as "a man of great preseverance and keen intellect, bold in action, experienced in judgment, and zealous in religion." He wrote a letter to the king of the Picts persuading him to celebrate Easter on the Roman date and sent along some masons trained to build churches of large stones as was done at Rome.

His joint monastery numbered 600 monks when he resigned and set off for Rome, hoping to die in the Holy City; but he got no further than Langres, France. He had with him as a gift for the pope a Latin Bible produced in his own scriptorium. This is the magnificent **Codex Amiatinus,** the earliest surviving complete Latin Bible.

1569   [*O.SS.T.*]

Bl. Mark Criado, who became a Trinitarian at fourteen and died a martyr at Almeria, Spain, tortured and slain by the Moors.

1824   [*C.P.*]

St. Vincent Strambi, Passionist, bishop of Macerata and Tolentino in Italy. A druggist's son, he served as seminary rector when only a deacon, and was a priest at twenty-three. The following year he became a Passionist through contact with St. Paul of the Cross, founder of the order.

A leading pulpit orator with a reputation for prayer and penance, he served as provincial superior for twenty years and then was appointed bishop. The sick, aged, and orphans were his special care; and he organized clergy and laity into an effective catechetical team. He spent six years in exile for refusing the fealty oath which Napoleon required. Macerata, headquarters of Murat's army, was spared both by the defeated French and by the Austrians, thanks to the bishop's pleading.

SEPTEMBER 26

Unknown date
STS. COSMAS and **DAMIAN,** early martyrs at Cyr in Syria, patrons of physicians. Their shrines became so popular for cures, especially after the Emperor Justinian was healed, that in Rome seven churches were dedicated to them and their names were inserted into the canon of the mass. Legend made them twin brothers, doctors who took no fees for their service.

ca. 1005
St. Nilus of Rossano. Near Frascati, a few miles from Rome, he founded Grottaferrata, which has since remained the center of Greek monasticism in Italy. After the sudden death of his wife and young daughter and some illness of his own, he experienced a profound conversion and entered one of the Byzantine monasteries of his native Calabria. He became an abbot, lived to nearly 100, moved his community several times to escape the Saracens and, just before his death, selected Grottaferrata. He refused the Archbishopric of Rossano, then capital of the Byzantine sector of Italy. He would not compromise through human respect or fear of the mighty, but he was a man of peace and once pretended to fall asleep during an interview in order to avoid an argument.

1323   [*Franciscan III O.*]
St. Elzear, Baron of Ansouis in his native Provence and Count of Ariano in southern Italy. He died at thirty-eight, and his

wife **Bl. Delphina** was present at his canonization. They were Franciscan tertiaries. He ruled his subjects with a remarkable combination of competence, kindness, piety, and good sense.

1838-46
The Korean Martyrs. Christianity was introduced by a group of Koreans who read Chinese Christian books and had a member of the 1783 delegation to Peking contact a priest for instruction and baptism. Ten years later, when the first Chinese priest smuggled himself into Korea, he found 4000 Catholics.

Of the many thousands martyred during the next century, seventy-nine have been beatified—thirty-two men and forty-seven women, all Korean except three Paris Foreign Missioners. Nine died on Sept. 26, 1838, including **Columba Kim,** an unmarried woman of twenty-six, and her sister **Agnes Kim,** twenty-four.

1885   [*R.C.*]
St. Marie Victoire Thérèse Couderc, foundress in France of the Religious of the Cenacle, a contemplative-active congregation, which in 1982 had eighty-four retreat houses for women and 1,000 religious. Mother Thérèse was superior of the institute from the age of twenty-three to thirty-three; the rest of her eighty years were a story of success through humiliation.

SEPTEMBER 27

1660
ST. VINCENT DE PAUL, founder; central figure of the seventeenth century renewal in Paris and, through his Daughters of Charity, the one mainly responsible for popularizing the non-cloistered way of life typical of modern feminine congregations. A peasant boy who received a good education, thanks to the vision and sacrifice of his parents, he was ordained at

twenty. A few years later, under the influence of Father Bérulle, the future cardinal, his spiritual life began to deepen.
By forty he was wholly a man of God ready to give himself to
the point of heroism in relieving the spiritual and bodily needs
he saw on every side. "I belong," he said, "to God and to the
poor."

The piety he taught and practised was simple, nourished on
the words and example of Christ, and oriented toward action.
He had excellent practical judgment, but his gift for inspiring
and working with others was in a special way the fruit of humility. He once said: "I have tried over and over again to find
out the best means of living in union with God and in charity
with my neighbors, and I have never found anything that helped
as much as humility—the lowering of oneself below everyone
else with the sense that one is really worse than others, and
the refusal to judge anyone." He made it a practice, whenever
two ways of saying something came to his mind, to choose
the less brilliant.

In one of the many dialogue conferences preserved in priceless notes by the sisters he said: "God has given me such a
high esteem for simplicity that I call it my Gospel. I have . . .
a special consolation in saying things just as they are" (Conference of Feb. 24, 1653). He was always himself, whether
with galley slaves or on the Council of Conscience selecting
bishops for France. He formed St. Louise de Marillac and received from St. Francis de Sales the care of the Visitation nuns
in Paris.

In 1625 he founded the Congregation of the Mission—also called
Vincentians or Lazarists—to preach in country places and educate
priests. When he died in his eightieth year, there were already 500
in his society. The 2,500 letters that remain are only a fraction of his
correspondence. In 1833 Ozanam and some companions founded the
St. Vincent de Paul Society to help the poor, but more generally St.
Vincent is patron of all charitable societies.

1457

Bl. Lawrence of Ripafratta, novice master of St. Antoninus and also of Fra Angelico whom he encouraged in his painting: "The most persuasive tongue becomes silent", he said, "but your pictures will go on speaking of religion and virtue throughout the ages."

SEPTEMBER 28*

929

ST. WENCESLAUS, best known of the first dukes of Bohemia and identified with the most dramatic phase of the Christianization of the Czech people and of their emergence as a nation of Europe. At his father's death, his mother and brother aligned themselves with the anti-Christian party, and his mother as regent reversed the religious policy. St. Ludmilla, the paternal grandmother who educated Wenceslaus in the faith, was put to death. Then Wenceslaus, though only about fifteen, assumed government, re-established a Christian rule, and—in the cause of peace—recognized the German king Henry I as over-lord.

He had governed only seven years and had just had a son assuring succession when his younger brother, Boleslaus I, through personal ambition as well as religious and political motives, assassinated him before morning Mass. "May God forgive you, brother", Wenceslaus murmured as he fell at the church door. His spontaneous veneration as a martyr did much to hasten the conversion of the nation and to convince Christendom of the legitimacy of the new Czech state. This youthful saint of twenty-two is the patron of Czechoslovakia.

780

St. Lioba, missionary abbess, sent with thirty nuns from the abbey of Wimborne in England to help her relative, St. Boniface, bring the faith to Germany. St. Thecla and St. Walburga

---

*O.S.A., O.A.E. see June 1 Japanese Martyrs.

were members of the same group. They settled at Bischofsheim and quickly spread to other convents, endearing themselves to all as holy nuns who could work in the fields, at the crafts, and also teach. Symbolic of their role as collaborators was the request of St. Boniface that Lioba be buried at Fulda to await the resurrection there together with him.

1494

Bl. Bernardino of Feltre near Venice, outstanding preacher who regularly ended his sermons with a bonfire of cards, obscene books, useless finery, and the like. He is particularly remembered for his part in establishing some thirty **Montes Pietatis**—a type of charitable pawn shop where the poor could get credit at a low rate of interest. Such interest, he maintained, was not usury—a position sanctioned a few years after his death by the Fifth Lateran Council in 1515.

1624   [*O.SS.T.*]

Bl. Simon de Rojas, Trinitarian, confessor to the Spanish queen. When an epidemic broke out in Madrid, King Philip III forbade Simon to help lest he bring back the infection. He answered: "A sick-bed is a more fitting place for me than a royal palace; and if I must give up one of them, it will be the palace."

SEPTEMBER 29

The Archangels, **STS. MICHAEL, GABRIEL,** and **RAPHAEL.** St. Michael has been honored on Sept. 29 since the fifth century. Sts. Gabriel and Raphael were added to the universal calendar only in 1921. Now all three —they are the only single angels mentioned by name in the Bible—are celebrated in a single feast.

St. John writes in the **Revelation** (12:7-9): "War arose in heav-

en, Michael and his angels fighting against the dragon. . . .
And the great dragon was thrown down, that ancient serpent,
who is called the Devil and Satan, the deceiver of the whole
world—he was thrown down to earth, and his angels were
thrown down with him." "Michael" means "who is like God?"
In the book of **Daniel** and Jewish tradition he is the guardian
of the chosen people, and the Church continues in the same
way to honor him as her special protector. In the East he is
particularly popular as healer of the sick.

St. Gabriel, whose name means "Hero of God" or "Power
of God" is best known as the angel of the Annunciation, speaking the first words of the **Hail Mary.** The "Angelus" gets its
name from him. He also appeared to Zechariah, and in the Old
Testament he stood by the prophet Daniel, and explained the
visions to him.

St. Raphael is mentioned only in the book of **Tobit.** His name
is "God has healed." He heals the blindness of Tobit and provides a husband for Sarah.

Only St. Michael is called an archangel in the Bible, but the
church following Jewish tradition gave that title to all three.

1484
Bl. John of Dukla, Polish Franciscan, guardian at Lvov; a
patron of Poland and Lithuania. He reconciled many to the
Catholic Church; and although blind in his last years, he continued to preach and hear confessions.

SEPTEMBER 30

420
ST. JEROME, doctor, unequaled among the Fathers as a student and translator of the Sacred Scriptures. Born of well-to-do
Christian parents at Stridon near present-day Trieste, he studied
classics at Rome under Donatus, and gradually developed his

genius as a writer of pure, vigorous Latin. He was baptized when about twenty. Asceticism, the Church, and Scripture studies would be the consuming interests in his life.

After a brief attempt at community life with some friends at Aquileia he started off for the Holy Land. His two companions died on the way and he too fell sick. In delirium he saw himself at the judgement seat of Christ. Asked who he was he answered, "A Christian." "You lie," was Christ's reply. "You are a Ciceronian; for where your treasure is, there is your heart also."

He perfected his Greek at Antioch, and during a period as a monk in the desert of Chalcis he applied himself to the ascetic life and to Hebrew. He was ordained a priest at Antioch with the understanding that he could follow his monastic vocation. At Constantinople he studied Scripture under St. Gregory Nazianzen and experienced a brief enthusiasm for Origen.

Back at Rome he served as secretary to Pope St. Damasus, and at the pope's request began to improve the Latin translations of the Scriptures. His intemperate criticism of Roman ladies and clergy aroused much antagonism.

He became the center of an ascetic group that included St. Paula and Eustochium, who built several convents and a monastery at Bethelem, where St. Jerome settled after Pope Damasus died. There in the rock-hewn cell he accomplished his greatest work: the Latin text of the Bible later known as the Vulgate. The only parts of the vulgate not translated or at least reworked by him are the books of **Wisdom, Sirach, Baruch,** and the two books of **Maccabees.** He wrote much and was often engaged in sharp controversy.

When refugees fled east during the sack of Rome he wrote, "I cannot help them all but I grieve and weep with them. And, completely given up to the duties which charity imposes on me, I have put aside my commentary on Ezechiel and almost all study. For today, we must translate the words of Scripture into deeds, and instead of speaking saintly words we must act them." He died there in 420.

ca. 332

St. Gregory "the Enlightener," honored as apostle and first Catholicos of Armenia, as well as principal national saint and hero.

OCTOBER 1

1897

ST. THÉRÈSE OF LISIEUX, French Carmelite, the most popular modern saint. "I feel that my mission is about to begin." she confided shortly before her death at twenty-four, "my mission of making people love God as I love him, of teaching them my little way." At her canonization only twenty-eight years later, Pope Pius XI urged everyone to study her carefully.

Within twenty years of her death her autobiography—three documents edited and combined into one book by the prioress, her second oldest sister, but now available in their unrevised form—had already been translated into thirty-four languages. On reading these intimate family and convent memoirs, ordinary people everywhere felt that sanctity was also possible for them.

Filial love issuing, despite faults and weaknesses, in total reliance on the infinite goodness of God, is the keynote of her message. From this supernatural trust she drew the practical consequences which made her life and teaching so attractive:

freedom of spirit, joy, courage, simplicity in prayer, and indifference to everything that could be considered extraordinary in the spiritual life.

"Sanctity," she said, "does not consist in this or that practice but in a disposition of heart which makes us humble and small in the arms of God." Drawing on the Church's teaching, the Scriptures, and her personal experience of divine help and family love, she portrayed, perhaps better than any other saint, what it means to have God as Father.

Her saintly parents, Louis and Zélie Martin, had nine children. Four died in infancy; the others, all girls, became nuns — four of them Carmelites at Lisieux. Thérèse was the youngest. At four she lost her mother. At ten she suffered a strange nervous illness but made a sudden recovery when she saw the statue of the Blessed Virgin smile on her.

She was touchy and suffered from scruples in her early teens; but at fourteen, overhearing her father's complaint about a childish Christmas custom, gained in a moment and for good a self-mastery she seemed to have lost at her mother's death. She determined to become a saint. The foreign missions attracted her, but she chose the contemplative life because of the missionary role of prayer — particularly the prayer for priests which the Lisieux Carmelites made their special work.

After taking her case personally to Pope Leo XIII, she succeeded in entering the convent at fifteen. The next nine years were spent in such an ordinary way — household and sacristy work, the training of novices — that nuns in her own community wondered what could be said of her in the obituary circular normally sent to the other convents of the order.

She once wrote to a cousin who would follow her into Carmel: "You want a means for reaching perfection. I know of only one: Love." To the very great joy of the millions who have come to know her, St. Thérèse has shown that the heroism of love is possible in the most humble and ordinary situations of daily life. She is patroness of foreign missionaries.

SAINT THERESE OF LISIEUX

OCTOBER 2

THE GUARDIAN ANGELS, good spirits assigned to help us while always remaining in the presence of God (Mt 18:10). Angels, according to the **Epistle to the Hebrews,** are "spirits whose work is service, sent to help those who will be the heirs of salvation" (1:14). The word "angel" means messenger. They are God's messengers first of all, but their service is broader and is ideally portrayed in St. Raphael, who accompanied the son of Tobit. "Do not worry, my sister," Tobit assured his wife, ". . . for a good angel will go with him. His journey will be successful, and he will come back safe and sound" (Tob 5: 20-21). During the first centuries angels were represented as men.

ca. 530

St. Remigius or **Remi,** apostle of the Franks, bishop of Reims for seventy years, remembered especially for his part in the conversion of King Clovis. Traditionally, the solemn baptism of Clovis and several thousand of his men in the Reims cathedral about the year 500 symbolized the militant vocation of Catholic France as "the eldest daughter of the church" among the new nations of the West, just as Clovis was called "the eldest son."

677

St. Leodegar or **Leger,** Benedictine abbot of St. Maxence; bishop of Autun; martyr. He helped Queen St. Bathildis and incurred the wrath of Ebroin, mayor of the palace. When an army came to capture him he gave himself up to save the city of Autun. Ebroin had him blinded, imprisoned, degraded, and finally beheaded. The saint once said that if monks were what they ought to be their prayers would preserve the world from public calamities.

OCTOBER 3

959

St. Gerard, abbot of Brogne, one of the principal restorers of monasticism in the tenth century. His reform extended to twenty Benedictine abbeys in Flanders and Lorraine. His own vocation became clear to him on the way home from a hunting expedition when he stopped to pray in a chapel while the rest of the party went on. There he had such an intense experience of joy during prayer that he came away with the conviction that it would be wonderful to have no other preoccupation than to praise God night and day, and to live always in his presence.

1572   [S.J.]

St. Francis Borgia, great grandson of Pope Alexander VI, cousin of Emperor Charles V, and superior general of the Jesuits—whose second founder he is sometimes called, because he did so much to expand the young order and crystallize its spirit. "It was when I was viceroy of Catalonia," he said, "that God prepared me to be general of the Society of Jesus. I then learned to decide important questions, to settle rival claims, to see both sides of an affair in a way I could not otherwise have done."

The eldest of fourteen children—two of whom became cardinals—he moved in the highest circles of the courts of Spain and Portugal and succeeded his father as Duke of Gandia. He became a Jesuit at the age of thirty-seven, a year after the sudden death of his wife Eleanor, by whom he had eight children. His profession was kept secret for three years until he had settled his family.

1684

Bl. Bonaventure of Barcelona, a shepherd who married at seventeen but lost his wife after two years and then became a Franciscan brother. To avoid the notoriety of his ecstasies he was sent out of Spain and became doorkeeper at a friary in Rome, but there he came to the attention of several cardinals who helped him establish houses of retreat, or hermitages, for members of his order.

OCTOBER 4

1226

ST. FRANCIS OF ASSISI, best known and most followed of mediaeval saints. In ten years he already had several thousand friars. Today, in their three branches, they are the most numerous religious order of men; his Poor Clares are the largest group of contemplative nuns; and the Franciscan Third Order, which he also founded, has been estimated at two million.

He wanted his friars to be identified by their following of Christ in poverty and by the rejection of every privilege. To all Christians he gave, more simply and fully than any other saint of the Middle Ages, the vision of a life lived wholly in the power and spirit of the cross.

As a young man, except for his considerateness and generosity, he differed little from other frivolous, well-to-do youths of Assisi. A year as hostage and a serious illness had their sobering effect. But the turning point came at twenty-five, when he began to care for the sick. "It seemed extremely bitter to me," he wrote in his **Testament,** "to look at lepers. The Lord led me in among them and I practised mercy with them. And when I came away from them what seemed bitter to me was changed to sweetness."

He soon adopted the ways of a hermit and began rebuilding dilapidated churches. Divine contemplation, which would increasingly dominate his life, culminated in the bestowal of the stigmata. His vocation to preach came clear to him, when he heard the Gospel passage in which Jesus sent his disciples to preach penance: they were to take only one tunic and go without money, shoes, or staff. Out of awe for the Holy Eucharist he did not advance beyong the order of deacon.

He always looked for success through the meekness of the Gospel and was ingenious in finding ways of serving, turning the other cheek, giving away what he had, welcoming insult and persecution. No other saint has so captured the popular feeling of his own times or inspired so many stories whose charm derives in great part from the fact that he had the courage and simplicity to take the words of Jesus literally.

Though he was uncompromisingly papal, he is a favorite among non-Catholics. Non-Christians, too, feel kinship with him, convinced that mankind has been greatly enriched by his all-embracing love, his joy, liberty of spirit, compassion, and kinship with every creature. His enthusiasm for God and everything but sin is expressed in the **Canticle to Brother Sun** and exemplified in his final greeting, "Welcome, Brother Death!" He was forty-four or forty-five and was canonized two years later.

OCTOBER 5

1399

Bl. Raymond of Capua, Dominican, spiritual director of St. Catherine of Siena. While assisting at his Mass Catherine heard an interior voice, "This is my beloved servant. This is the one to whom I will entrust you." Their first joint effort was the care of the plague-stricken. When Raymond himself succumbed and was near death, Catherine prayed an hour-and-a-half for him, and the next day he was well; so he began to have confidence in her supernatural mission.

During Catherine's last and most important years, Raymond was her confessor and the closest collaborator in her various projects, particularly the return of Pope Gregory XI to Rome and the healing of the subsequent schism. Raymond sometimes spent entire days hearing the confessions of those Catherine brought him. After her death he assumed fuller direction of the clerics, nuns, and laity who made up her "family" and wrote the story of her life. As master general of the Dominicans he was especially identified with reform movements to strengthen the spiritual life within the order.

1926

Bl. Bartholomew (Bartolo) Longo, a layman who brought a vital Christianity to the Valley of Pompei and gave a great impetus to Marian devotion, especially the Rosary. At 25 he obtained a degree in law at Naples where he also attended spiritualist seances and lost his faith, but regained it before long helped by a Dominican priest. He began to assist the aged and in his thirties started catechizing the peasants of the Valley of Pompei, a desolate region near Naples. He would also lead the Rosary before a picture of the Madonna and at the age of 35 laid the first stone for Mary's now famous Sanctuary of Pompei. An orphanage came next, then a place for the sons of the imprisoned and also a printery from which flowed about one hundred of his devotional booklets on Mary as well as appeals for the destitute, and a periodical **The Rosary and the New Pompei,** edited by Mr. Longo until his death at 85.

At 44 he married a charitable, rich widow whose affairs he had managed for a decade and whose property in the Valley of Pompei was the reason for his first coming there. At two stages just before and after the turn of the century he handed the Sanctuary and all his other property over to the Holy See and became the pope's administrator and delegate. A final institution was added in 1922 when Bl. Bartholomew Longo was 81 a hospice for the daughters of the imprisoned. He also founded a third order Dominican sisterhood, the Daughters of the Holy Rosary. He himself belonged to the lay third order of St. Dominic.

OCTOBER 6*

1101

ST. BRUNO, founder in 1084 of the Carthusians, the most strictly contemplative religious order. He was about fifty-five at the time and had distinguished himself at Reims as one of Europe's foremost teachers. He had also been chancellor of the diocese and had taken a leading but disinterested role in removing the incumbent simoniacal archbishop.

Though Bruno was the popular choice for the now vacant diocese of Reims, he retired with six companions to the Chartreuse forest in the French alps near Grenoble. There, among precipitous rocks in the complete solitude of a snowy valley at the 3500-ft. level, they embarked on a life of contemplative prayer and penance.

Bruno wrote no rule nor was it his intention to found a new order; but within forty years his life style and spirit had crystallized into a **Customary,** or set of usages, which gave the Carthusians their identity as a special way of organizing solitary life within a community framework.

Bruno had spent only six years at Chartreuse when he was called to Rome as adviser by a former pupil who had become pope, Bl. Urban II. He turned down another archbishopric, this time in southern Italy, and after a year was allowed to return to solitude, provided it was nearer to Rome. So he founded a monastery at Della Torre in Calabria, where he spent the final ten years of his life. He has remained one of the region's most popular saints.

His writings include the profession of faith made before his death, some sermons, a commentary on the Psalms, a commentary on the epistles of St. Paul, and two letters, one of them written to encourage the brothers of his beloved Chartreuse.

At their peak development during the first years of the Protestant Reformation the Carthusians had 195 monasteries. Today there are some 400 professed monks and about a third as many nuns. The Carthusian emblem is a globe surmounted by a cross and seven stars

---

*S.N.J.M. see Oct. 12 for Bl. Marie Rose Durocher.

BLESSED BARTOLO LONGO

with the motto, "While the world changes, the cross stands firm."

1791 [*Franciscan III O.*]

St. Ann Mary Gallo, also known as St. Mary Frances of the Five Wounds, whose father beat her and locked her up, but could not break her resolve to consecrate her virginity to Christ. She became a Franciscan tertiary, continued to live at home, and for thirty-eight years directed the household of a secular priest in Naples. Many supernatural phenomena, including the stigmata, were reported. While making the Stations of the Cross, particularly on Fridays, she experienced the pains of the passion, and sometimes her request to take on the sufferings of those in purgatory seemed to be granted.

OCTOBER 7

THE HOLY ROSARY, principal Marian devotion in the Western Church during the past 500 years. Contributing to its popularity were the Rosary confraternities initiated by the Dominicans in the late fifteenth century, the victory at Lepanto on Oct. 7, 1571, which led to the institution of today's feast, the apparitions at Lourdes and Fatima, and the appeals of many saints and pontiffs.

The objection, cited by Pope Pius XII, that the rosary is a boring formula repeated with monotonous, singsong intonations and useful only for children or the very old, is based on a misunderstanding; for, while the externals are fixed, the rosary has a remarkable flexibility deriving from the various mysteries that epitomize the life of Jesus and of Mary and are meant to be the primary object of attention, while the words and beads help to create a prayer setting and engage parts of the mind that can function without consciously willed effort. Against this background of vocal prayer the various elements such as reflection on the mysteries, affective, and even contemplative prayer, or concentration on the recited words, will dominate according to each one's possibilities and preferences.

Pope Leo XIII, the great advocate of the rosary, once described it as listening to the Blessed Mother explaining the mysteries and conversing at length with her about our salvation. In Mary's company one gazes lovingly on the Mystery of Christ. It's special suitability for the spiritually more advanced is suggested by the repetitive form characteristic of love-inspired prayer.

St. Dominic's connection with the rosary is legendary, but he did live at a time when the **Ave Maria** and its repetition were becoming a part of popular piety. The **Ancren Riwle,** already about the year 1200, directed the recluse to recite fifty **Aves** in sequences of ten. But at that time only the first half or greeting and congratulatory part constituted the **Hail Mary.** And it would be another two hundred years until, partly through the effort of Carthusians, lists of mysteries were mingled with the **Hail Marys,** and the **Our Father** was inserted between groups of ten. By then too, a petition was being appended to each **Ave** so that by the year 1500 the **Holy Mary** as said today was being used in various places.

Of the many ways of praying the beads prevalent in the sixteenth century, St. Pius V indulgenced the Dominican form used by the Rosary Confraternity, and thus generalized a rosary of fifteen decades and mysteries. The 1968 norms for indulgenced prayers prescribe that in public recitation the mysteries be announced according to the practice of the locality, while in private recitation it suffices that the meditation of mysteries accompany the vocal prayer.

OCTOBER 8

ca. 311

St. Pelagia, virgin and martyr at Antioch. At fifteen, to preserve her virginity when soldiers came to arrest her she threw herself to her death from the top of her house.

1595

St. Philip Howard, earl of Arundell and Surrey, one of the very attractive Elizabethan saints. At twenty-four, while neglecting his young wife and leading a dissolute life at court, he attended—out of curiosity—a theological disputation in the London Tower. The prisoner St. Edmund Campion made such a spirited defense of the Catholic faith that Philip soon returned to Arundell and three years later became a Catholic, but without telling his wife. And she too was received without telling him. When they discovered one another's faith their mutual fondness greatly deepened.

They tried to leave the country but were captured at sea. Philip was imprisoned. During eleven years he led a vigorous ascetic life in striking contrast to his earlier luxurious ways. He arose punctually at 5 a.m. to kneel at prayer on the flagstones of his cell. He fasted three days a week and daily recited the breviary and many rosaries.

The words he carved on the wall over the fireplace of his cell are still clearly visible: **"Quanto plus afflictionis pro Christo in hoc saeculo, tanto plus gloriae in futuro: Arundell 1587"** ("The greater the suffering for Christ in this life, the greater the glory in the next").

He wrote to his friend, St. Robert Southwell, that no sins grieved him so much as the neglect he showed to his wife.

Though he was condemned to death the sentence was never carried out and he died in prison on October 19, 1595, at the age of thirty-eight. He had written a letter to the Queen asking to see his wife and two children before he died. When the officer brought back the answer that he could do so and go free if he would attend church as prescribed, the saint said he could not accept the terms and added, "I am sorry I have but one life to lose for this cause."

OCTOBER 9

3rd cent.

ST. DENIS (or Dionysius) and **companions,** martyrs at Paris where St. Denis is honored as the city's saint **par excellence** and first bishop. He is also patron of France.

Denis probably came as a missionary from Rome, and was beheaded during the persecution of Valerian in 258. The great Parisian abbey of St. Denis, founded by King Dagobert in the seventh century, stood over his tomb. Excavations beneath the abbey church in 1957 show that the burial place was a pagan cemetery.

Through a series of confusions given universal currency in the West by Hilduin, ninth century abbot of St. Denis, today's saint was identified with Dionysius the Areopagite, whom St. Paul converted at Athens 200 years earlier, and with a philosopher-theologian — now called Pseudo-Dionysius — who wrote in Greek 200 years later. Abbot Hilduin and Scotus Erigena translated these fifth century Neo-Platonic works into Latin and until the fifteenth century everyone believed that they belonged to apostolic times.

1609

ST. JOHN LEONARD, a pharmacist's helper who grew up during the Council of Trent, began priestly studies at twenty-five, and founded at Lucca the Clerks Regular of the Mother of God to carry out the ideals of priestly ministry projected by the Council.

The Confraternity of Christian Doctrine had just been established at Rome, and St. Pius V was recommending it to bishops for their own dioceses. John Leonard would be the first to organize the confraternity at Lucca, where immediately after ordination he began to train lay leaders to teach catechism and in a short time wrote a compendium of Christian doctrine that would remain in use for three centuries.

At Rome, with John Baptist Vives, he established a seminary to train priests from missionary areas—an initial attempt at what became an enduring reality in the College of the Propaganda which Vives founded a few years later. John Leonard thought of sending his own community into the foreign missions, but St. Philip Neri persuaded him to have his priests keep Italy as their mission field, and they are still working there today.

1581 [*O.P.*]

St. Louis Bertrand, Spanish Dominican. He encouraged St. Teresa when she asked his advice about starting the reform and assured her that within fifty years her order would be one of the most famous in the Church. He was novice master for a long time and trained many excellent preachers, teaching them as the first lesson that prayer must always be their principal preparation. He spent seven years as a missionary in Spanish America, was recalled to Spain, and now is the patron of Colombia.

OCTOBER 10

644

St. Paulinus, first archbishop of York. A monk of St. Andrew's monastery in Rome, he was with the second band of missionaries Pope St. Gregory sent to England. After twenty-four years in southern England he went to York, for it was part of a marriage agreement that he would serve as bishop-chaplain to Princess Ethelburga, fiancée of Edwin, pagan king of Northumbria; because when Edwin asked for her hand, her brother Eadbald, the king of Kent, answered, "It is not lawful to marry a Christian virgin to a pagan husband lest the faith and the sacrament of the King of Heaven be profaned by the company of a king who does not know the true worship of God." Edwin promised he would do nothing contrary to Christian belief and would permit her and her entourage to practice their faith. He also said he would embrace her religion if, on examination by wise persons, it proved to be more holy and more worthy of God.

In bringing a bishop to the court of a pagan husband, St. Ethelberga repeated what her mother Bertha had done when she came from France to be the bride of King Ethelbert of Kent.

The mission of Paulinus prospered; Edwin and his nation were converted; and Pope Honorius I sent the archbishop's pallium along with letters that put York on an equal footing with Canterbury. But Rome's messengers arrived after the pagan Penda had killed Edwin and Ethelburga had fled back to Kent accompanied by Paulinus, who ended his days as bishop of Rochester.

1227　　　　　　　　　　　　　　　　　[*Franciscans*]

St. Daniel and **six Franciscan companions** martyred in Morocco eight days after they began to preach.

OCTOBER 11

ca. 600

St. Canice or **Kenneth,** abbot whose apostolic preaching left many traces in Ireland and Scotland.

1592　　　　　　　　　　　　　　　　　[*C.R.S.P.*]

St. Alexander Sauli, general of the Barnabites at thirty-three and for twenty years bishop of Aleria in Corsica, where there had been no bishop for three quarters of a century. He belonged to a noble family of Genoa and served as page to Emperor Charles V. At seventeen he was admitted to the new reform-oriented congregation of Barnabites; but he had first to pass the pre-novitiate trial of carrying a heavy cross through the crowded streets of Milan on Pentecost Sunday, dressed as a page, and then giving a sermon in the Piazza dei Mercanti.

When later as a priest he spoke in the Milan cathedral St. Charles Borromeo and Cardinal Sfondrati—the future Pope Gregory XIV—were so moved that both became the young missioner's penitents; and Cardinal Borromeo, after having him as confessor for many years, had the privilege of ordaining him bishop. St. Alexander long refused promotion to a larger diocese but under obedience transferred to Pavia at the age of fifty-seven, a year before his death.

1887

St. Mary Soledad Torres-Acosta, foundress at Madrid of the Sisters Servants of Mary. At twenty-four she was attracted by the project of Father Michael Martinez Sanz, and with six other women formed a religious community and began to care for the sick poor of the area. Departures, change of priest-director, refusal of the Spanish government to recognize the rule, and slanders that led to the saint's removal from office, brought the community to near extinction, until a new priest-director had Mary reinstated.

When she died at fifty-one, the congregation had forty-seven houses in Europe and Latin America. At her death bed the nuns begged, "Mother, bless us as St. Francis did." She shook her head, but a sister raised her in bed and the saint lifted her hand saying slowly, "Live together in peace and unity."

OCTOBER 12

1604 [*Franciscans*]

St. Seraphino of Montegranaro, Italy, Capuchin brother. He was a shepherd until his parents' death and then came into the service of his brother, a bricklayer, who treated him harshly.

He was minded to be a hermit but hearing of the Capuchins applied to them at Tolentino. After several refusals the provincial admitted him at the age of sixteen.

He made swift progress in the spiritual life but was a failure in the ordinary tasks assigned to brothers, and there were many complaints about his awkwardness. But his fidelity to the rule, devotion to the Blessed Sacrament, charity to all, and his miracles won him the devotion of the people. He died at Ascoli at sixty-four.

1849

Bl. Marie Rose Durocher, who died on her thirty-eighth birthday at Longueuil, Quebec, foundress, superior and novice mistress of the Sisters of the Holy Names of Jesus and Mary, a teaching order whose rule and habit came from a community of the same name established at Marseilles, France, under guidance of the first Oblates of Mary Immaculate.

Eulalie Durocher, the future Mother Marie Rose, the youngest of ten children, was thwarted by illness in her early attempts to become a nun; and so, from the age of 19 to 32, she served as housekeeper for one of her three priest brothers in the large rectory of Beloeil. The parish of Saint Hilaire, just across the Richelieu River, being temporarily without a priest, was also cared for by her brother. On December 8, within a week of the arrival of the first Oblates in Canada, Eulalie at the age of 30 met Father Pierre Telmon, O.M.I. Bishop Bourget of Montreal had given the Oblates Saint Hilaire as their first headquarters. Father Telmon recognized the housekeeper's extraordinary quality, made her superior of the Children of Mary association he organized, and described her and her rectory companion, Mélodie Dufresne, in a letter to Bishop de Mazenod of Marseilles as "two women of rare talent and virtue who desire to sanctify themselves by the practise of humility, obedience and poverty. They are sufficiently advanced to make the three perpetual vows of religion and the vow to make daily progress in perfection." Father Telmon permitted Eulalie to pronounce private vows and told her not to join any of the orders then in Canada but to form a teaching order under Bishop Bourget and lead into it the devout young women clustered about her. Her brother, the pastor, at first ridiculed the idea and her aged father, who also lived in the rectory, added his pleas; but the plan went ahead. In 1843, Eulalie Durocher and Mélodie Dufresne moved to Longueuil where Henriette Céré, a teacher animated with like ideals, kept a school for 13 boarders in her home. This house became the convent, novitiate and school. The Oblate Fathers had already located their novitiate in the same town and undertook the formation of the sisters. On December 8, 1844, the three took vows. When Bl. Marie Rose died, a consumptive, five years later, there were 3 houses, 23 professed sisters, 11 novices and 7 postulants. At her beatification in 1982 her sisters numbered nearly 3000.

OCTOBER 13

909

St. Gerald, count of Aurillac, a deeply religious feudal lord, outstanding for his delicacy of feeling and consideration for others. After a number of stories that illustrate the quiet strength of Gerald's meekness, his availability, mercy, and tact, St. Odo of Cluny, his biographer, sums his character up by saying, "He was loved by all, for he himself loved everyone."

Odo adds an incident of a malefactor who had escaped from the count's territory but after a time was accidentally discovered during Gerald's travels. The trembling man was brought before the saint who asked how things were going; and when he found that the man was held in high esteem by his new neighbors, the count would not allow his party to divulge what the man had been. Instead Gerald openly gave him some small gifts and paid him considerable public respect in talking to him at table so as to further enhance the man's good reputation.

The biographer also reports that the saint was not easily annoyed, as rulers generally are, by criticism. He remained celibate, and though he did not become a monk he founded the abbey of Aurillac. Its poor observance proved a disappointment to him; but it was in that monastery, thirty years after the saint's death, that Gerbert of Aurillac, the outstanding future Pope Sylvester II, began his studies and received his monastic training.

1012

St. Coloman, Irish or possibly Scottish pilgrim who was killed near Vienna, and became a patron of Austria. His body was soon transferred to the abbey of Melk, and the many churches dedicated to him in that part of Europe show his wide-spread cult in the Middle Ages.

1503

Bl. Magdalen Panattieri, virgin, Dominican tertiary who lived in her home at Trino and devoted herself to works of mercy. Her sermons to women became so popular that even priests attended. When dying she called the other tertiaries to her room and promised to intercede for them, for she said she would not be happy in heaven unless they were there too.

OCTOBER 14

ca. 222

ST. CALLISTUS I, pope and martyr, a one-time slave who became a deacon and the administrator of the Christian burial grounds at Rome. There is more information on him than on any other primitive pope, thanks to the schism Hippolytus began as a protest to his election.

The rigorists accused him of being lax, because he recognized the church's authority to absolve even the greatest sins and favored a policy of mercy towards those who had denied their faith by temporary apostasy. He condemned the teaching of Sabellius as over-emphasizing the unity in the Blessed Trinity.

He is the first pope after St. Peter whose name is on the

oldest martyrology of the church of Rome, the fourth century **Depositio Martyrum.** In 1960 his tomb was discovered in the remains of an oratory erected during the fourth century.

753 or 754

St. Burchard, an Anglo-Saxon Benedictine who joined St. Boniface on the German mission and became the first bishop of Würzburg. He was one of the principal agents Pepin the Short sent to Rome to secure papal recognition for his claim to be king of the Franks.

1060

St. Dominic Loricatus, who discovered that his parents had obtained his priestly ordination through a bribe and after that would no longer offer Mass but began to do penance and live as a hermit. He finally became a monk at Fonte Avellana under St. Peter Damian and was appointed prior of San Severino. He slept in a kneeling posture, and is called "Loricatus" ("the armored one") because of the metal breastplate he wore.

OCTOBER 15

1582

ST. TERESA OF AVILA, foundress in 1562 of the Discalced Carmelites—one of the greatest and most human of mystics. She was declared a doctor of the church in 1970 so that her teaching on prayer—her "message of prayer" as Pope Paul VI called it—might become increasingly authoritative throughout the world.

This message is contained principally in her writings: the **Way of Perfection**—composed for the nuns at St. Joseph in Avila, the first of the fifteen convents she personally founded—the **Interior Castle,** and her **Life.**

Drawing on her own experiences she has succeeded, perhaps

better than anyone else, in describing the life of prayer in its
various stages and in giving non-technical, practical advice
for anyone seriously working at the spiritual life. She has also
made the way of prayer uniquely attractive, not, however, because of visions and ecstasies, for she writes that "at the beginning one must not think of such things as spiritual favors, for
that is a very poor way of starting to build such a large and
beautiful edifice. If it is begun upon sand, it will all collapse:
souls which build like that will never be free from annoyances
and temptations" (**Interior Castle** II, 1).

Though she made a special contribution in mapping out the
higher stages such as the "prayer of quiet" and "union," she
was particularly persuasive in urging mental prayer. "No one,"
she writes, "who has begun this practice should ever forsake
it, no matter how many sins he may commit. For it is the
means by which we amend our lives again. . . . Mental prayer,
in my view, is nothing else but a friendly way of dealing in
which we often find ourselves talking, just two alone, with
Him Who we know loves us" (**Life** VIII).

To allay the sisters' fears she assures them that mental prayer
is neither dangerous nor anything unusual, but a quite normal
preparation for vocal prayer: "Whenever I remember to do so,
I shall always speak of mental and vocal prayer together. . . .
Who can say that it is wrong if, before we begin reciting the
Hours or the rosary, we think Whom we are going to address,
and who we are that are addressing Him, so that we may do
so in the way we should" (**Way of Perfection** XXII).

She belonged to an upper middleclass Avila family of three
girls and nine boys, and as early as the age of seven showed
qualities that would make her a tirelessly active contemplative:
"I had one brother almost my own age . . . whom I loved
the most. . . . We used to read the lives of the saints together.
. . . We agreed to go off to the country of the Moors, . . . so
that they might behead us there. . . . But our greatest hindrance seemed to be that we had a father and mother. It used
to cause us great astonishment when we were told that both
pain and glory would last forever. We would spend long peri-

ods talking about this and we would like to repeat again and again, 'Forever—ever—ever' " (**Life I**).

Thanks to her literary genius—for she could hardly write a dull sentence—the details of her career are well known: a Carmelite at twenty-one, serious illness, ups and downs at prayer, a "conversion" that gave her mastery of her desire to be appreciated and thought well of, help and hindrance from confessors, contact with the saints and theologians of Spain, encouragement by St. Peter Alcantara, secret foundation of her first community of nuns, her discovery of St. John of the Cross, opposition to the reform, and the bewildering confusion between the jurisdictions of papal nuncios, visitators appointed by King Philip II, and Carmelite superiors.

Unique as her other writings are, nothing gives such an insight into the richness of St. Teresa's personality as the correspondence of her final years when she settled into her full role as mother and foundress.

OCTOBER 16*

1243

ST. HEDWIG, duchess of Silesia. She was helpful, even valiant, in matters of state, fostered monastic, social and cultural institutions, and introduced the mendicant orders into the territory. After the birth of their seventh child she and her husband vowed continence. On her husband's death she retired to the Cistercian convent of Trebnitz which the royal couple had founded—the first community of women in Silesia.

1690

ST. MARGARET MARY ALACOQUE, Visitation nun at Paray-le-Monial, mystic, Our Lord's principal instrument in establishing popular devotion to the Sacred Heart. "I wished," she said, "to

---

Canada see Dec. 23 for Bl. Marguerite d'Youville.

be burnt away like a candle so as to give Him back love for love."

An incident at twenty-four just after her entry into the convent brings out her special calling to suffer with Christ. On asking her novice mistress for directions on how to meditate she was told, "Go and place yourself before God like a blank canvas." Puzzled, she went to kneel before the Blessed Sacrament and there received her answer: "My sovereign Master showed me that my soul was the blank canvas on which He wished to paint all the details of his life of suffering, entirely spent in love and poverty, solitude, silence, and sacrifice. . . . After emptying my heart and stripping my soul naked, he kindled in them so burning a desire to love and suffer that it allowed me no rest."

But her vocation had begun much earlier and she had long been accustomed to the supernatural. At eight, "without knowing what it was, I felt myself continually persuaded to say these words, 'O my God, I dedicate to you my purity and I make you a vow of perpetual chastity'. . . . I understood neither what I had done nor what the words 'vow' or 'chastity' meant." Suffering soon followed: "I fell into such a pitiful state that, for about four years I could not walk." But at fourteen she was instantly cured when, at her mother's suggestion, she vowed herself to the Blessed Virgin.

Early in her religious life she began to receive revelations concerning the Sacred Heart: a feast was to be established on the Friday after the octave of Corpus Christi; she should atone man's ingratitude, coldness, and indifference by frequent reception of Holy Communion, especially on first Fridays, and by an hour's vigil every Thursday night in memory of the agony and desertion in Gethsemane. There were also the promises and she was told to speak to the Jesuit Claude de la Colombière— now beatified—and tell him to do all he could to spread the devotion. A few months before her death at forty-three she remarked, "I will not live much longer, for I no longer suffer."

ca. 635

St. Gall, Irish monk and missionary. The most famous medieval abbey in Switzerland stood on the spot where he established his hermitage when he became too sick to follow St. Columban over the Alps.

1775 [*C.SS.R.*]

St. Gerard Majella, mystic, a Redemptorist brother with a great reputation as a wonderworker. He died at Caposele near Naples at the age of twenty-nine, after only three years of religious profession.

OCTOBER 17

ca. 110

ST. IGNATIUS, bishop of Antioch, known primarily through seven epistles he wrote to various churches while he was a prisoner on his way to martyrdom at Rome. He is the key witness to Church structures and to Christian belief and practice at the beginning of the second century, when some who had been taught by the apostles themselves were still alive.

An hour's reading of these letters provides an historical perspective and a sense of Church continuity that can be had in no other way. Ignatius witnesses, for example, to the Real Presence, warning the Smyrnaeans against heretics who do not participate "because they do not confess that the Eucharist is the flesh of our Savior Jesus Christ." He shows the ecclesial dimension of marriage by pointing out that it is proper that those who contemplate matrimony "enter the union with the sanction of the bishop." "Thus," he says "their marriage will be acceptable to the Lord."

The writings reveal St. Ignatius as an enthusiast for Christ of the stamp of John the Apostle or St. Paul. Referring to himself as the "wheat of Christ" he begged the Romans not to oppose his martyrdom: "Coax the wild beasts to become my tomb and leave no part of my person behind. . . . Fire, cross, . . . the crunching of the whole body, . . . let them come upon me, provided only I make my way to Jesus Christ."

After Christ the saint's main preoccupation is the holiness of the Church, a holiness that can be achieved only by keeping united with the bishop in faith, obedience, and love. Typical of this ever-recurring theme are his words to the Trallians: "When you obey the bishop as you would Jesus Christ, it is clear to me that you are not living the life of men but that of Jesus Christ. . . . Likewise, let all respect the deacons as they would Jesus Christ, the bishop as representing the Father, and the presbyters as God's high council and as the apostolic college. Apart from these no church deserves the name."

OCTOBER 18

ST. LUKE, evangelist, author also of the **Acts of the Apostles** and commonly identified with the Luke St. Paul mentions in his epistles, once as "my dear friend Luke, the doctor" (Col. 4:14). He was a gentile and is credited with the best Greek in the New Testament.

From the "we" passages in **Acts** it appears that he joined St. Paul at Troas (**Acts** 16:10) during the second missionary journey and went along as far as Philippi. Some years later he rejoined the missionary party at Philippi and remained Paul's traveling companion, not only as far as Jerusalem but also on the sea voyage that took Paul as a prisoner to Rome.

Though Luke gives the precise year in the reign of Tiberius when the Baptist began to preach, exact times and places are for the most part missing from his gospel. Under the vague heading of a trip to Jerusalem he weaves together ten chapters of his **Gospel** (9:51-19:27) out of materials almost wholly omitted by others.

He is careful to show Christ praying before every important step—giving eight instances not mentioned by the other evangelists—and he preserved the parable of the widow and the unjust judge (18:1-5) to inculcate perseverance at prayer. The canticles from his infancy narratives have long had the place of honor in the divine office at the hours of Lauds, Vespers, and Compline.

He is sensitive and sympathetic to the role of women and shows a sensitivity for minorities and the underprivileged: Samaritans, lepers, publicans, soldiers, public sinners, and the poor. Dante called his the "gospel of Christ's meekness," for only Luke includes the incidents of the sinful woman kissing Christ's feet (7:36-50), of Zacchaeus (19:1-10), of the good thief (23:39-43); only he recounts the parables of the lost coin (15:8-9), the pharisee and the publican (18:9-14), and the prodigal son (15:11-32). It is he who saved the words, "be merciful, even as your Father is merciful" (6:36), as well as the call to absolute renunciation and total discipleship: "Whoever of you does not renounce all that he has cannot be my disciple" (14:33).

The **Acts** and the gospel bring out the joy of believing and underline the role of the Holy Spirit in the first congregations and in the enduring life of the church. Recent New Testament studies give St. Luke a central place as the best witness to the changing theological perspective in the period immediately after the fall of Jerusalem as the primitive Christian community grew into the post-apostolic church.

OCTOBER 19

1642-1649
ST. ISAAC JOGUES and **COMPANIONS,** the North American

Martyrs, secondary patrons of Canada, six priests and two lay associates, all members of the band of French Jesuits who established the first permanent missions in Canada. Father Isaac Jogues and the Jesuit associates **René Goupil** — a surgeon — and **John La Lande,** were martyred by the Iroquois near Auriesville, New York; the other five priests, Sts. **Jean de Brébeuf, Gabriel Lalemant, Anthony Daniel, Charles Garnier** and **Noël Chabanel,** suffered in Huron Territory near Georgian Bay, and are now honored at the Jesuit Martyrs Shrine, Midland, Ontario.

The heroic labors of these missionaries were chronicled in the first volumes of the **Jesuit Relations** — annual reports sent by the Jesuit superior in Quebec to the provincial in Paris during the years 1632 to 1672 and intended for the general public. These vivid records caused a great sensation and stimulated priests, nuns, and colonists to come to New France.

The **Relation** of 1636 gave Jean de Brébeuf's lengthy description of what the missioner should expect. ". . . Our lives," he wrote, "depend on a single thread. . . . If you cannot make it rain, they speak of nothing less than making away with you. . . . What a satisfaction to negotiate these rapids and to climb these rocks, for one who has before his eyes the loving Savior harassed by his tormentors and ascending calvary laden with his cross. . . ."

Typical of the spirit of these martyrs is the incident Father Jogues reported to his provincial in Paris during his first Iroquois captivity. An old woman, also a prisoner, was ordered to cut off the priest's thumb. At first she refused but finally "she cut off my thumb at the place where it joined my hand. . . . She was a Christian, named Jeanne. It gives me happiness to receive such sufferings from those whom we have come here to save. . . . Then taking up in my other hand the severed thumb, I offered it to you my living and true God, in remembrance of the Sacrifices that I had offered in your church during the past seven years. . . " The captors had already gnawed off the saint's index fingers and otherwise multilated his hands. He escaped down the Hudson River and at New Amsterdam — now New York — one of the Calvinists knelt at his feet and kissed the mangled hands exclaiming, "Martyr of Jesus Christ!"

1775

ST. PAUL OF THE CROSS, mystic, spiritual director, founder in Italy of the Passionists, who promote devotion to the Sacred Passion and combine a vigorous apostolate of retreats and missions with penitential monasticism. The order has approximately 4,000 priests and brothers. He also founded the cloistered Passionist Nuns; a century later a flourishing active congregation of Passionist Sisters was started in England. The saint wrote his rule in five days after forty days of retreat and penance. He was then twenty-six.

OCTOBER 20

1411 [*Franciscans*]

Bl. James of Strepar, Polish Franciscan, guardian at Lvov, archbishop of Halicz, zealous preacher among the dissidents and pagans of western Russia at the time the Latin Church was expanding in those areas. He is especially remembered for his devotion to Mary.

1902 [*Franciscan III O.*]

Bl. Contardo Ferrini, jurist, professor of Roman Law at Pavia, leading authority on the Byzantine period of Roman Law and author of more than 200 monographs. At twenty-two while at the University of Berlin he made a vow of celibacy. Back in Italy he became a Franciscan tertiary. All his energies were devoted to God and he used to refer to work as his wife. He died at forty-three.

Pope Pius XI, who as a priest went mountain climbing with him, said, "my relations with him were purely scientific or were concerned with the beauties of high mountains. For him these were an inspiration to holiness and almost a natural revelation of God."

1922

St. Bertilla Boscardin, one of the most recent saints, a sister of St. Dorothy, who died of cancer at the age of thirty-four after spending most of her eighteen years of religious life nursing in a hospital at Treviso. As a nun she wrote in her diary: "I must keep myself in the last place, pleased to be put after others."

When reproved she would reply, "Always correct me. You do me a favor." "It is enough for me," she would say, "if I am useful." "To God all the glory, to my neighbor all the joy, to me the work."

To the doctor who removed a seven pound tumor she said, "For your sake I am sorry that I am not going to recover." "You are here with me," she told the sisters around her deathbed. "Perhaps some patient needs you more." The superior general asked, "What shall I tell your sisters when I return to the motherhouse?" "Tell them," St. Bertilla answered, "tell them to work only for Jesus, that everything else is nothing."

OCTOBER 21*

Probably 4th cent.   [O.S.U.]

The Cologne virgin martyrs. As early as the fourth century the city had a church dedicated to a group of virgin martyrs but nothing further is certain about them. Gradually a famous

---

*O.SS.T. see Dec. 17 for St. John of Matta.

C.P.P.S. see Dec. 28 for St. Caspar del Bufalo.

Franciscan II O. see Oct. 22 for Bl. Josephine Leroux.

BLESSED CONTARDO FERINI

legend developed. The name "Ursula" appeared in the ninth century. According to one version there were eleven martyrs, but the more impressive account had St. Ursula heading a band of eleven thousand virgins from England whose ships sailed up the Rhine as far as Cologne.

ca. 304

St. Philip, bishop of Heraclea in the Balkans, and his companions **Hermes,** a deacon and former magistrate, and the priest **Severus,** martyrs under Diocletian. On the way to prison the mob threw the bishop down, but he got up with joyful countenance. He was later dragged through the town by a cord tied to his feet, and these became so maimed that he had to be carried to the scene of martyrdom.

"Why should we be concerned about our feet," Hermes remarked, "since we will need them no more?" At the stake their legs were covered with earth up to the knees and the fires were lit. Sts. Philip and Hermes suffered on one day; and Severus, who voluntarily gave himself up, suffered on the next.

ca. 371

St. Hilarion, abbot, desert father known mostly through a life written by St. Jerome. After a short period under St. Anthony in Egypt he returned to his home near Gaza in Palestine, and though still a teenager he soon embarked on the solitary life in the nearby desert. Disciples flocked to him—he is credited with founding eremetical monasticism in Palestine—and to escape the fame of his miracles he moved from place to place: Egypt, Libya, Sicily, Dalmatia, and finally Cyprus, where he died at eighty. In the beginning he subsisted on fifteen figs a day; and though, for the sake of health, he later added several other ingredients to the scanty diet, he kept a life-long practice of not eating until sunset.

OCTOBER 22

1562 [*Franciscans*]

St. Peter of Alcantara, Spain, prodigy of austerity, founder of the discalced penitential branch of Franciscans known as the Alcantarines. He normally ate once in three days and looked to St. Teresa as if he were made of roots of a tree rather than flesh. For forty years he slept only an hour-and-a-half a day, and that in a sitting posture on a skin spread over the floor, his head leaning against the wall. He wrote a masterful treatise on prayer, and St. Teresa said she got more help from him than from anyone else.

1794 [*O.S.U.*]

The Valenciennes martyrs, eleven nuns of the Ursuline convent at Valenciennes in northern France, guillotined for illegally resuming religious life and for teaching the Catholic faith. Eight were Ursulines by profession, while the Bridgettines, **Bl. Lilvina Lacrois** and **Bl. Anne Mary Erraux,** and the Poor Clare, **Bl. Josephine Leroux,** lived with the Ursulines and wore their habit because their own communities had been disbanded.

Five Ursulines were tried and executed on October 17, and on October 23 it was the turn of **Bl. Clotilde Paillot,** the prioress, and the other five nuns. **Bl. Cordule Barré,** a lay sister, was overlooked by the commissioners; but she too climbed into the cart that was taking the others to execution in the market place. "We die," Bl. Clotilde Paillot attested, "for the faith of the Catholic, Apostolic, and Roman Church." The nuns kissed the hand of the executioner and, chanting all the while, bared their necks for the stroke of the blade.

OCTOBER 23*

1456

ST. JOHN CAPISTRAN, Franciscan, outstanding preacher and

---

*O.S.U. see Oct. 22 for Bl. Clotilde Paillot and companions.

SAINT BERTILLA BOSCARDIN

reformer who spent most of his life on various papal missions and is best remembered for his final service to christendom just after the fall of Constantinople, when he roused the people of Hungary to defend their country against the Turkish invasion. At the Battle of Belgrade on July 21, 1456, he so animated the troops with his courage and devotion that the siege of Belgrade was lifted and the invaders were driven from the land. He was seventy years of age and died of exhaustion and contagion at Ilok, Jugoslavia, three months later.

A native of Capistrano in the Abruzzi, he studied law at Perugia and soon attained a high government position; but imprisonment brought a complete conversion at the age of thirty and he became a Franciscan of the Observance. He was trained under St. Bernardine of Siena and during the year 1425 worked with him, hearing confessions while Bernardine preached. He defended Bernardine when he was accused of heresy, wrote his life, was present for his canonization, and attributed the many miracles that accompanied his own preaching to the relic of St. Bernardine which he carried.

He fostered the Colettine reform at Ferrara, obtained approval for Franciscan tertiaries to live in common, and was the first vicar general of the Observants in Italy when efforts to reunify the Franciscans failed. He spent several years on a mission to the Hussities in Bohemia, but the gates of the city of Prague were never opened to him.

877

St. Ignatius, patriarch of Constantinople. He abdicated after eleven years in office and was followed by Photius. A few years later he was reinstated, but Photius became patriarch again when Ignatius died.

These changes primarily reflected the policies of a succession of regents and emperors; but they entailed complicated sequences of synods, appeals to Rome, excommunications, and reconciliations that were differently reported by various factions and gave rise to partisan historical traditions.

Improved relations between Rome and the Eastern churches
and disinterested research are now facilitating a calmer ap-
praisal of the so-called "Photian Schism," especially as Photius
himself was no longer in schism at the time of his death and
is honored as a saint by the orientals.

Never was the Roman primacy so solemnly acknowledged in
any Eastern synod as at the Council of Constantinople con-
vened in 869 shortly after Ignatius was reinstated. This synod
was disallowed ten years later, but the West from the end of
the eleventh century has accepted it as ecumenical.

OCTOBER 24*

1870

ST. ANTHONY CLARET, archbishop of Santiago, Cuba, founder in Spain of the Missionary Sons of the Immaculate Heart of
Mary, better known as Claretians. The son of a poor weaver,
he worked in a Barcelona textile mill, learning printing and
Latin on the side. He was ordained at twenty-seven and tried
the Jesuit novitiate at Rome but returned to Spain and devoted
himself to retreats and missions, always emphasizing devotion
to the Blessed Sacrament and to Mary. As one of Spain's most
popular preachers he sometimes gave as many as twelve sermons a day.

The Claretians originated in a group of five young Catalan
priests who banded together with him for preaching purposes
in 1849. But the following year, when only forty-two, the founder was sent to Cuba as archbishop; and it was only after his
return to Spain that he wrote up some rules for the order.

In the much-neglected diocese of Santiago he initiated a
vigorous reform of clergy and laity and strove particularly to
combat the high rate of illigitimacy. No less than fifteen attempts were made on his life, and he was once wounded by a
man who was furious at the conversion of his mistress. He also

---

*O.H. see Sept. 29 for St. Raphael the Archangel.

fostered credit unions, sound farming methods, and the like, but after seven years was recalled to Spain to become confessor to Queen Isabella II. With this light assignment he combined a vigorous apostolate of the press. In Catalonia and in the city of Madrid he founded societies for the free distribution of Catholic literature and produced some 200 works himself.

The 1868 revolution banished the queen and her chaplain, and he died two years later in France. By then he had also taken vows in his own order. His last words were those of St. Paul, "I want to be gone and be with Christ" (Phil 1:23). The Claretians are devoted to preaching and other forms of the apostolate. Their traditional profession formula contains a special consecration to the Immaculate Heart of Mary.

446

St. Proclus, Archbishop of Constantinople, known for the mildness and tact with which he treated even obstinate heretics. Against Nestorius he defended Mary's title as Mother of God, saying, "We do not proclaim a deified man but we do confess an incarnate God."

OCTOBER 25

686

St. Eata, abbot and bishop. He was one of the twelve English youths St. Aidan trained in Celtic monasticism. He rose to the position of abbot of Melrose, Scotland. There he received St. Cuthbert as a novice, and when Eata became abbot at Ripon he took Cuthbert along as guest master.

After the Synod of Whitby Eata fully adopted the Roman observances and was one of the bishops ordained to take over the territory of York, when St. Wilfrid was driven from that see. Eata was bishop of the Bernicians, with his principal church first at Lindisfarne and then at Hexham. St. Bede describes him as "the meekest and mildest of all men."

1243 [O. Cist.]
St. Bernard, Cistercian abbot of Santa Cruz near Tarragona in Spain and the bishop of Vich, a vigilant guardian of the faith against the subtle Waldensian and Albigensian errors.

1506 [O.S.M.]
Bl. John Angelo Porro, Servite, a native of Milan, noted particularly for his zeal in teaching Christian doctrine. In his order he is patron of novice masters, so well did he fulfill that office at Florence.

1539 [O.S.A., O.A.R.]
St. John Stone, Augustinian friar of Canterbury who refused to acknowledge Henry VIII's headship of the Church and even after a year's imprisonment—according to the commissioner's report—"still held and still desired to die for it that the king may not be head of the church of England, but it must be a spiritual father appointed by God." He was hanged for his faith; and the chamberlain's accountbook at Canterbury still shows the charges for the timber of the gallows, the halter, and the cauldron in which the martyr's dismembered body was parboiled.

OCTOBER 26

1711 [Franciscans]
Bl. Bonaventure of Potenza in southern Italy, Conventual Franciscan, remembered for his priestly ministry and devotion to the Immaculate Conception. He was given his own way and never became a guardian, but he was forced to accept the position of novice master. His life was a convincing example of the humility and obedience he constantly recommended to those

who wished to become Franciscans.

1917

Bl. Mutien Marie Wiaux, who joined the Brothers of the Christian Schools at 15 but after his first teaching assignments seemed so unfitted for the work that the community council voted against him; and it was only through the efforts of an understanding confrere that he was allowed to renew temporary vows. He was humble and completely obedient: so he received a few months of training in drawing and music—subjects in which he had no special interest—and then was given beginners classes in these subjects along with prefecting, tasks that would be his main assignments for the remaining 55 years of his life, all at the college in Malonne, a town of his native Belgium. He was able to teach the rudiments of piano, flute, tuba and a few other instruments, and even in his 70's would still religiously be taking his own practise times on the harmonium which he would also at times play in choir when the organist was not there. He regularly supervised the play grounds and even in old age and in every kind of weather would always be there. Each morning found him kneeling before the Blessed Sacrament at 4:30 and then he would move to Our Lady's altar. The family Rosary had been the practise in his home and the normal thing was to see Br. Mutien, wherever he was, fingering the Rosary. At 75, shortly before his death agony, he confided with simplicity to those about him, "How happy a person will be, if like me now on the brink of the grave, he can say that he has a great devotion to Mary."

Extraordinary favors began to be reported from the day of his death, January 30, 1917; and in the course of the years the number of pilgrims increased to such an extent that Br. Mutien's remains were moved to the foot of the tower of the parish church in Malonne.

OCTOBER 27 *

ca. 380

St. Frumentius, venerated as the fourth century apostle of

°Franciscans see Nov. 28 for Bl. Francis Anthony Fasani.

the Aksumite kingdom in Ethiopia. He was a Syrian youth who, like St. Patrick a few years later, was carried off as a captive to the pagan country which he later converted. His consecration by St. Athanasius is the link between the Ethiopian Church and the Coptic Patriarchate of Alexandria. After his death he was called "Abuna" meaning "Our Father," which is still the title of the primate of the Ethiopian Church.

1915

Bl. Aloysius Guanella, founder of the Servants of Charity and the Daughters of St. Mary of Providence. A ninth son, he tended sheep in the Italian alps and entered the seminary at eleven. His two orders, one for men and one for women, grew out of pioneering efforts to solve the social question and relieve every kind of distress in the diocese of Como. He had earlier spent several years with St. John Bosco at Turin and tried to found a Salesian house at Como, but the effort failed and he was recalled by his bishop.

His congregations have both expanded beyond Italy, and he himself traveled to the United States in order to have his religious ·assist the Italian immigrants. He wrote some fifty popular works of piety, had a particular devotion to St. Joseph, and was ever confident in divine providence, saying, "It is God who does it." He continually taught his religious "to pray and suffer" as the best means of success. The beatification decree described him as joyful in serving, forgetful of self, simple, and frank. He died October 24, 1915.

OCTOBER 28

STS. SIMON and **JUDE,** apostles, whose names occur in the tenth and eleventh places in the New Testament lists of apostles, and if Thaddeus is another name for Jude then they have these places to themselves. **Simon** is called "the Zealot" (Lk

6:15) and so had probably belonged to the Zealots, a radical and extremely nationalistic anti-Roman revolutionary party, the group that would hold out longest against the Romans, Masada rock on the Dead Sea being their last stronghold.

St. Jude is called the son of James. In the discourse after the Last Supper he asks, "Lord, how is it that you will manifest yourself to us and not to the world" (Jn 14:22)? The traditional identification of these two apostles with the Simon and Jude who were Our Lord's brethren (Mk 6:3) is being increasingly rejected, nor does it seem that the Epistle of Jude was written by one of the Twelve, since verse 17 speaks of the apostles in the past tense.

ca. 670

St. Faro, a Burgundian, outstanding bishop of Meaux in France. In his thirties, with his wife's consent, he became a cleric. St. Burgundofara, first abbess of Faremoutier, was his sister.

1585

Bl. Thomas Alfield, convert, priest, and martyr. He apostatized on his first imprisonment. When released he went to France to make amends. He returned to England, was taken again and sentenced under Elizabeth I for circulating Dr. Allen's **True and Modest Defense.** This time, though offered freedom, he remained steadfast and was hanged at Tyburn.

OCTOBER 29

ca. 12th cent.

St. Abraham of Rostov, abbot, called the "Wonderworker" by the Russians. A youthful pagan convert at Halicz in the Ukraine, he left home to become a monk shortly after his conversion and went to Rostov in south eastern Russia, where he preached and established two churches and a monastery.

1910   **[*S.D.B.*]**

Bl. Michael Rua, St. John Bosco's inseparable helper and his successor as rector major of the Salesians. Under his self-effacing fidelity to John Bosco's ideals the society grew in twenty-two years from 800 to 4,000 members. "A frail figure of a priest," Pope Paul VI described him at the beatification in 1972, "all meekness and goodness, all duty and sacrifice."

On his deathbed John Bosco reminded Father Rua, "You see now what I meant when I used to tell you we would share everything;" for as a young priest he would give Michael—who was eight years old—candy or a holy card and make a slicing motion saying, "Here, let's go halves on this, you and I."

The two met shortly after Michael's father, a Turin mill-worker, died. At sixteen the boy began to attend the seminary and to live with John Bosco at the Oratory, where he was entrusted with the discipline and care of the funds. At eighteen he was the first of John Bosco's followers to take religious vows; and three years later he accompanied his master to Rome carrying the copy of the society's constitutions for Pope Pius IX, transcribed in his own neat hand.

On his ordination day at twenty-three he received this note from John Bosco: "You will see better than I how the Salesian Society will go beyond the boundaries of Italy and establish itself in many parts of the world. You will have much work to do and much to suffer. But you know, we reach the Promised Land only by crossing the Red Sea and the desert. Suffer bravely and even here you will not lack the Lord's comfort and assistance."

OCTOBER 30

298

St. Marcellus the Centurion, executed at Tangiers, Morocco.

During a banquet in honor of the Emperor's birthday he took the resolution that as a Christian he could no longer continue in his way of life. Casting the soldier's belt and centurian's insignia at the foot of the standards and condemning the banquets as heathen he declared, "I serve Jesus Christ the eternal King. I will no longer serve your emperors and I scorn the worship of your gods."

When asked at his trial, "Did you cast away your arms?" he answered, "I did, for it is not right for a Christian who serves the Lord Christ, to serve in the armies of the world." On admitting that the official report of his conduct was accurate, he was beheaded.

1292

Bl. Benvenuta Bojani, Dominican tertiary who lived with her family at Cividale in northern Italy and died at thirty-eight, a contemplative remembered for her devotion to Mary and her penances, as well as for the cheerfulness and confidence she habitually showed despite the grueling temptations to disbelief and despair by which God purified her soul. During a five-year illness her greatest cross was that she could but rarely assist at Mass or be present at compline when the **Salve Regina** was sung.

1583

Bl. John Slade, a lay schoolmaster educated at Oxford, martyred at Winchester for denying the supremacy of Elizabeth I in things spiritual.

1739

Bl. Angelo of Acri, Capuchin provincial in Calabria, an example of success despite failures and difficulties. The son of poor parents, he tried the Capuchins at eighteen but found their life too austere. With the help of much prayer he was professed on his third attempt after a stormy novitiate.

During his first sermon confidence and memory deserted him, and he left the pulpit in confusion. While meditating on his failure he heard our Lord say, "For the future, Angelo, preach simply and colloquially, so that all may understand you." He became one of the greatest preachers of his day, conducting home missions and the Forty Hours Devotions till his death. He wrote only one book, a collection of prayers on Christ's sufferings, for the Capuchin nuns he founded at Acritania.

OCTOBER 31

994

St. Wolfgang, bishop and patron of Regensburg. He was trained at Reichenau and Würburg and then directed the cathedral school at Trier. He later became a Benedictine at Einsiedeln Abbey in Switzerland and soon after receiving priestly orders set out for the newly opened Hungarian missions; but he was there hardly a year before he was appointed bishop of Regensburg.

For the next twenty-two years he preached, reformed monasteries, and earned a reputation as a zealous pastor and a man of prayer. His love of the poor became proverbial through southern Germany, where he remained a popular saint during the Middle Ages. He tutored Emperor Henry II and drew up the charter for the historic diocese of Prague which was carved out of his territory.

1617   [S.J.]

St. Alphonsus Rodriguez, who after the death of his wife and three children became a Jesuit brother at thirty-nine, and who is remembered as the patient, helpful and spiritually keen old porter at Montesione College in Majorca, where he spent every spare moment in prayer and inspired the young student St. Peter Claver with zeal for the missions. His childhood contacts with the Society of Jesus included preparation for first Communion by the. family guest Bl. Peter Favre and, at four- teen, a few months in a Jesuit college, until the death of his father made it necessary for him to return to Segovia to help his mother carry on the father's cloth business.

Deaths terminated a happy married life, and business failure caused him to sell out; so he undertook a retired way of life; and prayer soon became the most meaningful part of his day. On the death of his last child he thought of the priesthood; but the Jesuits refused his application because of his insuffi- cient education, poor health, and advanced years — though he would live almost another half century. The provincial, con- trary to the advice of the official consultors, received him as a brother and after six months sent him to Majorca, where he spent the rest of his life.

NOVEMBER 1

THE FEAST OF ALL SAINTS. The spirit behind the cult of martyrs in the primitive church is beautifully portrayed in the **Martyrdom of St. Polycarp** of the year 155, the oldest document to mention a celebration of the "birthday" of a saint: "We afterwards took up his bones, more precious than costly stones and more excellent than gold, and interred them in a decent place. There the Lord will permit us, as far as possible, to assemble in rapturous joy and celebrate his martyrdom — his birthday — both in order to commemorate the heroes that have gone before, and to train and prepare the heroes yet to come."

As martyrs increased in number it soon became impossible to commemorate them all separately, and as early as the fourth century St. Ephraem witnesses to a feast at Edessa on May 13 honoring "the martyrs of the whole world." From St. John Chrysostom we learn that Antioch at the same period had a similar feast on the first Sunday after Pentecost — which is still the "Sunday of All Saints" in the Byzantine rite.

Veneration of the holy martyrs and of all the saints received a special impetus, when the eighth century Iconoclasts (or "image-breakers") were put down in an ecumenical council called precisely to settle the question. In 787 the Second Council of Nicea declared: "Representations of the cross and the holy images, whether painted, sculptured or made in some other way, are to be placed on vessels, vestments, walls, houses and along roads. The images we mean are those of Jesus Christ, of his Immaculate Mother, the holy angels, and all holy persons. The more we behold these images, the more we call to mind the persons they represent; and we make a point of imitating them and showing them respect and veneration, without however, giving them worship in the proper sense which belongs to God alone. . . . Whoever venerates an image venerates the one represented by it." At the time of the controversy a solemnity of all saints was being celebrated at various places in the West; but it was not until fifty years after the council that, by the joint action of Pope Gregory IV and Emperor Louis the Pious, November 1 was fixed as the uniform date for this solemnity throughout the Western empire.

"In Catholic tradition," Pope John XXIII explained in one of his talks, "devotion to the saints is not merely a mark of respect or a brief prayer on certain occasions which seem to grow fewer as life proceeds, but a deeply felt spiritual communion, an attentive study of the precious examples and lessons which the saints give to cheer and encourage us."

NOVEMBER 2

COMMEMORATION OF ALL THE FAITHFUL DEPARTED, described by Pope John XXIII as a "meditation on eternal truths, enabling us to perceive what it is that passes away and what is destined to survive." The three Masses priests are permitted to offer on this day—the first according to their own intention, the second for all the faithful departed, and the third according to the Holy Father's intentions—reflect the deep and unbroken Catholic conviction that the Eucharistic Sacrifice has pre-eminence among the prayers, good works, alms, and acts of religion, which believers are encouraged to offer on behalf of the dead.

As early as the beginning of the third century Tertullian mentions the custom of celebrating Mass on the day of death and on the anniversaries; while St. Cyprian (**Letter** 1), a few years later, recalls a decision of the African bishops to the effect that official "prayers should not be offered nor the sacrifice celebrated for the repose of the soul" of anyone who in his will appoints a cleric to be a guardian or trustee and thus, by involving the cleric in secular affairs, withdraws him from prayer and the ministry of the altar.

Seventh century Spain had an All Souls day on Pentecost Monday; but the November 2 date grew out of an eleventh century decision of St. Odilo, abbot of Cluny that required Cluniac monasteries everywhere to have special prayers for all the dead on the day after All Saints.

The privilege of three Masses originated with the Spanish Dominicans, was generalized for all priests in the Kingdom of Spain during the eighteenth century, and was extended to every priest by Pope Benedict XV during the first World War.

The Church, as St. Augustine pointed out, shows herself a mother in making general supplications for all the faithful departed, "so that those who do not have parents, children, relatives or friends to render them this service receive it from the devoted and common mother of all."

1148

St. Malachy, archbishop of Armagh. He restored Church discipline after the Danish invasions and is credited with introducing the Roman liturgy as well as Cistercian monks into Ireland. On a return trip from Rome he died at Clairvaux Abbey, France, in the arms of his friend St. Bernard. The "prophecy" attributed to him is a sixteenth century forgery that characterizes each of the 111 successors of Pope Celestine II (1143-44) in a short epithet.

NOVEMBER 3

1639

ST. MARTIN DE PORRES, wonder-working Dominican brother in Lima, Peru, an example of universal charity. He was entered in the Lima baptismal register as of "unknown father" because John De Porres, a highborn Spaniard and future governor of Panama, refused to recognize the child when he saw his mulatto color; and for some years Martin shared the poverty of his unmarried mother, Anna Velasquez, a free Negress. His social handicap did not, however, embitter him and may even have helped him acquire the genuine humility which was such a striking life-long characteristic.

In time he won his father's heart and name, being open, gentle, sensitive to the needs of others and resourceful in finding them assistance. He was about twelve when his father took an interest in his education, and he was successfully apprenticed to a barber-surgeon, but in the meantime he became aware of his religious vocation.

The Dominicans received him as a lay helper and a tertiary— his humility not allowing him to aspire to vows—and it was nine years before he gave in to the community's wish that he become a fully professed member. He lived to his sixtieth year, interested only in prayer, self-denial, and being of assistance. He cared for the sick and the poor, particularly the negroes, and taught them the elements of their faith, their dignity as men and sons of God, and the equality of their race with others, Spaniards included.

His sympathetic care also extended to animals and he had a special influence over them. Pictures show him with an open basket collecting mice from church drawers. He would take them outside, give them food and tell them not to harm the crops or go back into the churches. He steadily refused advancement of every kind and remained to the end the brother in charge of the infirmary of Holy Rosary Priory.

727

St. **Hubert,** founder of the city of Liège and its first bishop.

753

St. **Pirmin,** Benedictine abbot and missionary bishop, patron of Alsace and Innsbruck, founder of several monasteries of which the most famous was Reichenau on an island in Lake Constance.

1211

Bl. **Alpais,** virgin, a peasant girl in the diocese of Orleans. She is the earliest person of whom it is reported on reliable evidence that she lived for years upon the Blessed Eucharist alone.

NOVEMBER 4

1584

ST. CHARLES BORROMEO, cardinal archbishop of Milan, the churchman who best personifies the reform associated with the Council of Trent. His enduring relevance can be seen in the several religious orders of men and women that are under his patronage and in the publication of his official acts by such prominent ecclesiastics as Achille Ratti (Pius XI) and Angelo Roncalli (John XXIII). Pope Paul VI, too, just before leaving Milan established the Academy of St. Charles Borromeo to promote study of his life and writings—including the 30,000 letters.

What is most remarkable is the youthful age at which St. Charles made his irreplaceable contribution to the pastoral life of the Church. From the age of twenty-two to twenty-five he was the one chiefly instrumental in reopening the Council of Trent, after a ten-year recess, and in bringing it through the final nine sessions—though he was not at the council but in Rome handling all the correspondence of his uncle, Pope Pius IV.

From twenty-seven until his premature death at forty-six, despite a certain severity in his uncompromising logic, he set an example in Milan of a model bishop and probably did more than any other person to have the decrees of the Council of Trent put into action throughout the Catholic Church. He wore himself out in pastoral work, ate practically nothing, slept little, spent long hours in prayer, and reached the point of heroism in charity to others, particularly during the plague of 1576-78. He promulgated and applied Trent's legislation in six provincial and eleven diocesan synods in northern Italy.

Angelo Roncalli, editing in five volumes the acts of Borromeo's visitation during 1575 of the diocese of Bergamo, would write, "Parish records in this region nearly all begin in 1576 when parishes began to follow the instructions given during that visit." Also on three occasions St. Charles made the rounds in parts of Switzerland and he is largely credited with the revival of Catholicism there.

Vocally somewhat handicapped, he spoke little and gravely in a voice that was barely audible. Though he accomplished so much, he never did anything in a hurry, least of all rush a liturgical prayer or ceremony. He initiated the Confraternity of Christian Doctrine—and is a patron of catechists today—but the clergy for whom he founded three seminaries were his special concern. "Ah," he said when a certain priest fell sick, "do you not realize the worth of the life of a good priest?" He himself was ordained at twenty-four when already a cardinal for two years. Pope John, after a lifelong study of the saint, called him "the teacher of bishops."

1031

Bl. Emeric, only son of St. Stephen of Hungary. His vow of chastity was set aside so that he could marry for reasons of state. He died in an accident while still young.

NOVEMBER 5

ca. 700

St. Bertilla, nun of Jouarre and then first abbess of Chelles, near Paris, when that monastery was restored by queen St. Bathildis. Great numbers flocked to the abbey during Bertilla's half-century of rule, including many Anglo-Saxon girls and two former queens.

1485 [*O. Carm.*]

Bl. Frances d'Amboise, duchess of Brittany, widow, Carmelite prioress. In 1463 she founded at Vannes the first cloister of Carmelite nuns in France.

1707

Bl. Gomidas Keumurgian, martyred in Constantinople under the Turks but at the instigation of brother Christians. He was beatified in 1929. A member of the Orthodox Armenian colony in Constantinople, Gomidas followed in the steps of his father and entered the priesthood. At forty, along with his wife and children, he became Catholic. He continued to minister in the parish and was an outspoken advocate of union with Rome. Before long five of the twelve priests in the parish also became Catholic.

It was a time of unrest, civil as well as religious, and the Armenian leaders began to take alarm. Gomidas was eventually denounced to the Moslem authorities as one who had embraced the religion of the Franks and advised others to do the same, and as a troublemaker disturbing the peace of the Armenian people within the Turkish realm. A mob clamored for blood; and the governor finally gave in, but only after offering to spare Gomidas if he accepted Islam. The martyr's sister broke through the crowd and begged him to feign compliance; his wife and children followed him to the place where he was beheaded. It was the Greek Orthodox clergy who gave him burial, as the Catholics were afraid to make a demonstration. The holy man's reputation and his noble conduct under persecution exercised a powerful influence on the local Armenian community, and many more sought union with Rome.

It is not enough for a priest, Bl. Gomidas said during his trial, to be in the right way himself—he must lead others into it as well.

NOVEMBER 6

1745-1861　　　　　　　　　　　　　　　　　　　　　　[*O.P.*]

Bl. Ignatius Delgado and **companions,** martyrs in Vietnam. In the 350 years since Christianity began to flourish there through the zeal of the French Jesuit Alexander Rhodes, Vietnam has been exceedingly rich in martyrs, and particularly during the fifty years just prior to the establishment of the French Protectorate in 1883, when an estimated 300,000 suffered death or extreme hardship as their homes and villages were destroyed.

After 1832, the Annamite king Minh Mang excluded all foreign missionaries and required native Christians to apostatize by trampling the cross underfoot. His edict of 1839 required all his subjects to take a personal part in the erection of pagan temples "in every village, and to sacrifice at stated times in honor of ancestors and the spirits. . . . After the publication of this edict, if there are still in our kingdom Christian rebels or those whose submission is but exterior . . . we shall punish without pity both the incorrigible Christian and the negligent official."

Up to the present, 117 Vietnam martyrs have been beatified. The Dominicans to whom the vicariate of eastern Tonkin was confided in 1693 account for thirty of these, six being bishops and nine, lay tertiaries.

In 1838 Bl. Ignatius Delgado, vicar apostolic who had come from Spain as a young Dominican nearly fifty years before, was sentenced to be beheaded; but before the sentence was carried out he died of hunger, thirst, and exposure to the sun in a cage that was so small that he could not even stand up.

Among the laymen who suffered at the same time were three soldiers who after a year gave in and trampled on the crucifix, but then recovered themselves and disvowed their action. Two were cut in half with a saw and the third strangled. They too are beatified: **Augustine Huy, Nicholas Bui The,** and **Dominic Dat.**

NOVEMBER 7

739   [*O.S.B.*]

St. Willibrord, apostle of Holland, first archbishop of Utrecht. He inaugurated a century of Anglo-Saxon Benedictine missionary activity on the continent, with the monks also serving as agents of civilization and solidarity with Rome and collaborating effectively with the rising Carolingian dynasty.

Willibrord had the earliest possible initiation into religious life, being entrusted as a mere infant to St. Wilfrid at Ripon. When Wilfrid was deposed, Willibrord, aged nineteen, joined Egbert, a mission-and-Roman-minded Englishman who was at the head of a monastery in Ireland.

Twelve years later Egbert sent him with eleven companions into Friesland, where Wilfrid had once spent a fruitful winter. They landed at the mouth of the Rhine and soon reported to Pepin of Heristal, who gave them Antwerp as a starting base. Four years later Pepin sent Willibrord to Rome—his second trip there—to be made archbishop of the Frisians. The saint also enjoyed the favor of Pepin's son, Charles Martel, and in turn baptized his grand-son, Pepin the Short.

St. Boniface, who arrived on the Frisian mission a generation later and worked for three years under St. Willibrord,
summarized the saint's career in this way: "Pope Sergius ordained him bishop and sent him to evangelize the pagan Frisians along the coast of the western sea. During fifty years of
preaching he converted the greater part of the Frisians to
Christ, destroyed their shrines and temples and built churches."

Willibrord received the pallium from Rome, inaugurating in
this northern region a practice St. Boniface would help gen-
eralize. Historians also note that it was hardly by accident
that the cathedral churches of Rome, Canterbury, and Utrecht
were all dedicated to the Holy Savior. Alcuin, in his life of
Willibrord, describes him—a close relative—as "handsome, joyous, of wise counsel and pleasant speech, . . . and energetic in
whatever had to do with the work of God."

At the time St. Bede was writing his **History,** Willibrord was
nearing his eightieth and final year. "Willibrord," he writes,
"is still alive, venerable with age, . . . sighing for the rewards
of heavenly life after the many spiritual conflicts he has waged."
He was buried at his favorite monastic foundation of Echternach in the Duchy of Luxembourg, a country where the saint's
memory remains particularly alive.

NOVEMBER 8

ca. 429

St. Sisoes, desert father in Egypt, known for his wisdom and
profound sense of the Divine Presence. One day a hermit said
to him, "Father, I always place myself in the presence of God."
"It would be much better," the saint replied, "to put yourself
below every creature."

789

St. Willehad, first bishop of Bremen. His feast on the day after St. Willibrord is coincidental but appropriate as he is the last important English missionary of the eighth century and died just 100 years after Willibrord arrived in Holland. Willehad also came from Northumbria and began his preaching in the vicinity of Dokkum at the extreme north of Holland, where St. Boniface and companions were massacred ten years earlier.

In 780, when Charlemagne conquered the Saxons, he sent Willehad to evangelize them; but soon the nation revolted against the Franks and Willehad withdrew, going first to Rome and then retiring for two years to Echternach abbey in Luxembourg. When the Saxons were again subdued he recommenced his mission in earnest. Two years before his death he was appointed bishop of the Saxons, and established his cathedral at Bremen, where he was also buried.

1917

Bl. Vincent Grossi, a model parish priest in the Diocese of Cremona, Italy. Ordained at 23, he served four years as assistant and then became a pastor, the first ten years in one parish and the remaining thirty-four in another. To assist in the pastoral work, especially of catechizing and forming the young, he founded the Daughters of the Oratory according to the spirit of St. Philip Neri. Among the qualities that endeared Bl. Vincent to his people were his ever-friendly and joyous dispostion, attentive care of the sick, zeal for the confessional, devotion to the Blessed Sacrament, his living in great poverty with no self-seeking, and the mortifications they knew he practised.

NOVEMBER 9

DEDICATION OF THE LATERAN BASILICA, Rome's oldest and highest ranking church. Though the present structure dates mostly from the sixteenth and seventeenth century, the original Lateran basilica along with palace, baptistery, and grounds was part of Emperor Constantine's grant to the Roman church; and for nearly 1000 years the popes made the Lateran their main residence. It was only after the Lateran was ruined by fire and neglect during the Avignon papacy that the Vatican became and remained the pontiff's permanent home.

The original title was the Basilica of the Savior, but in time John the Baptist was added and St. John Lateran became its accepted name. Today's feast has such high rank because the Lateran is the pope's cathedral as bishop of Rome. In the early centuries when stational churches were observed no one basilica was considered the cathedral, since the pope regularly celebrated Mass at various churches. His coronation as well as all ordinations took place at St. Peter's on the Vatican.

As the stational system gradually declined and as the pope's external authority increased in the eighth century, the Basilica of the Savior adjoining his residence began to be regarded as his cathedral and a symbol of his universal authority.

461

St. Benin or **Benen,** son of an Irish chieftain, honored as St. Patrick's dearest disciple and his successor as leading bishop of the Irish.

NOVEMBER 10

461

ST. LEO I, "the Great," whose chief characteristic during the twenty-one year pontificate—one of the longest and most significant in the early church—was a serene and uncompromising insistence on the Roman primacy, "the care which by divine institution we especially owe to all the churches." The doctrine had long been traditional with the popes; but no previous pontiff had taught it so fully, spelled out its structures with such precision, or reduced it to practice so frequently and effectively.

In 1870, the I Vatican Council had only to restate his teaching on the primacy in more technical terms.

Writing to Bishop Anastasius of Thessalonica he sketches the interrelationship of episcopal care in these terms: the bishops of each province are gathered around their archbishop, a number of provinces are under the supervision of certain great bishoprics, and "through these the care of the universal church converges in the See of Peter." "One who finds himself set over others," the pontiff adds, "should not take it amiss that someone else is over him rather he should render the obedience he himself requires of others." Ninety-six of his sermons, mostly short and preached on feast days, remain.

His deep spirituality, confidence in the enduring mission of St. Peter, and trust in divine providence gave hope to his brother bishops, to clergy and people at a time of general catastrophe.

Secular history recalls especially his meeting with Attila, king of the Huns, at Mantua in 452 and how he persuaded him to spare Rome for an annual tribute and to retreat beyond the Danube. His 123 letters show him clear-sighted, exact and methodical, with a genius for government and prudent decision, a staunch defender of Church law and tradition, unyielding on matters of principle, and careful not to compromise papal authority.

The achievement which earned him the greatest acclaim from both East and West was the sure guidance that led to the Council of Chalcedon in 451. When his letter—the **Tome** which has since become the classic statement on the two natures and the unity of the person of Christ—was read, the assembly of more than 600 bishops gave it near unanimous approval with the words "Peter has spoken by Leo!"

In an encyclical on the fifteenth centenary of the death of St. Leo, Pope John XXIII expressed the hope that scholars of churches not in communion with Rome would again sing the praises of this great pope and overcome the difference of opinion in his regard. He pointed out how clear-sighted the saint

was in opposing Canon 28 of Chalcedon, which recognized
Constantinople as the first see in the East; for he saw the
canon as an affront to the more ancient oriental churches, a
lowering of the prestige of Rome, and a threat to Church unity.
Pope John thought that the title which best sums up St. Leo's
life and work is "Doctor of the Unity of the Church."

NOVEMBER 11

397

ST. MARTIN, bishop of Tours, whose reputation as a miracle-
worker made his shrine the most popular in medieval France.
His **Life** by Sulpicius Severus, a disciple, was an immediate
success and became something of a model for later miracle-
laden lives of saints. Everyone knew how, at Amiens, this
eighteen-year-old soldier slit his cloak down the middle to cover
a shivering beggar, and how that night he saw Christ in a
dream and heard him say, "Martin, still a catechumen, covered
me with this cloak."

He is one of the first non-martyrs honored as a saint. St.
Benedict, early in the sixth century recognizing his contribution
as a founder and popularizer of monasticism in the West, dedicated a chapel to him.

Born in Hungary of pagan parents, Martin was raised at
Pavia, Italy, and on receiving military discharge went to Poitiers
to be trained by St. Hilary, the outstanding bishop of France.
After a period as hermit he founded at Ligugé near Poitiers
the earliest known monastery in France. When he came to
Tours as bishop he soon established another monastery there —
later called Marmoutier — where he could live in community.
But he travelled much, evangelizing the country areas, pulling
down pagan shrines, erecting churches, and showing a bishop's
solicitude for everyone, especially the poor.

Though he used a rough bench and never the episcopal
chair, he had an exalted sense of a bishop's dignity. It was

only after many refusals that he accepted an invitation to dine with Emperor Maximus; and if he had to speak on anyone's behalf to the emperor, "he commanded rather than pleaded." He failed, however, in 385, to save Bishop Priscillian and his several companions from execution as sorcerers—the first instance of heretics being put to death. "It is enough and more than enough," St. Martin told Emperor Maximus, who was responsible for the trial, "that these men should be declared heretics by the judgment of bishops and dismissed from their sees. It would be a monstrosity and unheard-of impiety for an ecclesiastical case to be tried by a secular judge."

His speech was ever salted with spiritual instruction. Noticing a newly sheared sheep he said, "See, she has fulfilled the precept of the Gospel: she had two coats, and one of them she has given to him who had none. This therefore you ought also to do." But the saint's best remembered words were spoken on his deathbed when disciples begged him not to leave them. "Lord," he prayed, "if I am still necessary to your people, I do not refuse the toil. Your will be done."

NOVEMBER 12*

1623

ST. JOSAPHAT KUNCEVIC, a native of Vladimir in the Ukraine, Basilian abbot at Vilna, archbishop of Polotsk, martyr for union with the Holy See and organizer, with Archbishop Rutski of Kiev, of the Catholic branch of the Order of St. Basil the Great which occupies such an important place among the Ukrainian Catholics of North America today. Josaphat was in his teens in 1596, when the famous Union of Brest brought the archbishop of Kiev and five other bishops of the Ukraine and White Russia into the Catholic Church—with a resulting division among the loyal Byzantine rite Christians.

Josaphat apprenticed as a merchant, became a monk, and by

---

*O.SS.T. see March 24 for Bl. Diego of Cadiz.

his mid-thirties as leader of the union party was appointed bishop. But within six years he was felled by an ax and a bullet. One of the rumors spread against him was that he had gone Latin, though in reality he was insisting on equal status for the Slavonic rite, and thus incurred the disfavor of the Polish Latins.

He loved the Old Slavonic prayers, was a strenuous ascetic, and had the Jesus Prayer, "Lord Jesus Christ, Son of God, have mercy on me," as his favorite devotion. Disregarding personal danger he worked tirelessly for union. His prayer that he might shed his blood for this cause was answered on November 12, 1623, when he calmly went out to meet a mob that was shouting, "Kill the papist!" "I am ready," he said, "to die for the holy union, for the supremacy of St. Peter and of his successor the Supreme Pontiff."

826   [*O.S.B., O. Cist., O.C.S.O.*]

St. Theodore called **"the Studite"** after Studios, Constantinople's leading monastery, which he revived, populated with over 700 monks, and launched on its period of maximum influence in studies, culture, and Church affairs. As the foremost mentor of Byzantine monasticism since St. Basil the Great, Theodore is principally responsible for making it more cenobitic, and in that way more "Basilian"; but he also succeeded in retaining much of the spirituality of the more solitary laura system.

Studios came into its own during the second and final Iconoclast persecution when Abbot Theodore, true to the great prophetic tradition of that monastery, had his monks go in solemn procession through the streets around the monastery carrying the sacred images and chanting a hymn which begins, "We reverence thy holy image, O blessed one. . . ."

Theodore, already twice exiled for reproving the injustices of previous emperors, was now banished by Leo V the Armenian, imprisoned, and cruelly abused; but he continued to animate orthodox resistance by his correspondence.

His letters, of which 550 remain, also show him to be the great Byzantine doctor of the papal primacy, a Greek "version" of St. Leo I. His constantly recurring theme is that Peter continues to govern the universal church through his successors in Rome. He sees the pope as the divinely appointed head of the patriarchs and the unshakeable rock of faith without whose approval no ecumenical council is possible. Seventeen years after his death, the Iconoclast controversy now over, St. Theodore's body was brought back to Constantinople in great triumph as champion of the holy images.

NOVEMBER 13*

867

St. Nicholas I, pope, remembered for his personal holiness and firm stand against injustice of every kind, as well as his leadership on the large issues of Church government in both the East and West. He is, however, a controversial figure because his nine-year pontificate coincides exactly with Photius' first term as patriarch of Constantinople—a stormy period that contributed much to later misunderstandings and hurt feelings between Rome and Byzantium. Nicholas insisted on a re-examination of the change-over at Constantinople and finally reached the decision that Ignatius must still be considered the legitimate patriarch as he had been condemned without a just trial.

Nicholas forcefully reasserted traditional papal teaching on the primacy and made some further applications such as denying emperors any role in ecumenical councils. He called powerful Western archbishops to account for their actions and by the threat of excommunication constrained King Lothair II of Lorraine to take back his legitimate wife.

The Pope's immediate successors would inherit some of his

United States see Dec. 22 for St. Frances Cabrini.

spirit and authority, but with the political chaos of the tenth century it would be nearly 200 years before the vigorous popes of the Gregorian reform would again shoulder the responsibilities of the Apostolic See in the tradition of the three holy pontiffs who are called "great": Leo I, Gregory I, and Nicholas I.

1004

St. **Abbo,** abbot of Fleury in France, outstanding teacher and author, champion of monastic exemption, and energetic promoter of Cluniac observance. He was killed at the abbey of La Réole in Gascony where he had gone to establish reform.

1568   [*S.J., S.M.M.*]

St. **Stanislaus Kotska,** who died at seventeen after nine months as a Jesuit novice and is now a patron of Poland. Second son of a Polish senator, he asked for admission to the Society of Jesus after several years at their school in Vienna. The provincial, however, was afraid of parental opposition; and so Stanislaus stole off to Germany, where St. Peter Canisius tried him at menial tasks for three weeks and then sent him on to the general in Rome. This was St. Francis Borgia. He accepted the novice despite the father's threat that he would have the Society expelled from Poland. Paul, an older brother, was sent to Rome to bring Stanislaus home at any cost—but found him dead.

Two weeks before the Assumption the saint said he hoped to be in heaven for the feast. He fell ill on the tenth and died on August the fifteenth, shortly after telling the priest he had seen the Blessed Mother.

NOVEMBER 14

1391   [*Franciscans*]

St. **Nicholas Tavelic** and **companions,** four European Franciscans martyred at Jerusalem after deliberately provoking the Moslem authorities. Their aggressive approach was a reason why their canonization was delayed until 1970—nearly 600 years— but their mode of action finds support in St. Francis, who wrote in his First Rule: the brothers who go on a mission among the infidels "may conduct themselves in two different ways. One of them is not to start strife and contention, but 'because of the Lord be obedient to every human institution' (I Pet 2:13) and thus show themselves to be Christians. The other manner is this: when they see it is God's will, to announce the word of God, to have them believe . . . be baptized and become Christians. . . ."

St. Nicholas, a native of Sibenik in Croatia, worked in Bosnia and Dalmatia before his superiors sent him to Jerusalem. And after he was there for eight years, during which the Moslem law left him very little scope for missionary zeal, he decided, along with three companions, to follow Christ's command that the Gospel be preached to every creature. They went to the Cadi and said, "We have come here, not sent by any man but by God, who has inspired us to come and teach you the truth and the way of salvation." As they would neither desist nor retract they were executed three days later.

1811   [*S.J.*]

St. Joseph Pignatelli. Except for Empress Catherine the Great —who kept the Jesuit order alive in Russia—he was the chief mainstay of the Society during its fifty years of expulsion and suppression. A Spanish grandee, he joined the Society of Jesus at fifteen, contracted tuberculosis by the time of ordination and was expelled from Spain along with 5,000 other Jesuits in 1767. Though then only twenty-nine he was given the authority of provincial over the Aragon deportees and settled them in Corsica and then at Ferrara.

With papal suppression of the order in 1773—it numbered 23,000—he retired to Bologna, prayed, studied, collected books of Jesuit history, and helped confreres who were in distress. In the Duchy of Parma, a vice-province affiliated with the Russian branch eventually became possible; and at the age of fifty-nine he again made solemn profession. He became novicemaster though candidates had to go to Russia for profession, and in time was named provincial for Italy. St. Joseph Pignatelli died in 1811, aged seventy-three, just three years before Pope Pius VII restored the Society for the whole Church.

NOVEMBER 15

1280

ST. ALBERT THE GREAT, Dominican, doctor of the Church, who today is best remembered as the teacher of St. Thomas but to contemporaries was known as "the Great"—a title none of the other schoolmen ever had. He gained this unparalleled reputation by supplying the Latin West with an organic exposé of all that was considered best in science and philosophy and thus took the lead role in "processing" the writings of Aristotle, which the Arabs already possessed and to which Averroes had given certain interpretations that made them appear dangerous to Christian faith.

In great part Albert paraphrased the individual works of Aristotle, correcting and augmenting them from other sources as well as from his own abundant observations and reflections. In this way he helped close the science gap between the Latins and the Arab world and provided theologians with a much better philosophic tool than they previously possessed.

But, as his contemporary and severe critic Roger Bacon pointed out, Albert did not give sufficient place to experimentation and exact mathematical observation as the means for making progress in science. And, since in the thirteenth century science and philosophy were not sufficiently separated, scholastic thought became too closely wedded to a physics that was already, to some extent, outmoded.

The eldest son of a powerful Swabian lord, Albert became a Dominican, probably at the age of sixteen, and spent most of the next fifty-seven years studying, teaching, and writing—except for short interludes, such as three years serving as provincial in Germany and two years as bishop straightening out the affairs of the Regensburg diocese. He put in considerable time at the University of Paris, but is especially identified with Cologne.

The most prolific mediaeval writer—his edited works run to thirty-eight quarto volumes—he allotted almost equal space to Scripture commentaries, to theology, and to the sciences. He also wrote more on the Blessed Virgin than anyone else of his time. He took part in the II Council of Lyons and made his last intervention as a theologian by traveling from Cologne to Paris to defend the teaching of St. Thomas, who had died three years before. He is patron of scientists.

1539

Bl. Richard Whiting, Benedictine abbot of Glastonbury, martyred in his eightieth year along with two of his monks, **Bl. John Thorne** and **Bl. Roger James;** and also **Bl. Hugh Faringdon,** abbot of Reading, who was executed with two companions outside his abbey gate.

NOVEMBER 16

1093

ST. MARGARET, queen and patroness of Scotland. A daughter of the highest English and continental royalty, she was religiously brought up in Hungary at the court where the memory of St. Stephen I was still fresh. She came to England in her early teens, to the court of another saint, Edward the Confessor.

After the Battle of Hastings her party found asylum in Scotland, where her beauty and gentle, strong personality soon captivated the heart of Malcolm III. As queen she gradually softened his ferocity and so influenced national policy that she and her son St. David I are in great part responsible for ushering in two centuries of progress in religion and culture. She set the nation an example in personal care of the sick and in bringing up a family. Among her eight children are three kings of Scotland and Good Queen Maud of England.

Typical of her practical methods is the semi-religious embroidery club she organized among ladies of the court to provide vestments and church furnishings; and Dumfermline Abbey, her foundation and place of burial, is an example of her benefactions.

1302

ST. GERTRUDE THE GREAT, mystic, a nun at Helfta, Saxony, under the rule of St. Benedict. She was entrusted to the sisters at five and at twenty-five had a vision of Christ, which made her realize for the first time in a meaningful way that Christ was a Person and that he took pleasure in dwelling within her "as a friend in living with a friend or a bridegroom with his bride" (**Herald II,** 23). The experience was deepened before the feast of the Annunciation and again before Ascension, so that Christ's familiar companionship during the remaining twenty years of her life was a vivid fulfillment of his promise: "If anyone loves me he will keep my word, and my Father will love him, and we shall come to him and make our home with him" (Jn 14:23).

"I want your writings," Christ told her, "to be indisputable evidence of my goodness" (**Herald II,** 10). The presence of her feast in the calendar gives meaning to these words, for it was through her writings that Gertrude became known. Saints have been inspired by her **Herald of Divine Love**—also called **Revelations,** Book Two is written by herself—and her **Spiritual Exercises,** while scholars marvel at the wealth and rigor of the incarnational and trinitarian theology contained in her uninhibited outpourings of love and praise.

1628 [*S.J.*]

Bl. Roque González and two young priests from Spain, Jesuits, known as **the Paraguay Martyrs.** Father González, a seasoned missionary born in Paraguay, had an important part in spreading the famous "reduction" system of Paraguay. Deep in the jungle he established six of these Christian Indian settlements. He was felled by a tomahawk at his last colony in what is now Rio Grande do Sul, Brazil.

1136

St. Leopold, 'Leopold the Good,' patron of Austria which he ruled for forty years and where his feast is a national holiday. He was educated under St. Altman of Passau, was nephew of Emperor Henry IV, refused the imperial crown and had eighteen children, among whom are Bishop Otto of Freising, the historian, and Archbishop Conrad II of Salzburg. St. Leopold fostered monastic institutions and is buried at Klosterneuburg which he established for the Canons Regular of St. Augustine.

NOVEMBER 17*

1231

ST. ELIZABETH OF HUNGARY, an example of devotion to her husband and to the poor, she died at the age of twenty-four with such a reputation of piety and miracles, of services to the sick—she set up three hospitals—and of wrongs patiently borne, that she was canonized within four years.

As daughter of King Andrew II she is called Elizabeth of Hungary; but it would be better to identify her with Thuringia, for at the age of one she was engaged to the future Louis IV of Thuringia—a boy a few years older than herself—and at four she was sent to that country to be raised in the same

---

*O.S.B., O. Çist. see Nov. 16 for St. Margaret of Scotland.

O.C.S.O. see Nov. 16 for St. Gertrude of Helfta.

R.S.C.J. see Nov. 18 for Bl. Philippine Duchesne.

castle with him. Their marriage, which took place when he came of age and she was thirteen or fourteen, proved most happy despite the fact that a jealous mother-in-law, finding Elizabeth over-pious, tried to prevent the wedding.

Louis, however, died of malaria as he was setting out on a crusade. Elizabeth, who was then only twenty, was apparently turned out with her three children by a usurping brother-in-law; and so she experienced something of the poverty she had done so much to relieve. When reinstated she provided for her children — Bl. Gertrude, abbess of Altenburg, is one of her two daughters — freed herself of her possessions, submitted totally to a severe spiritual director, donned the habit of a Franciscan teritary, reputedly the first lady in Germany to do so, and gave herself to the care of the sick-poor and to prayer. She is patroness of the Franciscan third order and of charitable organizations of women.

680

St. Hilda, abbess of Hartlepool and then of the double monastery she founded at Whitby, Yorkshire, where she trained many scholars including five future bishops, Saints Wilfrid and John of Beverley among them, and encouraged Caedmon — the first English poet — to cultivate his gift. In 664 the most important synod of the Anglo-Saxon period was held in her monastery to settle the differences between the Celtic and Roman observances. She is one of the greatest English women of all time.

A grandniece of King Edwin of Northumbria, she was baptized at thirteen; and at thirty-three on the advice of St. Aidan undertook monastic life in her home province instead of following her sister to Chelles in France. She had the talent both to receive and give instruction. St. Bede writes, "Bishop Aidan and the religious people who knew her, because of the great wisdom and love to serve God that were in her often visited her, cherishing her deeply and instructing her with much care.... She was of such wisdom that . . . at times even kings and princes sought and found counsel in her. . . . All that knew her were wont to call her 'Mother' for her notable grace and godliness.'' She died at sixty-six after a lingering illness of six years, instructing by word and example to the very last.

NOVEMBER 18

DEDICATION OF THE BASILICA OF ST. PETER AND OF THE BASILICA OF ST. PAUL in Rome, a joint feast that helps give the Latin Church a sense of continuity with her origins as she honors the temples which enshrine the remains of her glorious apostle founders.

1852

Bl. Philippine Duchesne, who left France at forty-nine and founded, mostly in the vicinity of St. Louis and New Orleans, the first American houses of the Religious of the Sacred Heart. Because of her long hours before the Blessed Sacrament, she is best characterized by the name given her by the Indians, "The Woman-Who-Always-Prays."

Already at the age of twelve this second of seven daughters in a wealthy and politically-important Grenoble family showed many of her outstanding, life-long traits: zeal for the missions, devotion to the Sacred Heart and Blessed Sacrament—learned as a boarding pupil in the local Visitation convent founded by St. Francis de Sales and St. Jane de Chantal—enthusiasm for religious life, an unswerving conviction concerning her own vocation, a penchant for ascetic ways with a will of steel to carry them through, and a readiness to be guided provided it was toward sanctity.

At eighteen, as the family was thinking about her marriage, she stole off without telling either parent and joined the Grenoble Visitation nuns; but the French Revolution disbanded the convent before she took vows. Under Napoleon, for three heart-breaking years she was the moving spirit in an effort to re-establish community life. "Gossip had it," she later wrote, "that I had driven the religious away, that I would not yield in anything, that no one could bear to live with me." The situation was saved when some interested priests, mostly future Jesuits, arranged to have St. Madeleine Sophie Barat, foundress of the Religious of the Sacred Heart, incorporate the Grenoble community as the second house of her new congregation.

Madeleine Sophie and Philippine differed in almost everything except what had to do with saintliness. Mother Barat at twenty-five, and ten years younger than Philippine, became her novice mistress and then for nearly fifty years was her superior general, confidante, and directress. As their correspondence —one of the priceless treasures of hagiography—shows, they understood, loved, and trusted one another from first to last. Mother Duchesne had enough impetuosity, sensitivity, impatience, failures, and in old age, difficulties in accepting changes she didn't like—such as the removal of the picture of her favorite Saint, John Francis Regis—to make it easy for different types to identify with her and be inspired by her heroism and religious ideals.

"Our Lord, in His goodness," Mother Barat once wrote to her, "wants you to become a great saint. . . . I know you cannot correct yourself suddenly. How could you become meek, stripped of all attachment to your own judgment, etc., when the contrary faults have been rooted in your character for so long?" And again she wrote, "Because we both want to love and to suffer, Jesus brought us together."

NOVEMBER 19

1253   [*Franciscan II O.*]
St. Agnes of Assisi, abbess, whose religious vocation was St. Clare's first conquest after her "conversion," for among the

prayers Clare offered at the very beginning of her new way of life was the request that as she and her fifteen-year-old sister had been of one heart and soul in the world, so now they might again be one in the service of God.

Turning aside from a proposed marriage, Agnes stole away from home just sixteen days after Clare's departure and joined her at the convent of San Angelo di Panzo, three-and-a-half miles from Assisi. Also in her case the family tried to bring her home by violence, but God answered Clare's prayer once again. About six years later St. Francis sent Agnes to be abbess at Monticelli in Florence. She is credited with several other foundations.

The few facts of her life attest heroism in her love of God, deep affection for Clare and fidelity to the ideals of St. Francis —qualities which help explain her reputation for inculcating the true spirit of the Order. She returned to Assisi to be at St. Clare's deathbed and heard from her these parting words: "It is God's wish, dearest sister, that I go. But cry no more, for you will come to the Lord soon after me and before you die the Lord will grant you great consolation." St. Agnes died at Assisi before the year was out.

1298   *[O.S.B., O. Cist., O.C.S.O.]*
St. Mechtilde of Hackeborn, mystic, spiritual mother of St. Gertrude the Great. She is not to be confused with St. Mechtilde of Magdeburg, also a mystic, who lived in the same convent. She was entrusted to the nuns at Rodarsdorf at seven. The convent was soon moved to Helfta, a property belonging to the Hackeborn family.

Mechtilde became first chantress and was only twenty but already in charge of the abbey school, when the future St. Gertrude, a child of five, was put under instruction. The girl made rapid progress in studies and, in time, assisted Mechtilde as second chantress; but it is especially their intimate partnership as mystics of identical inspiration that is unique. Gertrude compiled the **Book of Special Grace,** an account of the visions and favors of St. Mechtilde.

While going about their daily round of work and prayer and without falling into ecstasies, these two contemplatives lived in familiar conversation with God and the saints, particularly with the Incarnate Word. They received intimate disclosures regarding the Sacred Heart four centuries before St. Margaret Mary. The Helfta writings provide the classic example of a life of prayer harmonized with the daily liturgy and the feasts of the Church year.

NOVEMBER 20

870

St. Edmund the Martyr, king of East Anglia, slain in battle at twenty-nine by Danish invaders and given the title of martyr in the belief that he was offered peace but in terms that would have compromised his faith and the welfare of his people.

1922

Bl. Fortunata Viti, whose seventy-one years in a Benedictine convent at Veroli, Italy, read like a collection of mediaeval **fioretti:** a providential last minute change of convents, mind-reading and helping others in their secret temptations, physical experience of some incidents in the Passion, birds obeying her, molestations by the devil, and a flood of favors after her death.

The third child, she became, in her middle teens, the home-maker for six younger brothers and sisters. When all were provided for, she entered the local convent, being then twenty-four.

Her father was a once-well-to-do merchant whose gambling and carousing brought his wife to an early grave and his family to destitution. He died six years after his daughter's entry into the convent. In one of her prayer-books a paper was found on which she had written, "Our beloved father Luigi died on March 22, 1857."

Another of her early convent notes reads, "As I have the happy chance of becoming a saint I wish to profit by it; because if I fail now I fail forever. . . . O God, give me the strength to fulfil my desires." Her formula would be prayer—with particular attraction to the Passion—and humble service. She made a promise, for love of Mary, never to refuse anyone a service; and her superior could testify that "she seemed to live exclusively for the purpose of serving the community."

To another lay sister who was sad because she was not a choir nun, Sister Fortunata confided that she had the chance to be a choir nun, and while she valued the vocation to sing the divine office, "yet the state of a lay sister is a still greater gift from God, for we have the advantage of remaining in the background with more opportunities to practice humility for the love of God."

Her life-long assignment—she lived to nearly ninety-six and worked till a few days before her death—was the care of the clothing and linens of the community, with mending—in which she kept the worst articles for herself—and spinning taking up most of her time. Her characteristic response to anything marvelous was, "O the power and the love of God!"—an aspiration which one day turned on a newly installed electric light.

NOVEMBER 21

PRESENTATION OF THE BLESSED VIRGIN MARY. This feast, which has become symbolic of self-offering and religious consecration, commemorates Mary's dedication to God and has meaning independently of the apocryphal account of her being confided to the temple at the age of three.

496
St. Gelasius I, of African origin, the leading fifth century pope after St. Leo I. His statements on the primacy and on various

points of Church government became well known because they had a prominent place in the collection of canon law edited by the pope's contemporary, Denis the Short.

Gelasius is especially remembered for his letter to Emperor Anastasius I. There are, he told him, two powers "by which the world is mainly ruled: the sacred authority of bishops and the royal power." In matters religious the emperor should learn from the bishops and instead of supporting the schismatic tendencies of the patriarch of Constantinople in the monophysite dispute—now known as the Acacian schism—the emperor should use his influence to bring his people back into unity on terms dictated by the episcopate under the leadership of the successor of St. Peter.

In a Roman synod under St. Gelasius there is the first record of the term "vicar of Christ" applied to the pope. He decreed that the revenues from Church property should be apportioned four ways: to the bishop, the clergy, the poor, and to the maintenance of buildings. He insisted that Holy Communion be distributed under both species and composed a number of Mass texts, which were later included in the Verona Sacramentary. The so-called Gelasian Sacramentary is misnamed, for it was compiled at least a century after the saint's death.

NOVEMBER 22

ST. CECILIA, virgin and martyr of unknown date, mentioned in the Roman canon. Her legendary **Acts** made her very popular throughout the centuries, but nothing certain has been preserved about her life or martyrdom.

ca. 270

St. Gregory the Wonderworker, apostle of Cappadocia and first bishop of Neocaesarea in Pontus. He became a Christian while studying under Origen in Palestine and returned to his native Neocaesarea full of enthusiasm for the faith. He soon became its bishop. It is said that there were seventeen Christians there when he began his ministry and only seventeen pagans in this important town when he died. According to St. Gregory of Nyssa, he was favored with a vision of Our Lady.

594

St. Gregory of Tours, a leading bishop of sixth century France, collector of religious legends, and author of the celebrated **History of the Franks.** On him in large measure depends our insight into the social history, language, and religion of France in that epoch. He died on Nov. 7th.

1597

B. Joseph (José) de Anchieta, Jesuit, Apostle of Brazil, and linguist. Born in the Canary Islands, he became a Jesuit in Coimbra, Portugal, at 17. Two years later, 1553, he arrived in Brazil in time to be one of the founders of São Paulo (1544), where he taught humanities in the college the Jesuits opened. He would be principally a man of action, but during these early years he applied his talent for languages to mastering Tupi, the language spoken along the coast, and he composed a grammar as well as songs, plays, and catechism in Tupi and Portuguese. Ordained at 32, he was soon superior over a region, and from the age of 42 to 52 he was provincial for all of Brazil. Beritiba, where he died at 63, was renamed Anchieta in his honor. The popular account which credits him with two million baptisms, the marvelous stories of religious heroism, and the veneration the Brazilians have always had for him, all attest in their own way to the legitimacy of the enduring and unchallenged title of "Apostle of Brazil," which the Bishop of Bahia gave to Bl. Joseph de Anchieta in the funeral eulogy. He died June 9, 1597.

NOVEMBER 23

ST. CLEMENT I, bishop of Rome, usually considered the third successor of St. Peter. He is remembered for a long letter written about the year 95 in the name of the church of Rome, reprimanding the church of Corinth for its quarrels and jealousies.

The occasion of this earliest of Christian documents outside the New Testament was a schismatic group at Corinth who ousted the legitimate authorities and set up their own leaders. "Our Apostles," the letter says, "were given to understand by our Lord Jesus Christ that the office of bishop would give rise to intrigues. For this reason, equipped as they were with perfect foreknowledge, they appointed the men (bishops and deacons) mentioned above, and afterwards laid down a rule once for all to this effect: when these men died, other approved men shall succeed to their sacred Ministry" (44).

The first signs of the primacy of the Apostolic See are found in this letter. Its authoritative tone is impressive: "Should any disobey what has been said by Him (Jesus Christ) through us, let them understand that they will entangle themselves in transgression and no small danger; but for our part we shall be innocent of this sin" (59). The letter was held in great honor in the early Church and in some places was considered as inspired Scripture.

615

ST. COLUMBAN, author of a strict monastic rule and of a penitential, the greatest Irish missionary on the continent. Along his paths through France, Switzerland, and northern Italy there sprang up a chain of dynamic institutions that would give the main impetus to seventh century Christianity in those parts.

After thirty years as a monk at Bangor under St. Comgall, he left Ireland with twelve companions and reached France about 590. He kept his own date of Easter and other Celtic usages; but what made him particularly popular and unpopular —he was put on a ship for deportation after twenty years in France—was his scathing denunciation of court immorality and the compromising silence of local bishops.

At the end of his life, writing to the pope for support, he said: "We Irish, living at the furthest extremity of the world, are the disciples of St. Peter and St. Paul, and of the other apostles who have written under the dictation of the Holy Spirit. . . . In Ireland there have never been either heretics . . . or schismatics. The native liberty of my race gives me boldness. With us it is not the person but the right which counts. We are bound to the chair of St. Peter; for however great and glorious Rome may be, it is this chair which makes her great and glorious in our eyes."

His warm spirit comes through in the parting letter to his monks at Luxeuil: "My soul is torn asunder. I wanted to serve everybody, I trusted everybody, and it has made me almost mad. . . . While I write, they come to tell me that the ship is ready, the ship which is to carry me back against my will to my country. . . . The end of my parchment obliges me to finish my letter. Love is not orderly: it is this which has made it confused."

A storm would drive the ship back to France and he died at the great abbey he founded at Bobbio in Lombardy. One entry in his rule reads: "No matter how wise a man is, if he talks much he will say many things that were better left unsaid."

NOVEMBER 24*

851

Sts. Flora and Mary, virgin martyrs at Cordoba. Flora had a Moslem father but was raised a Christian by her mother; Mary was a nun and had a younger brother already a martyr. The two young women spontaneously came forward in quest of martyrdom and publicly professed their faith. The archbishop of Seville, however, urged them to compromise for the sake of peace. Their resolve began to weaken at the prospect of slavery in a harem and it was to bolster their courage that the priest St. Eulogius, also a prisoner, wrote his **Documentum Martyriale.** "Keep before your eyes the example of Christ's passion," he

---

*O.S.B., O.Cist., O.C.S.O. see Nov 23 for St. Columban.

wrote, "think of it continually, and all the pain of this life will become a pleasure. It may be hard and bitter, but it must be short." "They threaten to sell you into a shameful slavery, but do not be afraid: no harm can come to your souls whatever infamy they inflict on your bodies. Cowardly Christians will tell you that churches are empty and without the Sacrifice because of your obstinacy, and that if you will only yield for a time all will be well. . . . You cannot now draw back and renounce the faith that you have confessed." They remained firm and were beheaded at three o'clock in the afternoon of November 24th. On receiving the news the other prisoners gathered and sang the office of virgin martyrs, "concluding," Eulogius writes, "with the sacrifice of the Mass to the honor and glory of the new saints."

NOVEMBER 25

1555   [O.S.A., O.A.R.]

St. Thomas of Villanova, a miller's son who became archbishop of Valencia and earned the title "Father of the Poor."

He joined the Augustinian Friars at twenty-eight after teaching philosophy at Alcalá, was a priest at thirty, provincial a few years later, and—by constraint—became archbishop in his middle fifties. He arrived at Valencia on foot dressed in his monastic habit and accompanied by one servant. Seeing his poverty the cathedral chapter gave him a large sum for house furnishings, but he passed it on to outfit a hospital instead. When the canons remonstrated about his clothes, he replied, "I do not see how my religious habit interferes with my dignity as archbishop." But he did exchange his twenty-five year old cloth hat for a silk one; and this he would sometimes display saying, "Look at my episcopal dignity!"

He spent much time before the Blessed Sacrament, but wished to be called as soon as anyone wanted to see him. Several hundred poor were cared for at his door daily, usually receiving a meal, a cup of wine, and some money. On being reminded that there were loafers in the crowd he answered that this was the concern of the civil authorities. "My duty is to assist and relieve those who come to my door."

"If you desire that God should hear your prayers," he told the rich, "then hear the voice of the poor. . . . Anticipate especially the necessities of those who are ashamed to beg; to force these to ask an alms is to make them buy it."

Of a theologian who objected to his delay in using legal penalties against concubinage he said, "He is without doubt a good man, but one of those fervent ones mentioned by St. Paul as having zeal without knowledge. . . . Let him inquire whether St. Augustine and St. John Chrysostom used anathemas and excommunication to stop the drunkenness and blasphemy which were so common among the people under their care. No; for they were too wise and prudent. They did not think it right to exchange a little good for a great evil by inconsiderately using their authority and causing aversion in those whose good will they wanted to gain in order to influence them for good."

When struck down with a heart condition he gave his money to the poor and all his goods to the college rector, keeping only a bed which he gave to the jailer for prisoners and then borrowed it back until he would need it no longer. He died at sixty-six.

NOVEMBER 26

1267 [*O.S.B.*]

St. Silvester Guzzolini, founder at Monte Fano in central Italy of a penitential and preaching branch of the Benedictine order now known as Silvestrines. A zealous canon at Osimo, he finally at fifty gave in to his longing for solitude. Disciples soon came and when he died at ninety there were eleven monasteries following his observance. He insisted particularly on strict poverty.

1621 [*S.J.*]

St. John Berchmans, Flemish Jesuit scholastic who once said, "If I do not become a saint when I am young, I shall never become one." He died of a contagious disease in Rome at the age of twenty-one. His father, a shoe-maker at Diest, Belgium, became a priest after his wife's death.

In some notes John made for himself he wrote, "Take care to avoid doing the kind of things that displease you in others." Included are such entries as, "Frequent contradictions displease me. Being too dainty displeases me. . . . An ironical way of speaking displeases me." And on the positive side he tells himself, "Notice what pleases you in others and imitate them in that. . . . In Father Provincial, his love of literature. In Father Rector and the spiritual director, their being always the same." His list includes twenty-one other priests and fellow students, and in each he found one or two outstanding qualities such as ". . . delight in the progress of his scholars in their studies . . . patience in sickness . . . love of his room . . . joyousness, even with all his spirituality . . . cleanliness . . . giving everything its own allotted time." He concludes the catalogue with a number of things he likes. Among them are: "I like exterior gladness with great regularity. . . . I like giving the companion who shares your room leave to do what he pleases without minding you. . . . I like doing heartily and for all you are worth whatever you do."

1751 [*Franciscans, C.P., O.M.I.*]

St. Leonard of Port Maurice on the Italian Riviera, Franciscan, patron of those who give popular missions—a work he carried on throughout Italy for more than forty years. To gain the attention of the hard-hearted he would sometimes use the discipline on himself in public; but the devotion he principally fostered was the Way of the Cross, and it is to him that much of its later popularity is due. Wherever he went he spread devotion to the Blessed Sacrament, to the Sacred Heart, and to the Immaculate Conception.

NOVEMBER 27

399

St. Siricius, pope for fifteen years, remembered especially for his important part in promoting the authority of the Apostolic See and in establishing the Western discipline of clerical celibacy. His reply to Himerius of Terragona is the first papal letter—it will technically be called a "decretal"—included in the early collections of canon law.

"We bear within us the burden of all who are weighed down," he wrote to the Spanish bishops as he sent them answers on fifteen points of Church discipline, "but it is rather the Blessed Apostle Peter who bears these burdens in us; since, as we trust, he protects us in all the matters of his administration and guides us as his heirs." Nearly a century earlier, Spain in the Council of Elvira had passed a law demanding total continence of deacons, priests, and bishops; but now the pope's authority was added and strict penalties imposed. During the saint's pontificate regional councils were held in Spain, Africa, Italy, and France endorsing the program: so that celibacy may well be the first instance of general legislation based on Roman decretals and supported by local synods.

Another of the pope's encyclicals condemns Jovinian who taught the equality of marriage and Gospel virginity. Siricius also censured Bishop Bonosus of Sardica for denying the perpetual virginity of Mary. He denounced the Spanish bishops who counseled the death penalty for the heretic Priscillian and excommunicated Felix of Trier, whom they ordained bishop.

In many areas he acted in concert with St. Ambrose, the dominant Western churchman of the period. A letter from the

Council of Milan in 390, signed by nine bishops and probably written by St. Ambrose, commends Pope Siricius: "You are truly the good shepherd, keeping a loving watch over the sheep-fold of Jesus Christ and defending it with energy. . . . You deserve to have the sheep of the Savior hear your voice and follow you." Little is personally known about St. Siricius. In 390 he consecrated the basilica of St. Paul-outside-the-walls and his name can still be seen on one of the pillars preserved from the fire that destroyed the church in 1823.

NOVEMBER 28

1476   [*Franciscans*]
St. James Gangala, also called St. James of the March, after the March of Ancona, his native territory. He and St. John Capistran were students under St. Bernardine of Siena and the three of them are remembered in Franciscan history as particularly ardent promoters of the Observant branch of the order.

He preached in Italy, Yugoslavia, and central Europe, had a part in the Councils of Basel and Florence, carried out many papal missions, and succeeded St. John Capistran as nuncio to Hungary. He was once offered the archbishopric of Milan but preferred to continue his mission work as a simple friar. Bl. Bernardine of Fossa and Bl. Bernardine of Feltre were attracted to the order by his preaching. He died at eighty-two.

1508   [*O.S.A., O.A.R.*]
Bl. Gratia of Cattaro in Yugoslavia. He was a sailor who, at the age of thirty, attended church in Venice and was so moved by the sermon preached by an Augustinian that he spent his remaining forty years as a brother in that order.

1742
Bl. Francis Anthony Fasani, who took vows as a Conventual

Franciscan at fifteen and after lengthy studies returned to his native Lucera in southern Italy, where he remained the rest of his life. He taught theology at the Franciscan college, was rector and then provincial. He was particularly devoted to prisoners and started a custom of collecting Christmas gifts for the poor who were continually after him with requests of every kind.

In the beatification address Pope Pius XII gave a vivid picture of the saintly friar in his sixty-second year: "The last days of his holy life, how poetic they were! A round of visits to families to whom he wished to bid a last farewell, his supreme effort to get up at night, trembling with fever, to answer the appeal of one of his penitents who was seriously ill, a morning of confessions, a last day of faithful observance of community life, and finally, when obedience kept him in bed, his serene preparation to render an account to God for his life and work." Not long before, still apparently in good health, he had foretold the time of his death. It came on the first day of the solemn public novena he annually kept at Lucera in preparation for the feast of the Immaculate Conception.

NOVEMBER 29

1638 [*O. Carm., O.C.D.*]
Bl. Dionysius of the Nativity, a priest, and **Bl. Redemptus of the Cross,** a brother, Discalced Carmelites martyred at Sumatra. Bl. Dionysius was thirty-seven, just ordained and only four years a Carmelite. He had previously been a professional navigator and cartographer. Some of his maps are now preserved in the British Museum.

Born in Normandy, Pierre Berthelot by name, he went to sea and was captured by Dutch pirates on his first trip to the Indies. After gaining freedom from his prison on Java he went to Malacca, did some trading on his own and assumed com-

mand of a Portuguese ship. It was at Goa that he came into
contact with the Carmelites.

He was appointed chaplain for a Portuguese expedition at
Sumatra; and Bl. Redemptus, who had served as a soldier in
India before becoming a brother, was assigned as his assistant.
They were taken prisoners almost immediately on their arrival
and put to death when they refused to embrace Islam.

1891

Bl. Mary Ann Sala. When Pope John Paul II beatified her in 1980
he placed before the Church a rather typical holy and capable teaching
nun. Her life was not particularly marked by the extraordinary, though
finding her body incorrupt after 30 years caused a stir. She put into
practise, the Holy Father remarked, the words of Our Lord, that one
"who is faithful in what is very little, is faithful also in much." (Lk 16:10)

One of ten children, she was always devout and helpful. Her religious
vocation made itself strongly felt at the boarding college of the Sisters
of St. Mercellina near Milan, where she obtained a teacher's certificate.
She was a novice at 20 and made profession three years later along
with 24 others, when the young congregation was finally permitted to
admit sisters to vows.

An extremely competent teacher, she spent most of forty years in
that apostolate at Cernusco sul Naviglio, Milan, and Genoa. She was
always available and interested in her pupils, one of whom was Guiditta
Alghisi, mother of Pope Paul VI. "I'll be right with you," was her
characteristic response. The girls sensed that she lived in the presence
of God, not only when she knelt in chapel or before the crucifix at
night in the dormitory, but also in the classroom.

She spent her final thirteen years in Milan where, among other
things, she served as assistant superior general, novice mistress and
librarian. Bl. Mary Ann Sala died November 24, 1891, at the age of 62,
bearing heroically all the pain and distress of cancer of the throat.

NOVEMBER 30

ST. ANDREW, apostle. He is generally mentioned with Peter, James, and John, the three closest to our Lord. The Greek Church underlines his special place by calling him the "Proto-clete," the "First-called," combining in this way the gospel of St. John which shows Andrew as a disciple of John the Baptist discovering the Messiah and the next day bringing Peter (Jn 1:40-42), and the synoptic account which shows Peter and Andrew as the first to receive the invitation to follow Christ (Mt 4:18-20).

St. Andrew acted as mediator between Jesus and the Greeks who wanted to see him (Jn 12:22). Andrew also called attention to the boy who had the five barley loaves and two fish with which the 5,000 were fed (Jn 6:8-9).

Eusebius reports a tradition that St. Andrew evangelized part of Russia north of the Black Sea. He is patron of Russia and of Scotland.

1283

Bl. John of Vercelli, master general of the Dominicans during nineteen of the most brilliant and dynamic years of the young order. He was attracted to the friars as a secular priest who had taught law at the University of Paris and at Vercelli.

The pope had him draw up a **schema** for the II Council of Lyons and gave him a special commission to propagate devotion to the Holy Name of Jesus in reparation for the blasphemies of the Albigensians. Bl. John required the Dominicans to establish confraternities and to have an altar of the Holy Name in each of their churches. He declined the patriarchate of Jerusalem. Though he asked to be relieved of office he was persuaded to continue until his death.

1577

St. Cuthbert Mayne, the first martyr of the English College,

Douai. At Oxford, as a minister of the Church of England, he came under the influence of Dr. Gregory Martin and Edmund Campion. He served in Cornwall for a year, was arrested under Elizabeth I and executed for treason. When Campion heard the news he wrote to Gregory Martin: "How that novice outdistanced me! May he be favorable to his old friend and tutor! I shall now boast of these titles more than ever."

1835

Bl. Joseph Marchand, a Paris Foreign Missioner martyred in Vietnam after six years on the missions. He refused to trample on the cross and during preliminary tortures, as his flesh was being torn with hooks, he was taunted about the sacraments: Why do Christians tear out the eyes of the dying? Why do people who are going to marry come before a priest at the altar? What is this magic bread they eat after going to confession? He died at thirty-two.

DECEMBER 1

1581 [*S.J.*]
St. Edmund Campion, England's first and most famous Jesuit martyr. Son of a London bookseller, he was a junior fellow of Oxford at seventeen and soon the most popular speaker and most influential leader in the university. He took the Oath of Supremacy and deacon's orders, but a study of the Fathers brought him back to the Catholic faith.

He studied theology and taught rhetoric at Douai and became a Jesuit at Rome about the age of thirty-three. Five years later he was ordained in Prague and in less than two years, disguised as a jewel merchant, arrived in England and along with Father Robert Persons launched the historic Jesuit mission. He would be captured a year later; but by then his sanctity, gaiety, personal charm, eloquence, and aggressive pen had given new heart and courage to the Catholics of the land.

With characteristic verve he composed a letter to the Privy Council stating his purpose in coming to England. He left it in an unsealed envelope to be produced in case he was taken. But the nine-point document was filled with the spirit of chivalry and copies were circulated to bolster Catholic morale. Soon the government too had the letter and within a few weeks of his arrival Campion's name became a household word throughout the land.

The Jesuits, he wrote, will "cheerfully carry the cross you lay upon us while we have a man left to enjoy your Tyburn. . . . The expense is reckoned, the enterprise is begun; it is of God, it cannot be withstood. So the faith was planted: so it must be restored." He wrote to the Jesuit General: "I ride about some piece of country every day. The harvest is wonderful great. On horseback I meditate my sermon, when I come to the house I polish it. . . ."

He published secretely his **Ten Reasons** for challenging the most learned divines to religious debate, a book that would go into over forty editions. Three weeks later he was caught. At one point he was brought before Queen Elizabeth I and some ministers and was offered a high post if only he would cease being a Papist. "Which," he replied, "is my greatest glory."

To the court just before sentence was passed he said, ". . . In condemning us you condemn all your own ancestors—all the ancient priests, bishops and kings. . . . God lives; posterity will live; their judgment is not so liable to corruption as that of those who are now going to sentence us." After five months in prison and repeated rackings he was hanged at Tyburn, his age probably forty-one.

1595   [*S.J.*]

St. Robert Southwell, English missionary and poet, martyred for his priesthood at thirty-three. **The Burning Babe** is the best known of his more than sixty poems. A Jesuit at seventeen, he worked on the mission for six years and spent three more in prison. Tortured a dozen times, he gave no information but would simply say, "My God and my all." Though he died Feb. 21, the Society of Jesus celebrates his feast today with St. Edmund Campion.

DECEMBER 2

1381

Bl.John Ruysbroeck, author in Flemish of some of the Church's best mystical theology. He came of a humble family in Ruysbroeck, six miles south of Brussels, was ordained at twenty-four, and at fifty retired to Groenendael with his uncle and another cleric. Though clumsy, he was fond of manual labor. Their hermitage soon grew into an abbey of Augustinian canons with Ruysbroeck as prior. He was widely read and contributed much to the milieu that produced the **Imitation of Christ.** He died at eighty-eight.

His writings of set purpose counteract a false mysticism that tends to identify the soul with God and to neglect Church discipline, the sacraments, and good works. Much of his work contains instruction also for beginners, and he writes in a way that is intelligible to them and also attractive. Thus he recommends three books for reading each evening: "a dirty, old, crumpled book" in black ink, our life filled with sins; "a white, pleasing book written in red with blood," the life of our Lord; and "a blue-green book with letters all of pure gold," eternal life in heaven (**Book of the Seven Enclosures,** 21).

A good sample of Ruysbroeck is the long description of three groups of people who seek God in everything: faithful servants, secret friends, and hidden sons. In ascending order, with the higher always including the lower, they represent the active, the interior and finally, the contemplative Christian.

The faithful servant loves God and seeks him in all he does, but he is "more occupied in what he does than with God for whom he does it. . . . What the secret friends of God experience remains to him hidden and unknown. And this is why . . . he is always judging and finding fault with inward men, because it seems to him that they are lazy. This was why Martha complained to our Lord about her sister Mary. . . . But nowadays we find men so obstinate that they want to be so inward and so unoccupied that they refuse to work and help the needs of their fellow Christians. You may be sure that such men are neither our Lord's secret friends nor yet his faithful servants. . . . And this is why our Lord's secret friends are always his faithful servants too when there is need. . . .

"Yet there is still a higher and finer distinction, and that is between the secret friends and the hidden sons of God. Both of them alike stand upright in the presence of God; but his friends have attachment to the interior life, for they choose a loving cleaving to God as the best and highest which they can attain or desire. . . . And this they will not give up because they feel attachment to it; but they have no experience of how God is possessed above all exercises, in a naked, empty state of love" (**Book of the Sparkling Stone**).

DECEMBER 3

1552

ST. FRANCIS XAVIER, patron of foreign missions. A Basque like his spiritual father St. Ignatius, he capitulated to that saint's heroic ideals at twenty-eight after sharing a room with him and Bl. Peter Favre during four years at the University of Paris.

As a last-minute substitute for another of the original seven Jesuits, Francis became the order's first foreign missionary. "The work is yours," Ignatius told him. Francis had to leave Rome for Portugal in twenty-four hours. He accepted "with great joy and set to work patching an old pair of trousers and a soutane," showing at the very start the joyful readiness, the poverty and simplicity, and the search for the will of God through obedience and prayer that would characterize all his work on the missions.

He had no ability for languages and knew nothing of native peoples. On the thirteen-month voyage from Lisbon to Goa he wrote to Ignatius: "One of the things that greatly comforts us and makes us hope increasingly for the mercy of God is the complete conviction we have of lacking every talent necessary for preaching the Gospel in pagan lands."

During his ten years on the missions he traversed the greater part of the Far East as papal nuncio and Jesuit superior, everywhere leaving behind him flourishing churches that have generally endured to the present day. He died without sacraments or Christian burial, while waiting on the island of Sancian near Hong Kong for the merchant who had promised to smuggle him into China. He was forty-six.

"There is no better rest in this restless world," he wrote shortly before opening the first Christian mission in Japan, "than to face imminent peril of death solely for the love and service of God." "Do not," he instructed his friend Mansilhas, "fix your residence in any one spot, but go round all the time from village to village visiting each and every one of the Christians, as I did when I was there." He reminded him of the adage, "that if the water does not come to the mill, the miller must go to the water."

"I entreat you," he told him in another letter, "to bear yourself very lovingly towards those people; . . . for if they love you and get on well with you, you will do great service to God. Learn to pardon and support their weaknesses very patiently, reflecting that if they are not so good now, they will be some day. If you fail to accomplish with them all that you might wish, be satisfied with such results as you can bring about, which is what I do myself."

After a year-and-a-half in India he wrote Ignatius a 4400-word letter that was widely publicized in Europe. "My arms," he said, "are often almost paralysed with baptizing and my voice gives out completely through repeating endlessly in their tongue the creed, the commandments, the prayers, and a sermon on heaven and hell." He thought of those in the universities back home: "If while they study their humanities, they would also study the account which God will demand of them for the talents He gave, many might feel the need to undertake spirtual exercises that would lead them to discover and embrace the divine will rather than their own, and they would cry to God, 'Lord, here I am! What would you have me to do?' "

DECEMBER 4

ca. 750

ST. JOHN DAMASCENE, a monk of Mar Saba near Jerusalem, priest, outstanding preacher, doctor of the Church and author of the **Fount of Knowledge,** a handy, clear, and solid synthesis of dogmatic theology, far surpassing anything done up to this time. "I shall add nothing of my own," he wrote in the introduction, "but shall gather together into one those things which have been worked out by the most eminent of teachers and make a compendium of them." Except for St. Leo I, his sources are the Greek Fathers, Nicene and post-Nicene, with St. Gregory Nazianzen as his favorite theologian.

In the opening part he makes an attempt, the first in history, to provide theology with an adequate supply of the relevant logical and metaphysical concepts developed by Greek philosophers and Church fathers. The second section describes 103 heresies, the first eighty were compiled by St. Epiphanius, twenty more are from another source, and three are his own, including a long, interesting chapter on Islam in which he shows his thorough first-hand knowledge of the Koran and the earliest Moslem traditions. The third and final portion, translated into Latin in the twelfth century under the title **De Fide Orthodoxa,** gives an organic exposition of the Catholic faith—a first try at a **Summa** of theology—though certain important topics are missing, such as the Church, the theological virtues, and some of the sacraments. The Holy Eucharist, however, is the subject of one of the finest chapters. John Damascene is pre-eminently the theologian of the Incarnation, the mystery to which he gave most thought.

He was born in Damascus, where he succeeded his father as a trusted official of the Moslem caliph; but he withdrew from court and embraced monastic life. His writing and brilliant preaching during the first Iconoclast controversy made him the champion of orthodoxy in Palestine, where he was beyond the reach of the emperor of Constantinople. Four years after his death an Iconoclast synod condemned him, but in 787 the Second Council of Nicaea completely vindicated his memory.

He composed religious hymns and is particularly remembered for sermons on the Assumption of the Blessed Virgin. "By what name," he asked, "must this mystery be known? Shall we call it death . . . ? For it pleased Him who took his flesh from a virgin in order to become man, . . . it pleased Him, when she went forth from this world, to honor her pure and spotless body in preserving it from corruption and carrying it to heaven before the general resurrection. . . . Your most pure body, then free from every stain, O Virgin, has not been left beneath the ground, but you have been raised with Him to celestial regions; you are truly queen, truly sovereign, and truly Mother of God."

DECEMBER 5

532   [*O.S.B., O. Cist., O.C.S.O.*]

St. Sabas, one of the great monastic figures in the East, founder in Palestine of several hermit colonies, especially of Mar Saba in the bleak Kedron gorge ten miles southeast of Jerusalem.

As a mere boy he slipped from under the guardianship of an uncle and entered a monastery in his native Mutalaska near Caesarea in Turkey. At eighteen he went to Jerusalem, where he soon placed himself under St. Euthymius. At the age of thirty he was permitted to spend five days a week as a solitary in prayer and manual labor. He would leave the monastery on Sunday evening with bundles of palm branches and return Saturday morning with as many as fifty baskets.

After the death of Euthymius, he withdrew further into the wilderness and eventually, like St. Benedict in distant Italy twenty years later, found himself an almost inaccesible cave on the side of a cliff. The cenobium he finally established on the other side of the ravine for the disciples who gathered about him is the present Mar Saba, one of the oldest and most venerable monasteries in the world, the home of St. John Damascene and many other saints.

The colony of hermits soon numbered 150 and the patriarch of Jerusalem required Sabas to accept priestly ordination to serve the community. He was then fifty-three, the patriarch also made him archimandrite with responsibility for all the hermit monks of the region. Some of his subjects found him too withdrawn, for like St. Euthymius he would retire into complete solitude for lent, and sixty of them left to form a laura of their own. Sabas himself withdrew on another occasion in deference to a faction, but the patriarch insisted on his return.

He traveled through Palestine to preach against the Eutychian heresy and went to Constantinople to try to convince the heretical-minded Emperor Anastasius. On another delegation to the capital to ask redress for people in Palestine, the saint left the audience chamber to keep a scheduled hour of prayer. To a companion who thought they should remain in the Emperor Justinian's presence Sabas replied, "My son, the emperor does his duty, and we must do ours." St. Sabas died at ninety-three.

His body was later carried off to Venice; but in 1965 the Holy Father in concurrence with the patriarch of Venice transferred the precious relics to the Greek Orthodox Patriarch of Jerusalem, who handed them over to the community of fifteen monks at Mar Saba.

DECEMBER 6

4 cent.

ST. NICHOLAS, bishop of Myra in Asia Minor After Our Lady, probably no saint was more frequently represented in Christian art than St. Nicholas. While he was popular throughout the East and West, the nation that honored him most was Russia, where he is patron along with St. Andrew. He is also patron of Greece, Sicily, and Lorraine. In the East, sailors wished one another a safe voyage with, "May St. Nicholas hold the tiller!" But except for his being a bishop nothing is historically certain in his regard. In the eleventh century when the Saracens took possession of Myra the saint's relics were secretly removed to Bari in southern Italy, so that he is often called Nicholas of Bari.

The principal miracle legends show him freeing three unjustly imprisoned officers, saving innocent youths who were condemned to death, and producing three bags of gold for dowries to save the honor of three young women. In Germany the dowry story was combined with folklore to make St. Nicholas into the bringer of gifts on the eve of his feast; in English speaking countries the legend became associated with Christmas and the holy bishop became known as Santa Claus.

1876

Bl. Frances Schervier, 'Mother of the Poor,' foundress at Aachen, Germany, of the Franciscan Sisters of the Poor. Her life was one of generous service to others: as a child giving away the rich presents her godfather Emperor Francis I of Austria would give her, at 14 heading up a household after the death of her mother and two older sisters, at 21 joining a parish society of women pledged to visit the sick and poor and to care for abandoned children, at 22 operating a popular canteen sponsored by the parish curate, at 26 shortly after the death of her industrialist father renting a house and starting her order with five like-minded young women. At 28 she had the hardihood to dress as a man and enter a brothel to save a poor girl. During the Franco-Prussian

War she earned the Award of Merit for the service she and her sisters did caring for the wounded at the front. When Bl. Frances Schervier died at 57 on December 14, 1876, there were 41 houses of the order, a number of them in the United States, a country she twice visited during her five terms as superior general.

DECEMBER 7

397

ST. AMBROSE, archbishop of Milan and doctor, outstanding preacher and pastor, the most effective and respected churchman the West had yet seen. He converted St. Augustine, defended orthodoxy, and popularized papal primacy in the West. He is one of the founders of devotion to Mary as the ideal and patron of the consecrated life and spoke so persuasively on holy virginity that mothers tried to keep their daughters away from his sermons.

Of his many writings some are important: **De Officiis** — the first comprehensive presentation of Christian ethics — the various treatises on virginity, and the **De Mysteriis** and the **De Sacramentis** which are sets of sermon material with much valuable information for the history of the liturgy.

Ambrose is also author of the first and some of the best Latin church hymns. St. Augustine tells how he initiated congregational singing during the struggle with the Arian Empress Justina (**Confessions** 9,7): "The devoted people had stayed day and night in the church, ready to die with their bishop. . . . It was at this time that the practice was instituted of singing hymns and psalms after the manner of the Eastern churches, to keep the people from being altogether worn out with anxiety and want of sleep. The custom has been retained from that day to this, and has been imitated by many, indeed in almost all congregations throughout the world."

St. Ambrose was the youngest child; the other two, Satyrus and Marcellina, are also saints. Their father, as prefect of Gaul, held an office just below the emperor in rank. Ambrose was born at Trier, but after his father's death the family returned to Rome. He completed his studies there and soon rose to the position of governor of two provinces with residence at Milan.

Such was his reputation and eloquence that while keeping order at the episcopal election in which Catholics and Arians were at odds, he himself was chosen by both parties, though he was still a catechumen and probably only thirty-five. It was a crucial election, for during a good part of his twenty-three years as bishop Milan would be the principal seat of the empire.

Through his various confrontations with emperors — particularly the excommunication and unprecedented public penance of Theodosius the Great for the slaughter of thousands of innocent reprisal victims at Thessalonica — Ambrose became for all time the pattern of episcopal courage against evil in high places. "I dare not offer the Holy Sacrifice," he wrote to Theodosius, "if you intend to be present." He did much to establish in the West the principle that the Church is independent in her own domain and that in matters of faith and morals even emperors are subject to bishops. "The emperor," he said, "is in the Church not above it."

St. Ausutine left a charming picture of the bishop: "I was kept from any face to face conversation with him by the throng of men with their own troubles, whose infirmities he served. The very little time he was not with these he was refreshing either his body with necessary food or his mind with reading. When he read, his eyes traveled across the page and his heart sought into the sense, but voice and tongue were silent. No one was forbidden to approach him nor was it his custom to require that visitors should be announced; but when we came into him we often saw him reading and always to himself; and after we had sat in silence, unwilling to interrupt a work on which he was so intent, we would depart again" (**Confessions** 6,3).

He died on April 4, Holy Saturday. December 7th marks the day of his episcopal ordination.

DECEMBER 8

THE IMMACULATE CONCEPTION OF THE BLESSED VIRGIN MARY. On December 8, 1854, Pope Pius IX solemnly defined it as an article of faith "that, in view of the merits of Jesus Christ the Savior of the human race, the Blessed Virgin Mary in the first instant of her conception was, by a unique grace and privilege of almighty God, preserved from all stain of original sin."

Explicit belief in this doctrine developed gradually through centuries of devotional and theological reflection on the holiness of the humble and obedient handmaid of the Lord whom all ages would called blessed (Lk 1:48). The second century saw her as the new Eve; the fifth, at the Council of Ephesus, vindicated her title "Mother of God"; by the eighth her personal sinlessness was generally acknowledged and the feast of her Conception, though not specifically as "immaculate," was being celebrated in the East.

In the twelfth century, Eadmer of Canterbury produced the first treatise on the Immaculate Conception and sparked the earliest theological debates over the nature of Mary's freedom from sin. It was the English Franciscan Duns Scotus who overcame a final objection which theologians, including St. Thomas, had, that if Mary had been totally preserved from all sin Christ would not have been her Redeemer. "Mary more than anyone else," Scotus answered, "would have needed Christ as her Redeemer, since she would have contracted original sin . . . if the grace of the Mediator had not prevented it."

The feast was introduced into the Roman calendar in 1476, and by the seventeenth century the Catholic world was agreed and increasingly enthusiastic regarding this singular prerogative of the Blessed Virgin. Thus in 1846, eight years before the definition, the bishops of the United States declared the Immaculate Conception as the patronal feast of the nation.

DECEMBER 9

1640

St. Peter Fourier; for thirty years pastor of Mattaincourt, Lorraine; reformer and educator; co-founder of Bl. Alix Le Clercq's teaching nuns; and superior general of a congregation of Augustinian Canons.

A canon regular at twenty, he pursued advanced theological studies after ordination. When given his choice among three of his monastery's parishes, he took the poorest and most neglected, the one where he would have most work to do.

Arriving at Mattaincourt for the feast of Corpus Christi, he held a procession and on the return to the church gave an impassioned sermon that brought many to tears. He had come, he told them, for the single purpose of serving them and would, if necessary, give his life to save their souls. Pastoral zeal, poverty, and mortification backed up his words. His house, for example, would not be heated unless he had a guest. Using the confessional for spiritual direction he formed three separate confraternities: for women, for men, and for girls, with monthly confession as one of the requirements.

After failing in his attempt to start a free school for boys, he turned his attention to the education of girls as even more important. He was hardly in the parish a year before Bl. Alix and three other girls were launched on what would become the Augustinian Canonesses of the Congregation of Notre Dame. He gave them daily instructions in pedagogy and generally supervised the growth and spread of the new congregation. He composed dialogues on important virtues and vices and had the children dramatize them for the instruction of the parish on Sunday afternoons. He built up a fund from which parishioners could be given assistance, the only condition being that they repay if they prosper.

His bishop had him appointed papal visitor for the canons regular of Lorraine with the responsibility of establishing good discipline and of uniting the monasteries into a single congregation. Peter Fourier was then in his late fifties. He succeeded, and at sixty-two was elected superior general. His group was known as the Congregation of Our Saviour.

DECEMBER 10

ca. 304
St. Eulalia of Merida, Spain's most celebrated virgin martyr, a girl of twelve who perished when her hair caught fire during torture. The first French poem, a ninth century composition, is in her honor.

1455   [*O.S.M.*]
Bl. Jerome Ranuzzi, retiring but universally helpful Servite priest at Sant' Angelo in Vado, a village near Urbino in Italy. The local population had such devotion to him that his body was at once enshrined over an altar in the church.

1591
St. Swithin Wells; a London gentleman hanged in front of his home along with **St. Edmund Genings,** a priest of only twenty-four who was apprehended in the house while saying Mass. At Tyburn, some distance away, there died on the same day **St. Polydore Plasden,** priest; together with **Bl. John Mason** and **Bl. Sidney Hogdson,** laymen; all three captured while as-

sisting at that same Mass. The laymen were convicted of receiving priests.

Mr. Wells, fifty-five, was a teacher who for years had devoted himself to the service and safety of priests. He happened to be away when the pursuivants carried off his wife and the martyrs; and when he demanded that his wife and the key to the house be returned, he too was taken into custody.

At the hanging, St. Edmund, the young priest, screamed when they began to dismember him; but St. Swithin, awaiting his turn, said, "Thy pain is great indeed, but almost past; pray now, most holy saint, that mine may come." His widow died ten years later, still in prison; and his daughter Margaret became a nun.

1610

St. John Roberts, a Welshman who left Oxford to study law, became a Catholic in Paris, and in Spain became a priest and a Benedictine of the Valladolid Congregation. He returned to England about the age of twenty-six. Arrested five times in the remaining seven years, he is remembered for his buoyant if quarrelsome disposition, his devotion to the stricken in the London epidemic, and his many conversions. Downside Abbey venerates him as its first martyr, for he was one of the principal founders of the original community at Douai, France. A secular priest, **Bl. Thomas Somers,** was executed at Tyburn with him.

The Spanish heroine, Lady Louisa de Carvajal, through bribing the jailer, was able to hold a great supper the previous evening in the company of twenty Catholic prisoners with the two priests at her right and left at the head table. "Do you think," Father Roberts asked her, "that I may be causing disedification by my great glee? Had I not better withdraw and give myself to prayer?" "No, certainly not," she answered, "You cannot be better employed than in letting them all see with what cheerful courage you are about to die for Christ."

DECEMBER 11

384

ST. DAMASUS I, pope for eighteen years, effective patron of the Roman martyrs and the catacombs. Most of his pontificate was harrassed by a faction under the anti-pope Ursinus. Epitaphs he composed show that his father was a bishop, that his mother lived sixty years in dedicated widowhood, and that his sister Irene was a virgin "vowed to Christ."

He was an outspoken defender of the primacy of the Apostolic See; and St. Jerome, who had been baptized at Rome and was then living as a young ascetic in the Syrian desert, expressed the same preoccupation when he found it hard to choose between the three rival bishops of the local see of Antioch. "I exclaim," he wrote to Pope Damasus, "Whosoever is united with the chair of Peter is my ally. Meletius, Vitalis, and Paulinus say they are on your side. I might believe it if one of them made the claim. As it is, either two of them are lying or all three" (Letter 16). Again he wrote: "Inasmuch as the orient . . . has torn to pieces . . . the seamless robe of our Lord . . . I have decided that I must consult the chair of Peter. . . . I crave food for my soul from that source whence I originally obtained the vestments of Christ. . . . I speak with the successor of the Fisherman. . . . Following none but Christ as my primate, I am united in communion with Your Beatitude, that is, with the chair of Peter. Upon that rock I know the Church is built. Whosoever eats a lamb outside this house is profane" (Letter 15).

Damasus had been pope thirteen years, when Emperor Theodosius on February 28, 380, issued the momentous decree which established the Catholic religion: "It is our will that all the peoples who are ruled by the administration of Our Clemency shall practice that religion which the divine Apostle Peter transmitted to the Romans, as the religion which he introduced makes clear even to this day. It is evident that this is the religion that is followed by the Pontiff Damasus and by Peter, Bishop of Alexandria, a man of apostolic sanctity. That is . . . we shall believe in the single Deity of the Father, the Son, and the Holy Spirit, under the concept of equal majesty and of the Holy Trinity. We command that those persons who follow this rule shall embrace the name of Catholic Christians."

The'epitaph the saint composed for himself reads: "He whose steps calmed the bitter waves of the sea, who gives life to the dying seeds of earth, who had the power to free Lazarus from the chains of death and after three days' darkness restore him to his sister Martha in this upper world, He, I believe, will raise Damasus after death."

DECEMBER 12

1641

ST. JANE FRANCES DE CHANTAL, devoted wife and mother, and then co-founder with St. Francis de Sales of the Visitation nuns. Their first convent at Annecy in Savoy combined contemplative life with the visitation of the sick, but the traditional enclosure soon became the rule. St. Francis de-emphasized bodily austerities in favor of interior mortification and kept the order open to widows, the elderly, the crippled, the infirm, and the very young. There were eighty-five monasteries when St. Jane died.

She and Francis de Sales are one of the famous teams of canonized saints. When they first met—after she had already seen him in a vision—she was thirty-two, the deeply religious widow of Baron de Chantal, devoted to the sick and to the upbringing of her four children: two others had died in infancy. "She is simple," St. Francis said of her, "and sincere as a child, with solid and noble judgment, a lofty spirit and the courage to undertake holy enterprises."

The household soon felt the effect of the new director's all-embracing but unobtrusive spirituality. "Madame always prays," they remarked, "yet she is never troublesome to anyone." Francis moderated her tendency to severity, especially with herself, and restrained her desire to enter religion, saying that "nothing so prevents us from perfecting ourselves in the vocation we have as wishing for another." When the time for entry did come at thirty-eight, she could not be held back even by her own son who had thrown himself down to block her path.

Her bishop-director made light of what she believed were temptations against faith; and St. Vincent de Paul, to whose guidance St. Francis bequeathed her, singled out faith as her special characteristic. Not long before her death at sixty-nine, speaking to a friend about her work as foundress she said, "It is twenty-seven years since I have thought only of others with no time to think of myself."

1308   [*O.S.A., O.A.R.*]

Bl. James of Viterbo, Augustinian theologian who became archbishop of Benevento and then of Naples. It was his opinion that God had sent three teachers especially to enlighten the universal church: St. Paul, St. Augustine, and his own near contemporary Thomas Aquinas.

1531   [*United States*]

Our Lady of Guadalupe, patroness of Mexico and all Latin America as well as the Philippines and a special favorite in many other places, particularly the United States. In 1531, according to reliable accounts, the Blessed Virgin appeared on Tepeyac hill to Juan Diego, an Aztec convert in his middle fifties. She wished a shrine built on that site, then three miles from Mexico City; but Bishop Zumarraga wanted a sign. Three days later, on December 12, she appeared again and asked Juan Diego to pick roses and take them to the bishop. He gathered them; and the Virgin arranged them herself in his **tilma,** his coarse six-by-three foot mantle. When the roses were presented to the bishop, there on the **tilma** was the picture of Our Lady of Guadalupe, the beautiful girl of fifteen who had appeared on Tepeyac. The church of Guadalupe, where this treasure is kept, is the world's most frequented Marian shrine.

DECEMBER 13

304

ST. LUCY, virgin martyr of Syracuse in Sicily, where she inspired warm personal devotion within a few years of her death. She became so popular that her name was inscribed in the canon of the mass at Rome and Milan.

1671

Bl. Anthony Grassi, who at sixteen joined St. Philip Neri's oratory at Fermo, Italy. He was a brilliant student with a severe case of scruples that lasted until he celebrated his first Mass, but from then on he was characterized by imperturbable serenity.

While praying in the Holy House of Loretto, he was struck by lightning and left immobilized but conscious. On recovering a few days later, he felt that henceforth his life belonged in a very special way to God. The confessional became a major apostolate. He was chosen superior of his community at Fermo for a three-year period and was then re-elected for eleven successive terms, till his death at seventy-nine.

He used to say, that in forming an estimate of a man, one should not just look at an individual trait, but take all of that person's qualities together and then more good than bad will generally be found. So he was a very gentle superior; and when asked why he didn't show more severity, he said he did not know how. When questioned as to whether he wore a hair shirt, he replied that he had learned from St. Philip that it was better to begin with spiritual mortifications, like humbling the mind and will. He would go at once, day or night, when someone was sick or in need of help; but he would not accept social or ceremonial engagements.

DECEMBER 14*

1591

ST. JOHN OF THE CROSS, the most authoritative postpatristic mystic theologian and St. Teresa's closest associate in founding the Discalced Carmelite Friars. His poetry ranks with the best Spanish literature, and his books in the form of commentaries on these poems combine personal experience and traditional theology to give an exact exposition of the whole course of the interior life of prayer.

No one before him had analysed so clearly the transition from more active forms of meditation and mental prayer to the simpler general and loving sense of God's presence which prayerful people tend to have. It is a cornerstone of his teaching that this change is brought about by God giving himself at a deeper level of consciousness in a contact that is a genuine experience of God—though at first it may hardly be noticed. In a famous passage of the **Ascent of Mt. Carmel** (II, chapter 13), he gives three signs by which one can know that it is time to discontinue discursive meditation in favor of this state of "dark contemplation."

St. John is best remembered for his teaching on "All and nothing": loving God with all one's heart, soul, mind, and strength, and being totally detached from every countrary desire. The saint's intransigent expressions are, however, subject to the same misunderstanding as Christ's words: "If any one comes to me and does not hate his own father and mother and wife and children and brothers and sisters, yes, and even his own life, he cannot be my disciple" (Lk 14:26). The saint's

---

*C.O. see Dec. 13 for Bl. Anthony Grassi.

doctrine is eminently positive, however, and one of his best remembered maxims is; "Where you do not find love, put love and you will find love."

He was the youngest of three sons and was raised in poverty by his widowed mother. He was educated by the Jesuits, spent some time as a weaver—his father's trade—became a Carmelite at twenty-one, and then attended the university of Salamanca.

He first met St. Teresa, when he came to Medina del Campo to celebrate his first Mass. He was twenty-five, Teresa fifty-two. She was planning a community of friars to help her nuns whose reform she had launched five years before. She had heard of this penitential young friar who had already received permission to observe the primitive rule. She urged him not to join the Carthusians, as he was minded to do, but to join her, as she was planning to open a house of friars as part of her reform. He agreed on condition that it would be soon. The house was opened at Duruelo a year later, and John was the first friar to wear the Discalced habit.

"Although he is small of stature," Teresa wrote at this time, "I believe he is great in God's eyes. . . . He is . . . suited to our way of life. . . . For although we have had some disagreements about business a few times, and I have been the occasion of them and have been vexed with him several times, we have never seen an imperfection in him. He has courage. . . . He is greatly given to prayer and is intelligent."

His name in religion had been John of St. Matthias; he now chose "John of the Cross" as more expressive of his vocation. He would serve the Reform through important offices and by his example for twenty-three years. And he often made these three requests in prayer: that he might not pass a day without suffering something, that he might not die in office, and that he might end his life in humiliation and contempt. And so he died, shelved if not disgraced, while the leading party among the Discalced was gathering evidence to expel him from the Reform.

St. Teresa once wrote of him: "I have found no one like

him in all Castile nor anyone who inspires people with so much fervor on the way to heaven."

DECEMBER 15

956

St. Paul, a hermit on Mt. Latros in Turkey, where he at-attracted many disciples. Had he not been prevented he would have sold himself into slavery in order to relieve some unfortunates. When asked why he appeared sometimes joyful and sometimes sad, he replied, "When nothing diverts my thoughts from God my heart so overflows with joy that I often forget my food and everything else; and when there are distractions I am upset."

1315   [*O.S.M.*]

Bl. Bonaventure Buonaccorsi, a leader of the powerful Ghibelline faction in Tuscany. He was converted by St. Philip Benizi, became a Servite, and went about preaching peace.

1855

St. Mary di Rosa, foundress at Brescia of the Handmaids of Charity to care for the sick. At seventeen she began to devote herself to social and apostolic work, including the opening of a school for deaf and dumb girls; and after ten years she began to form her co-workers into a religious community to look after the sick in hospitals, not simply as nurses but as giving all their time and concern to the suffering and the dying.

She herself died at forty-two, her frail health totally spent in the service of others. "I can't go to bed with a quiet conscience," she once said, "if during the day I missed any chance, however slight, of preventing wrong-doing or of helping to do some good."

1856

Bl. Charles Steeb, a priest of the Diocese of Verona who, without any significant ecclesiastical appointment, spent himself tirelessly for 60 years helping wherever he saw a need: helping the poor, tending the sick, hearing confessions, teaching, and in his late 60's founding the Verona Sisters of Mercy. Born of staunch Lutheran parents, he left his native Tuebingen, Germany, to study business and trade at Paris and then at Verona, where at the age of eighteen he became a Catholic, forfeiting his family ties for life. At 23 he was a priest, a man of few words and many deeds. Pope Paul VI saw Bl. Charles as exemplifying Our Lord's words, "Unless a grain of wheat falls into the earth and dies, it remains alone; but if it dies it bears much fruit." (Jn 12:24)

DECEMBER 16

999

St. Adelaide, an empress thoroughly dedicated to peace and to the religious and cultural works of the Church. Twice widowed, she had one child by Lothair of Provence, her first husband, and four by Otto the Great whom she married at twenty and outlived by more than a quarter of a century. She was ill-treated by a son and a daughter-in-law.

Discerning in her choice of advisers, she worked closely with such churchmen as St. Adalbert of Magdeburg, St. Willigis of Mainz, and especially Sts. Majolus and Odilo, abbots of Cluny, whose monastic reform she did much to promote. She died in the monastery of Seltz on the Rhine, one of her own foundations.

1496

Bl. Sebastian Maggi of Brescia, noted Dominican preacher. He was for a time Jerome Savonarola's confessor and appointed Savonarola novice master at Bologna. Bl. Sebastian served as superior in a number of houses and had the reputation of being gentle and indulgent when treated with openness as a father, but of being severe when the friars dealt with him merely as a master.

1717   [O.C.D.]

Bl. Mary of the Angels or **Mary of Turin,** a Carmelite mystic much consulted by those outside the cloister. The daughter of the Count of Fontanella, she entered the Turin convent at fifteen and in the beginning experienced great homesickness along with aversion for her new way of life and for her novice mistress. She experienced sublime states of prayer and practised harsh and unusual penances.

When about to be elected prioress for the fifth time, she no longer felt equal to the task, and prayed that if it be God's will she might soon die. Within three weeks she was very ill. "I have so stormed the Heart of Jesus to get my desire," she told her sisters, "that He has granted it. It cannot be changed now." She was fifty-six.

DECEMBER 17

779

St. Sturmi, earliest recorded German Benedictine, abbot and founder of Fulda. St. Boniface sent him as young monk to find a site for a monastery, and he selected the vast tract of forest where the Greizbach empties into the Fulda. Boniface himself went there with workmen to see to the building of the abbey church and took a personal role in the training of the monks. He had Sturmi and two companions go to Rome, Monte Cassino, and Subiaco to study Benedictine monasticism at its sources.

Fulda flourished, particularly after the martyred remains of

St. Boniface were deposited there; and during the lifetime of Sturmi the community grew to nearly 400 monks. It was soon a center of learning and culture, a model abbey that served as a seminary of priests for all Germany. The abbey lands in time were transformed into the town of Fulda.

1213 [*O. SS. T.*]

St. John of Matha; a native of Provence; founder of the Trinitarians, an order of contemplative-active friars whose original apostolate was the ransom of Christians who were held captive by the Moslems in Spain, Africa, and the Near East. The order combined features of monasticism with an international organization to purchase Christian slaves, bring them back to their homes and provide for their spiritual and temporal needs during the period of repatriation. When slavery was abolished, the order undertook educational work along with the usual forms of pastoral ministry, but always with a primary emphasis on devotion to the Holy Trinity.

DECEMBER 18

605

St. Venantius Fortunatus, bishop of Poitiers, gifted and prolific poet. He is the first to combine Christian theology and sentiment with a poetic view of nature.

Born near Treviso, Italy, and educated at Ravenna, he moved through parts of Germany and France—many of his 300 poems mark stages of this journey—on a pilgrimage whose ultimate destination was Tours, where he went to thank St. Martin for curing him of an eye disease. At Poitiers St. Radegund—the former queen—and her nuns persuaded him to stay on, to take priestly orders, and to become their chaplain.

He was a gracious gentleman with a facility for turning all

his experiences—friendships, food, the towns he passed—into poetry.

Among his best-known hymns are two that became part of the Holy Week liturgy, the **Pange lingua** and the **Vexilla Regis**—the latter originally written to mark the solemn reception of a relic of the true Cross, which Emperor Justin II had sent to St. Radegund.

761

St. Winebald, third member of an apostolic English family that helped St. Boniface on the German mission. He was abbot of Heidenheim in Wurttemberg, a double monastery built with the help of his brother St. Willibald, bishop of Eichstätt. Their sister St. Walburga was abbess of the monastery's nuns.

The two brothers had originally set off from England to accompany their father on a pilgrimage to Rome. There Winebald eventually became a Benedictine and met St. Boniface on one of his visits to the pope.

DECEMBER 19

1370

Bl. Urban V, a Benedictine, the only Avignon pope raised to the altar. A native of Grisac in southern France, he became abbot of St. Germain in Auxerre, attained a wide reputation as professor of law at Montpellier and Avignon, and was elected pope in 1362, when the cardinals could not agree on one of their own number. His continuing interest in education was shown in the foundation of the universities of Cracow and Vienna.

He set an example of simplicity and integrity, was free of every taint of nepotism, and worked earnestly for Church reform. The great act of his pontificate was his return to Rome, where a pope had not set foot in sixty years; and he threw himself with energy into rebuilding the great basilicas which had fallen into ruin. But after three years, harrassed by local disorders, he yielded to various pressures as well as his personal love of France, and returned to Avignon despite St. Bridget's warning that he would soon die if he left Rome—a prediction that came true in less than three months after his departure.

Historians agree with Petrarch's written comment on hearing the news: "Urban would have been reckoned among the most glorious of men if he had caused his dying bed to be laid before the altar of St. Peter and had there fallen asleep with a good conscience, calling God and the world to witness that if ever the pope had left this spot it was not his fault, but that of the originators of so shameful a flight."

DECEMBER 20

1073

St. Dominic, Spanish Benedictine abbot who was so popular as a wonder-worker that three years after his death the king, prelates, and a large throng came to transfer his relics to the abbey church and to change the name of his monastery at Silos from St. Sebastian to St. Dominic. This church soon became the most important pilgrimage shrine in Castile.

The saint began his monastic career at San Millán de la Cogolla, but was banished by the king of Navarre for refusing to surrender some monastic lands into the hands of the king. Dominic was, however, welcomed by King Ferdinand I of Old Castile, and was given the run-down monastery at Silos which he soon turned into one of the greatest abbeys in Spain. Until the revolution in 1931 it was the custom for the abbot of Silos to leave the staff of St. Dominic at the bedside of the queen of Spain when she was in childbirth.

This saint has always been cherished by the Dominican order, because a century later, St. Dominic Guzman, their founder, came from the neighborhood of Silos, was named after the holy abbot, was educated in his school, and was traditionally believed to have been born in answer to his mother's prayers to the saint. Silos is still an important abbey today.

1831

Bl. Vincent Romano, secular priest who spent nearly all his fifty-six years of priesthood in his own home town of Torre del Greco, near Naples. He was particularly assiduous in teaching and preaching, and many young men followed him to the altar. But even after twenty-four years as a priest, he was unwilling to assume the responsibility of pastor and it took a formal order from his bishop to make him accept the office. He was a model shepherd. Among other things he saw to it that his local sailors received a fair wage. When he died at eighty the whole town came out to pay homage to its generous, loving father in Christ.

DECEMBER 21

1597

ST. PETER CANISIUS, Jesuit, doctor of the Church. His three catechisms went through more than 200 printings and were translated into fifteen languages during the author's lifetime, making him central Europe's leading Catholic voice in the counter-reformation. He is called the second apostle of Germany.

The son of the mayor in Nijmegen, Holland, he became firmly attached to the Catholic party during his studies at Cologne in his middle teens through the influence of the priest Nicholas Van Esch. "With him for guide," Peter wrote in his **Confessions,** "I gradually began to make small surrenders of my own pleasure that I might better please God. . . . Every night before going to bed, I used to tell him . . . all the falls and follies and stains of the day's experience, that he might be their judge and sentence me to whatever penance he thought best."

At twenty-two he made the Spiritual Exercises under Bl. Peter Favre and at the end of the first week resolved to enter the Society of Jesus. About the time of his ordination at twenty-five Peter brought out an edition of the works of St. Cyril of Alexandria and of St. Leo the Great, thus becoming the first "literary" Jesuit.

At Messina, Italy, he was on the first staff of the first Jesuit college, but he was soon sent on the German mission to teach theology at the university of Ingolstadt. He soon reformed the school and in time became its rector. The emperor wished to make him archbishop of Vienna, but St. Ignatius permitted nothing more than that he administer the diocese for a year. When Peter arrived there in 1552, Vienna had not had a priestly ordination in twenty years. It was there he wrote his catechisms.

While provincial in southern Germany he founded Jesuit colleges in six cities. For dealing with boys he once gave this advice: "The usual result of pushing boys too rapidly, in excess of the right measure, is to break their spirits rather than to correct them." He advocated schools of Jesuit writers; for "one writer," he maintained, "is more valuable in Germany than ten professors."

With his great capacity for friendship and his concern for virtue and the purity of doctrine, he left a prodigious correspondence—8,000 pages in the printed edition. To a friend he wrote, "I have never learnt to be elegant as a writer: but I cannot remain silent on that account. I just pour out to my friends the first thoughts that come into my head."

His last years were spent in Switzerland, where he selected the site for the university of Fribourg and by his preaching and presence did much to keep that canton Catholic. He died at seventy-six.

DECEMBER 22

1917

St. Frances Cabrini, foundress of the Missionary Sisters of the Sacred Heart, patroness of immigrants, and the first citizen of the United States to be canonized. Born in Lombardy, the youngest of thirteen, she was fired with missionary zeal as a little girl through family reading of the **Annals of the Propagation of the Faith;** and she would do without sweets because she would also be without them in China.

She earned a teacher's certificate and applied to two orders with missionary houses but was rejected because of health. Reluctantly, at the request of her bishop, she tried to save an orphanage and turn its staff into a religious community; but after six hard years the work collapsed; and Frances, now thirty, began her own missionary community with seven associates from the orphanage. Bishop Scalabrini suggested they work with Italian immigrants, especially in the United States, as his own Congregation of St. Charles was doing; but Mother Cabrini's heart was set on China; and she asked Pope Leo XIII. "Not to the East," he told her, "but to the West."

Founding schools, hospitals, and charitable works of every kind, she would cross the ocean thirty times bringing bands of young Italian sisters to North and South America. Her community letter during her second trip to New York gives a typical picture of these missionary voyages: "This morning all the sisters woke up very ill. Some of them thought they were going to die. Sister Cherubina lost her speech, Sister Egidia was almost in convulsions. All the others were sea sick. It was a scene of perfect desolation. . . . Those who trusted my words arose and tried to eat and presently were looking quite well. The others who thought that death was at hand stayed in bed awaiting it without opening their mouths the whole day. As for Sister Egidia, not being able to find any remedy and not even a doctor, I had to have recourse to one of my usual tactics, a good scolding, and immediately the convulsions disap-

SAINT FRANCES CABRINI

peared. The effect was such that I became ill myself."

The letters are filled with the practical motherly instruction of a foundress who knew she was loved and imitated by her sisters. "When you are corrected do not justify yourself. Keep silence and practice virtue whether you are right or wrong, otherwise we may dream of perfection but will never reach it" (Oct. 17-20, 1892). "Love is not loved, my daughters! Love is not loved!" (Aug. 21, 1890). "Renounce yourselves entirely if you wish to enjoy peace. . . . She who is not holy will make no one holy" (Oct. 17, 1892).

Explaining why she did not accompany some sisters on a boat excursion she wrote, "I admit my weakness, I am afraid of the sea; and if there is no very holy motive in view I have no courage to go where I fear danger, unless I were sent by obedience, and then, of course, one's movements are blessed by God."

Mother Cabrini died at sixty-seven, suddenly and alone in one of her Chicago hospitals, while preparing Christmas presents for 500 children.

DECEMBER 23

1473

ST. JOHN CANTIUS or John of Kety, secular priest, dean of philosophy and then professor of Sacred Scripture at the University of Cracow, a patron of Poland. His university became so proud of its intimate association with the holy priest that his doctoral gown was for a long time used in conferring degrees. His mortified, prayerful life was also characterized by a special love of the poor. He gave his scholars this advice: "Fight false opinions, but let your weapons be patience, sweetness and love. Roughness is bad for your own soul and spoils the best cause."

1771

Bl. Marguerite d'Youville, Canadian-born foundress of the Grey Nuns. The eldest daughter of Captain Christopher Lajemmerais, Marguerite at the age of twenty was married in Montreal to Francis d'Youville, a selfish man who died nine years later, despised in Canada and France for defrauding both Indians and merchants through illegal fur and liquor trade. By opening a small store Marguerite was able to pay off her husband's large debt and educate her two sons, who both became priests—four other children had died in infancy.

On December 31, 1737, she and three companions committed themselves to serve the needy. A year later they began to live together in her house and also to take in the destitute. But the d'Youville name had a bad reputation, and there was also a fear that these women would take over Montreal's general hospital. At one point they were publicly refused Holy Communion. They were jeered in the streets as **les soeurs grises,** the "tipsy sisters," as if they too were trafficking in liquor; but Mother d'Youville would perpetuate the jibe as a symbol of humility by adopting the name in its literal sense of "Grey Nuns." Their official name, however, once the hospital did come into their hands, was the Sisters of Charity of the General Hospital of Montreal.

Mother d'Youville opened the first foundling home in North America, and with unfailing ability and charity set about to relieve every form of distress. At her beatification in 1959, less than 200 years after her death, some 8,000 sisters in six autonomous congregations could look to her as foundress. In Montreal itself some 4,000 nuns had affixed their name to the solemn commitments which she was the first to sign, promising "to live together... in perfect union and charity ... to consecrate our lives ... our work ... for the poor."

DECEMBER 24

1865

Bl. Paula Cerioli, widow, foundress in Italy of the Institute of the Holy Family to care for orphans. She was the last of six-teen children. At the age of nineteen her parents arranged a marriage with a wealthy widower of sixty. She bore him three children, but two died in infancy.

After her husband's death she devoted her fortune and the large mansion at Seriate in Lombardy to the welfare of orphans. When told that people thought her crazy, she replied, "So I am, with the foolishness of the cross."

She made religious profession in 1857 and organized her helpers into a religious community. A few years later a branch of brothers was established to care for boys. She died in her sleep on Christmas eve. Her life had been especially marked by devotion to St. Joseph.

1898

St. Sharbel Makhlouf, Lebanese Maronite monk and priest, a modern desert father. The son of poor peasants, he became a monk at thirty-three. He served others so readily that no one knew his preferences—except for things like solitude, mortifica-tion, and obedience. Others approached him with great confi-dence. Marvels were reported during his life-time and many cures after his death.

Totally dedicated to divine contemplation, he progressively sought greater solitude and spent his last twenty-three years on a mountain with one companion. He slept little and ate but a few morsels once a day. In 1898, just after receiving the Precious Blood at Mass, he had a stroke and was taken to his cell where he died eight days later, being about seventy years of age.

DECEMBER 25

FEAST OF CHRISTMAS. In Bethlehem, six miles south of Je-rusalem, the place of the nativity cave is indicated on the floor of the basilica with a silver star and the words, "Here Jesus Christ was born of the Virgin Mary."

In 274 Emperor Aurelian proclaimed the Sun God as the principal patron of the Roman Empire; and a great festival honoring the Unconquered Sun was regularly kept on December 25, the day of the winter solstice in the Julian calendar. As Christ is the true "light of the world" (Jn 9:5), his birthday fittingly replaced the pagan festival.

In recognition of the fact that he is "the beginning and the end" and came "to make all things new" (Rv 21:5-6), the year of his birth was eventually reckoned as the year one—a mode of calculating time that was introduced by Dionysius Exiguus at the beginning of the sixth century.

1907

Bl. Teresa Wuellenweber, or, as she was known in religion, Mary of the Apostles, co-foundress at Tivoli in 1888 of the Salvatorian Sisters, a missionary society for establishing the kingdom of the divine Savior in every part of the world.

She was born at Myllendonck in the Rhineland, daughter of a Baron. She tried three religious orders but did not find what she was looking for. This troubled her. Many people, including her father, thought she did not know what she wanted and that she would never become settled about her vocation. In the meantime, as the oldest daughter, she took the place of her deceased mother in the home. For a period she also tried to form her own congregation, but the venture failed because the ladies who joined tired of the life and left one by one.

Finally she heard of the work of Father John Jordan in far off Italy and recognized immediately that his missionary project was what she was looking for. It was as if her youth had been restored and new energies released, as she offered herself and all she had should he wish to start a feminine branch. There would still be long periods of waiting, but at the age of fifty-five she made religious profession. In the next twenty years she founded twenty-five flourishing feminine mission houses and died very peacefully on Christmas Day.

DECEMBER 26

ca. 34

ST. STEPHEN, deacon, the first martyr. When the Greek-speaking brethren in Jerusalem complained that their widows were being neglected in the daily distributions the apostles said, "It is not right that we should give up preaching the word of God to serve tables. Therefore, . . . pick out from among you seven men of good repute, full of the spirit and of wisdom, whom we may appoint to this duty. But we will devote ourselves to prayer and the ministry of the word. . . . And they chose Stephen, a man full of faith and of the Holy Spirit" (Acts 6:2-5) along with six others.

Stephen also found time to preach and addressed himself to his own group of Greek-speaking Jews. Some believed; others found his message blasphemous; for he taught that the Law and the temple were replaced and spiritualized in Christ. The saint's dying words, as the stones rained in upon him, were, "Lord Jesus, receive my spirit" and "Lord, lay not this sin to their charge" (Acts 7:59-60). The youthful Saul of Tarsus stood by and approved the stoning; but he would one day become the chief herald of the same message, proclaiming to every one that Christ is the fulfillment of the Law.

1890

St. Vincentia Lopez y Vicuña, foundress at Madrid of the Daughters of Mary Immaculate, a congregation that has now spread through Europe and Latin America and conducts hospices for working girls and teaches domestic arts. For some years Vincentia helped her aunt maintain a home for orphans and working girls; and at nineteen, with her confessor's consent, she made a vow of chastity. "I'll marry neither a king nor a saint" was the way she expressed her decision.

But she was not clear on whether her own vocation lay in the cloister or with youth, and so she went to a Visitation convent to pray and reflect. 'The girls won out," she said, explaining her return to the orphans. But her father, a lawyer, would not go along with this vocation; for he favored either marriage or the Visitation Nuns. So he recalled her to the family home at Casante. There she became sick, and as the doctor prescribed a change of climate she returned to Madrid where she eventually organized community life with her aunt and a few others at the orphanage. She died at forty-three.

DECEMBER 27

ST. JOHN THE APOSTLE, the son of Zebedee and brother of James. He should still be identified, as he has traditionally been, with the "disciple whom Jesus loved" (Jn 13:23) and with the "author" of the fourth gospel and the Johannine epistles. The Apocalypse, too, should be understood in relationship to him. His writings show that same remarkable combination of contrasting qualities which the apostle himself possessed: the simple words of an unlettered man and the profound meditation of the contemplative; a burning love and an uncompromising insistence on doctrinal truth; the intensity and fire of a "son of thunder," as Jesus called him (Mk 3:17); and the tenderness of the disciple who leaned on the breast of Jesus (Jn 13:25) and who alone of the sacred writers declared "God is love" (I Jn 4:8). Jesus had foretold that John would drink a chalice like his own (Mt 20:23). He was the only apostle at the foot of the cross, and it was to him that Jesus entrusted his mother (Jn 19:25-27).

John's great preoccupation is to be a faithful witness to God's revelation of Himself through Jesus Christ; for "no one has ever seen God; it is the only Son, who is in the bosom of the Father, he has made him known" (Jn 1:18). "That which was from the beginning, which we have heard, which we have seen with our eyes, which we have looked upon and touched with our hands: the Word, who is life—this is our subject. That life was made visible: we saw it and we are giving our testimony, telling you of eternal life which was with the Father and has been made visible to us. . . . We are writing this to you to make our own joy complete." (I Jn 1:1-4).

DECEMBER 28

THE HOLY INNOCENTS. This feast honors the male children whose slaughter in or near Bethlehem under King Herod is recounted in the second chapter of the gospel of St. Matthew. The Innocents were honored as the first who died because of Christ; they even died in his place—buds, as St. Augustine says, killed by the frost of persecution the moment they showed themselves.

1837
St. Caspar del Bufalo, founder in Italy of the Society of the Precious Blood. He wanted the most neglected district in each diocese to be confided to his priests, and Pope Pius VII assigned them the task of converting the brigands who were ravaging the Papal States—an apostolate in which they were eminently successful. After an exhausting mission St. Caspar would say, "If it is so gratifying to tire ourselves for God, what will it be to enjoy him?"

At Rome, even as a seminarian he catechized, visited hospitals, and reactivated the Santa Galla hospice for the homeless. His priests and brothers lived a common life but without vows and were held together solely by the bond of charity—but time proved the organization unstable, and a promise of fidelity was eventually introduced.

The congregation fosters devotion to the Precious Blood and engages in the various works of the ministry. It has approximately a thousand members, half of whom are in the United States.

DECEMBER 29

1170

ST. THOMAS BECKET, archbishop of Canterbury, felled in his cathedral by four of King Henry II's men; the most famous martyr of the Middle Ages. During most of his fifty-two years he was worldly and ambitious—he would remain harsh and impetuous to the end—but with his episcopal ordination at forty-four he was transformed, to use his own words, "from a follower of hounds to a shepherd of souls." And during his exile in France, he experienced the deeper conversion to sainthood. A hairshirt was found under the magnificence of his blood-spattered robes, and miracles occurred in such numbers that canonization hardly took two years. The king himself soon came in public penance. Pilgrims arrived from afar and also the poor whom Archbishop Thomas had washed and fed before dawn, thirteen a day. "I accept death," he had murmured as he fell, "for the name of Jesus and in defense of the Church."

London-born, a merchant's son of Norman stock, he was educated in the liberal arts and law in Europe's best schools. He was energetic and handsome, a master of debate and extemporary speech. Integrity, personal charm, generosity, judgment, and capacity for affairs won him the patronage of Archbishop Theobald, who made him archdeacon of Canterbury and then proposed him as chancellor to the new twenty-one year old king, Henry II. Thomas was thirty-six. He guided Henry in the art of kingmanship; handled his correspondence; became his bosom companion, trusted adviser and most successful diplomat.

Then the archbishopric fell vacant. "If I should chance to be promoted," he remarked to the prior of Leicester, "I would either lose the favor of my lord the king . . . or neglect the services of the Lord God." And Thomas warned Henry, "The affection which is now so great between the two of us would soon be changed to violent hatred."

On the way to the ordination Thomas charged his faithful

friend, Herbert of Bosham: "Hereafter, I want you to tell me, candidly and in secret, what people are saying about me. And if you see anything in me that you regard as a fault, feel free to tell me in private. For from now on people will talk about me, but not to me. It is dangerous for men in power if no one dares to tell them when they go wrong."

Henry, with his talent for law and government, wanted to consolidate the realm by making his closest and most capable adherent primate of the church in England, particularly as the secular and ecclesiastical domains divided England into two virtually independent legal and fiscal structures.

But Thomas, now archbishop, was firmly attached to the pope, accepted the principles of the Gregorian Reform, gave primacy to priestly concerns, and saw the temporalities and freedom of the Church as necessary for her spiritual functions and her charities to the poor.

One of his first acts, and it hurt and angered the king, was to resign the chancellorship. Soon there was open conflict over Church properties and the privilege of clerics to be tried only in Church courts. At one point Thomas weakened and led the bishops to accept the restrictions of Church freedoms contained in the Constitutions of Clarendon; then he backed off and refused to sign the document. He fled to France, spent six years in exile, returned during a period of reconciliation, only to be slain, the victim of angry expostulation rather than of an explicit order to kill.

The travelers in **Canterbury Tales** were on their way to the tomb of St. Thomas, one of the most popular pilgrimage spots in Europe until the Reformation.

DECEMBER 30

1876
    St. Catherine Labouré, the unknown and unassuming Sister

of Charity of St. Vincent de Paul to whom the Blessed Virgin revealed the Miraculous Medal. It was the subject of a series of visions at Paris just a few months after her entrance into the convent at twenty-four.

On November 27, 1830, she saw Our Lady as in a picture, standing on a globe and encircled with the words, "O Mary, conceived without sin, pray for us who have recourse to you." Then Our Lady showed her the reverse side with a capital "M," two hearts, and a cross. Catherine heard a voice telling her to have a medal struck and that those who wore it would have Mary's special intercession.

She told her confessor everything but would never allow him to divulge her name. He became convinced, obtained authorization from the Archbishop of Paris, and two years later had 1,500 medals made. Among the marvels soon reported, was the conversion of Alphonse Ratisbonne, an Alsatian Jew who reluctantly wore the medal, had a vision of the Blessed Virgin, and eventually founded the Fathers and Sisters of Zion.

Catherine spent forty-five years at the Hospice de'Enghien on the outskirts of Paris, as portress, tending the aged, and unobtrusively doing household chores. But eight months before her death, she told her revelations also to her superiors in order to have a statue made that the Blessed Virgin requested. She was matter-of-fact and even seemed cold, but her death sparked a wave of popular enthusiasm.

Catherine was the ninth child of a prosperous farmer. From the age of twelve, after her mother's death and older sister's entrance into a convent, she had charge of the household for her father and brothers, so that she was the only one of the seventeen children who received no formal education. To discourage her religious vocation her father sent her to Paris at the age of twenty-two to work as waitress in her brother's cafe, but it only strengthened her resolve. She died on December 31, at the age of seventy.

DECEMBER 31

335

ST. SYLVESTER I, whose pontificate from 314 to 335 coincides almost exactly with the reign of Emperor Constantine I, that decisive quarter-century when the Church, newly emerged from persecution, passed from toleration to a privileged status under the patronage of a powerful emperor to whom state religion in the Roman tradition seemed the only normal thing. Sunday was declared an official holiday; churches were authorized to accept legacies; priests were exempted from public service; numerous basilicas were constructed including St. John Lateran, Santa Croce, and St. Peter's in Rome, and several in Palestine.

Constantine looked on bishops as colleagues, and in certain localities bishops' courts received jurisdiction to handle civil cases. He convoked synods in East and West, and acted as president at the Council of Nicaea. All the while Pope Sylvester stood by, possibly impressed by all the good that was being done by this first Christian emperor and apparently making no protest against intrusion on episcopal or papal authority. Two priests represented him at Nicaea, but no trace remains of any decision or strong action he took during his long pontificate—in sharp contrast to Pope St. Julius I, a champion of the rights of the Apostolic See, who was elected barely a year after St. Sylvester died.

439 and 431

St. Melania the Younger and St. Pinian, an attractive couple noted for their charities and enthusiasm for the ascetic life. Melania was a Roman lady of great wealth, granddaughter of St. Melania the Elder and married at fourteen against her will to her cousin Valerius Pinian. After their two infants died, Melania won her husband over to a life of continence; and they devoted their wealth and influence to help the poor. Melania's house on the Appian way was converted into a hostel for pilgrims.

They traveled, both to flee the Goths and to improve their spiritual life. At St. Augustine's Hippo in northern Africa, Pinian so impressed the people that a riot was quelled only after he promised that, if ever he was ordained a priest, he would come to minister to them. The saintly pair settled in the Holy Land, where Melania founded and governed a large community of virgins on Mt. Olivet.

Index of Names and Dates

The date is the date assigned in the **Roman Sanctoral** (Roman Martyrology). This is generally the day of death.

When two dates are given the one in parentheses is the day of death, the other is the day on which the entry will be found.

An asterisk (*) marks entries that are not expected to be in the **Roman Sanctoral.**

A

Abbo, St.	Nov. 13
Abraham of Rostov, St.	Oct. 29
Acacius, St.	May 8
Accursio, St.	Jan. 16
Achilleus, St.	May 12
Adalbert, St.	June 25
Adalbert of Prague, St.	Apr. 23
Adamnan, St.	Sept. 23
Adelaide, St.	Dec. 16
Adelhelm, Bl.	Feb. 25
Adjutus, St.	Jan. 16
Aelred of Rievaulx, St.	Jan. 12
Agapetus I, St.	Apr. 22
Agatha, St.	Feb. 5
Agathangelo, Bl.	Aug. 7
Agatho, St.	Jan. 10
Agnellus, Bl. (Mar. 13)	Apr. 27
Agnes, St.	Jan. 21
Agnes of Assisi, St.	Nov. 19
Agnes Kim, Bl.	Sept. 26
Agnes of Montepulciano, St.	Apr. 20
Agnes of Prague, Bl. (Mar. 6)	Mar. 2
Agostina Pietrantoni, Bl. (Nov. 13)	Jan. 18
Aidan, St.	Aug. 31
Alban, St.	June 22
Aban Roe, St.	Jan. 21
Alberic of Molesmes, St.	Jan. 26
Albert the Great, St.	Nov. 15

Albert of Jerusalem (Sept. 14)	Sept. 17
Albert Trapani, St.	Aug. 7
Aldhelm, St. (May 25)	Apr. 20
Alexander Sauli, St.	Oct. 11
Alexis Falconieri, St.	Feb. 17
Aldyeis, St. (June 11)	June 12
Alferius Pappacarbone, St.	Apr. 11
Alice, St. (June 11)	June 12
Alix le Clercq, Bl.	Jan. 9
All Saints	Nov. 1
All Souls	Nov. 2
Aloysius Gonzaga, St.	June 21
Aloysius Guanella, Bl.	Oct. 27
Aloysius Orione, Bl. (Mar. 12)	Mar. 16
Aloysius Palazzolo, Bl.	June 15
Alpais, Bl.	Nov. 3
Alphege, St.	Apr. 19
Alphonse Ligouri, St.	Aug. 1
Alphonse Navarrette, Bl.	June 1
Alphonse de Orozco, Bl.	Sept. 19
Alphonse Rodriguez, St.	Oct. 31
Altman, St. (Aug. 8)	Aug. 9
Alypius, St. (*)	May 16
Amadeus IX, Bl.	Mar. 30
Amand, St.	Feb. 6
Ambrose, St.	Dec. 7
Ambrose, Barlow, St.	Sept. 10
Ambrose of Siena, Bl.	Mar. 20
Anastasius the Persian, St.	Jan. 22

Anatolius, St.	July 3
André Bessette, Bl.	Jan. 6
André Grasset de Saint-	
Sauveur, Bl.	Sept. 2
Andrew the Apostle, St.	Nov. 30
Andrew Bobola, St.	May 16
Andrew Corsini, St.	
(Jan. 6)	Apr. 2
Andrew of Crete, St.	July 4
Andrew Dotti, Bl.	Aug. 31
Andrew Fournet, St.	May 13
Angela of Foligno, Bl.	
(Jan. 4)	Jan. 7
Angela Merici, St.	Jan. 27
Angelina of Marsciano,	
Bl. (July 14)	July 13
Angelo of Acri, Bl.	Oct. 30
Anne, St.	July 26
Anne of St. Bartholomew,	
Bl.	June 7
Anne Mary Erraux, Bl.	Oct. 22
Anne Mary Gallo, St.	Oct. 6
Anne Mary Javouhey, Bl.	
(July 15)	July 17
Anne Line, St. (Feb. 27)	Feb. 26
Anne Michelotti, Bl.	Feb. 1
Anne Mary Taigi, Bl.	
(June 9)	June 10
Annunciation of the Lord	Mar. 25
Ansegisus, St.	July 20
Anselm of Canterbury, St.	Apr. 21
Anselm of Lucca, St.	Mar. 18
Ansgar, St.	Feb. 3
Anthelm, St.	June 26
Anthony, St.	Jan. 17
Anthony of the Caves,	
St.	July 10
Anthony Claret, St.	Oct. 24
Anthony Daniel, St.	Oct. 19
Anthony Deynan, St.	Feb. 6
Anthony Gianelli, St.	June 7
Anthony Grassi, Bl.	Dec. 13
Anthony Neyrot, Bl.	Apr. 10
Anthony of Padua, St.	June 13
Anthony Primaldi, Bl.	Aug. 14
Anthony Mary Pucci, St.	Jan. 12
Anthony of Stroncone, Bl.	
(Feb. 7)	Feb. 8
Anthony Zaccaria,	
St.	July 5

Antoninus of Florence, St.	
(May 2)	May 10
Apollonia, St.	Feb. 9
Apollonius, St.	Apr. 21
Archangels	Sept. 29
Arnold Janssen, Bl.	Jan. 15
Arsenius, St.	July 19
Athanasius, St.	May 2
Athanasius of Mt. Athos,	
St.	July 5
Attalus, St.	June 2
Audrey (Etheldreda), St.	June 23
Augustine of Canterbury,	
St.	May 27
Augustine Chevreux, Bl.	Sept. 2
Augustine Gazotich, Bl.	Aug. 3
Augustine of Hippo, St.	Aug. 28
Augustine Huy, Bl.	Nov. 6
Augustine Novello, Bl.	May 19
Augustine Webster, St.	May 4
Avitus, St.	Feb. 5
Ayalà, Bl.	June 1

B

Babylas of Antioch, St.	
(Jan. 24)	Jan. 23
Baptista Varani, Bl.	
(May 31)	May 30
Barachisius, St. (Mar. 29)	Apr. 7
Barbara Acarie, Bl.	Apr. 18
Barnabas, St.	June 11
Bartholomea Bagnesi, Bl. (*)	May 28
Bartholomea Capitanio,	
St.	July 26
Bartholomew the Apostle,	
St.	Aug. 24
Bartholomew Amidei, St.	Feb. 17
Bartholomew Longo, Bl.	Oct. 5
Bartholomew Pucci, Bl.	May 6
Basil the Great, St.	Jan. 2
Bathildis, St.	Jan. 30
Beatrice da Silva, St.	
(Aug. 16)	Sept. 1
Bede the Venerable, St.	May 25
Benedict of Aniane, St.	
(Feb. 12)	Feb. 13
Benedict dell'Antella,	
St.	Feb. 17

C

Clare of Pisa, Bl.
(Apr. 17) — Apr. 20
Clare of Rimini, Bl. — Feb. 10
Claude de la Colombière,
Bl. — Feb. 15
Clelia Barbieri, Bl.
(July 13) — May 6
Clement I, St. — Nov. 23
Clement Mary Hofbauer,
St. — Mar. 15
Clement of Osimo, Bl.
(Apr. 8) — May 19
Clothilde, St. — June 3
Clotilde Paillot, Bl. — Oct. 22
Cloud, St. — Sept. 7
Colette, St. (Feb. 6) — Feb. 7
Coloman, St. — Oct. 13
Columba (or Columcille),
St. — June 9
Columba Kim, Bl. — Sept. 26
Columba of Rieti, Bl. — May 20
Columban, St. — Nov. 23
Comgall, St. — May 10
Conrad of Parzham, St. — Apr. 21
Conrad of Piacenza, St. — Feb. 19
Conrad of Seltenbueren,
Bl.(°) — May 2
Contardo Ferrini, Bl. — Oct. 20
Corbinian, St. — Sept. 8
Cordule Barré, Bl. — Oct. 22
Cornelius, St. — Sept. 16
Cosmas (with Damian), St. — Sept. 26
Crescentia Höss, Bl. — Apr. 5
Cunegund (Kinga), Bl.
(July 24) — July 23
Cunegund, St. — Mar. 3
Cuthbert, St. — Mar. 20
Cuthbert Mayne, St. — Nov. 30
Cyprian, St. (Oct. 12) — June 24
Cyprian of Carthage, St. — Sept. 16
Cyril (with Methodius)
St. — Feb. 14
Cyril of Alexandria, St. — June 27
Cyril of Jerusalem, St. — Mar. 18

D

Damasus I, St. — Dec. 11
Damian (with Cosmas) St. — Sept. 26

Daniel (martyr) St. — Oct. 10
David, St. — Mar. 1
David I of Scotland, St. — May 24
Dedication of the Lateran
Basilica, — Nov. 9
Dedication of St. Mary
Major, — Aug. 5
Dedication of Sts. Peter
and Paul, — Nov. 18
De Mazenod, Charles Joseph
Eugene, Bl. — May 21
Delphina, Bl. — Sept. 26
Denis, St. — Oct. 9
Deogratias, St. (Jan. 5) — Mar. 22
Desideratus, St. — May 8
Diana, Bl. (June 10) — June 8
Didacus (or Diego) of
Cadiz, Bl. — Mar. 24
Dionysius of the Nativity,
Bl. — Nov. 29
Dominic, St. — Aug. 8
Dominic Barberi, Bl.
(Aug. 27) — Sept. 6
Dominic Dat, Bl. — Nov. 6
Dominic Loricatus, St. — Oct. 14
Dominic Savio, St.
(Mar. 9) — May 6
Dominic of Silos, St. — Dec. 20
Dunstan, St. — May 19

E

Eata, St. (Oct. 26) — Oct. 25
Edmund (martyr) St. — Nov. 20
Edmund Campion, St. — Dec. 1
Edmund Genings, St. — Dec. 10
Edward the Confessor,
St. — Jan. 5
Edward Shelley, Bl. — Aug. 30
Elijah the Prophet (°) — July 20
Elizabeth of Hungary,
St. — Nov. 17
Elizabeth Picenardi, Bl. — Feb. 19
Elizabeth (or Isabella)
of Portugal, St. — July 4
Elizabeth Bayley Seton,
St. — Jan. 4
Elphege, St. — Apr. 19
Elzear, St. (Sept. 27) — Sept. 26

Gabriel Lalemant, St.	Oct. 19
Gabriel Possenti, St.	Feb. 27
Galdinus, St.	Apr. 18
Gall, St.	Oct. 16
Gall of Clermont, St.	July 1
Galasius I, St.	Nov. 21
Gaspar Bertoni, Bl.	June 12
Gemma Galgani, St.	Apr. 11
Genevieve, St.	Jan. 3
George, St.	Apr. 23
George Gervase, Bl.	Apr. 11
Gerald, St.	Apr. 5
Gerald of Aurillac, St.	Oct. 13
Gerard of Brogne, St.	Oct. 3
Gerard of Clairvaux, Bl. (June 13)	June 14
Gerard of Csanad, St.	Sept. 24
Gerard Majella, St.	Oct. 16
Gerard Sostegni, St.	Feb. 17
Gerasimus, St.	Mar. 5
Germain of Auxerre, St. (July 31)	Aug. 3
Germaine Cousin, St.	June 15
Germanus, St.	May 12
Germanus (or Germain) of Paris, St.	May 28
Gertrude of Helfta, St.	Nov. 16
Gertrude of Nivelles;, St.	Mar. 17
Gervase (with Protase), St.	June 19
Gilbert of Sempringham, St. (Feb. 4)	Feb. 16
Gildas, St.	Jan. 29
Giles of Assisi, Bl.	Apr. 23
Giles Mary, Bl.	Feb. 7
Gleb, St.	July 24
Godehard (or Gothard), St.	May 5
Godfrey of Kappenberg, St. (Jan. 13)	Jan. 16
Godric, St.	May 21
Gomidas Keumurigian, Bl.	Nov. 5
Gratia of Cattaro, Bl.	Nov. 28
Gregory I, St.	Sept. 3
Gregory VII (Hildebrand) St.	May 25
Gregory X, Bl.	Jan. 10
Gregory Barbarigo, St.	June 18
Gregory the Enlightener, St.	Sept. 30

Gregory Grassi, Bl. (July 9)	July 8
Gregory of Langres, St. (Jan. 4)	Jan. 18
Gregory Nazianzen, St.	Jan. 2
Gregory of Nyssa, St.	Jan. 10
Gregory of Tours, St.	Nov. 22
Gregory the Wonderworker, St.	Nov. 22
Guardian Angels	Oct. 2
Guerricus, Bl.	Aug. 19
Guy, St.	Mar. 31

H

Hallvard, St.	May 14
Hedda, St.	July 7
Hedwig, St.	Oct. 16
Helen, St.	Aug. 18
Helen Duglioli, Bl.	Sept. 23
Helen Guerra, Bl.	Apr. 11
Helen of Udine, Bl.	Apr. 23
Heliodorus, St.	July 3
Henrietta Dominici, Mary, Bl. (Feb. 21)	Feb. 20
Henry II, St.	July 13
Henry de Ossó y Cervelló. Bl.	Jan. 27
Henry of Treviso, Bl.	June 10
Heribert, St. (Mar. 16)	Mar. 4
Herman the Cripple, Bl.	Sept. 24
Hermenegild, St.	Apr. 13
Hermes, St.	Oct. 21
Hilarion; St.	Oct. 21
Hilary of Lerins, St.	May 5
Hilary of Poitiers, St.	Jan. 13
Hilda, St.	Nov. 17
Hildegard, St.	Sept. 17
Hippolytus of Galantini, Bl.	Mar. 20
Hippolytus of Rome, St.	Aug. 13
Honoratus of Arles, St.	Jan. 16
Hormisdas, St.	Aug. 6
Hubert, St.	Nov. 3
Hugh of Bonnevaux, St.	Apr. 1
Hugh of Cluny, St. (Apr. 29)	May 11
Hugh Faringdon, Bl.	Nov. 15
Hugh of Fosses, Bl.	Feb. 10
Hugh of Grenoble, St.	Apr. 1

John Francis Burté, Bl.	Sept. 2	John of Rieti, Bl. (*)	Aug. 12
John Cantius, St.	Dec. 23	John Roberts, St.	Dec. 10
John Capistran, St.	Oct. 23	John Roche, Bl.	Aug. 30
John Cassian, St.		John Rochester, Bl.	May 11
(July 23)	July 28	John Ruysbroeck, Bl.	Dec. 2
John Chrysostom, St.	Sept. 13	John of Sahagun, St.	
John Climacus, St.	Mar. 30	(June 11)	June 12
John Colombini, Bl.		John of Salerno, Bl.	Aug. 9
(July 30)	Aug. 5	John Sarkander, Bl.	Mar. 17
John of the Cross, St.	Dec. 14	John Slade, Bl.	Oct. 30
John Joseph of the Cross,		John Soreth, Bl.	June 25
St.	Mar. 5	John of Spain, Bl.	June 25
John Damascene, St.	Dec. 4	John Stone, St.	Oct. 25
John Dominic, Bl.	June 10	John Thorne, Bl.	Nov. 15
John Duckett, Bl.	Sept. 7	John of Vercelli, Bl.	Nov. 30
John Dukla, Bl.	Sept. 29	John Vianney, St.	Aug. 4
John Eudes, St.	Aug. 19	John Wall, St.	
John Fisher, St.	June 22	(Aug. 22)	July 12
John Forest, Bl.	May 22	Jonas, St. (Mar. 29)	Apr. 7
John of God, St.	Mar. 8	Jordan of Pisa, Bl.	Mar. 6
John of Gorze, St. (*)	Mar. 7	Jordan of Saxony, Bl.	
John Grande, Bl.	June 3	(Feb. 13)	Feb. 12
John Gualbert, St.	July 12	Josaphat Kuncevic, St.	Nov. 12
John Haile, Bl.	May 4	Joseph, St.	Mar. 19
John Hewett, Bl. (Oct. 5)	Sept. 6	- the Worker,	May 1
John Houghton, St.	May 4	Joseph de Anchieta, Bl.	
John the Iberian, St.	July 12	(June 9)	Nov. 22
John Jones, St.	July 12	Joseph Cafasso, St.	June 23
John Kemble, St.	Aug. 22	Joseph Calasanctius, St.	Aug. 25
John Lalande, St.	Oct. 19	Joseph Cottolengo, St.	Apr. 30
John du Lau, Bl.	Sept. 2	Joseph of Cupertino, St.	Sept. 18
John Leonard, St.	Oct. 9	Joseph Freindametz, Bl.	
John Lloyd, St.	July 22	(Jan. 28)	Jan. 29
John Mason, Bl.	Dec. 10	Joseph of Leonessa, St.	Feb. 4
John Masías, St.		Joseph Marchand, Bl.	Nov. 30
(Sept. 16)	Sept. 18	Joseph Moscati, Bl.	
John of Matha, St.	Dec. 17	(Apr. 12)	Mar. 29
John Nepomucene Neumann,		Joseph Oriol, St.	Mar. 23
St.	Jan. 5	Joseph Pignatelli, St.	Nov. 14
John Ogilvie, St.	Mar. 10	Joseph Tommasi, Bl.	Jan. 1
John of Parma, Bl.	Mar. 19	Josepha Rossello, St.	
John of Gabriel Perboyre,		(Dec. 7)	Feb. 5
Bl.	Sept. 11	Josephine Leroux, Bl.	Oct. 22
John William Plessington,		Jude the Apostle, St.	Oct. 28
St.	July 19	Julia Billiart, St.	Apr. 8
John Angelo Porro, Bl.	Oct. 25	Julian of St. Augustine,	
John Prado, Bl.	May 24	Bl.	Apr. 8
John Francis Regis, St.		Julian Maunoir, Bl.	
(Dec. 31)	June 16	(Jan. 28)	July 2
John of Ribera, St.	Jan. 7	Juliana Falconieri, St.	June 19

Stephen of Rostov, St.	
(Apr. 26)	June 1
Sturmi, St.	Dec. 17
Swithbert, St.	Mar. 1
Swithin Wells, St.	Dec. 10
Swithun, St.	July 2
Sylvester I, St.	Dec. 31

T

Tarasius, St.	Feb. 25
Tarsicius, St.	Aug. 15
Teresa of Avila, St.	Oct. 15
Teresa of Jesus Jornet	
e Ibars, St.	Aug. 26
Teresa of Lisieux, St.	Oct. 1
Teresa of Portugal, St.	June 17
Teresa Margaret Redi,	
St. (Mar. 7)	Sept. 1
Teresa Verzeri, Bl.	Mar. 3
Teresa Wuellenweber,	
Bl.	Dec. 25
Theodore of Canterbury,	
St.	Sept. 19
Theodore of Chernigov,	
St.	Sept. 20
Theodore the Studite,	
St.	Nov. 12
Theodosius, St.	Jan. 11
Theodosius of the Caves,	
St. (May 3)	July 10
Theophane Venard, Bl.	Feb. 2
Theophilus of Corte, St.	
(May 19)	Aug. 10
Theotonius, St.	Feb. 18
Thomas the Apostle, St.	July 3
Thomas Aldfield, Bl. (July 6)	Oct. 28
Thomas Aquinas, St.	Jan. 28
Thomas Becket, St.	Dec. 29
Thomas of Cori, Bl.	Jan. 11
Thomas Corsini, Bl. (*)	June 27
Thomas Kasaki, St.	Feb. 6
Thomas More, St.	June 22
Thomas Reynolds, Bl.	Jan. 21
Thomas Somers, Bl.	Dec. 10
Thomas of Tolentino, Bl.	
(Apr. 1)	Apr. 9
Thomas of Villanova, St.	Nov. 25
Thomas Whitebread, Bl.	June 20

Timothy, St.	Jan. 26
Titus, St.	Jan. 26
Toribio de Mogrobejo, St.	Mar. 23
Transfiguration of the Lord	Aug. 6
Turibius, St. see Toribio	

U

Ubald Adimari, Bl.	
(Apr. 9)	July 4
Ulric, St.	July 4
Urban II, Bl.	July 29
Urban V, Bl.	Dec. 19
Ursula, St.	Oct. 21

V

Vaast (or Vedast), St.	Feb. 6
Venantius Fortunatus, St.	Dec. 18
Veronica of Binasco, Bl.	Jan. 13
Veronica Giuliani, St.	
(July 9)	July 10
Victor I, St.	July 28
Victor III, Bl.	
(Sept. 16)	Sept. 23
Victoria Fornari-Strata,	
Bl.	Sept. 12
Villana de Botti, Bl.	Feb. 28
Vincent Ferrer, St.	Apr. 5
Vincent Grossi (Nov. 7)	Nov. 8
Vincent Pallotti, St.	Jan. 22
Vincent de Paul, St.	Sept. 27
Vincent Romano, Bl.	Dec. 20
Vincent of Saragossa, St.	Jan. 22
Vincent Strambi, St.	
(Jan. 1)	Sept. 25
Vincentia Gerosa, St.	June 28
Vincentia Lopez y	
Vicuña, St.	Dec. 26
Vladimir of Kiev, St.	
(July 15)	July 16

W

Walburga, St.	Feb. 25
Wandrille, St.	July 22
Wenceslaus, St.	Sept. 28
Wilfrid of York, St.	Apr. 24

15 Nov 83